D0900812

The world's largest collection of visual travel guides

auSTRIa

Edited by Wilhelm Klein

Managing Editor: Dorothy Stannard

Editorial Director: Brian Bell

APA PUBLICATIONS

Part of the Langenscheidt Publishing Group

L

INSIGHT GUIDES

austria

© 1998 APA Publications GmbH & Co. Verlag KG
(Singapore Branch), Singapore. *All Rights Reserved*

NO part of this book may be reproduced, stored in a
retrieval system or transmitted in any form or means
electronic, mechanical, photocopying, recording or
otherwise, without prior written permission of Apa
Publications. Brief text quotations with use of
photographs are exempted for book review purposes
only. Information has been obtained from sources
believed to be reliable, but its accuracy and
completeness, and the opinions based thereon, are not
guaranteed.

CONTACTING THE EDITORS: Although every effort
is made to provide accurate information in this
publication, we live in a fast-changing world and would
appreciate it if readers would call our attention to any
errors or outdated information that may occur by
writing to us at Apa Publications,
P.O. Box 7910, London SE1 8ZB, England.
Fax: (44) 171-620-1074.
e-mail: insight@apaguide.demon.co.uk.

First Edition 1991
Updated Edition 1998

Distributed in the United States by
Langenscheidt Publishers Inc.
46–35 54th Road
Maspeth
NY 11378
Fax: (718) 784 0640

Distributed in the UK & Ireland by
GeoCenter International Ltd
The Viables Centre, Harrow Way
Basingstoke, Hampshire RG22 4BJ
Fax: (44) 1256-817988

Worldwide distribution enquiries:
APA Publications GmbH & Co. Verlag KG
(Singapore branch)
38 Joo Koon Road
Singapore 628990
Tel: 65-8651600
Fax: 65-8616438

Printed in Singapore by
Insight Print Services (Pte) Ltd
38 Joo Koon Road
Singapore 628990
Fax: 65-8616438

Mention Austria and what springs to
mind are its mountains and lakes,
winter skiing or summer hiking,
deep valleys and pretty villages crouching
before snow-capped peaks. "The chief crop
of provincial Austria is scenery," said John
Gunther, a traveller in the 1930s. Others may
think of names and places associated with
the country's unique cultural heritage: of Wolfgang Amadeus Mozart and Salzburg; of the
Habsburgs and Vienna; of Johann Strauss
and the Blue Danube.

Whether drawn by the rich legacies of the
past or lured by the magnificent scenery, the
visitor to Austria is spoilt for choice. Indeed,
there is more here than can be digested in
one go; you don't have to have studied the
tourism statistics to know that Austria has
long been an integral part of any journey to
Europe, and that most people, having been
here once, tend to return.

Klein

The task of putting together *Insight Guide:
Austria* fell to project editor **Wilhelm Klein**.
who had already produced a number of books
for Apa Publications, including *Burma, Moscow, St Petersburg* and *Vienna*. He himself
hails from Austria and therefore found that
the challenge of producing a comprehensive
guidebook to the country was close to his
heart and set about putting together an expert team of writers and photographers.

One of the contributors, **Jutta Kohout**,
another old Apa hand, had worked with Klein
on *Insight Guide: Vienna*. In *Insight Guide:
Austria* she took another close look at her
home city of Vienna and examined the de-

Fischer

lights of the Austrian cuisine, one of those
aspects of the country that – apart from
Weiner schnitzel – outsiders probably know
least about. It was in Vienna that Kohout
studied history and political science for her
doctorate. She now works as a freelance journalist and writes for a number of magazines.

The task of unravelling the tangled web of
the country's history – especially the machi-
nations that went into preserving the
Habsburg dynasty – fell to **Rowlinson Carter**,
another regular contributor to this series. A
widely-travelled English journalist, television

Maier

Carter

elyn Feichtenberger

Neuhold

Kölbel

documentary maker and historian, Carter believes that history is not mainly about dates and events but a story about people, their glory, bravery, villainy, vanity, lechery and greed. Given such a philosophy, what meatier material could he have wished for than the melodramatic saga of Mayerling?

Carter is also responsible for the feature discussing the Austrians themselves, their virtues and vices, what is so special about them and what makes them tick. He was quick to clear away various myths about them and fully endorses the following comment by Richard Bassett, a foreign correspondent with the London *Times*: "It is often thought that the Austrian is a born musician... this is an extravagant misconception, as anyone who has spent five minutes at a service in an Austrian village church will testify."

Marton Radkai, previously project editor of *Insight Guide: Hungary*, is an American of German-Hungarian descent who now lives in Vienna, and has studied history, German and journalism. Here he describes the fascinating cultural and artistic development of the country in his article *The Austrian Muse*.

Many people who travel to Austria do so in order to marvel at the legacies of its glorious past. And what more splendid or prodigious epoch was there than the Austrian Baroque, the physical manifestation of the glories of the Habsburgs' Empire and the power of the Church? The country is dotted with magnificent palaces and abbeys, the most important of which are highlighted in the chapter *Baroque Masterpieces* by **Ute Fischer**, a freelance travel journalist living in Hesse in Germany.

Dr Dieter Maier is primarily an expert on German, although he also studied Romance languages and the history of art. He blends his expertise in these fields with his love of the Alps and is a specialist on the culture and history of the Alpine region. As a freelance author, he has written a number of books and articles on the subject. Here he looks at the west of the country, at the delightful city of

Salzburg, the Tyrol and Vorarlberg, regions that he knows every bit as well as his native Bavaria on the other side of the border.

But Austria is not just Salzburg and the Tyrol – and most certainly not just Vienna. The centre of the country is dominated by the mighty mountains of the East Tyrol, crowned by the country's highest peak, the Grossglockner. The Alps then become lower the further east one gets, but continue all the way through Styria, finally petering out in the lowlands of the Burgenland and Lake Neusiedler on the Hungarian border. To the south is Carinthia, bordering on Slovenia, and to the north are the hills of Upper and Lower Austria, providing the basin for the River Danube flowing resolutely towards the Black Sea.

Each of these regions has its own particular distinctive character and charm, its own rich store of things to discover. Each is vividly described by **Evelyn Tambour-Feichtenberger** and **Kurt Feichtenberger**, two journalists from Vienna whose articles on different aspects of the country have appeared in numerous magazines.

To many sport enthusiasts, Austria is more than anything else the home of skiing, but it is not just the excellent pistes and exciting off-piste powder snow which attract the intrepid. Mountaineering, white river rafting, skijoring and ice-climbing are just a few of the other adventure sports available. **Christian Neuhold**, editor of the Vienna trend-magazine *Basta*, is an expert in a variety of sports – the ideal man to contribute to the *Great Outdoors* chapter. He was helped by **Alfred Kölbel,** who has written several books about hiking in Austria. Here he shares his knowledge of many of the most beautiful routes between Vienna and Bregenz, and provides valuable tips for those who want to head off into the mountains.

The original translation into English was supervised by **Tony Halliday** and produced in Apa's London editorial office by **Dorothy Stannard**. Vienna resident and art historian **Chris Clouter** updated this edition, which was edited in Apa's London office by **Clare Griffiths**.

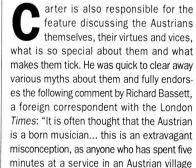

CONTENTS

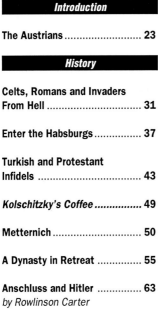

Introduction

The Austrians 23

History

Celts, Romans and Invaders
From Hell 31

Enter the Habsburgs 37

Turkish and Protestant
Infidels 43

Kolschitzky's Coffee 49

Metternich 50

A Dynasty in Retreat 55

Anschluss and Hitler 63
by Rowlinson Carter

Features

The Austrian Muse
by Marton Radkai 75

Baroque Masterpieces
by Ute Fischer 80

Austrian Cuisine
by Dr Jutta Kohout 86

The Great Outdoors
by Christian Neuhold and
Alfred Kölbel 102

Places

Introduction
by Wilhelm Klein 114

Vienna
by Dr Jutta Kohout 124

The Burgenland
by Evelyn Feichtenberger and
Kurt Feichtenberger 154

Lower Austria
by Evelyn Feichtenberger and
Kurt Feichtenberger 167

Upper Austria
*by Evelyn Feichtenberger and
Kurt Feichtenberger* **184**

The Salzkamnergut
*by Evelyn Feichtenberger and
Kurt Feichtenberger* **194**

Styria
*by Evelyn Feichtenberger and
Kurt Feichtenberger* **204**

Carinthia
*by Evelyn Feichtenberger and
Kurt Feichtenberger* **225**

East Tyrol
*by Evelyn Feichtenberger and
Kurt Feichtenberger* **241**

Salzburg
by Dr Dieter Maier **249**

The Tyrol
by Dr Dieter Maier **270**

Vorarlberg
by Dr Dieter Maier **294**

Maps

Austria **114**

Vienna and Surroundings **122**

Vienna **134**

East Austria **150**

South Austria **200**

Graz **214**

Klagenfurt **228**

West Austria **244**

Salzburg **251**

Innsbruck **273**

Vienna Metro **319**

TRAVEL TIPS

Getting Acquainted
The Place 314
Topography 314
Climate 314
The Economy 314
Government............................ 314
Historical Overview 314

Planning the Trip
What to Wear......................... 315
Entry Regulations 315
Currency 315
Public Holidays 315
Getting There 316
Maps 317
Tourist Offices 317
Embassies Abroad 317

Practical Tips
Business Hours 317
Tipping 317
Religious Services 317
Media 317
Postal Services 318
Telephone 318
Tourist Offices 318
Consulates 318
Emergencies 318

Getting Around
Public Transport..................... 318
Vienna Rail Map 319
Private Transport 320
Mountain Railways 321

Where to Stay
Private Accommodation 321
Hotels 321
Campgrounds 324
Youth Hostels 324

Eating Out
What to Eat 325
Where to Eat 326
Drinking Notes 327

Attractions
Culture 328
On the Baroque Trail 329
Museums 329
Festival Performances 331
Nightlife 332

Sports & Leisure
Participant 332

Further Reading
General 336
Other Insight Guides 336

Art/Photo Credits 337
Index 338

It is the common belief of diplomats and spies that if they wish to be truly mis-informed about a country they should ask someone who has lived in it for 20 years. It is certainly true that Austrians are least qualified to field such questions as "Who are you?" or "What are your special qualities?" Nevertheless, it is in the national character to try to offer opinions on such matters.

"A mixture," one might cheerfully reply, "of bad-tempered pig-headedness, witty charm, cosmopolitan snobbishness, good-natured optimism, petty-fogging jingoism, acerbic spleenishness, naffish indifference, melancholia, bibulousness and pretentious philosophising." Anything else? "We're the ones that make this golden heart beat?" Which golden heart is that? "The golden heart of Central Europe."

Golden hub: Austria's geographical position is in fact one of the keys to a very complicated question. The other is history, because the golden hub of the Habsburg (i.e. "Austrian") empire tended to wander, and it was the cultural swirl around the shifting centre that set the style for the aristocracy in all the corners as well. It was thus that for quite a long time after the Emperor Charles VI the Austrian nobility rather fancied themselves as Spaniards, and Spanish etiquette was rigorously observed at court. Some emperors were anxious to absorb as much as they could from their Italian possessions; others looked favourably on the Hungarians.

The German fashion: The Spanish and other fashions were merely interludes. Before and after them, the inhabitants of the land which is now the Second Republic of Austria weighed up the components of empire with which they most wished to identify themselves, and that choice generally boiled down to being, or not being, German. While the indubitable Germans were still a confused jumble of states crying out for leadership, the Austrians went to extraordinary lengths – including blatant forgery concerning the genealogy of their ruling family – to prove that they were more genuinely German than half-baked imposters who came from places such as Bavaria. When that particular contest was ultimately lost to the Prussians, the guardians of the empire decided that their future lay among the assorted Slavs to the east, and in that respect it was advantageous to be rather less German and more like them.

By the time the First Republic of Austria was formed in 1919, the pedigree Germans had long established themselves in Germany and the World War I peace settlement had provided independent countries for the Hungarians and Slavs to the east. For the Austrians left behind in the rump of the old empire, the question of who they were became infinitely more difficult.

Hitler brought the issue to a head, and it is at this stage in the evolution of the modern Austrian identity that the geography of the rump becomes critical. It is indeed at the heart of Europe. The Brenner Pass spears through the Alps as a natural highway to

Preceding pages: girl with snowball; a sign in Vienna flea market; house facade in Vienna; Viennese ball; snowboard acrobatics; the Gosau Valley; Jakob's Cathedral, Innsbruck; an ancient fresco; a day out on the crags. Left, the popular image is of a nation of musicians. Right, star actor, the late Helmut Qualtinger.

Bavaria and Italy, an ancient road curves south-east down the Adriatic coast, and the Danube is the greatest artery of all. The river had always been an open sesame (in both directions) to the Balkans, the eastern steppes and the Black Sea. The magnetic effect of a great imperial capital like Vienna therefore merely reinforced what was a natural rendezvous for Germans, Italians, Slavs, Magyars, Jews and to some extent even Poles. They came in all shapes and sizes and intermarried to produce a distinctive blend of features. Visitors are advised to find a suitable pavement table, order coffee, and verify the phenomenon for themselves

The language and culture of the melting

these matters as any Austrian could possibly be) came along first with the suggestion and then the order that they were all Germans. A few months of Anschluss under the Third Reich were sufficient to persuade most Austrians that this was not the case. The Jews, of course, were given no choice in the matter. Most of those who did not escape abroad were sent to Dachau and Buchenwald and Austria lost for ever the greatest single generator of its intellectual and artistic achievement. Britain and America were the principal beneficiaries.

The new persona: Emerging from the wreckage of Anschluss, Austrians knew that they were not the sort of Germans the unlamented

pot was German, and when emperors were not trying to be Spanish the German stamp was applied with a fairly firm hand. After World War I the rump of the empire – the Germans having gone one way, the Slavs the other – sounded German but neither in the faces of the people nor in the architecture did it look particularly German. There had been far too many outside influences for that, and even today the Vienna telephone directory has a healthy proportion of Czech and other "foreign" names.

The post-war Austrians were still not sure what they were, or even what they ought to call themselves, when Hitler (as confused in

Hitler had in mind, so they set about assembling a new persona out of the pieces of the imperial Identikit that were still lying around. It is in this extremely complex context that the obliging Austrian needs a moment to think on being asked what might otherwise be the simple question "Who are you?"

The answer they have cobbled together – once the enquirer has digested "bad-tempered pig-headedness, witty charm…" etc – is to work hard at the image of being softer and more charming than their northern neighbours. The international searchlight that bore down on them in 1986 because of President Kurt Waldheim's somewhat enigmatic career in the Wehrmacht was a shock. Most Austrians had persuaded themselves, and they hoped others, that a veil had been securely drawn over unsavoury events. They had leapfrogged back into a past where, thank heaven, the Imperial Army was almost certain to lose a war, Johann Strauss was in full swing, and everything in the garden was Gemutlichkeit.

If that leap is allowed – and who is left on earth who has not once occupied a glass house? – one may give due consideration to the issues raised in a slim volume by Jorg Mauthe, *Cogitations for Austrians.*

"The production of geniuses in our little country exceeds comparable achievements

"It is often thought that the Austrian is a born musician," says Richard Bassett, an astute observer of contemporary Austrian life. "This is an extravagant misconception, as anyone who has spent five minutes at a service in an Austrian village church will testify." Bassett is not here referring to the renowned Vienna Boys' Choir or the magnificent orchestras, but to ordinary people. He believes their great talent is acting, as revealed in debates between waiters and customers about the amount of milk they want in their coffee.

Bassett is impressed, too, by the way motorists in Austria handle, for example, rival claims to a parking space. "In this respect

of other countries considerably..."

Who would argue with him? In music alone the names reel off like a pantheon of gods: Brahms, Mozart, Haydn, Schubert, the Strausses, Schoenberg, Bruckner. Beethoven and Mahler represent a slight problem; they were not born in Austria but they blossomed in the unrivalled atmosphere of Vienna created by local aristocrats competing with one another to secure the services of the best musicians, not to mention the architects and painters as well.

Left, Heinz Schimanko, Vienna's nightclub king. **Above**, cool café.

Vienna is unrivalled. Posturing, exaggeration, threats which instantly crumple up into spineless submission... The Austrians are born improvisers, happy to storm with rage one moment but equally content to smile innocently at the next."

While the Habsburg dynasty left by far the clearest impression on the make-up of the modern Austrian, there are extant strains of an earlier existence. The Miracle Plays in the Tyrol began as religious folk festivals in the early days of Christianity. They evolved into gigantic Baroque spectacles lasting several days. The plays are presented on a more modest scale today, although beneath the reenactment of Christ's Passion there is still an atavistic streak of medieval hanky panky.

Participants in the Vierbergelauf (Four Mountain Course) in Carinthia might as well come clean and admit that it is pagan with only a dash of Christianity added. Starting at midnight on the second Friday after Easter, the "faithful" charge about the mountains to anticipate and then follow the path of the sun. They are joined in this commendable devotion by lost souls trying to escape some awful fate to which they have previously been condemned.

Pig's dance: The pig enjoys in Austria a degree of respect and affection not accorded to it in all other cultures. The pig still ends up

being slaughtered, usually as the climax of pig chases and the "pig's dance", long a very acceptable excuse for young men and women to make the most of the festive atmosphere. Johann Strauss contributed a jaunty ode to the pig, probably not his greatest work and in any case one which may suffer unfairly in translation:

My aim in life,
White, pink and big,
It's lard and pork,
And piggy-wig!

For a people who attach so much importance to frivolity (when they're not producing philosophers like the distinctly unfriv-olous Ludwig Wittgenstein), the Austrians have a ghoulish preoccupation with death, although they seem to have registered some progress since the days when Emperor Franz II ordered the body of a black man, one Angeli Soliman who had rendered sterling service as an adviser to the nobility, to be stuffed and mounted among flora and fauna as a museum piece. Other skinned and stuffed corpses were put on display by Joseph II supposedly to generate interest in anatomy.

Today a last resting place, with a romantic view and shade-providing trees, is selected as carefully as a holiday villa on a Spanish costa and funerals are as lavish as any wedding. "We love the sickly, morbid scent of chrysanthemums," enthuses one Austrian champion of death. Even these days the coffin is nearly always of oak, with plenty of elaborate in-lay.

The Emperor Joseph II thought things had gone too far in this respect and that his subjects wasted too much oak on coffins with pharaonic pretensions. He personally designed a reusable coffin (the bottom unhinged to let the corpse drop into the grave) and was only prevented from making its use compulsory by popular outrage. A model of his invention is on display in Vienna – in a museum which honours the nation's undertakers. Vienna boasts of having the largest cemetery in the world, the Zentralfriedhof, and there are not a few Austrians who seem strangely smug about the country's position in the first division of suicide statistics.

It is to the statisticians that in the end one must turn for a satisfactory solution to the riddle of the average Austrian. "The popularity and consequent usage of numbers has become increasingly popular in the last few years…" The official publication devoted to this subject continues with advice on how to pursue the elusive goal and says its records are open for inspection. "Should you decide to attend personally," it tells prospective callers, "you will find the central information desk on the ground floor, to the left of the entrance. It is recommended that you contact this service either in writing or by telephone should you have a problem that requires a complex, comprehensive solution." Quite.

Left, Styrian pig farmer. **Right**, Art Nouveau relief in Vienna's Barnabitengasse.

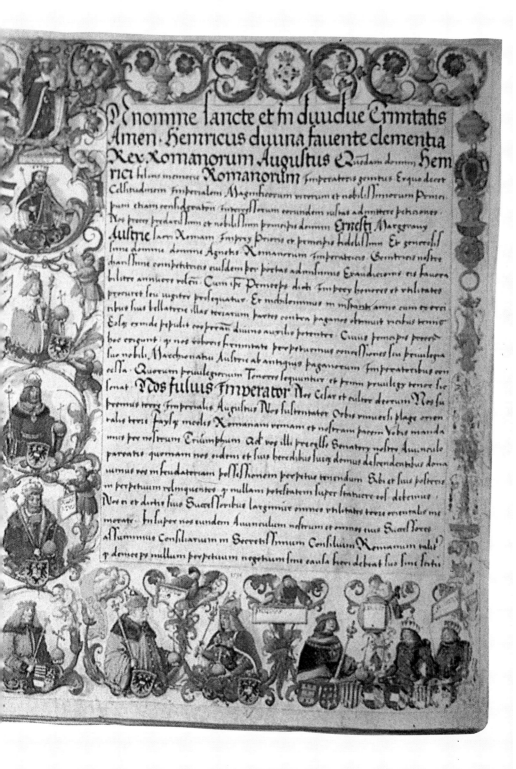

In nomine sancte et in dividue Trinitatis Amen. Henricus divina favente clementia Rex Romanorum Augustus Quondam domini Henrici felicis memorie Romanorum Imperatoris genitus Erga decet Celsitudinem Imperialem Magnificorum virorum et nobilissimorum Principum etiam consideratione Successorum eorundem iustas admittere petitiones Nos preces predicti Ioannis et nobilissimi principis domini Ernesti Marggravii Austrie sacri Romani Imperii Prioris et principis fidelissimi Et generosissime domine domine Agnetis Romanorum Imperatricis Genitricis nostre charissime cohibitricis eiusdem per portas admissimus Exaudiemus eis favorabiliter annuere volens Cum se Princeps dicti Imperii honores et utilitates procuret seu iugiter prosequatur Et nichilominus in instanti anno cum ex ovibus Eosque ex inde populos eos prout divino auxilio petentes Cuius principis procedit sue nobili Macchenatus Austrie ab antiquis paganorum Imperatoribus conservat Quorum privilegiorum Tenores sequuntur et prius privilegii tenor sic premius terre Imperiales Augustus Nos Sustentator Orbis universi plage orientalis terre faylis medis Romanam vienam et nostram pacem Vobis mandamus per nostrum Triumphum Ad vos illi precelse Senatori nostro Avunculo parentis quoniam nos eidem et suis heredibus suisque domus descendentibus donavimus vos in feudatoriam possessionem perpetuo tenendum Sibi et suis posteris in perpetuum relinquentes et nullam potestatem super sententie eos debemus Nos et dictis suis Successoribus largimur omnes utilitates terre orientalis memorate hii super nos eundem Avunculum nostrum et omnes eius Successores assummimus Consiliarium in Secretissimum Consilium Romanum tali quod deinceps nullam perpetuum negotium sine causa fieri debeat suis sine factis

So ich nun auff die zeÿtt Otto des kaÿsers pin ko
men· so wil ich von den dingen sagen· die zu sei
nen zeÿtten zu auffspring geschehen send· Do sich d
kaÿser otto beraÿttet wider berengancium den künig vo
lamparden als wider ain wietrich· vnd geitigen vn
der alle gerechtikait vmb gelt gab· Doch so forcht
in der selb wietrich· wan er die mächtikait des kaÿ
sers wol wisset· vnd durch ratt des hertzogen vo lüth
ringen· kom er zu dem kaÿser vnd begeret frid· Do

CELTS, ROMANS AND INVADERS FROM HELL

Comparatively little is known about the earliest inhabitants of the future Austria. The Celts arrived in roughly 390 BC, the year in which they also conquered Rome, as yet an insignificant town. Elsewhere at the time of their arrival, Athens had just passed the apex of its Golden Age and was about to be engulfed by the Macedonians under Alexander the Great. While the Macedonians conquered Greece and then pushed east through Persia towards India, the Celts drove in the opposite direction. In coats of mail, armed with huge shields and iron swords, equally happy fighting on foot, horses or from chariots, the Celts were irresistible as they tore through Austria, Northern Italy, Gaul, Spain and Britain.

For all their ferocity in battle, the Celts were evidently quite benign in victory and quickly assimilated. The original Austrians introduced the Celts to their well-developed techniques of iron and salt mining, the latter reciprocated by providing a new language, religion and a taste for urban settlement. Noreaia, the name given to the Celtic "kingdom", corresponded with all but the western extremities of modern Austria.

Germanic tribes to the north were a constant threat to Noreaia but it was eventually to the Romans that it lost its independence. Possibly because they feared the Germanic tribes more than the Romans, the Noricans were pleased to be included in plans for an empire which would stretch from the Rhine in the west to the Danube in the east.

Fortified Vienna: For 50 years or so the Romans were content to let the Noricans run their own affairs under traditional leaders, but incessant harassment by northern tribes necessitated putting the province, re-named Noricum, on a more military footing. The future Vienna, among many other settlements, was fortified with an earth rampart and garrisoned by a contingent of 1,000 British cavalry in the Roman army.

Rome kept up a lively trade with all corners of empire and beyond, and as the Danube was the principal eastern artery, Noricum was bound to be in the thick of it. The supplementary network of roads and mountain passes carried a heavy traffic in Austrian gold, iron, salt and cattle south. Italy supplied olive oil and wine, although it was not long before the Romans introduced wine-growing (and bee-keeping) to the province.

Christianity was another import. Legend attributes the first teaching to St Florian, a soldier and early convert who escaped with 40 followers from Diocletian's persecution

in Rome. Hoping that Noricum would be more tolerant, he sat down to explain his religious convictions to the governor. The governor's response was to have him drowned. The statue still to be seen in many Austrian villages of a saint pouring water over a burning house is of this St Florian.

Rome's military might was ultimately insufficient to keep the northern tribes out. They were in turn eclipsed by Asiatic tribes who were even more terrifying. Short, squat and muscular, the newcomers ate roots and raw meat, leading to the assumption that they could only have originated in hell. Some of these tribes remained for a generation or two

Preceding pages: the *privilegium majus*. **Left,** the Battle of Lechfeld, 955. **Right,** Venus of Willendorf, ancient fertility symbol.

and then moved on, but there were always others waiting to fill their space. From the 6th century onwards, most of the intruders were Turko-Finnish Hvars and Slavs.

Charlemagne rose in the 8th century to impose Christian order on a confusion of squabbling kingdoms and wild tribes. He subdued the Saxons in the north-east and the Lombards in northern Italy. He withdrew inconclusively from an expedition against the Moors in Spain but established a "Spanish March" south of the Pyrenees to keep the infidel at bay. The Eastern March, or Ostmark, in the middle Danube basin was his buttress against the Hvars and later the Magyars.

For services to Christianity and in particu-

burgs, preferred to see themselves – semi-divine and grudgingly only second to the pope as champions of Christianity against whomever threatened it.

On Charlemagne's death, the empire disintegrated but the idea behind it lived on. The German nobility, who had emerged as the hard core of Charlemagne's support, decided among themselves who would be their overall monarch under the title of King of the Romans. The throne was not hereditary – although reigning Kings of the Romans were forever scheming to make it so – but it was the recognised stepping stone to becoming emperor, a transition which required the pope's endorsement and a coronation.

Charlemagne

lar for helping Pope Leo III in his difficulties with rebellious Romans, on Christmas Day, 800, Charlemagne was crowned Emperor of the Romans, a title which distinguished him from the eastern emperor in Byzantine Constantinople. In more familiar terms, he became "Holy Roman Emperor".

When Charlemagne was buried at Aachen (Aix-la-Chapelle) in 814, his body was embalmed in a sitting position on a golden chair, a gold sword at his side, a golden volume of the Gospels on his knees, a gold chain around his neck and a piece of the wood of Christ's cross in a crown on his head. That is how his successors, including a long line of Habs-

Contested title: Over the centuries, the rules of succession were modified. The election of the king was vested in an electoral college (or Diet) of seven princes whose membership of the college was a fiercely contested honour. A new King of the Romans was elected and kept in the wings during an emperor's lifetime in order to speed up the eventual succession. Any Christian ruler, not merely the Germans, became eligible for the throne, and this tended to make the competition hotter and less manageable.

Not to appreciate the prestige and complications of the imperial succession is, alas, to run the risk of being thoroughly confused by the flow of European history which was central to the making of modern Austria. It caused many more wars than anything else over a thousand years, and the chance to become Holy Roman Emperor was a mouth-watering prospect even to a hardened atheist like Napoleon. A perennial claim to the imperial throne, abetted by a talent for arranging useful marriages, was the mainspring of the House of Habsburg.

Babenberg dynasty: The laborious build-up to the Habsburgs' near monopoly of the throne began in 955 when Emperor Otto the Great, one of the Germans, defeated the Magyars at the historic Battle of Lechfeld. They retreated to what is now Hungary,

built on claims to the Babenberg inheritance.

The Babenbergs were adept at making the most of the chronic three-cornered contest between the Pope in Rome, the Holy Roman Emperor, who was supposed to be loyal to him but often had other ideas, and the German princes who effectively put the emperor where he was. The Babenberg policy of supporting the King of the Romans, in other words the emperor-elect, at a critical point in this contest earned them a duchy in 1156. The Babenberg in question was Henry, better known as "Jasomirgott", a contraction of his favourite saying: "God help me!" The freshly-minted duke announced that he would take his seat at Vienna.

where they have remained. The rescued eastern marches were in 976 put in the charge of Count Leopold of Babenberg, who was elevated to the rank of margrave but remained officially subject to the Duchy of Bavaria. A document of 996 makes reference to the margrave's lands as "Ostarrichi", only a short cry from the later "Österreich". By then the Babenbergs were well on their way laying the foundations of a dynasty which was to last 300 years. The Habsburg fortunes were

His son, Leopold, amassed great wealth for the Babenbergs. He was one of the so-called Robber Barons, the German princes who plundered the armies of the Crusaders on their passage to the Holy Land to repel the Mohammedan threat. Inevitably, such wealth attracted predators. The last of the Babenbergs, known as Frederick the Quarrelsome, was caught between a Holy Roman Emperor threatening the duchy from the west, warlike Magyars from the east, and jealous princely rivals all around. He lost Vienna to the first, his life to the second (at the battle of Leitha in 1246), and his dominions to Ottokar II of Bohemia.

Far left, Iron Age figure. **Left**, Charlemagne, Emperor of the Romans. **Above**, the death of Duke Frederick II, the last of the Babenbergs.

Haupt Ansicht der Residenzstadt Wien,
und des gröften Theils ihrer Vorftädte, von Belvedere anzusehen.

Maria Hilf.   St. Ulrich.   Rochkirche.   Augustiner Hofkirche.
Stadlmaus auf der Wieden.   Pfarrkin in der Josefstadt.   Pfarrkirche in der Alsergrund.

Vûe de la Capitale de Vienne, et d'une grande partie de ses Fauxbourgs, prise du coté du Belvedere.

St Stephan, Domkirche. de Universitæt. Salesianerinnen auf dem Rennweg, Elisabethanerinnen,
die Leopoldstadt. Pfarrkirche zu Erdberg, Augustiner auf der Landstraße,

W-I/45

The Babenbergs were not the only victims of a period of utter anarchy as the Robber Barons turned on one another. Pope Gregory became so alarmed by the "Terrible Times" that in 1273 he warned that if they did not settle their differences long enough to elect a new King of the Romans to restore order, he would impose one himself.

The most obvious contender was King Ottokar of Bohemia whose flourishing kingdom had expanded so that it stretched from Bavaria to Hungary and from the Baltic to the Adriatic. While the princes felt obliged to obey the pope, a king actually able to call them to order was the last thing they wanted. They cast around for a suitable nonentity who would not impede their rampaging ways, and their eyes settled on a minor count, Rudolf of Habsburg.

Rudolf was 55 years old at the time. He was amazingly tall, all of 7 ft (2.1 metres), and as thin as a rake. His tiny head was completely bald and thrown out of balance by a nose so enormous that (the story went) it prevented other riders from passing on narrow mountain tracks. His complexion was pale, his expression grave, and he tended to wear peasant dress, a notable eccentricity in an age of resplendent feudal regalia. He had inherited only a half-share of the land which bore the family name and a few scattered estates. He had since managed to wrest back some ancestral lands from the church, but he was not well-off. His election as king would change that. "I am not he that once before ye knew," he declared ominously as he rose from his knees after the coronation.

Acre maker: His first success was to defeat Ottokar and take over all his lands. As the undisputed master of the Austrian provinces, Rudolf parcelled them out to his sons and went off in Habsburg pursuit of "more acres". He bought out the residual Babenberg claims in the region, persuaded Henry of Bavaria to cede him land above the Enns, and took over Carinthia. His dynastic ambitions took a significant step forward in 1282 when the

electors agreed at the Diet of Augsburg that Austria, Styria, Carinthia and Carniola would pass to his two sons as a joint inheritance. Swabia, Alsace and Switzerland were earmarked for a third son, Hartman, but on a journey to England with a view to marrying Joanna, Edward III's daughter, Hartman fell into the Rhine and drowned.

The pacification of the pugnacious German barons was a formidable task, and in one year alone Rudolf destroyed 70 castles belonging to them. Encouraged by his success,

Rudolf advanced on the Counts of Burgundy and Wurttemberg, who appealed to Philip IV of France for protection. The French king sent ambassadors to tell Rudolf to get off French territory. "Tell Philip," he replied languidly, "that we await his arrival, and will convince him that we are not here to dance or make merry, but to give law with the sword." In reality, his army had run out of supplies was practically starving and about to be defeated. With a sure instinct for the morale-boosting gesture, Rudolf pulled a turnip out of the ground and ate it raw, saying he could not remember a better meal.

Rudolf was invigorated at the age of 64 by

Preceding pages: Vienna, seat of the Habsburgs, in 1784. **Left,** Maximilian I. **Right,** the Zollfeld ducal throne.

a second marriage to Agnes of Burgundy, a lovely girl of 14. But his last desire on reaching the age of 73 was to secure his son Albrecht's future. The plum would have been to get him elected as King of the Romans and therefore in line to become emperor, but the electors were not keen on Albrecht. Their rejection is said to have broken Rudolf's heart so that he died soon afterwards in deep depression.

But in time Albrecht managed to win election as King of the Romans on the strength of his own merits in putting down revolts in Vienna and Styria and, in league with others, deposing Adolphus of Nassau, who had succeeded his father. Pope Boniface VIII hesi-

his reign, Charles of Bohemia published a Golden Bull which stripped the Habsburgs of their vote in the electoral college, an almost essential platform from which to mount another bid for the throne.

Rudolf IV, then head of the Habsburg House, retaliated with the discovery of a cache of documents which proved beyond the shadow of doubt that the Habsburgs were the most illustrious family in Christendom, so exalted in fact that they outranked even the collective authority of the electors. The documents were forgeries, of course, but the various Habsburgs wore their windfall of new titles with considerable aplomb. Rudolf let it be known that if the electors continued

tated before confirming the election, but Albrecht did not live long to enjoy the throne. He lost his life in a war with the Swiss, whose numbers included the celebrated William Tell. The cause of death was not one of William's well-aimed arrows but a mighty blow with an axe which split Albrecht's head. On that gruesome note, the imperial crown slipped off Habsburg heads and was not to be regained for a century.

Counterfeit glory: Alarmed at the thought that in Rudolf and Albrecht they had inadvertently sown the seeds of a power beyond their control, the princely electors set about cutting the Habsburgs down to size. During

to bar his path to the imperial throne, he was empowered by God to establish a new one.

The contest for the throne became a personal battle between Rudolf and Charles of Bohemia, whose capital was Prague. News of the construction of St Vitus's Cathedral in Prague goaded Rudolf into reconstructing St Stephen's in Vienna on an even grander scale. A university in Prague? Vienna must have one too, and better.

The Habsburgs eventually regained the imperial throne in 1438. The Hussite uprising in Bohemia at the beginning of that century was the first intimation of religious revolt which, under Martin Luther, still lay another century ahead. It was recognised at once, though, as a threat to much of what the empire stood for, and the Emperor Sigismund was grateful for any help, even from the Habsburgs. Albrecht V, then head of the House, was willing to give it, but at the price of marriage to Sigismund's daughter and, on Sigismund's death, the kingdom of Hungary. With the extra crown firmly on his head, Albrecht could no longer be denied the coveted title.

In his dual capacity as King of Hungary and Holy Roman Emperor, Albrecht was immediately called upon to defend his lands against a threat from the Turkish Ottomans. They had already conquered much of Asia Minor, laid siege to Constantinople and invaded Serbia. Hungary was next in line, and any doubts the Hungarians might have harboured about their new king were overshadowed by the need to rally round him. The actual confrontation, however, fizzled out because dysentery laid both sides low. Albrecht himself contracted it. "I shall recover," he declared confidently, "if I can only once more behold the walls of Vienna." He couldn't and he didn't, dying in the village of Gran on his way there.

Relieved to have the imperial throne back, the Habsburgs and the nobility beholden to them called their hero "Albrecht the Magnanimous", but the glory did not filter down to their ordinary subjects. Vienna seethed with economic unrest. Albrecht blamed the Jews, who were thereupon persecuted and massacred in fearful numbers. The Hungarians had no cause to love him either, and immediately after he died they snatched back their throne.

Conditions hardly improved under Frederick III. He was at loggerheads with his quarrelsome neighbour, Matthias Corvinus of Hungary, fought wars against his brother and was twice besieged with his family in the Hofburg by the Viennese themselves. The wretched royals were forced to eat the palace pets and even vultures, which gathered hungrily but unwisely on the roof.

He was buoyed up throughout these trials by sublime confidence in the efficacy of his royal blood. As ingenious in matters of

Left, Walther von der Vogelweide, poet at the time of the Babenbergs. **Right**, Rudolf IV, claimed to be empowered by God.

geneology as Rudolf IV had been, Frederick was able to trace his line to Augustus Caesar and thence to King Priam of Troy. Steeped in magic and the occult, he had all his possessions engraved enigmatically with the letters A E I O U. To the naive eye, these looked like the alphabet vowels, but Frederick was able to reveal with smug satisfaction that they stood for *Austriae Est Imperare Orbi Universo*, or "Austria [by which he meant the House of Austria, the Habsburgs] is Destined to Rule the Whole World".

The practical side of Frederick's nature knew that if the Habsburgs were going to rule anything at all their coffers would have to be replenished massively and without

delay. Moreover, the previous bloodline was in jeopardy. All but two of his children were dead. The only hope lay in negotiating an advantageous marriage for his son Maximilian, a name he had invented through some astrological formula, a combination of Fabius Maximus and Paulus Aemilius.

Maximilian and marriage: Maximilian, then 14, was taken along to wait in the wings while Frederick negotiated for Marie, daughter of Charles the Bold, the Duke of Burgundy and the richest man in Europe. Innumerable suitors were jostling for Marie's hand, and Charles was in no mood to let her go for an iota less than she was worth. On financial grounds, Frederick would have stood absolutely no chance, but he had something in his gift (Charles believed), the only thing which was more important than money. Frederick could make him King of the Romans, his heir-apparent. As such, in one glorious bound, he would soar in rank over the despised King of France. Confident that Frederick would have to accept his terms, Charles called in his jewellers to have his head measured for a crown.

Charles over-estimated Frederick's ability to influence the electors. They were as usual open to bribery, but Frederick was in no position to bribe them. The whole purpose of marrying Maximilian to Marie was

LOUIS XI

Fils de Charles VII, né à Bourges en 1423.
Très jeune, il eut la soif du pouvoir, se révolta contre son père
et à sa mort, en 1461, se fit sacrer à Reims. Malgré ses défauts,
Louis XI reste un des créateurs de l'unité nationale.
Nul ne connut mieux les ruses de la politique, les passions des hommes,
et les moyens de les dominer. Grâce à sa ruse, à sa patience,
et sa mauvaise foi, il abaissa les grands, surtout le Duc de Bourgogne,
Charles le Téméraire et réussit non seulement à leur enlever leurs pouvoirs,
mais à accroître le territoire de la Couronne.
Il mourut en 1483, au Château de Plessis-les-Tours,
livré à toutes les Terreurs du remords et de la superstition.

4   ND

to make money, not give it away. On the very eve of the convention at which the electors were supposed to choose the next King of the Romans, Frederick slipped away and the election had to be postponed.

Stuck with an unbetrothed daughter and a half-finished crown, Charles seemed to lose his senses, launching himself into a series of gravely misjudged and ultimately ruinous wars. Frederick sat and waited for the inevitable. By 1476 Charles was a broken man, willing to let Marie go to Maximilian unconditionally. Within days of his decision, his body was dragged out of a frozen lake; by then it had been half-eaten by wolves. In

order to forestall any designs the son of Louis XI of France might have on the fatherless Marie, the Duke Ludwig of Bavaria played the part of the proxy groom in a ceremony which required him to lie next to her on a bed with one leg bare. The rest of his body was covered, awkwardly it would seem, in armour.

Marie gave Maximilian an heir, Philip, and a daughter Margaret, and was then killed in a riding accident. Maximilian was devastated, his gloom compounded by news that the skinny Dauphin who had once been his rival for Marie's hand was now Charles VIII of France and lobbying furiously for the Kingdom of the Romans which Maximilian considered his own.

With France looking even more dangerous than the Turks, Maximilian surveyed the options among states capable of making the King of France think again. As he could hardly marry another Burgundy, he looked at the next best, and that was Brittany. Anne, the 15-year-old heiress to Brittany, fitted the bill perfectly. The necessary arrangements were concluded without fuss and an ambassador despatched to lie in bed with Anne, a leg bared.

Desperate search: Charles VIII, the proverbial bad penny, understood what was going on and refused to acknowledge the preemptive rights of the proxy marriage. While Maximilian was detained in Frankfurt on electoral college business, he marched into Brittany, seized Anne, summoned a priest for a perfunctory ceremony, and consummated the marriage there and then. Still desperately short of money, Maximilian was forced to think again and lower his marital sights. In the eyes of his peers, his sights could not have gone much lower than his next quarry, Bianca Sforza, niece of the Duke of Milan. The Sforzas were regarded as jumped-up peasants; still, they appeared to be rich. The Sforzas were keen on the marriage, and Maximilian must have noted with some satisfaction that the preparations for the proxy wedding, not even the real one, were entrusted to Leonardo da Vinci.

Getting to know Bianca was full of surprises which seemed to confirm misgivings about her background. She had to be taught, first of all, not to eat her meals on the floor. Most disconcerting of all, however, was the dawning truth that Bianca was not nearly as rich as he had imagined and, moreover, that any money she had was spent with frivolous abandon. On a journey through the half-starved Netherlands, she insisted on goose tongues for every meal.

It was noted at court that he took to seeing other women, and it was not long before they formed a queue at his door with the illegitimate issue. One of these was a future Bishop of Salzburg.

Maximilian's uninhibited frolics with the large number of "travelling ladies" then drawn to Vienna were the light-hearted side of what with hindsight was the dawn of a Renaissance spirit. The atmosphere in the capital also attracted intellectuals and artists,

In addition, he was physically very brave.

In retrospect, though, the most breathtaking feature of Maximilian's reign is the way he manipulated marriages, not only his own but also those of his relatives. He could be relied upon to come up with a suitable bride or groom for almost any situation. By the end of his reign he had secured a member of his family in almost every House in Europe.

Maximilian's last official function as emperor was to attend the Diet of 1518. In characteristic fashion, he used the occasion to ensure that the imperial succession went to his grandson, the future Charles V. In equally characteristic fashion, he did so by buying the requisite number of votes with money

setting a precedent for the life and times associated with Paris hundreds of years later. He himself was a reasonable example of the so-called Renaissance man. He was well versed in Latin, French, German and Italian, skilled in various arts and sciences and the author of works on such diverse subjects as religion, military matters, hunting, hawking and cookery. He was also an able administrator who established local government in the 10 districts of empire, overhauled the legal system and abolished many oppressive taxes.

Left, Maxmilian's opponent, Louis XI of France. Above, Vienna in 1530.

which he did not possess. Two other items of business on the Diet's agenda that year were ominous. One was the Turkish threat, then looming so large that the Pope was calling for another crusade. The other, which Maximilian did not consider of great significance, concerned a meddlesome Augustinian monk who the previous year had affixed to the door of the church at Wittenberg 95 propositions condemning the Church's dubious raising of funds through the sale of indulgences. Maximilian died with little intimation of what the Turks and Martin Luther would mean to the Habsburg fortunes his arranged marriages had nurtured.

Charles V, Maximilian's heir and grandson and a Habsburg, albeit of the Spanish branch, was forced to spend at least $20 million on bribes to see off challenges for the imperial throne from Francis I of France, who spent even more, Henry VIII of England, Lajos of Hungary and Sigismund of Poland. In victory, however, he could survey the fruits of Maximilian's matchmaking: in addition to his Spanish inheritance, which included Naples and Sicily, he had an aunt Margaret who was Regent of the Netherlands, he shared the German-speaking lands with his brother Ferdinand, he had sisters who were queens of France, Portugal, Hungary, Bohemia, Denmark, Norway and Sweden and another aunt, Catherine of Aragon, who was married to the King of England.

Charles presided over the Diet at Worms in 1521 whose outcome was the famous Edict of Worms which denounced Martin Luther and was famously ignored by him. With Charles frequently distracted by other imperial business, especially Turkish incursions in Hungary, the Archduke Ferdinand was left to grapple with the intractable problem of Protestantism in Austria not only among the masses, who rose in what became known as the Peasants' Wars of 1525–26, but also at the University of Vienna and among the aristocracy

Turkish breakfast: An even more dangerous threat to the faith which Charles was pledged to defend came in 1526 with the news that a Turkish army "sufficient to exterminate the world" under the command of Suleiman the Magnificent had advanced to the Hungarian border. This time Suleiman withdrew but he was back three years later with the intention of taking Vienna. His army reached the walls of the city with only trifling opposition and laid siege. "On the third day," a message to the motley defenders promised, "we will breakfast within your walls." Turkish sappers moved their trenches forward and tunnelled under the walls to lay mines. If Vienna fell, there was no knowing where or how the Turks could be stopped. As days and then

Left, Martin Luther, seen as a Protestant threat.
Above, Kara Mustapha, leader of the Turks.

weeks passed with the situation unchanged, the Viennese commander was emboldened to signal the Turks: "Your breakfast is getting cold." So was the weather, and the Turks knew better than Napoleon would about the perils of feeding 250,000 mouths in frozen conditions 700 miles from home. With the first snow of winter, the Turks struck their tents and departed.

Even so, by 1555 Charles was a broken man. The Turkish and French threats, coupled with German princes who saw Luther-

anism as a tool to undermine the central authority of the empire, sapped him of the will to continue in office. He resigned the crowns of the Netherlands and Spain to one of his sons, and took the unprecedented step of abdicating the imperial throne as well. He then retired to a convent.

While the Counter-Reformation was pursued vigorously, not to say brutally, in the Spanish half of the Habsburg empire, Charles's easy-going heir Maximilian was far more tolerant of Protestants. An ambassador commented that in Austria "the question is seldom asked whether anyone is Catholic or Protestant". The relative calm lasted until 1618 when in Prague, not for the first or last time, a political altercation ended in defenestration, a dignified term for the business of throwing people out of windows.

The victims in this instance were two Roman Catholic imperial envoys who had gone to Prague for a meeting with Protestant leaders. Tempers frayed and the two envoys in full regalia were hoisted out of a window of the Hradcany castle 60 feet above the ground. They managed to cling to the window ledge by their finger tips for a while, but a bang on the knuckles broke their hold and sent them plunging in howling descent. They landed, as luck would have it, in a pile of dung and made good their escape to report

the insult to Vienna. The result was the Thirty Years' War, one which engulfed Europe as had never happened before and the likes of which would not be seen again until Napoleonic times, or even World War I.

Behind the rhetoric, the battle between Protestants and Catholics, was the House of Habsburg settling old scores with France, and it only ended through the sheer exhaustion of all concerned.

Siege of Vienna: When the dust of the Thirty Years' War settled, the Habsburg fortunes were in the hands of a 14-year-old who had impressed his Jesuit teachers in his nursery by making little chapels out of wooden blocks

and pretending to be a priest celebrating mass. His personal qualities were not otherwise alluring. Young Leopold was undersized, a weakling, ugly beyond belief, almost toothless and so short-sighted as to be practically blind. Nonetheless the sickly youth rallied to log one of the longest reigns in Austria, and against two of the wiliest opponents of all time – Louis XIV of France and Kara Mustapha, Grand Vizier of Turkey – he steered his domain into joining the first rank of European powers.

The early years of Leopold's career were occupied by what might be described as routine business. His Jesuit advisers were let loose to conduct the Counter-Reformation, he survived an attempt on his life by Hungarian Protestants and Turks who sent him a poisoned pigeon pie, Vienna was struck by plague in 1679, and all the time Louis XIV was trying to encroach on his territory.

The passage of Halley's comet in 1682 heralded something extraordinary, the nature of which he did not yet know. "May God will that I do nothing wicked," Leopold wrote, "for I know myself as a great sinner, and just now it is high time to appease the godly majesty, who shows his anger, for we see a comet that to all pious-minded people is clearly seen as a warning to make atonement before our new sins are punished with a well-deserved lash…"

The lash in question was wielded by the Grand Vizier Kara Mustapha. He would not relax, he announced, until his horses were stabled under the dome of St Peter's in Rome, and with that objective in mind a Turkish army 250,000-strong began the long march through the Balkans.

By July 1683 the Turks were only hours away from Vienna and blind panic set in. The sight of the Carmelite convent on the Kahlenberg burning told the population just how close the Turks were. Peasants poured into the capital and the nobility tried to flee in the opposite direction. Surrounded by subjects imploring him not to desert them, Leopold wept and held out a hand to be kissed even as he backed into a carriage. Palace courtiers and servants bolted from the Hofburg in such haste that they neglected to close the gates.

The lives of the 60,000 people left in Vienna rested on a mixed force of 20,000 infantry and armed civilians backed up by artillery of untested quality. The city was enclosed by the walls on three sides, the river took care of the fourth, and the bridge across it was destroyed as the Turks approached. The imperial army, such as it was, was held in reserve further up the Danube under the command of Leopold's brother-in-law, Duke Charles of Lorraine. Luckily, King John Sobieski of Poland, recognising that the fall of Vienna would leave the road open to Poland, offered to help.

On 4 September a tremendous explosion destroyed part of the wall near the Hofburg. Thousands of Turks protected their heads with sacks as they scaled the walls crying "Allah! Allah!". They were able to plant two

tember, Polish cavalry executed a brilliant manoeuvre which ended the siege that day.

Leopold was on a boat on the Danube when he learned of the lightning victory. His immediate orders were to postpone any celebrations until he got to Vienna. He was candid about the reason: "It is true I have commanded that I must be the first to enter the city, for I fancy that otherwise the love of my subjects for me would be diminished, and their affection for others increase."

Political alliance: On the other flank of the empire, the problem was as usual France. Louis XIV was determined to win for his son Philip the Spanish crown which the Habsburgs had come to regard as family

standards on the wall before being driven back. The defenders patched the hole in the wall with rubble, furniture, wine-presses, mattresses – anything that came to hand.

The Grand Vizier could probably have taken the city by force, but he preferred to wait for a capitulation. It was a mistake. Before then a salvo of rockets from the Kahlenberg signalled the approach of the relief column. As a mixture of Saxons, Schwabians, Bavarians and Bohemians charged down the Kahlenberg on 12 Sep-

Left, officer cadet in the Thirty Years' War. Above, the Siege of Vienna.

property. England was absolutely opposed to a union between France and Spain, the newly imported King William of Orange especially so. Such a union would imperil his birthplace, Holland.

The Grand Alliance therefore created one of history's most famous military partnerships, the patrician Duke of Marlborough, Winston Churchill's ancestor, and little Prince Eugene, destined to become Austria's most famous soldier. They could not have been more different. When Marlborough once spotted some of his men apparently leaving the field of battle, he extended an arm and cried out: "Gentlemen, the enemy lies that way." In exactly the same circumstances, indeed during the same battle, Eugene whipped out a gun and shot his men. As a team, however, Marlborough and Eugene were devastating. They destroyed the French at Blenheim and won honours at Oudenarde, Malplaquet and Ramillies. Eugene went on alone to capture Turin.

The English were being slightly duplicitous in their alliance. Their objective was to defeat France, not to win Spain for the Habsburgs. As soon as the French were beaten, England broke off the alliance. Charles VI, Leopold's successor, therefore did not get Spain, although under the Treaty of Utrecht he was compensated with Spanish

possessions in the form of Naples, Milan, the Spanish Netherlands and Sardinia, the last later exchanged for Sicily. On the other hand, the French Philip did get Spain, but only on the condition that he forfeited rights to the French throne.

As if to make up for his disappointment over Spain, Charles introduced what was to become an enduring feature of the Habsburg court in Vienna. Etiquette and ritual followed Spanish custom, and king and courtiers wore Spanish dress. Fisher von Erlach, the young Austrian architect largely responsible for rebuilding Vienna after the siege, strove to incorporate Spanish touches in his work,

notably the twin pillars of his Karlskirche. The other preoccupation was to improve on anything the wretched French could do. Schönbrunn, as he originally conceived it, was meant to outdo Versailles. Such extravagance drew attention to the yawning gulf between rich and poor and raised questions about the source of aristocratic wealth.

The disparity was particularly glaring in Bohemia where confiscated land belonging to Protestants had been parcelled out to the Roman Catholic noblility, who were expected to reciprocate with unswerving loyalty to the Habsburgs and not decamp with their estates into the arms of some rival power. As time went by, the Habsburgs had to sweeten the bonds by exempting the nobility from taxation.

Pragmatic sanction: As the empire was held together by the pampered self-interest of the respective nobilities rather than geographical or cultural links, Charles even at the age of 28 was fretting over his apparent inability to produce the male heir without which the whole thing would very likely fall apart. There was no provision for the throne going to a daughter, so the empress's bed-chamber was stuffed with male charms of the type which could well have been supplied by a witchdoctor. When these failed to work, Charles resorted to "Pragmatic Sanction", a loophole which enabled him to promulgate certain laws without reference to the Electoral Diet. In this instance, the Pragmatic Sanction went against all precedent by permitting the crown if necessary to pass to a daughter – a solution which raised a chorus of objection from those countries keen to see the Austrian Empire disintegrate. As Charles was to learn, the willingness of some to turn a blind eye came at a price.

Charles wanted to see Maria Theresa, his threatened heiress, secured as far as possible by a good marriage. The Prussian Crown Prince Frederick was considered, as was a Spanish Bourbon prince, but the 15-year-old archduchess was single-minded about marrying Franz Stephan, the heir to the Duchy of Lorraine and grandson of the commander at the siege of Vienna. France rubbed its hands at the prospect; it was time to play its Pragmatic Sanction card. The bridegroom would

Left, Prince Eugene, Austria's greatest soldier.
Right, the formidable Maria Theresa.

MARIA THERESIA
HVNGARIAE   BOHEMIAE REGINAE
AVGVSTAE   CONIVGI
ORBIS   DELICIIS
NOSTRI TEMPORIS   PALLADI

MARTIN DE MEITENS PINXIT.
PHIL. ANDR. KILIAN SVMPTIBVS SOCIETATIS SCVLPSIT

D D D
OMNIVM HVMILLIMA
DEVOTISSIMA
AA LL SOCIETAS

have to surrender his Lorraine inheritance to France. The young duke was appalled at the blackmail. On being told to sign, he thrice picked up the pen, stopped himself, and threw it down. "No renunciation, no arch-duchess," taunted one of Charles's ministers. He signed.

Empress in waiting: The couple were married in 1736 and within four years they produced three children, all girls. During those four years, the emperor went from bad to worse. The Pragmatic Sanction imbroglio dragged him into two disastrous wars, as a result of which he lost Serbia. He had grown fat and suffered from gout. His final act was to raise his arms in a gesture of benediction

towards the ante-room where Maria Theresa was waiting.

An Empress rules: "I found myself," Maria Theresa wrote of her succession, "without money, without credit, without an army, without experience and knowledge…" Especially without money. The funds in the exchequer stood at 100,000 florins, her army had not been paid for months, and the national debt did not bear thinking about. Fabulously rich subjects who could have settled her financial needs at a stroke were the nobility who paid no taxes and expected things to remain that way. The peasants who did pay tax had already been bled dry. Added to the

gloomy economic prognosis was a new phenomenon in European politics: the rise of Prussia under the man once thought a suitable husband, the future Frederick the Great.

Frederick had just succeeded his father and was busy studying the map of Europe. "Silesia is the portion of the imperial heritage to which we have the strongest claim and which is most suitable," he declared to his aides. "It is consonant with justice to maintain one's rights and to seize the opportunity of the Emperor's death to take possession."

Maria Theresa never forgave Frederick for the rape of Silesia, the opening move in the War of the Austrian Succession. "You had better realise," she remarked darkly, "that nobody is to be trusted less than a Prussian." Her geriatric advisers could not see far worse writing on the wall. France was preparing to dismember the Habsburg empire: "There is no more House of Austria," Cardinal Fleury announced prematurely. The French plan was to give Bohemia and Upper Austria to the Elector of Bavaria, who would then be crowned emperor; Moravia and Upper Silesia to Saxony; Lower Silesia and Glatz to Prussia; and Lombardy to Spain.

In the meantime Maria Theresa gave birth to the child she had been carrying at the time of her succession. Recent Habsburg failure in the matter of male heirs was reversed with spectacular emphasis: the boy, Joseph, was a 16-lb (7-kg) giant at birth and apparently normal in every respect. Clutching the infant, Maria Theresa set off on a last desperate gamble to fend off imminent invasion by both Bavaria and France. Riding a white charger and armed with a sabre, Maria Theresa appealed to her Hungarian subjects for help. Her speech, in Latin, was a classic example of playing to ingrained Hungarian chivalry. There she was, a young woman still in deep mourning for her father and nursing what looked like a promising child.

The Hungarians voted her six regiments, enough to repel the Bavarians and persuade the French to make peace. She never regained Silesia, but she did in due course retrieve the crown of the Holy Roman Empire from the Elector of Bavaria. Ineligible to wear it herself, she did the next best thing and gave it to her husband. The Kingdom of the Romans was reserved for her strapping son.

Left, the unforgivable Frederick the Great.

KOLSCHITZKY'S COFFEE

In the early days of 1683, the Turkish siege had reduced Vienna almost to the point of capitulation. Each day the Viennese commander climbed the tower of St Stephen's to scan the horizon for signs of the relief column. What he saw instead was a Turkish camp larger and more populous than Vienna itself, "crowded not only by soldiers but by the merchants of the East, who thronged thither as to a fair deal in the plunder of the Christians."

The hero of the dangerous task of running messages through the Turkish camp to and from the imperial forces awaiting reinforcements was a Pole named Kolschitzky, who had worked for the Levant Company and spoke fluent Turkish. He relied on brassy boldness and disguise to pass through the Turks. He evidently sang well in Turkish and would cheerfully accept numerous invitations to stop for coffee, a drink he developed a taste for on his travels but was unknown in 17th-century Vienna. While Kolschitzky sipped the endless cups, he was making a mental note of the Turkish deployments.

Kolschitzky's observations were passed on to the Duke of Lorraine and Sobieski and were of inestimable value in the plans drawn up by the Polish king for a lightning strike by his cavalry. With the Turks routed, the besieged population rushed out and fell on the food stores the Turks left behind. Kolschitzky was among them, but he knew exactly what he was looking for – sacks of a certain brown bean. Viennese who saw them asked whether they were best eaten baked, boiled or fried. The intrepid Pole knew otherwise and was rewarded for his services with a licence, the first of its kind in the Holy Roman Empire, to open Kolschitzky's "Kaffee Schrank", later the Blue Bottle in Singerstrasse. There was hardly a business deal, illicit romance or diabolical perfidy in Central Europe thereafter which was not hatched in one or other of hundreds of imitations. The coffee house was born.

In the department of diabolic perfidy, Vienna's Café Central ran absolutely true to form in 1913.

One of the regulars during the especially cold winter of that year was a Herr Bronstein, playing chess with a partner who, if noticed at all by the legions of secret police, was noted for his bushy moustache. If their true identities had been known, they would not have added up to much, but their patronage was recalled when news broke of the Russian revolution. The joke went round that it had been cooked up in the Café Central. "Bronstein" was Trotsky; his partner, Stalin.

The 4,000 coffee houses which Vienna could boast before World War II have shrunk to about 400 at present. Coffee house connoisseurs have strong, although possibly perplexing, views on what constitutes a worthy establishment. It is important, for example, to have staff with character. Attractively-wrapped Amazonian waitresses are considered a plus, but the thoroughbred is a waiter with the right combination of "a harrassed manner and a hint of cynical rapacity". The Bräunerhof has waiters who, it is approvingly said, could easily cause a saint to lose his temper.

Correct deportment in these august surroundings is clearly essential, so strangers ought to be aware that the Austrian's interest in their coffee "amounts almost to a scientific discipline, in which every possible combination of milk and coffee is obsessively categorised". Simply to order "a coffee" would be considered pathetically unimaginative, if not imbecilic. The rudimentary progression from pitch black to milky goes through three stages: Mokka to Kapuziner to Franziskaner. Poised somewhere between the last two is the Melange, and this is to venture on to the thin ice of whether a particular establishment thinks the extra ingredient should be a precise measure of milk or a blob of cream. An Einspanner is definitely cream, masses of the whipped variety.

It is to be wondered whether Herr Kolschitzky could not have persuaded the Turks to go home simply by inventing and serving them the Kaiser Melange. It consists of black coffee and two egg yolks. A studiously polite tourist was recently seen to order a Kaiser Melange with no idea of what to expect. His expression after a gulp was an invitation to solicit his verdict. "Rather..." he began weakly, "no, not rather... *unbelievably* vile."

Joseph, the boy on whom the hopes of the empire rested, grew up to share the throne with his mother as co-regent. The gulf between them was apparent. She was a devout Roman Catholic who, however enlightened, always believed in absolute rule. He was a student of radical French philosophy and wished to revolutionise the entire empire.

On becoming Joseph II he put his liberal theories into practice. The press was given unprecedented freedom, Jews no longer had to identify themselves by wearing yellow

stripes and sleeves, and education was made compulsory for all, including women. Where Joseph's instincts ran into difficulties was in accepting that intellectual freedom also included the right to question his legitimacy as ruler. His successors were confronted with what appeared to be the logical conclusion to unfettered liberty, the French Revolution. The only way to avoid that ghastly scenario in Austria amounted to a backlash.

Austria and France were poles apart: a conservative Roman Catholic monarchy versus a brash, atheistic republic. Both were championed at the beginning of the 19th century by young men who were born within a year of one another in foreign parts. Franz II, the Habsburg emperor, was born in Tuscany, Napoleon in Corsica. Each dreamed of expansive empires; Europe was clearly not big enough for both of them.

Napoleon's occupation of Vienna in 1805 after his lightning victories in Italy was a terrible shock and sent the imperial family packing with all its treasures and archives to the fortress of Olmutz. The stunning French victory over Austria at Austerlitz was handled by Franz with remarkable, although not uncharacteritic, stoicism. A note to his wife read: "A battle was fought today which did not turn out well. I pray you consequently to withdraw from Olmutz to Teschen with everything that belongs to us. I am well."

End of empire: Napoleon crowned himself Emperor of the French and a group of German princes seceded to join him in the Confederation of the Rhine. This was precisely the kind of defection which the Pragmatic Sanction had sought to prevent. Franz simply laid down the imperial crown and declared that the Holy Roman Empire was over. He would henceforth be Franz I of Austria, a Habsburg empire which owed nothing to the Holy Roman one. The title which had fomented countless cunning marriages and numerous wars for 1,000 years dropped out of currency as simply as that.

Franz's immediate concern was to check Napoleon before he could do further damage to the redefined empire. Emboldened by French reverses in Spain, Austrian forces mobilised and, against all odds, inflicted a single-handed defeat at Aspern. Franz watched the victory from a nearby hill. He could be as laconic in triumph as he was in despair. All he said after the battle was: "Now we can, I think, go home."

There then emerged in Austrian affairs a man whose first actions in office bore the stamp of his style. Prince Clemens von Metternich bought peace with Napoleon – "the Corsican ogre" – by persuading him to marry Marie Louise, Franz's daughter (when Napoleon was told that she was in love with another, his reply was: "May princesses fall in love? Why, they are nothing but political merchandise"). A proxy wedding took place in Vienna in March 1810. It was quintessentially Metternich's doing that, having bought peace with the marriage, Austria then declared war on France.

Napoleon was, of course, defeated at Waterloo, and immediately afterwards the Austrian, Russian, Prussian and British allies set about carving up his conquests at the Congress of Vienna. Austria emerged from the peace conference with Salzburg and Venice but had to give up the part of the Netherlands which later became Belgium. It also ben-

blocks of ice to his room; the King of Wurttemberg, too fat to reach the table, required a semi-circular hole cut out of it to accommodate his stomach.

Metternich had larger ambitions than could be satisfied by the congress settlement, but for the moment it served his purposes to remain dutifully at the foot of the throne and bide his time. A glance into the Hofburg nursery was enough to see that the next-in-line was a totally hopeless case. The heir Ferdinand, everyone agreed, was a friendly

efited from the prestige and fast-flowing money of 100,000 visitors and 215 princely delegates to the congress, but the cost and complications of putting up all the reigning sovereigns, their families and servants at the Hofburg were awesome. The Hofburg guests were fed each day at 40 banqueting tables; a transport pool of several hundred carriages was kept in readiness in the palace stables round the clock. Many of the guests had quirks: the Czar Alexander had some unexplained need for a regular supply of large

Left, Joseph II is crowned. **Above**, Napoleon rides through.

little fellow but an imbecile in the clinical sense of the word. With Ferdinand on the throne, Metternich could look forward to running the empire with a free hand. It remained to get Ferdinand on to it and keep him there. In short, Metternich had to preserve the monarchy in order to exploit it.

Assisted by Joseph Sedlnitzky at the Ministry of Police, Metternich sought to preserve the existing social and political order with draconian controls. The freedom of the press was swept away and political activity totally prohibited. The effect of the repression on ordinary people was to make them banish serious issues from their minds. They settled for 'Gemütlichkeit' and the trivial diversions of the so-called Biedermeier age. Superficially, it was the emergence of a prosperous, urban middle class swept along by crazes for operetta, the waltz, floral wallpaper, beer and sausages. No fewer than 65 factories churned out pianos in Vienna, which then had a population of 200,000. An archduke did the unthinkable by marrying a postmaster's daughter, but of course the marriage had to be morganatic.

In the spring of 1831, Metternich blandly announced that there was no reason why Ferdinand should not marry (he thought it would make him more plausible imperial material). Metternich had the perfect wife

standing by. She was the extremely plain and virtuous Princess Marianna of Sardinia. On clapping eyes on her imminent husband, Marianna turned white. Even the doddering Emperor Franz was heard to mutter at the wedding, "May God have mercy."

Foreign ambassadors were aghast at the prospect of having to do business with the new emperor. The cleverest thing he ever said, one of them remarked, was "I am the emperor and I want dumplings." And yet Vienna genuinely loved him; he was such a guileless, good-natured antidote to the Metternich and his frightful secret police.

With the dim-witted emperor in his pocket,

Metternich could use the emperor's personal power as his own, so he made sure he had plenty of it. The Family Law promulgated in 1839 was breathtaking. It first defined the family as all the archdukes (plus wives and widows) and all the archduchesses descended in the male line from Maria Theresa. They were to observe a code of conduct which amounted to undebatable obedience to the emperor's will. If they failed to do so they would forfeit all imperial honours, titles, privileges – and income. If they married without the emperor's permission, they lost all rights for themselves and their children.

The ordinary citizens of Austria were hardly better off than the besieged members of the family. Writers were the first to stick their heads above the parapet, and they did so in 1845 with a petition against censorship. Their defiance broke the false tranquility of Biedermeier and people took to the streets. The National Guard was called out, but the students of Vienna kept up the pressure. The Paris Revolution of 1848 inspired the population to stage a general uprising. Metternich quickly packed and escaped, reputedly hidden in a laundry basket, to England.

It became clear to the Habsburgs that their survival depended on more ingenuity than Ferdinand could bring to the task. The whole clan assembled in his apartment in the early morning of 2 December 1848 and told him he would have to go. A deed of abdication was put before him. Franz Josef, who stood beside him to take over the throne, had just turned 18. Ferdinand, who had once complained that governing was easy, "what is difficult is to sign one's name", took up a pen and laboriously scratched out his name.

A monarch of the old school: Franz Josef reigned from 1848 to 1916, a Habsburg record. It was only with the humiliating help of 200,000 Russian troops that he restored order in his unruly inheritance, and for 68 years thereafter, a period of momentous change in Europe, he rowed against the tide.

On paper, Franz Josef's empire included nine kingdoms, and in time-honoured Habsburg fashion he was in every instance the king as well, all of this at a time when groups of people who spoke the same language and had a common culture were beginning to think of themselves as separate nations who, if they wanted a king at all, preferred to make their own arrangements.

The Austrian Empire was held together by a number of pins, primarily bureaucracy, the Army and the German language. But this last was double-edged. The feeling among the urban classes that they were, or had become, "German" was to drive a wedge between them and more conservative peasants who clung to their ethnic roots. As time went by, the rift grew ever wider. Ultimately, it gave Hitler an excuse for the Austrian Anschluss and the seizure of the mainly urban and industrial (and therefore "German") Czech Sudeten. All these people, Hitler said, were really Germans. Some agreed with him.

The seeds of Hitler's theory were sewn in Maria Theresa's reign, when the rise of its Germanic nature to Hungary and to Slavic infuence in the east, or so people thought. A succession of military defeats against Napoleon III and then the Prussians led to what Franz Joseph most feared – "We are going to have a little parliamentary life, it is true," Franz Joseph wrote to his mother in 1860.

Franz Joseph believed in *fortwursteln* (muddling through) and his half-hearted acceptance of a parliament was characteristic. A gesture here and there would, he thought, lower the pressure for fundamental reform.

The cure for his Hungarian difficulties was "Dualism". Hungary and Austria, which is to say Hungary as opposed to the rest of the empire, would each have their own parlia-

Prussia under Frederick the Great offered the German Austrians an alternative spiritual home. Prior to that, Germany existed, in any sense at all, as a jumble of states which could not singly or even collectively hold a candle to the mighty Habsburgs. The industrialisation of the 19th century was manufacturing more and more self-consciously German Austrians, and all the time the new German state to the west was looking more teutonically impressive. The Austrian empire, on the other hand, was gradually ceding

Left, antique passport. **Above**, the 1848 Revolution was crushed by troops.

ments, however perfunctory, but the army, foreign affairs and finance would remain under joint control. In other words, there was still a pyramid and the emperor was at the top of it. He had the Austrian half of his Dual System relatively well sewn up: "a standing army of soldiers, a seated army of officials, a kneeling army of priests, and a creeping army of informants," according to one of his critics. Hungary was slightly more difficult. The masses were compliant, but he could never be certain of the loyalty of the fabulously rich aristocracy. Luckily, he discovered, he only had to whisper one word to make the nobility back down: "Democracy."

Franz Josef's marriage to a vivacious Bavarian Wittenbach called Elisabeth had been the 22nd between the two families and there was some concern about the blood running too thin, especially when their son Rudolf proved a sickly child. By the age of 10, however, Rudolf had banished doubts about any congenital flaws. He was bright, articulate and said to have excellent manners. "I hear you exercise yourself with history," he remarked to an eminent historian, "history is my favourite subject too, but I have not got further than Servius Tullius." At 14, he unsettled his tutor with opinions which did not bode well for a future emperor. "The aristocracy and the clergy manipulated the masses," he wrote in an essay, "through enforced ignorance and superstition."

Not many years afterwards he was party to an anonymous pamphlet portentously entitled "The Austrian Aristocracy and its Constitutional Function. A Warning to Aristocratic Youth". The warning was, bluntly, that they were stupid, lazy and no competition for the bourgeoisie. But Rudolf continued to collect compliments from all sides. "Most easy to get on with," Queen Victoria of England noted.

Public indiscretion: Rudolf's marriage to Stephanie of Coburg got off to a good start, and by the end of a year he brought himself round to saying that he loved her. He was genuinely pleased when in 1883 she gave birth to a daughter. But Stephanie was evidently a poor conversationalist, and the search for more convivial company steered Rudolf towards what Franz Josef considered the worst conceivable circle of friends and drinking companions, journalists, many of whom were Jews. Rudolf was invited to expand on some of his ideas as articles for publication, anonymously of course, and these duly appeared in *Neues Wiender Tagblatt*. He had access to most of the state papers on home and foreign affairs; his indiscretion in using this privileged information was staggering. All the time he was drifting further from his father's policies. "Our Emperor has no

Left, Emperor Franz Josef. Right, Rudolf, his problematic son.

friend," he wrote to his old tutor, "he stands alone on his pinnacle...he knows little of what people think and feel...He believes that Austria is now in one of its happiest epochs: this is what he is told officially, and he only reads the paragraphs which are marked for him in the newspapers."

Although Franz Josef's creation of the Dualism with Hungary was an implicit acknowledgement of the loss of German supremacy to the Prussians, Rudolf felt much more strongly than he that the empire's fu-

ture lay in the east. Like his mother, he felt a strong affinity with the Hungarians and they, sensing that, sounded him out on the possibility of assuming the Hungarian throne. As Franz Josef happened to be the reigning Apostolic King of Hungary, the slightest suggestion of any such thing was dynastic treason of the worst possible kind. Under the strain of being party to this kind of talk, Rudolf cracked up.

Rudolf's breakdown was apparent to his wife. "Not only was his health undermined," she wrote in her memoirs, "but his restlessness had also increased." The word "restlessness" may have been her euphemism for the pursuit of other women. There were dozens of them, but only one of permanence. She was Maria Caspar, known as Mitzi, variously described as a dancer, singer or model but in fact a *Süsses Mädel* or "sweet girl", of whom there were plenty in Vienna.

Rudolf, Mary and Mayerling: The marriage disintegrated, although in public they kept up appearances. They thus appeared together at a reception given by the German ambassador on 27 January 1889 in honour of Kaiser Wilhelm II's birthday. In a blaze of hindsight because of what followed, everyone present had something to say about the occasion. The British ambassador's wife thought Rudolf looked "dejected, sad, and only just

fought back his tears". Someone else remembered Rudolf bowing with exaggerated deference to the Emperor. Everyone claimed to remember the Baroness Mary Vetsera. They argued about which was more eye-catching: the ripe "development" of one so young – she was 17 – or the seductive sway when she walked.

Mary Vetsera was the daughter of the Baroness Helene Vetsera, nee Baltazzi, who was determined that Mary should do better than marry a lightly-titled obscure diplomat as she had done.

Once launched into Vienna's social whirl, it was inevitable that Mary and Rudolf would

eventually cross paths. Such a meeting in fact occurred at the Burg theatre in October 1888, three months before the Kaiser Wilhelm's birthday party.

This was an introduction her mother would not have sought to develop. Rudolf was the crown prince, but as long as the apparently robust Stephanie lived, he was in no position to marry Mary. The baroness would have been appalled to know that some weeks after that meeting Mary had been approached by Countess Marie Larisch-Wallersee, Rudolf's cousin and occasional procuress. Mary had soon afterwards been smuggled into Rudolf's rooms at the Hofburg. A cigarette case had passed as a gift from Mary to Rudolf. It was inscribed "13 January", exactly two weeks prior to Kaiser Wilheim's birthday. The inscription, it transpired, was to commemorate the day on which she had given herself to him "completely". Only the countess and Rudolf's valet might have guessed.

After leaving the Kaiser Wilheim reception, Rudolf had a clandestine assignation, but it was not with Mary. Instead he met his old flame, the "sweet" Mitzi Caspar, and they sat up until 3 a.m. drinking champagne. He amused Mitzi with what she took to be a joke, that they go outside and shoot themselves. The conversation turned to other matters, and Rudolf mentioned that later that morning he would be off for a couple of days, a shooting trip. He expected some friends along. They would meet up at his shooting lodge, Mayerling.

Later that morning, the Countess Larisch called at the Vetsera house to take Mary "shopping", the cover they were using for her visits to Rudolf. They went off together in a carriage but, unusually, the countess was back in an hour, alone and agitated. Mary, she said, had slipped away while she was in a jeweller's. The note she had left behind in the carriage, evidently for her mother, was alarming. "I cannot go on living," she had written. "Today I have gained a lead on you; by the time you catch up with me I shall be beyond rescue, in the Danube. Mary." In fact she was in Rudolf's carriage, gaily on her way to Mayerling.

His brother-in-law Prince Philip of Coburg and Count Hoyos were Rudolf's shooting guests. They made their own way to Mayerling the following day. There was no sign of Mary when they arrived, and Rudolf said nothing to indicate that she was at the lodge. The plans for the evening were that Rudolf and Philip would return to Vienna overnight for a family dinner they were required to attend. Hoyos would stay at Mayerling – not in the lodge itself but in a cottage about 500 yards from it. Rudolf and Philip would take the early train and be back for breakfast and, after that, a second day of shooting. Rudolf then cried off. He said he did not feel strong enough for the journey and asked Philip to extend his apologies both to the emperor and Stephanie, who was expecting him to join her.

Philip having left, Rudolf and Hoyos sat down to dinner. Exactly what happened at

Staying in the next room, Loschek could hear Rudolf and Mary talking late into the night but not what they were saying. His next recollection was of Rudolf walking into his room fully dressed at about 5.40 a.m. with the request that he get horses and a carriage ready right away. Loschek got up, dressed, and made his way to the stables some distance from the lodge. He had not gone far when he heard two shots. Racing back to the lodge, he could smell powder. He tried Rudolf's door; it was locked.

Not sure what to do next, Loschek went to fetch Count Hoyos from the cottage. Hoyos told him to break in, and with a hammer he managed to smash a hole large enough to

Mayerling thereafter was not fully revealed for 50 years. Rudolf, we now know, was not quite ready for bed when Hoyos went off to the cottage that night. He wanted some entertainment, and Bratfisch his coachman was summoned. Mary emerged from hiding for his performance of songs and, at the end, his speciality – whistling. When Rudolf and Mary withdrew to the bedroom, it was with instructions to the valet Loschek not to allow anyone in, not even the emperor. Rudolf never locked his bedroom door.

Left, Baroness Mary Vetsera. Above, the Crown Prince with Bratfisch, his coachman.

reach in and unlock the door from the inside. "What an appalling sight," he said in a memorandum taken down by his son many years afterwards. "Rudolf, fully dressed, was lying on his bed, dead; Mary Vetsera, likewise fully dressed, on her bed. Rudolf's army revolver was by his side. The two had not gone to bed at all... It was clear at first sight that Rudolf first shot Mary Vetsera and then killed himself."

The news of Rudolf's death was circulating on the stock exchange long before it reached the Hofburg. The Empress Elisabeth was the first at the Hofburg to hear, and it was her unenviable job to tell the emperor and

Baroness Vetsera, who was pacing about her ante-room demanding to know where the crown prince was and whether her daughter was with him. Going on information provided by Hoyos, she told the baroness that Mary had murdered Rudolf and then killed herself. She had used poison to do so.

Elisabeth then added another layer to what would become a mountain of obfuscation and outright deception. For public consumption, she told Baroness Vetsera, Rudolf had died of heart-failure. There was to be no murder, no suicide, and no Mary. Newspapers brought out special editions announcing Rudolf's death. They put it down to Elisabeth's heart-failure or, in some cases, a frequently absent Sisi, as he called Elisabeth. While on holiday in Switzerland with her lady-in-waiting she was assassinated by a half-crazed Italian anarchist, who, deliberately bumping into the empress, slid a sharpened file through her rib-cage. Sisi did not appear to feel it, but it had gone through her heart. Franz Josef never got over the shock of her death, but ever the conscientious emperor he focused his attention on his remaining heir, his nephew the Archduke Franz Ferdinand. Of particular concern were his marital prospects, which would clearly have to conform to the still active Family Law.

The Archduke Frederick and Archduchess Isabella's bevy of lovely daughters had

hunting accident. No one suspected the involvement of an 18-year-old mistress.

The Crown Princess Stephanie printed Rudolf's farewell letter to her in her memoirs. "Dear Stephanie: You are rid of my presence and plague; be happy in your own way. Be good to the poor little girl [their daughter] who is the only thing that remains of me. Give my last regards to all friends… I am going calmly to my death which alone can save my good name. Embracing you most warmly, your loving Rudolf."

Franz Josef's heir had been shot out from under him, so to speak, and in 1898 the unthinkable happened to his beloved though the necessary qualifications, so when Franz Ferdinand made a practice of spending weekends at their Pressburg estate the only question in the archduchess's mind, and a nagging one, was not knowing which of the daughters he preferred. He seemed to be remarkably even-handed in dealing with them, but Isabella liked to think it was her eldest, Marie Christine.

The solution to the mystery seemed at hand when Franz Ferdinand inadvertently left his watch behind at Pressburg. Instead of a normal chain, it was attached to a string of the trinkets he collected and one of them was seen to be a locket of the kind in which lovers kept miniature portraits of their dearest. Isabella prised open the locket and stared at the portrait in total disbelief. It was Countess Sophie Chotek von Chotkova und Wognin, her lady-in-waiting.

Sophie was sacked on the spot, and the emperor would not hear of Franz Ferdinand marrying her. Her family had a resectable Bohemian background and her father was a Czech diplomat but that was not enough, and Franz Joseph wheeled out the Family Law. Eventually, but only under pressure from Pope Leo XIII, Kaiser Wilheim and Czar Nicholas, he agreed to a morganatic marriage, which meant that the wife would not assume her husband's title, rank or privi-

waited to step into his uncle's shoes was to make up for the loss of power to Prussia in the west by consolidating the empire's hold in the east, in particular on Bosnia and Herzegovina, acquired from Turkey at the 1878 Congress of Berlin. He envisaged a multiplication of the Dual System with Hungary so that other parts of the empire could enjoy a certain degree of self-rule within the umbrella of empire.

Road to Sarajevo: The ironic flaw in Franz Ferdinand's thinking was that he had enemies who believed it might work, that scattered peoples would settle for limited autonomy and drop demands for full independence. These misgivings were especially acute

leges, nor would any children. The emperor boycotted the wedding, but he relented slightly in promoting Sophie to Princess of Hohenberg. The title was small compensation for slights at court, like not being allowed to share her husband's box at the theatre or sit next to him at dinner if more authentic Habsburgs were present. Despite these restrictions, Franz Ferdinand was delighted with his choice.

Franz Ferdinand's preoccupation while he

Left, removing the bodies from Mayerling. **Above**, Archduke Ferdinand and Sophie coming down the Town Hall steps.

among extremists in Bosnia's large Serb population who wanted full independence in order to break away and join up with Serbia to form Greater Serbia. Franz Ferdinand was aware of rumblings in Bosnia and was therefore delighted to receive an invitation to observe military manoeuvres which were to be held there in the summer of 1914.

The royal party arrived at Ilidze on 25 June 1914. The trip had been publicised well in advance and the resort was festooned with flags and bunting. Fully aware of Franz Ferdinand's antique collection, the Sarejevo dealers had craftily decorated his hotel with their wares to entice him to visit their shops.

Franz Ferdinand fell for the ruse and decided to visit the antique shops of Sarajevo that very day. At one point during their walk to the bazaar they passed close to, but probably did not notice, a thin-lipped, pale youth who was not cheering.

Gavrilo Princip was 19 years old, born the fourth of nine children to the postman in the village of Oblej in the wild, mountainous region separating Bosnia from the Dalmatian coast. An ethnic Serb, he was by nationality Austro-Hungarian and had been to school in Sarajevo. In 1912 he had gone off to live in the Serbian capital, Belgrade, and had returned to Sarajevo only four weeks prior to the Archduke's visit. Only a handful of people knew that his time in Belgrade had been spent with the Black Hand, Serbian nationalists who in the interest of a Greater Serbia had made the assassination of Franz Ferdinand their top priority. Princip's mission in Sarajevo was to do just that, three days later on Sunday 28 June, the anniversary of Turkey's victory over Serbia at Kossovo in 1389. The choice of this date was to signify a recovery from that defeat.

The first attempt on the Archduke's life that Sunday was bungled by one of Princip's accomplices. Franz Ferdinand saw the bomb tossed at the imperial carriage as they made their way to the civil ceremony at the town hall and deflected it into the road, where it injured a handful of spectators. With considerable *sang-froid* the outraged duke carried on to the reception, where the mayor, completely thrown by the assassination attempt, could not bring himself to deviate from the prepared text of his speech. Franz Ferdinand's reply showed more command of the situation: "It gives me special pleasure to accept the assurances of your unshakable loyalty and affection for His Majesty, our Most Gracious Emperor and King. I thank you cordially, Mr Mayor, for the resounding ovations with which the population received me and my wife, the more so since I see in them an expression of pleasure over the failure of the assassination attempt..."

While the Princess Sophie went upstairs to talk to a delegation of Muslim ladies, the archduke received local dignitaries in the vestibule. He was assured that the bomber had been arrested. Under the circumstances, however, aides suggested that the Archduke should take an alternative route to the city museum, the finale to his tour. Inexplicably they failed to inform the carriage driver.

War is triggered: After the first bomb attack the assassins further down the route either thought the job had been done or panicked; in any case they scattered – all but Princip. Seeing another chance as the carriage made its way to the museum, he stepped forward, drew his revolver, and at a range of 5 feet (1.5 metres) fired two shots. One hit Franz Ferdinand in the neck, the second Sophie in the stomach. Within minutes they were dead.

Not far beneath the outpouring of public and family grief over the couple's death were intimations of cataclysmic consequences. In saying privately that "world peace will not be any worse off", the Italian Foreign Minister could not have been more wrong. An Italian journal took a different line: "Hail to the gun of Princip and to the bomb of Cabrinovic." The author was the young Benito Mussolini.

The assassins were quickly rounded up and under questioning revealed the part played in the assassination by senior Serbian officials and the Black Hand in particular. On 23 July Vienna presented Serbia with an ultimatum: no more anti-imperial activities on its soil and the arrest of one of the implicated officials. The official in question was arrested but even more quickly "escaped", never to be found again. On 28 July, exactly one month after Franz Ferdinand's death, Austria declared war.

War on Serbia brought in Russia, which was pledged to defend the interests of the Slavs. In mobilising against Austria, Russia triggered the Austro-Germanic mutual defence pact of 1879. Germany duly declared war on Russia and, knowing that this would activate an alliance between Russia and France, decided to get in first with an attack on France. Great Britain was still technically neutral, but when Germany invaded Belgium in order to attack the French flank, Britain could not countenance the threat to the Channel coast and threw in its lot with France and Russia. At the end, with the United States also drawn in, the body count was some 10 million with another 20 million seriously wounded.

As far as the Habsburgs were concerned, World War I effectively spelled the end.

Right, The Archduke's blood-spattered uniform.

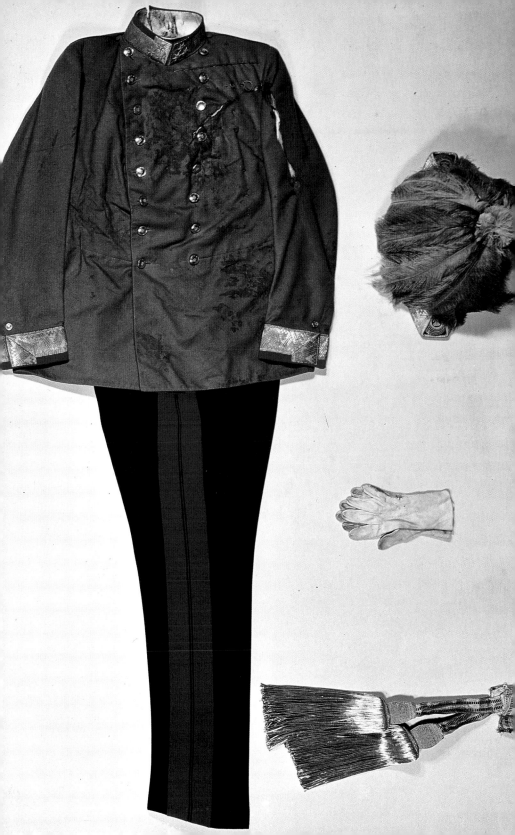

A large number of Austrians sprang a surprise on the architects of the new Europe after World War I. They did not want independence, not on their own; they wanted to be incorporated either in the German Weimar Republic or in some kind of union with Bohemia and Moravia, which the architects insisted belonged to the new Czechoslovakia. Others, mainly the land-owning Roman Catholic peasants, did not want democracy if it meant the country being run by the Social Democrats, who were seen to be against the Church and against private property.

To a considerable degree the division was "Red Vienna" versus the rest of the country, and both sides formed paramilitary organisations, the pro-socialist Schutzbund against the Roman Catholic Heimwehr, one of whose leaders was Goering's brother-in-law.

The impasse had not really been resolved when the Great Depression took hold in 1931. It was particularly severe in Austria because no adequate substitutes had yet developed for its former industrial base, now part of Czechoslovakia, or its mineral and agricultural wealth, which had vanished with the loss of Hungary. The army and the Schutzbund fought a pitched battle in February 1934. The fighting lasted four days, the army won, the Social Democrats were banned, and Austria was back to the kind of authoritarian rule with which Franz Josef would have felt at home. Austrian democracy had lasted all of 15 years.

Bad allies: To Austria's most notorious émigré across the border in Germany, these developments were excellent news. By suppressing democracy and the labour movement, the right-wing Chancellor Engelbert Dollfuss removed the natural opposition to pro-Nazi Austrians, who more loudly than ever were banging the drum of annexation to Germany, saying it was the only hope of setting the economy right. Adolf Hitler agreed completely. Dollfuss saw the threat to Austria's independence and sought to safeguard it with a foreign alliance. He could hardly have chosen a worse ally – Benito Mussolini.

Left, Austria's most famous son. **Right**, a poster advertising a speech by him in Vienna in 1938.

Dollfuss did not live to see the gravity of his error. He was assassinated by Nazis in 1934; Hitler and Mussolini reached their understanding two years later. Dollfus's successor as chancellor, Kurt Schuschnigg, tried to appease the Austrian Nazis with the offer of a couple of ministries in the government. Hitler was adamant that one of these should be the Ministry of State Security, which he proposed to hand over to Austria's leading Nazi (after himself), Artur Seyss-Inquart. Kurt Schuschnigg was summoned to Berch-

tesgaden and made to understand that he had no choice in the matter.

Schuschnigg handled the meeting with a tempestuous Hitler with quiet aplomb. When he reached for a cigarette, Hitler screamed that smoking was not permitted in his presence. Schuschnigg lit up anyway and casually flicked the match across Hitler's table. On returning to Vienna, Schuschnigg lifted the ban on the socialist parties and announced that Austria was definitely in favour of democracy and independence. He invited the country to confirm that commitment in a plebiscite to be held on 13 March 1938.

Hitler did not want any such signal to go to

the outside world. Two days before the plebiscite, Germany closed its borders with Austria. The following day, Hitler invaded.

Austria gave up even its name on being absorbed into the Third Reich. It reverted to "Ostmark", as it was under Charlemagne, which may have been Hitler showing that he knew a thing or two about history and particularly conquerors. Predictably, the Jews were the first victims of the German invasion. A British newspaper described scenes in Leopoldstadt, where the majority of Vienna's 200,000 Jews lived. "Now day after day, Nazi storm-troopers, surrounded by jostling, jeering and laughing mobs of 'golden Viennese hearts', dragged Jews from shops,

Anschluss were enough to convince them that, as demonstrated by the way a generous dosage of Slavic blood had altered their facial features, they were not quite so German after all. "The sweep of the Nazi scythe continued to cut down ruthlessly the flower of the intellectual and professional life in Vienna," the British report continued, "impatient to destroy the last traces of that cultured civilisation which for 500 years had marked out the distinction between Austria and Germany." A great number of Jews and anti-Nazis managed to escape, but within the first 10 days of Nazi occupation 90,000 Austrians were rounded up; most of them ended up in Dachau and Buchenwald.

offices and homes, men and women, put scrubbing brushes in their hands, splashed them well with acid and made them go down on their knees."

Strong reactions: From the moment of Hitler's entry into Vienna and for weeks afterwards, more than 100 people per day committed suicide. The reaction in other quarters was different. The Catholic Bench of Bishops under Cardinal Innitzer issued a proclamation praising the "splendid services of Nazism in the social field" and calling on all Christians to "proclaim themselves as Germans for the German Reich".

For the majority, however, a few weeks of

The country went to war in 1939 as an integral part of Germany, and while the loyalty of the Austrian officer corps to the Third Reich was considered suspect, Austrians were conscripted into the army like everyone else.

Little is said about Austrian resistance, the nature of which tended to vary according to which group was responsible. Communists on the left and monarchists on the right both attempted active resistance; socialists in the middle were more inclined to be passive. Factory workers were encouraged to compete to see who could do their jobs worst, and the Vienna fire brigade managed to achieve such a high level of incompetence that the

Gestapo transported more than 700 of its members to a firing range to watch two of the most hopeless cases being shot.

The various resistance groups gradually pooled their resources, a process accelerated by the Moscow Declaration of 1943 which said that whether Austria was judged after the war to have been willingly on Nazism's side or forced on to it would be determined by "her own contribution to her own liberation". Austrians had already played a prominent part in the Count van Stauffenberg plot to kill Hitler. At a prearranged signal, undercover agents in Vienna took the brave gamble of snatching a number of senior Nazi commanders and locking them up in the

Szokoll, the officer who had "dissolved" the SS, not only survived the reprisals but managed to get himself promoted to the rank of major in the Wehrmacht. As such, he produced forged postings and contrived other tricks which resulted in packing the Wehrmacht ranks in Vienna with secret resistance sympathisers. As the end of the war approached, the idea was that these units would coordinate with whichever of the Allied armies arrived to liberate Vienna and attack the SS divisions. In the event, the Russians got to Vienna first and the plot failed when one of the Austrians lost his nerve, but it was a wonderful scheme while it lasted and Vienna was promptly liberated.

former Imperial War Ministry on the Ringstrasse. A Captain Szokoll had even gone to the length of issuing orders for the dissolution of the SS when it was learned that the putsch in Germany had failed. The incarcerated commanders managed to get themselves released and immediately ordered arrests. Every Austrian in the Wehrmacht in Vienna who had aristocratic connections was dismissed. Many were executed.

Left, German troops gather on the Ringstrasse in 1938. Above, the *Staatsvertrag* of 1955 accorded to Austria the withdrawal of the armies of occupation in return for guaranteed neutrality.

The Allies partitioned Austria into four zones, Vienna having a bit of each of them. The harsh attitude adopted by the occupation troops in the Soviet sector was one of the explanations offered for the poor communist showing in the elections held in November 1945: four seats out of 165. The Allied victory had persuaded people that they would rather be Austrians than Germans; meeting the Russian troops evidently persuaded them that they'd rather be in the Western camp.

For the first decade of the Cold War there was considerable concern about Austria's ability to stay neutral. Russian had shown in Czechoslovakia that the Iron Curtain could be lifted, moved west, and dropped again – with a new acquisition squirming behind it. In 1955, however, Molotov announced that the Russians would evacuate Austria on receiving adequate guarantees that there would be no future Anschluss between Austria and Germany. These were quickly given and on 15 May Austria was again independent as the Second Republic. This may have been effected just in time. Events in Hungary the following year revealed a very different mood in Moscow.

Enfeebled aristocracy: The Second Republic of Austria obviously had a very much clearer vision than the First of what it was and what it ought to be. "We know all too

More than any other foreign newspaper, *The Times* of London has provided a close and not uncritical commentary on the Austrian mentality since the 19th century. Richard Bassett, one of a distinguished line of Vienna correspondents, brought the coverage up to date in 1987: "Years of socialist administration have distanced people's minds from its less socialist history. The Habsburgs are sufficiently remote and the present Austrian aristocracy so excessively enfeebled as to permit a warm nostalgia for distant imperial days. More disturbing recent events are submerged and simply not addressed...

"Thus, while on the one hand Kreisky gave the Austrians a voice in international

well what happens if there is unemployment in Austria," a favourite saying of Bruno Kreisky, the towering politican of the period, was the pointer to domestic policy: the construction of a social welfare state which at times had even the Scandinavians gasping. Job security, high rates of pay, family allowances and subsidies were paramount, the question of paying for them a secondary consideration. Externally, Kreisky raised Austria's profile as an international mediator, in recognition of which Vienna was able to compete with Geneva as the European centre for international agencies and their flashy headquarters.

affairs and an important role to play in Europe, coupled with a degree of comfort those who had experienced pre-war Austria would never have thought possible, it was achieved at the expense of any serious appraisal of Austria's role in events earlier this century..."

Bassett's sombre mood was brought on by a quick succession of events which had rocked the image of Strauss waltzes, Sachertorte and Christopher Plummer, in *The Sound of Music*, tearing up a swastika outside the von Trapp family mansion. The discovery of huge quantities of Austrian wine which owed its kick to anti-freeze uncorked a series of scandals which collectively suggested that the country was unusually corrupt. The World Jewish Congress stormed out of its convention in Vienna, the first time it had been held there, on learning that an Austrian war criminal, the SS officer Walter Reder, was simultaneously receiving a warm welcome on being repatriated from an Italian prison as an act of mercy. There was also the curious business of the Austrian Military Academy erecting a memorial to General Lohr, a World War I air ace, true, but in the second war personally responsible for the massacre of Yugoslav civilians, a war crime for which he was executed in Belgrade in 1947. The Yugoslav government issued a reminder, and the memorial was removed.

of Benjamin Disraeli of all people, the 19th-century British prime minister usually thought of in connection with foppish manners and buying the Suez Canal. He kept the portrait, he said, "as a reminder of the great services to the Austrian empire performed by Disraeli in supporting Austria's occupation of Bosnia-Herzegovina 100 years ago." The man from *The Times* needed a moment to collect his thoughts, but he was wonderfully impressed.

Since World War II Austria has behaved as a thoroughly Western nation, though it was prohibited by the *Staatsvertrag* of 1955 from joining any military or other political alliance. Its membership of the European

Even a stern critic like Bassett, however, confesses to being easily reconciled to a country he is actually very fond of. Many, perhaps most, modern visitors are attracted to Austria by the magnificence out of doors and the conviviality within, but as the preceding pages have tried to show, there is history galore. On that point, who would not be bewitched, as Bassett was, on running into an old man in Graz who was sitting, a glass of schnapps in hand, beneath a portrait

Left, President Klestil takes the oath in the National Council. **Above**, "Yes to Europe" in the 1994 plebiscite.

Union or even NATO was out of the question.

In 1994 a referendum brought Austria into the EU with a two-thirds majority and since then, despite a degree of misgiving amongst the population, Austria has taken its commitment seriously and is also set for monetary union in the year 2000. The future role of Austria as a member state of NATO is still a matter of heated debate however, and is an important issue in the 1998 presidential campaigns, particularly in view of EU expansion into Eastern Europe and Austria's post-war neutral status. One thing is certain, joining the EU has meant a lot of changes, many of which have brought dissatisfaction with them.

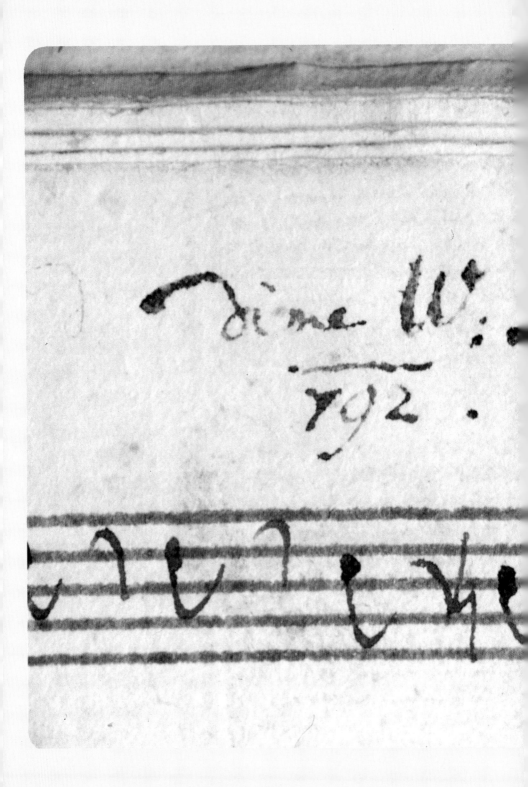

74

THE AUSTRIAN MUSE

Austria has provided the world with legions of musicians, painters, sculptors, writers and architects: the city of Salzburg is synonymous with Mozart, arguably the world's greatest composer; the capital Vienna has been home to more geniuses per acre than perhaps any other place on earth, and – for better or for worse – it was the birthplace of modern psychiatry.

Cultural legacies: Austria's cultural wealth owes much to its receptiveness to artistic movements originating in other parts of Europe. Designed to serve as both defence and buffer on the southeastern extremities of the Carolingian and later Frankish empires, Austria lived and breathed under the heavy influence of other cultures for centuries. Crusaders who crossed Austrian territory to reach the Holy Land and returned the same way, brought valuable booty and Byzantine culture. The fine Romanesque frescoes to be seen at Lambach, between Salzburg and Linz, and Friesach in Carinthia show pronounced Byzantine traits, as do the miniature paintings in manuscripts, an art form centred mainly in Salzburg.

Around the middle of the 13th century Gothic, introduced by the monks from the mendicant orders, in particular from France, and wandering artists from Italy, became the dominant influence. Church towers grew to vast heights. The spire of St Stephen's Cathedral in Vienna reached 450 ft (137 metres). Structural innovations enabled solid stone walls to be replaced by walls of glass, and light poured into the churches through tall arched windows. The altar developed from a functional table into a complex structure with wings and rear panels.

Artists and architects were no longer anonymous figures. They became recognised master craftsmen and some of the best known were Austrians: Hans Puchsbaum, Michael Knab, Anton Pilgram and painters and sculptors like Jakob Kaschauer and Micheal Pacher (who worked a great deal in the western part of the country).

Preceding pages: Mozart's signature; the composer's statue in Stadtpark; the artist Arnulf Rainer. Left, poster design by Oskar Kokoschka.

Increased trade brought greater prosperity to the towns. Much like his 20th-century counterpart, the wealthy burgher exhibited his financial standing by adding such features as golden-roofed bay-windows to his house (witness the "Goldenes Dachl" in Innsbruck). This was the age of the guilds, and handicrafts flourished especially under the aegis of public funds. Richly decorated Gothic furniture can be seen in castles and museums all over Austria. Even the design of fortresses changed with the times: walls were made thicker and defensive systems improved. Hohensalzburg, Hochosterwitz in Carinthia and the late 16th-century Hohenwerfen are fitting tributes to the great skills of their builders.

A new sense of realism marked Gothic art. As if to emphasise this, statues were made to stand separately from the walls, natural themes became important elements in paintings and sculpture, and historical events were represented in modern terms. Painters from Austria and southern Germany, collectively belonging to the so-called Danube school, such as Albrecht Altdorfer (1480–1538), who painted the altar in St Florian, Lukas Cranach the Elder (1472–1553) and Jörg Breu (1480–1537) carried the naturalist approach to the extreme. They depicted a society overburdened with the depraved, the sick, the drunk and the deformed.

Any sense of comfort disappeared completely at the end of the 15th century. The Turks arrived from the south, science was shaking Catholic postulates, and the Reformation split Europe. These times of troubles prevented the calmness of the Italian Renaissance from fully settling on Austrian soil. Mannerism, on the other hand, a peculiar distortion of the new sense of order, was particularly popular in Austria. Castles came to serve as a measure of prestige rather than fulfil any defensive purpose. Pretty arcades around courtyards replaced the grim ramparts. Barbicans and bartizans served as a kind of *retro* fantasy.

Austria sprouted few of its own artists during this period. The painters Jako Seisenegger (1505–67), Josef Heintz (1564–1609) and Bartholomäus Spranger (1546–

1611) are exceptions. Instead it tended to collect art and artists from the outside world – Italians at first and later a battery of Germans and Dutch.

It is the age of the Baroque, beginning around the 1620s, which has left the most impressive legacy. While the style is not to everybody's taste, nobody can deny its ability to overwhelm every sense and every emotion. It conjures up visions of excessive decoration and mirrors, symbols of undisguised vanity, of contrived exoticism, of acres of stucco and frescoes.

The Baroque was in many ways a direct extension of the previous age; many of the architectural elements were carried over from by Pietro Antonio Cesti for which a theatre had to be purpose-built on the old ramparts of the old fortress (Burg) in Vienna. The Burgtheater was born. Not until Gluck and Mozart did the tide start to change. The Italian craze even compelled some composers to change their names: Rösler became Rosetti and Jan Vacláv Stich became Giovanni Battista Punto (albeit the latter was trying to hide from an irate employer).

The high point of the Baroque age coincided with the costly defeat of the Turks in 1683. Composers suddenly discovered the appeal of the Ottoman army's music. A century later it still exerted influence, as exemplified by Mozart's "Turkish March" from

the Renaissance but given new stimulus through ornamentation and organisation. Italian artists and architects revelled in the Baroque. Santino Solari built the Cathedral in Salzburg and Carlo Antonio Carlone, associated with the baroquisation of the Kremünster church, was also responsible, among others, for the churches in Pöllau and St Florian and for the castle of Prince Esterházy in Eisenstadt.

Opera craze: The theatre came alive with Italian comedies and Italian opera became a century-long rage. The marriage of Leopold I to Margherita of Spain in 1667 was celebrated by a performance of *Il Pomo d'Oro* the Sonata KV. 331, the "Rondo" from his Violin Concerto in A, and Beethoven's "Ruins of Athens".

Towards the end of the 17th century Joseph Bernhard Fischer introduced a touch of Germanic sobriety into the wild party. Johann Joseph Fux, Kapellmeister at St Stephen's and a reputed music theorist and composer, harked back to the severe north German counterweight at the risk of appearing old-fashioned. The age of the Rococo dawned in Austria. Gentility replaced garishness; freshness, order and transparence were the elements of good taste. Exoticism remained an important theme especially in the light of trade links with the East, but it appeared lighter, less heady.

In 1705 the painter and sculptor Peter Strudel von Strudendorff founded the Vienna Arts Academy. It was here that Paul Troger was to educate a generation of great painters including the famous Franz Anton Maulbertsch (born in Swabia) and the less well-known Bohemian artist Jan Vaclav Bergl, whose frescoes in the Goesser apartments in Schönbrunn are some of the most splendid examples of Rococo art.

Then came the age of *Empfindsamkeit* sensibility, suggesting that art could convey emotions. Subject matter grew more serious. *Sturm und Drang*, a literary affectation,

Franz Schubert, "the most beautiful and lively thing that we had," wrote Moritz von Schwind, attempted for a while to copy Beethoven's Promethean voice.

Brahms v. Bruckner: The battles for musical superiority between the "old" and the "new", the proponents of Wagner and those of Brahms, raged throughout the 19th century, particularly in Vienna. Brahms even caught the spirit and called Bruckner's symphonies "giant snakes" (*Riesenschlangen*). Bruckner, the boy from St Florian still bathed in Catholicism – more at ease in clodhoppers and wielding a hoe than a baton – begged the Kaiser himself to do something about the violent attacks by Eduard Hanslick, the Vi-

spread quickly to music where the drama of minor keys was rediscovered.

Political absolutism ruled the day and law and order reappeared on the cultural scene. The exponents of Viennese Classicism, Joseph Haydn, Mozart and the lesser known Ditters von Dittendorf made music together in the capital and set revolutionary standards in their field. Even at his most unbuttoned, Beethoven, their natural heir, never destroyed the delicate balance between structure and content, between emotion and reason. Even

Left, Franz Grillparzer and Franz Schubert. **Above**, an evening with Johann Strauss.

ennese critic who set the tone for what was serious music and what wasn't. The music of Wagner, Liszt and Bruckner was not.

In literature and art the Romantic age meant a return to roots, to the magical qualities of the soil. The Carinthian-born Peter Rosegger was the movement's natural exponent. Painters like von Schwind, Franz Eybl, Rudolf Thoma and Leopold Kupelweiser endowed the common man and rustic scenes with all the colours and freshness once reserved for crowned heads. Meanwhile the industrial revolution was digging its claws into the social fabric.

Vienna became the nerve centre of a massive empire with more nationalities than it could count; it also served as a cultural centre on a European scale. While everyone danced to Strauss waltzes, made money, made love, or made art, a battalion of dismal governmental *geheimrats* tried to keep the ship afloat. While Baroque and Classicism still covered most of the country fairly evenly, new styles appeared in the country's capital. Historicism, a peculiar hodge-podge made up of a variety of past styles, suddenly became all the rage. When the Minister of the Interior, von Bach, decided to redesign Vienna, Eduard van der Nüll, August von Siccardsburg, Heinrich Ferstel, Gottfried Semper and others went to work creating

Heuer, "inventor" of tropes, created an uproar by dispensing with the classic notion of harmony in music altogether. Freud stalked the Viennese dreamworld and Stefan Zweig gave it a literary interpretation. Arthur Schnitzler examined the realities of *fin de siècle* society. But the real *bêtes noires* were Jaroslav Hásek, with his biting *Good Soldier Schweik*, Ödön von Horvath, author of the anti-militaristic *Child of our Time*, and Franz Kafka, a bureaucrat by day, who turned into an author of the bizarre by night.

The Hungarians were generally kinder; they provided Vienna's many stages with reams of operettas and scores of fine actors.

One flowering generation engendered an-

neo-Gothic, neo-Renaissance and neo-Baroque facades.

It was facade only. By the first years of the 20th century a cultural revolution had broken through the entire front. At first came Secession, a fantastic mixture of exoticism, orientalism and eroticism. They railed against the old and the creaky, against architecture that failed in even being functional, at the hordes of "kulturanalphabeten" who seemed to be running the Academy in Vienna. The leaders of the uprising, Olbrich, Wagner and Klimt risked their good reputations and sizeable sums of money to make their point.

Arnold Schoenberg and Joseph Matthias

other. Egon Schiele, writer at first, then painter, carried his teacher Klimt's visions a few steps further. The expressionist painters Oskar Kokoschka, Herbert Boeckl and Alfred Kubin were raised on Secession, as were the esoteric author Gustav Meyrink and the symbolist poet Georg Trakl.

Anschluss and after: World War I shocked Austria, but what truly brought this ebullient age to a halt was the Anschluss in 1938. The concentration camps swallowed most of the Jews, who had provided so much of its cultural life, while forced exile banished the rest. The knell sounded in Toscanini's voice when he screamed three times "*Mai piu!*"

(never again!) as he was seated next to Franz von Papen, the German envoy to Austria, at the post-festival banquet in Salzburg in 1937. He never returned.

But even World War II failed to destroy Austria's cultural vitality. Franz Salmhofer, director of the State Opera after the war, employed the artists themselves to get the extremely run down Theater an der Wien in shape again while the bombed out opera house was being restored. By the beginning of October 1945 Joseph Krips was conducting Beethoven's *Fidelio*.

After the war the Carinthian born authoress Ingeborg Bachmann wrote: "No new world without a new language." Austria in utilitarianism, the result of which can be seen in the eyebrow-raising Hundertwasser House in Vienna. Another individual of note is André Heller, writer, poet, singer, a painter with fireworks and impressario.

In literature Hans Weigel's attempt to create a Viennese school in the Café Raimund in the postwar years failed in the face of larger national strivings. The West German "Club of 47" had a much wider and more attractive appeal for young authors. However, Austria has been as productive as ever in the literary field, from Bachmann, already mentioned, to Peter Handke, Elfriede Jelinek, Alfred Kolleritsch, Barbara Frischmut and Thomas Bernhard (died in 1989), who prohibited his

the second half of the 20th century offers essentially everything from the typically sterile block building of the 1950s and 60s to the prurient sexcapades of one Otto Mühl who spread his orgiastic art philosophy to the distant Canary island of Gomera. Pop, avant-garde and the absurd filled the interval.

Among others, Anton Krejcar, Richard Matouschek and Friedensreich Hundertwasser combined not only the characteristics of previous artistic movements but also, in the case of the latter, art, architecture and

Left, Johannes Brahms. **Above**, ballet at the Opera Ball.

plays from being performed in Austria after his death, but was forced into a "reluctant" comeback by the controversial German director of the Burgtheater, Klaus Peymann.

The performaning arts remain popular with visitors not only in the more traditional centres of Vienna, Graz and Salzburg, but also in the provinces with the Bruckner festival in Linz, the Haydn festival in Eisenstadt and the summer lake-side opera festivals at Bregenz, Ossiach and Mörbisch. Apart from this the tradition of cabaret in the city feasts on political and religious scandals and indulges itself on the morbid and self-deprecatory Viennese charm.

All of Austria has something of the baroque about it: the cuisine and its delicatessens, the effusive kissing of hands, the olde-worlde atmosphere of the coffee-houses. The architecture is the backdrop for the "Baroque experience". No other country in Central Europe displays a comparable abundance of constructions in the baroque style

The style of the early-Austrian baroque (1620–83) was greatly influenced by the Counter-Reformation. Deep-rooted piety still permeated the Dominican, Franciscan, Paulinian, Carmelite and Jesuit churches: they were built without transepts or drum cupolas and many were without spires. The High baroque (1683–1740), in contrast is resplendent, almost theatrical. Inaugurated after the victory over the Turks, it symbolised the Empire as protector of Christianity.

Monumentality is the prime characteristic of the architecture that symbolises the authority wielded by the court, church and nobility after the Thirty Years' War. Spires and steeples sit like dabs of whipped cream on succulent wedding cake churches. Pompous portals, over-sized sculptures and expansive flights of stairs characterise the country mansions of the period. The style held until well into the 18th century. Then between 1740–80 the Austrian Late baroque made way for the French rococo.

The great architects of the Austrian baroque were Johann Bernhard Fischer von Erlach, his son Joseph Emanuel, Johann Lukas von Hildebrandt and Jakob Prandtauer. Equally influential was the Italian family Carlone: the father, Pietro Francesco, the sons Carlo Antonio and Giovanni Battista and their relatives Carlo Martino Carlone, Domenico Carlone, Joachim Carlone were all important baroque architects; Carlo Carlone a great painter and Bartolomeo Carlone a stuccoist.

The baroque road: Most visitors to Austria entering the country via the Salzburg border drive along the so-called "Baroque road" that leads via Vienna to the South of Austria. **Schloss Mirabell** in Salzburg evinces all the characteristics of Hildebrandt's style, though it is, in fact, a reconstruction by Peter von Nobile, which was built after the destructive fire of 1818. Hildebrandt also contributed to the main facade of the Imperial Residence. The original Schloss Mirabell was constructed during the time of the Archbishop Wolf Dietrich (1587–1612) and Markus Sitticus (1612–19).

Johann Bernard Fischer von Erlach built **Schloss Klessheim** and **St Mark's Church**. But splendid buildings can be found dotted throughout the Salzburg area. The **Pilgrimage Church of Maria Plain**, for example, exhibits wood carvings by Thomas Schwanthaler. In **Michaelbeuren** towers the immense, still inhabited Benedictine abbey.

In **Mondsee** the late Gothic parish church of the former Benedictine monastery has an early baroque interior. In St Georgen an der Mattig (near Braunau) is its daughter church containing three early baroque altars dating from 1650, created by the brothers Martin and Michael Zürn. Continuing to Traunkirchen, the visitor will come to the **Parish Church Mariae Krönung**. The church is built in the so-called Jesuit baroque, and contains the "fisher pulpit" representing the draught of fish by the apostles. The **Benedictine Abbey of Lambach** contains the only extant baroque monastery theatre.

Also in the region is Paura with its **Dreifaltigkeitskirche** (Trinity church) built by Johann Michael Prunner. Carlo Battista Carlone carried out some of the work on the Augustian monastery in Reichersberg.

Antique treasures in Kremsmünster: The next important centre of the baroque is Kremsmünster. Founded in the year 777, the **Benedictine Abbey** is one of the oldest cultural centres in the Bavarian-Austrian area. Where the monastery meets the secular buildings there is an architectural jewel: the so-called Fish Tank. At the edge of the minster compound stands the oldest high-rising building in Europe, the 160-ft (50-metre) high "mathematical tower", dating from the year 1759. In seven of its eight storeys there are museums devoted to natural science. The original abbey church in Kremsmünster was built in 1232. Its baroque renovation as well as the construction of the new monastery buildings was carried out between 1613 and 1731. The architects were Jakob Prandtauer and Carlo

Antonio Carlone, who was also responsible for the church in the **Augustinian Monastery of St Florian**. Prandtauer is also linked with the town of **Christkindl** near Styr. He completed the pilgrimage church, first begun by Giovanni Battista Carlone. But Prandtauer buildings can also be found in Lower Austria. His pilgrimage church first planned in 1706 in Sonntagsberg was, however, only completed in 1732 by his nephew, the Tyrolese architect Josef Munggenast. The two had already

Melk Monastery: The Abbey of Melk towers heavenwards. Its architect, Jakob Prandtauer, is said to have located his architectural works of art in the landscape in such a manner that nature and art combine in perfect harmony. In Melk the sacred aspects are especially emphasised. In contrast to other baroque monasteries, it is the church itself that dominates the complex.

The Abbot, Berthold Dietmayr – at the time a mere 30 years old – was an enthusiastic supporter of Prandtauer. Not only did he

worked together on the Augustinian Monastery in Hertogenburg, to the west of Vienna.

Jakob Prandtauer's influence is evident throughout this region, from the **Benedictine Abbey of Melk** to St Pölten, where, apart from various churches, there is also a Bishop's residence, the **Institut der Englischen Fräuleins** and the City Hall with its splendid Lord Mayor's chamber. The **Benedictine Monastery in Göttweig** was built in accordance with the plans of Johann Lukas von Hildebrandt.

Above, the Upper Belvedere, Prince Eugene's baroque residence in Vienna.

always know exactly what he wanted, he also knew the ways and means to impose his ideas, despite the objections and resistance he constantly encountered from his own monastery. For almost 40 years – between 1702 and 1736 – Prandtauer summoned the most important baroque artists to Melk. Especially impressive are the ceiling frescoes by Johann Michael Rottmayr in the monastery church: they illustrate the life of St Benedict; the combat of evil; the dove as the soul of St Benedict's sister, Scholastika, flies heavenwards; Benedict in God's divinity.

Paul Troger painted the ceiling fresco in the library. Here belief is depicted allegorically: a woman holds the book with the seven seals and the lamb of the Apocalypse in one hand, in the other a shield. Around her hover the four cardinal virtues – wisdom, justice, strength and moderation. Troger also painted the ceiling frescoes in the Marble Hall. In a chariot drawn by lions, Pallas Athena leaves the realm of dark, evil and brutality to enter the realm of light, goodness and beauty. Concerts of baroque music are frequently performed here.

Maintainence of the building has cost a great deal. The Gutenberg Bible was sold in order to finance renovation of the facade.

Melk has been a thriving religious community for almost 900 years. Nowadays, vation included restoring the church interior to its original blue colour, which over the years had been covered by many layers of yellow.

Dürnstein is actually the only monastery that was built in accordance with the religious concepts of a monk. The abbot, Hyronium Übelbacher, kept precise diaries about the design and the progress of the building. He himself supervised the execution of his plans. Almost all architectural features can be sub-divided into four: four seasons, four continents, four gospels, four elements, four portals. Unlike the customary norm, the main entrance is not in the middle axis of the church but rather on the northern

most of the monks live outside the actual monastery and carry out agricultural tasks on the land belonging to the community. Monastery life is run on the proceeds. The monks run a grammar school and a secondary school as well as a boarding school.

Rhapsody in blue: The former **Augustinian Monastery in Dürnstein** is one of the highlights of any journey through baroque Austria. The ruins of the castle in which King Richard I (Richard the Lionheart) was kept prisoner from 1192 to 1193 stand sentinel above the town, and, above the Danube, the blue monastery church clings to the cliff. Despite objections from some quarters, reno-side. An additional entrance hall is intended to highlight the contrast between the dark courtyard and the lightness of the interior. By entering the church, man enters life, the four continents – and these are blue.

Vienna is the baroque capital of Central Europe. In order to experience the splendour of baroque Vienna to the full it would be advisable to engage the services of one of the guides (usually female) employed by the city tour office. Not only do they tell you all the historical facts, but they also recount many entertaining – and sometimes scandalous – anecdotes associated with the buildings, including tales of envy, love and seduction.

Among the oldest of the early baroque buildings is the **Kirche am Hof** dating from 1662. Carlo Carlone was responsible for the facade. Vienna's most important clergymen have preached from the pulpit of this church, which is one of the oldest Jesuit churches in the city. Built in the style of the Jesuit churches in Rome, it is a jewel of the early baroque.

Fischer von Erlach took over as chief architect in Vienna in 1682. He had already been working on the **Plague Column** for 10 years, and applied to become the architect of the triumphal gate in honour of the entry of Josef I to Vienna. The designs he submitted were judged to be superior to those of his Italian competitors.

Hildebrandt took over as leading architect.

At around this time the splendid aristocratic palatial buildings were constructed, such as **Schwarzenberg** near the Karlskirche. The dual-winged **Schloss Belvedere** was built between 1714 and 1723 for Prince Eugene who, it was reported, lived in greater splendour than the Emperor. **Schönbrunn Palace** was built 20 years after Fischer's death by Nikolaus Pacassi and the plans were influenced by the Rococo style.

In 1733 Hildebrandt completed the **Church of St Peter**. Immediately afterwards he designed what is now the present-day residence of the Federal Chancellor, a building which took only two years to complete.

This event was regarded by his contemporaries as being a veritable victory for German art. Fischer received his commissions from the Emperor himself, and the aristocracy. According to his own statements he was occasionally working on as many as 14 buildings simultaneously. But then his fortunes took a sudden change for the worse. His plans for Schloss Schönbrunn were rejected and he subsequently lost the favour of Prince Eugene, who until then had been his patron.

Left, the National Library in Vienna. **Above**, baroque in the Tyrol: the ceiling fresco in the abbey church in Stams.

Fischer von Erlach was successful again with his plans for the **Karlskirche**, but he died in 1723 and his son, Josef Emanuel, completed the church, the design of which is heavily influenced by St Peter's in Rome – thus lending further credence to the idea that Vienna was supposed to become a third Rome. The mighty dome serves as an ecclesiastical symbol, and the crowns on the columns are signs of secular power.

The pond in front of the church was intended to mirror the splendour of the building, but because of the ever-prevailing winds that ruffle its waters, that seldom happens.

Josef Emanuel took over from where his

father left off. He built the **Winter Riding School** and then completed the **Hofbibliothek** (court library) that he had begun with his father. Today it houses the Austrian National Library.

Around Vienna: To the north of Vienna there is the splendour of the **Augustinian Monastery of Klosterneuburg**; to the southwest, there is the **Church of the Assumption** together with the palace with its imposing flight of stairs. A good 24 miles (40 km) in the direction of the Hungarian border there is the **Schlosshof**, the hunting lodge of Prince Eugene. This, too, was built by Johann Lukas von Hildebrandt, whose influence is also evident at **Schloss Halbturn** (about 30 miles/

50 km to the south of Vienna, in the Burgenland). Also here is the masterpiece of the baroque painter Franz Anton Maulbertsch, the *Allegory of Time and Light*.

Only 2 miles (4 km) further to the south is the most important ecclesiastical building in the Burgenland: the pilgrimage church in **Frauenkirchen**. By way of Loretto, with its Servitenkirche, you should make your way to Eisenstadt to the **Esterházy Castle,** built in the style of the upper Italian early-baroque, as represented by Carlo Martino Carlone who also worked on the Leopoldinian section of the Vienna Hofburg. The humanoid gargoyles on the inner facades of the

courtyard are based on the faces of the servants who supplied victuals to the construction workers, lining their pockets to the detriment of the artisans in the process.

In a southwesterly direction the baroque road leads to Vorau, with its Augustinian monastery, through the Fischbach Alps. From Kapfenberg to **Mariazell** it is about 34 miles (56 km). Here in the pilgrimage church is the famous high altar with a globe as a tabernacle. It was designed by Johann Lukas Bernard Fischer von Erlach. The so-called Gnadenaltar (the altar of divine mercy) was designed by his son Joseph Emanuel.

Graz also has a plethora of baroque buildings. In **Schloss Eggenberg**, built by Laurenz van der Sype (1623–33), there is a baroque museum. In Styria are the **Barmherzigkeitskirche** (1735–40, Johann Georg Stengg); the **Mausoleum of Ferdinand II** (1614–36) and the **Mariahilfkirche** (1607–11) both built in accordance with the plans by Giovanni Pietro de Pomis; the **Ursulinenkirche** (1696–1700, Bartholomäus Ebner); the **Welsche Kirche** (1721–25, Joseph Carlone); the **Palais Attems** (1702–16, Andreas Stengg); the **Palais Welserheim** (1689–94, Joachim Carlone) and the **Pilgrimage Church Maria Trost** (1714–24, Andreas and Johann Georg Stengg).

A worthwhile detour from Graz to the south (approximately 24 miles/ 40 km on the Autobahn) will take you to Ehrenhausen and the **Mausoleum of Ruprecht von Eggenberg**, scourge of the Turks. The design for the interior was the work of the great Johann Lukas Bernhard Fischer von Erlach.

In Carinthia, the baroque style flourished more modestly. Some pretty parish churches can be seen in Wolfsberg and St Veit an der Glan. Also worth visiting is the parish and former cathedral **Church of the Assumption** in Gurk, and in Villach, the parish and pilgrimage church **Heiligenkreuz**, with its central dome and twin spires, built in 1735 by Andreas Siegel, after the plans of Hans Eder. The highlight is the parish and former **Benedictine Monastery Church** in Ossiach; it is a baroque-revised Romanesque column basilica. Concerts and recitals are held here during the Carinthian Summer Festival.

__Left__, a detail of Michael Pacher's high altar in the Church of St Wolfgang in the Salzkammergut. __Right__, the library of Melk Abbey.

Fashionable refinements notwithstanding, Austrian cooking is firmly based on a collection of traditional recipes handed down over generations. Occasionally, as the empire expanded, these were supplemented by dishes from neighbouring cooking pots: damson dumplings from Bohemia, paprika goulash from Hungary, spicy braised peppers from the Balkans and rich pasta dishes from Italy. The Austrians zealously imitated all these specialities and in the end confidently claimed to have invented them.

The best example of this culinary plagiarism is the world-famous Wiener schnitzel, the breaded escalope of veal which every self-respecting Austrian housewife insists was discovered by her great-grandmother. Historical research in the National Archives reveals, however, that when Field-Marshal Radetzky returned from Italy in the year of the 1848 Revolution, he brought back tidings not only of the quashing of the uprising, but also of a certain *costoletto alla Milanese*, a recipe which he immediately passed on to the chefs at the Imperial Court – as a closely guarded secret, of course. Ever since then, the breadcrumb coating for veal, pork, chicken or fish has been regarded as typically Austrian.

The Austrians love to eat. This fact is clearly evident even as you walk down the street. The nation is proud of its hard-earned extra kilos; scrawny health-food addicts are regarded with mild amusement. To overhear someone say, "Waiter, bring me a pint of beer and a little goulash, or I shall die of starvation," at a time when most people are having a cup of coffee and a biscuit isn't as unlikely as you might think.

This devotion to gastronomic pleasures has been cultivated across the centuries. Ancient cookery books bear witness to the catholic appetites of previous generations: Tyrolean eagle with dumplings, roast squirrel with salad, or hedgehog in vinegar sauce with noodles were all great delicacies. During times of war and pestilence, when most of the people were starving, the nobility hardly noticed. When Empress Maria Theresa and her entourage visited the Monastery of Melk for just one day, the cook's duties were

awesome. His shopping list included – among other things – 587 lbs of beef, 743 lbs of veal, 9 calves' heads, 40 calves' feet, 4 lbs of marrow and 4 oxen's tongues. He also required 1,404 eggs, 138 litres of dripping, 9 sticks of cinnamon and 5 new roasting spits. Contemporary portraits show a correspondingly plump Maria Theresa (though that could have been because she was almost constantly and not unhappily pregnant); the gallant court painters endeavoured to hide the Mother of the Nation's double chin behind a large cloud of lacy frills.

Two and a half centuries later, even ordinary folk can enjoy a feast fit for an empress. The recipes have been slightly modified, but more exotic ingredients than were formerly available – such as oriental spices – have become within the reach of everyone. The Austrians have, on the whole, little time for newfangled fads. When it comes to food, they tend to be rather conservative. The old adage that "the farmer won't eat what he doesn't recognise" still applies – even in that international metropolis, Vienna, not to mention the provincial capitals. The average Austrian is as suspicious of nouvelle cuisine as a medieval cup-bearer faced with a goblet of hemlock. Fortunately, however, the variety of specialities on offer between Lake Constance and the Neusiedlersee is so extensive that even the most cosmopolitan guest will find plenty of novelties to sample.

Regional differences: In the Vorarlberg, the most westerly province, many inns still serve meals prepared from old recipes handed down across the generations. *Kässpätzle*, for instance, are home-made noodles prepared with flour, milk and egg and served with butter and cheese. A generous portion of Gouda or Emmenthaler cheese is an essential ingredient in the *marend*, the Vorarlberg mid-afternoon snack; traditionally it is served with bread and a mug of cider. Special delicacies are the trout, whitefish and pike – some weighing as much as 22 lbs (10 kg) – from Lake Constance, where Romans once fished for their supper.

The cuisine of the Tyrol is both substantial

Right, Austria is renowned for its cakes.

and nourishing. The province, through which travellers have passed for centuries on their journey northwards or southwards across the Alps, has a long tradition of hospitality – even though much of the region's produce had to be laboriously won from the bleak mountain soil. The principal ingredients are bacon and cured pork – for genuine Tyrolean bacon dumplings or a hearty Tyrolean snack. The latter is usually accompanied by a measure of gentian spirit, fruit schnapps or rowan *eau-de-vie* (home-distilled and guaranteed to knock your hat off). It tastes best served in a remote mountain hut after an arduous hike. With the wind whistling through the shingles outside and the warmth of the stove within,

from all over the world, not least for its scenic beauty and works of art. But the region has far more to offer than Mozart, the Festival and its celebrated churches, especially when it comes to food.

Travellers should leave some time to visit the historic inns of the Old Town; here, beneath ancient vaulted ceilings or in a shady inner courtyard, you can try Salzburg braised beef, cooked in beer, or a larded veal olive – followed by bilberry soufflé or a sweet baked pudding. No one should miss the excellent local beer, which is usually served in half-litre *krügerl* or tankards. In times past the archbishops of Salzburg acquired brewing rights in order to improve their precarious

the attractions of a three-star menu in a plush hotel dining-room are eclipsed by such simple delights.

For the truly ravenous there is the traditional *bauernschöpsernes*, tender braised lamb. It is first seared with fried onion rings, then braised for half the required cooking time. Quartered potatoes are added, with parsley, a bay leaf and a glass of red wine as flavouring, and it is cooked until tender. *Guten Appetit*! The meal ends with special doughnuts or freshly stewed apple, and a final tot of fruit schnapps for the road.

The neighbouring province of Salzburg is an attractive holiday destination for visitors

financial situation; for many years now, beer production has been a flourishing economic sideline in this enterprising city.

Sweet music: Confectionery is another Salzburg speciality. Here even the revered Wolfgang Amadeus is celebrated by balls of marzipan and plain chocolate – the famous and delicious "Mozartkugeln".

A detour into the nearby Salzkammergut is always worthwhile – especially a visit to Zauner, the baker in Bad Ischl near the former villa of the Emperor Franz Joseph. It is a paradise for the sweet-toothed, bursting with gâteaux, *stollen*, sweets and chocolate.

Upper Austria extends from the Alps across

the Salzkammergut Lake District to the Bohemian Forests, following for some distance the course of the Danube. This was once an exclusively agricultural region, as can be seen in its typical specialities. Cured pork, *sauerkraut* and dumplings are an essential component of every menu, as is the substantial *bauernschmaus* – which also includes sausages and bacon.

Upper Austria is considered to be the true home of the dumpling; many an inn holds an annual Dumpling Week, during which every imaginable form of the fluffy dough – savoury, piquant or sweet – will be served. The region's dumpling capital is the Innviertel, where any lunch without dumplings, how-

thick slice of bread topped by moist bacon.

Carinthia, the southernmost province of Austria, is shaped like an enormous shell; mountains slope away from the central region to the west, north and east, whilst the massive rocky wall of the Karawanken blocks the southern border. Nestling in between are warm lakes with sheltered bays for bathing, making the area a popular summer holiday destination. Fresh fruit and vegetables from the south appear on the market earlier here than elsewhere and are given due respect in the kitchens of the region. One local favourite is *krauthappelsalat*, a crisp and crunchy salad of lettuce and endive.

Game served in every imaginable form,

ever lavish it may be, is considered at best a paltry snack.

In the neighbouring Mühlviertel no meal is complete unless it includes a generous measure of cider or perry. This fermented juice of apples or pears is not really intended for refined palates, for it is mostly rather rough in texture. Even today, many farmers ferment their own cider; the juice is squeezed from the fruit in autumn, and allowed to settle in oak barrels. Traditionally, cider is served in a stone tankard, accompanied by a

Left, a helping of *Kaiserschmarrn*, perhaps?
Above, delicious apricot doughtnuts.

often cooked in red wine, fish from the clear waters of the lakes, and milk and cheese specialities adorn the menus of restaurants between Villach and Klagenfurt. Best known and best loved are undoubtedly the *kasnudeln*, pockets of dough filled with curd cheese and mint leaves and served with brown butter and fried diced bacon. A sweet variation is stuffed with prunes and chopped dried pears. The district around the Wörthersee is a busy tourist centre, but a few miles further on the traveller can still find peaceful meadows and little inns offering good plain cooking of excellent quality. If you are lucky the landlady may even bake the bread herself, from

a mixture of wheat and rye flour. One of these rustic loaves may weigh as much as 6–7 lbs (3–4 kg), with a diameter of up to 20 inches (50 cm). A thick slice, hacked off with a pocket knife and topped with bacon or dripping, or just fresh farmhouse butter and honey, makes a substantial snack.

In Styria, better known as the "Green March", locals and visitors alike feast on the hearty, down-to-earth dishes typical of a region in which the pleasures of life are enjoyed to the full. Characteristic is the *heidensterz*, fried dumplings and crackling prepared from buckwheat flour, pork dripping and water – not to be counted as a low-calorie dish. Classic, too, is *klachlsuppe*, a

ascribe the exotic flavour to the use of black pumpkin oil. For a long time it was scorned as "carriage grease"; today the darkly shimmering oil with its inimitable nutty taste is found in the most fashionable restaurants of Vienna, where it adds the finishing touch to many an elegant salad buffet.

Mushroom goulash and braised cabbage, poulardes and pork in every variation are other tempting – and fattening – specialities of Austria. If you decide on a fruit diet to repair some of the damage done to your waistline on your visit, you should head for the southern part of the province, along the border with Slovenia. Fruit trees form guards of honour along the roads; their harvest goes to

soup prepared from slices of leg of pork, herbs and vegetables, juniper berries and peppercorns. It is seasoned generously and served with boiled potatoes and grated horseradish. Guests who insist on something lighter, however, will find that the local market gardens can supply a huge range of fresh vegetables. The local pumpkin specialities earn eulogies from visiting gourmets.

If the salad you ordered seems different here from elsewhere in the world, you must

Left, Liesl Wagner-Bacher, one of Austria's supercooks. **Above**, in the hunting lodge "Graf Recke in Wald" in Pinzgau.

make apple juice and warming pear schnapps.

Wine and woods: In Lower Austria, the region, like the wine, is measured in quarters: those lying above and below the Manhartsberg, those above and below the Vienna Woods, and the Wine and Woodland Quarters. The cuisine of the region is just as varied. Many dishes have been handed down from the former woodland dwellers to the present-day inhabitants. Former peasant dishes have become favourite dishes of the most cosmopolitan gourmets. *Stosuppe* is a delicious and calorie-laden soup made from milk, full cream and boiled potatoes.

The River Danube and the region's lakes

and streams are teeming with fish. A perennial favourite is trout *à la meunière*, in which the fish is fried in butter, seasoned with lemon and served garnished with sprigs of parsley. Game dishes – from "pheasant in a bacon jacket" to roast wild boar – are a culinary sensation. For dessert, the sweet cream *strudel* has achieved national fame. As a *digestif*, the recommended choice is a fine liqueur or apricot brandy from the Wachau, with its excellent country inns and above all its ambitious cooks.

Ancient spice: The culinary skills of the Burgenland, Austria's youngest province, are as colourful as its population. Here live Croats, Hungarians and Gypsies whose tra-

ries-old culinary tradition which makes it a fitting final stop on this gallop through the kitchens of Austria. The Viennese are secretly convinced that all Austrian cuisine is really Viennese in origin, although they tend to keep their opinions to themselves when travelling through the provinces.

In addition to the Wiener schnitzel, whose praises we have already sung, the most famous speciality in this city of gourmets is the *tafelspitz*. This lean cut of beef is cooked in broth and served – surrounded by roast potatoes – with chive sauce, spinach and horseradish and apple purée.

The devotion to beef dates back to the last century, when a famous restaurant near the

ditional dishes are gathered together under the collective title of "Pannonian cuisine". Many specialities – such as the Esterházy Roast – can trace their names back to the ancient aristocratic families of the region. Hungarian cooking is not only represented by its spicy *gulyas* and other stews, but also by delicious sweet and savoury pancakes, *palatschinken*. The heady local wine can best be sampled as an accompaniment to a crispy fried *fogosch*. The Burgenland specialises in sweet wines; those from the shores of Neusiedlersee, "Vienna's sea", are particularly fine.

Vienna, the nation's capital, has a centu-

Kohlmarkt offered a daily selection of 26 beef dishes. Boiled beef and vegetables can be found on the menu of every restaurant today, from the smallest *beisel* (bistro) to the temples of haute cuisine. A true Viennese gourmet, incidentally, is a great soup fan. A lunch menu without a steaming bowl of broth with semolina dumplings, liver dumplings or sliced pancake lurking in its depths is not a proper meal. To follow, he or she may choose roast pork, perhaps, with bread dumplings and sauerkraut. Or – better still – eat *beuschel*, with veal heart, lots of root vegetables, herbs and spices. The favourite beverage is likely to be a cool "G'spritzter", equal quantities of white wine and sparkling mineral water. Pudding will be an apple strudel, made with a dough stretched out so thinly that you can read the newspaper through it, filled with a mixture of sliced apple, cinnamon and raisins, rolled up and baked crisply.

Famous cakes: Alternatively a meal may end with a choice of *torten,* cakes, for which Austria, and particularly Vienna, is famous. *Sachertorte,* the rich dark chocolate one, named after the place of its invention, Hotel Sacher in Vienna, is the best known, but others include *dobos-torte,* with a caramelised top, and *Linzer torte,* with nuts.

It is best to abandon all thoughts of calorie-counting, especially when it comes to genu-

With a population of roughly 7 million, it nevertheless boasts no fewer than 50,000 restaurants. It would be a remote corner indeed where the traveller could not be within easy reach of a range of establishments to suit every mood and every wallet. A common or garden inn is probably the best place to still the normal pangs of hunger or thirst. In country areas it is likely to tend to rustic comfort, with little in the way of fashionable decor; in towns, to welcoming intimacy. Vienna has developed its own variation on the inn theme: the *beisel.*

A genuine Viennese *beisel* serves lovingly seasoned plain cooking, crisp wines and fresh draught beer along with a generous portion

ine Czech yeast dumplings. They are a type of dumpling made of yeast dough, filled with damsons and painted with melted butter. If they are rather on the small side, they are known as "Ducat dumplings" and are served with vanilla sauce. And what do the Austrians say if they have particularly enjoyed a lovingly prepared meal? "It was poetry." This is the aptest description of Austrian cuisine in general.

Austria is known as an hospitable country.

Left, Chanteuse Juliette Greco in the Café Demel. **Above**, singer and artist André Heller in the Tiergartencafé in Schönbrunn Palace.

of native wit. Visitors can test this for themselves at the Pfudl in the Bäckerstrasse or the Zu den drei Hackn in the Singerstrasse. Austrian cuisine for the most discriminating gourmets with a wallet to match is served in Korso, the restaurant of the luxurious Hotel Bristol. Also at the summit of the nation's gastronomic ladder is the Steirereck in the 3rd postal district; it also possesses one of the best-stocked wine cellars in the land. The chef is called – appropriately enough – Helmut Österreicher; every evening he creates a succession of specialities to delight his guests: mushrooms au gratin, sliced black pudding, or simply a selection of perfectly ripe cheeses served with thick slices of pumpkin seed bread. It is no rarity for a standing ovation to greet the maestro when he enters the dining-room.

This renaissance of traditional cuisine has spread from the capital to the remotest corners of the provinces. These days one can experience Austrian cooking at its best in the Mesnerhaus in Mauterndorf (Styria), in the Villa Hiss in Badgastein, in the Bleiberghof in Carinthia or in the Schafelner in Haag (Upper Austria).

Fortunately, the past few years have seen the quiet demise of an ancient prejudice: the assertion that women are capable of producing acceptable plain cooking for her family

ceived due credit for her achievements and was elected Chef of the Year.

The feasts of rural life: An old adage goes: "One must celebrate feasts as they fall". In Austria in particular, this holds very true. Be it baptism, wedding or funeral, the ensuing party with family and friends is an essential part of the proceedings. On church festivals, or the name day of the local patron saint, celebrations are held as in times past; sliding over barrels, walking along tree trunks and other traditional tomfoolery follow the meal. Typical of such holidays is St Martin's Day, 11 November, marked by a festive dinner at which a crisply roasted "Martin's goose" is served with apple and chestnut stuffing.

or the clientèle of a simple inn, but not of ascending the heights of *haute cuisine,* the culinary Olympus. Ambitious women cooks include Lisl Wagner-Bacher, in her country house Landhaus Bacher at the gateway to the Wachau, and in the neighbouring village of Göttweig her sister, Gerda Schickh. The two young proprietresses of the Goldener Strauss in picturesque Dürnstein enchant visitors with their gourmet cuisine naturelle, and Sissy Sonnleitner has risen like a comet to the heights of the culinary firmament. Her most remarkable feat is in establishing a top-class restaurant in Kötschach-Mauthen, a remote Carinthian village. In 1990 she re-

In Austria as elsewhere, a new trend in favour of lighter, healthier food is becoming increasingly evident. Large hotels in all the provinces are introducing organic and health food, with appetising salad buffets, fresh muesli and low-fat fish dishes.

The guru of this new fitness wave is Willi Dungl, the former masseur of ex-Formula One World Champion Niki Lauda. He organises rejuvenating cures for body and soul in Gars am Kamp, in the Waldviertel. His prominent clientèle, from the realms of sport, politics and show business, pays dearly for

<u>**Above**</u>, **Pinzgau specialities.**

the privilege of sipping mineral water and jogging through the woods at the crack of dawn. Less ascetic but just as effective at burning off those extra calories are the numerous sporting activities which Austria offers – sailing, golfing, skiing, kite-flying, parachute jumping, hiking and riding to name but some of them.

Such activities, however, are helped along by their own particular refreshments. As darkness falls on the sun terraces of the skiing huts around the Arlberg a perfect day is capped by a *jagatee*, a brew of schnapps, wine and a drop of tea. Similarly, an essential part of the grape harvest, when town-dwellers flock out to the Neusiedlersee, southern Styria, the Weinviertel or the hills surrounding Gumpoldskirchen to help with the hard labour in the vineyards, are the open air lunches of bacon, sausages and freshly pressed grape juice.

But it is advisable not to try the stronger fermented brew known as "storm" unless there is at least an earth-closet in the vicinity. From grape juice via the "storm" it is only a small step to the *heurige*, the Austrian's favourite cure for all ills. Enjoyed in short draughts, it it is said to sort out body and soul and make you cheerful and contented.

The *heurige*, or new wine, is best sampled in an establishement of the same name, an *heurige* – if possible in the vicinity of Vienna, in Grinzing, Salmannsdorf, Kahlenbergerdorf or Nussdorf. To mention specific addresses would defeat part of the pleasure of the exercise. It is better to set out to discover them for yourself. If you see a low vintner's cottage, with the sound of laughter and the clinking of glasses echoing from the little inner courtyard, then you will know you've found a likely place. Some wine growers also invite travellers to a tasting in their cool cellars, among the acid smell of wooden barrels and fermented grapes, where the candlelight flickers romantically against the vaulted ceilings.

Equally inviting are the attractive whitewashed houses in the vintners' districts in the Weinviertel and in the south Burgenland. Many an elderly farmer can be seen still wearing his blue apron as he sits on the bench at the top of the terrace steps smoking his pipe and reflecting on the day's labours.

The cellars: Louder and livelier are the cellar bars in the nation's capital. Way below ground level, the Piaristenkeller in the Josefstadt, and the Matthias, Augustiner and Zwölf-Apostel-Kelle in the First Postal District are the most popular establishments. Roast pork, pig's trotters and roast chicken are served gleaming with fat to the sound of zither music and vintners' songs. Sometimes even a real Gypsy violinist can be heard fiddling away. These much-loved Austrian institutions have been copied all over the world by homesick emigrants and astute businessmen. And yet, for whatever reasons, these imitations are a poor substitue for the real thing.

The coffeehouse: The secret recipe for a genuine coffeehouse, for example, has still not been fathomed. At best, the prerequisites for its success can be listed. It should, if possible, be situated in Vienna – although Salzburg, Linz or Graz might be acceptable alternatives. Red velvet banquettes and marble tables, mirrors and crystal chandeliers, and a grumpily superior head waiter are pretty well vital, as is the smell of fresh coffee, butter croissants and poppyseed cake, and the rustling of newspapers from all over the world. It is a mixture to which one can easily become addicted. In Salzburg you can sample exactly the right blend of all these elements at Tomaselli or Café Bazaar, where worthy officials share ashtrays and sugar sprinklers with youthful music students from the nearby Mozarteum

In Vienna, locals and visitors alike are spoiled for choice. They may decide to head for the Prückl on the Stubenring, where on Saturday afternoons elderly ladies play bridge, or they may choose the Café Museum, an oasis beloved of students, artists and poets where yellowing posters for exhibitions and theatrical performances adorn the walls and the waiter hovers watchfully over his guests like a Sicilian godfather over his extended family. The continued popularity of Hawelka in the Dorotheergasse owes much to its illustrious past and the lady chef's warm yeast dumplings – only available, please note, after 10pm.

Many of the coffee houses are open late into the evening, and not just in the main towns. For a change, it is often a good idea to skip dessert in your hotel or restaurant and adjourn to one of the local coffee house for a slice of Sachertorte, a cup of coffee and a glass or so of schnapps.

The mecca of winter sports lies in the Eastern Alps. Resorts like Lech am Arlberg, Kitzbühel, St Anton, Innsbruck or Saalbach have become world-famous through competitions such as the World Cup, the Olympic Games and the World Championships in Alpine Skiing. These villages are the homes of the superstars of the skiing world – triple Olympic medallist Toni Sailer and downhill champion Franz Klammer.

Facilities for every kind of winter sport are available, from Nordic skiing to skijoring, can look back on a similarly long tradition of winter sports. But in Austria, skiing is not just a winter sport. The country possesses the greatest density of all-year-round glacial ski regions. Areas like the Dachstein, the Kaunertal, the Pitztal or the Mölltal offer skiing with all amenities whatever the weather. It is possible to ski in a swimming costume in the summer.

Testing piste: In 1990, in Kitzbühel – by far the most famous ski resort in Austria – aficionados celebrated the 50th anniversary of

from snowboarding to ice mountaineering, from sledging to so-called skeleton riding.

A nation of skiers: Austria is the home of modern skiing. At the turn of the century, in the little village of Lilienfeld in Lower Austria, the ski pioneer Matthias Zdarski invented the now world-famous stem turn which even today causes every fledgling skier so many problems.

Since then Austria has become one of the finest winter sports centres in the world. The resorts are strung out like pearls on a necklace right across the Alps: Lech am Arlberg, St Anton, Innsbruck, Kitzbühel, Saalbach, Obertauern, Schladming. Only Switzerland the notorious Hahnenkamm downhill race on the Streif Run, the most difficult and dangerous descent in the world. In skiing circles a victory in this race is more prestigious than a gold medal in the world championships. All great downhill skiers have stood on the starting line at the top of the run, which is over 2 kilometres long. The winners' names have gone down in the annals of skiing history: Toni Sailer, the first man to win a gold medal in all three alpine ski disciplines, Karl Schranz, the Austrian downhill champion of the 1960s, and the Olympic medallist from Carinthia, Franz "The Emperor" Klammer, who completed the course one-thousandth of a second faster than the famous Italian, Gustav Thoeni.

For the average skier the Streif Run can only be tackled from start to finish under perfect snow conditions. Even then it is an adventure which only those with considerable experience should attempt.

The Streif makes no concessions. Even at the beginning the piste is rock-hard. For approximately 100 metres past the start it slopes gently downhill. Then comes the most dangerous section, the infamous "mouse-

competitors reach the edge of the Hausberg, the entrance to the home straight and the second key section in the Streif Run. The "flat" middle section turns out to consist of very uneven, difficult terrain far more taxing than that usually classified as a "black" or "advanced" run. The home straight, extra fast and extra steep, allows top skiers to reach speeds of more than 82 miles (130 km) per hour; it is even more difficult than the preceding section. It seems incredible that the competitors can keep going at such ex-

trap". It is so steep that it is only covered with snow during exceptionally hard winters; for the race it is specially coated with a mixture of snow and ice. The competitors, crouching low as they hurtle downhill at speeds of almost 68 miles (100 km) per hour, have the utmost difficulty in adjusting to the slanting angle of the Mousetrap.

The middle section of the course is also very testing. After about one minute the

Preceding pages: a Styrian pays homage to the mountains; snowboard take-off; winter hang-gliding. **Left**, a high-level tour in the Ötztaler Alps. **Above**, look, no hands.

cessive speeds. Franz Klammer completed the Streif Run in just 2.04 minutes.

Off-piste on the Dachstein: During the past few years off-piste skiing in powder snow has become increasingly popular. Ski touring was for many years treated with derision as the hobby of a handful of extremists; today it is considered one of the most exciting winter sports, though it should always be undertaken in the company of experienced guides (in view of the high risk of avalanches, it would be extremely dangerous to venture out without their help).

The Dachstein offers the best off-piste skiing. Take the first cable car of the day up to the Dachstein glacier, as it is a long haul to reach the starting point. At the top you will have to shoulder your skis and trudge uphill through deep snow for over an hour to a snowy gully barely 320 ft (100 metres) below the Dachstein peak. The incline is steeper than 60 percent, and a mixture of deep drifts of powder snow and treacherous ice. The gully itself is about 160 ft (50 metres) wide, bordered by high walls of rock and littered with jagged rocky outcrops and ridges through which you must pick your way.

Leaning backwards as far as possible, and making short, rapid swings to left and right in order not to gain too much speed, you will experience an intoxicating sense of euphoria as you descend into the valley. Usually one guide leads the group whilst a second brings up the rear, ready to assist those who need help. The deep-snow adventure will last all of 10 minutes, during which you may often sink up to your neck in snow. You may feel weak at the knees from exertion, but the experience of skiing through deep snow is simply far more exhilarating than that on the manicured pistes.

The rest of the descent runs fairly gently through a beautiful mountain forest. To avoid damaging the young saplings, try not to use the sides of your skis more than necessary. Trees in the central Alps are of vital importance; they provide avalanche protection in winter and prevent mountainslides and mudflows in summer. Foolishness or exaggerated demonstrations of prowess are not appreciated. Austria can claim the highest number of deaths from avalanches.

For ski acrobats: During the past few years the innovative branch of the ski industry has invented a number of demanding alternatives to alpine skiing. Snowboards, monoskis and swingbos are the new stars of the slopes. Of the three, the monoski is without doubt the one which requires the most sophisticated technique and an almost acrobatic sense of balance. Two bindings are mounted in parallel on a very broad alpine ski. The grade of difficulty is virtually the same as waterskiing on a monoski.

The fun element is undoubtedly greater in the case of the swingbo and snowboard. The swingbo functions like a skateboard without wheels. The binding is mounted on a small pedestal slightly above the surface of the ski; it responds immediately to the slightest body movements. Riding a snowboard is like surfing. Wearing normal mountain boots, one stands in overshoes which are mounted directly on the snowboard. Centrifugal force enables the expert snowboarder to take spectacular curves, braking as he does so with his fists; on humpbacked slopes he can even leap in the air. Both items of equipment are suitable for beginners.

For some years now, virtually all Austrian ski schools have offered courses in swingbo, snowboard and monoski. Specialists such as the Dachstein-Tauern Region Adventure Club have abandoned alpine skiing altogether. Apart from the snow sports mentioned above they also provide an introduc-

tion to snow rafting, in which the boldest sports enthusiasts hurtle down the pistes in huge inflatable rafting boats. The descent takes place at breakneck speed, but unfortunately there is absolutely no way of steering the snow raft. Every excursion inevitably ends with a tumble.

Down in the valleys, many resorts provide skijoring, another popular alpine variation in which a team of two are pulled round an icy course by horses; the exceptionally bold do the same behind souped-up cross-country motorbikes or rally cars. The lakes of Carinthia and Styria, which acquire a deep layer of ice in winter, are the main skijoring centres. The sport is, however, only recommended for experienced skiers.

Ice pursuits: Austria has a long history of skating. Skating rinks such as Engelmann, or the Stadhalle or the Southern Ice Rink in Vienna or the stadia in Graz, Klagenfurt or Villach, are well patronised during the winter months. But Austria's lakes provide the most exciting skating to be had.

When there is a hard frost Lake Neusiedler is transformed into the largest natural expanse of ice in Europe. The ice freezes to a depth of several metres and offers an area of almost 15 sq. miles (40 sq. km) for skating and other ice sports. From the end of December until the beginning of February you can

Carinthia is also the location of the Weissensee, Europe's only golf course on ice – when the weather is cold enough. Golfers putt on the "white" instead of on the "green". There is just one disadvantage – once the ball is in the hole it is lost for ever, for the Weissensee is over 320 ft (100 metres) deep in places. Once a year the Weissensee is transformed into the setting for the Carinthian Ice Marathon, during which skaters must complete a course of over 125 miles (200 km) on ice. The only other place in Europe where such a race is possible is on the frozen canals of Holland.

South of the main Alpine ridge, ice hockey is the most popular sport. The matches of

usually skate across the lake from Pamhagen to Rust. Lake Neusiedler also serves as the national centre for ice-sailing. Although they are fragile vessels weighing only a few kilograms and supported on skids, ice yachts can reach top speeds of more than 50 miles (80 km) an hour in a good wind, which makes them faster than any other form of sailing boat. Ice-sailing requires a high degree of technical proficiency as a sailor. The sport is not without hazard for participants; dangers include sudden gusts of wind and a capsize if the ice sheet suddenly gives way.

Left, climbing a waterfall. **Above**, dog sledging.

world record holders KAC (Klagenfurt) and their perpetual challengers from Villach are perennially popular and arouse support which matches that of the American Football League Superbowl in the US. The ice hockey stadia are always packed, and the atmosphere is better than in any football stadium. In Austria, ice hockey is played only at club level; there are no opportunities for non-members to try this fast and challenging sport.

By contrast, everyone, can try their skills at curling. This sport has won many thousands of enthusiasts, especially in the western provinces of Austria. There are two kinds of curling: firstly, long-distance curling, in which the aim is to slide the curling stone – a metal plate weighing some 11 lbs (5 kg) with a handle – as far as possible across the ice. The present world record is held by an Austrian, who achieved a distance of over 640 ft (200 metres). In the more sophisticated version of the game the curling stone must be placed as close as possible to the the tee. In winter the Sunday curling match is one of the highlights of the week. Most tourist-oriented villages have a curling pitch where visitors may join in.

Much smaller and therefore more exclusive is Austria's circle of bobbers. The Olympic bobsleigh and toboggan run in Innsbruck-Igls is the only artificial ice run in the includes jet-set personalities like Gunter Sachs, but the steep walls of the Innsbruck run result in record times. The public particularly appreciates races on natural toboggan runs, which are usually narrow defiles or forest tracks with an artificial surface of ice. Here the sledges achieve top speeds of over 38 miles (60 km) per hour. Throughout Austria, sledging is a popular alternative to skiing as well as a much-loved *après-ski* pastime. Many an evening of merrymaking in one of the numerous ski huts culminates in a toboggan ride by torchlight along woodland paths to the valley.

The newest winter sport trend, dog sledging, imported from Canada and the US, has

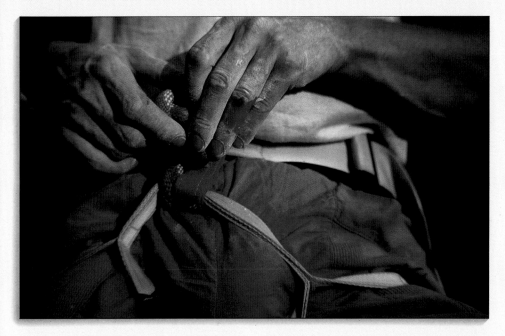

country. Nonetheless, Austria's bobbers occupy top place in the world rankings. In 1990 two Austrians won the gold and silver medals in the European Bobsleigh Championships. Austria's bobbers first achieved national recognition in 1976, when the former Chancellor, Dr Fred Sinowatz, who was Minister of Sport at the time, careered down the newly completed ice run on a four-man bob before the opening of the Winter Olympic Games.

The real heroes of Innsbruck are, however, the skeleton riders. The town's skeleton club may lack the cosmopolitan flair of the skeleton club in St Moritz, whose membership become one of the most popular spectator sports in Austria. The country's mushers are some of the continent's best. Horst Maas, the sportsman-adventurer from Linz, was the first man to cross the Himalayas and the previously almost unknown kingdom of Sanskar with a dog sledge. He was also one of the few European dog sledgers to take part in the notorious Iditarod race in Alaska.

The call of the mountains: Austria is one of the cradles of mountaineering. During the last century, most of the country's 9,800-ft (3,000-metre) peaks were conquered for the first time by English climbers, but native mountaineers have more than made up for this in the 20th century. Some of them – Habeler, Fritz Morawetz, Heinrich Harrer and Edi Koblmüller – have achieved world fame; together, they have conquered all the 26,000-ft (8,000-metre) giants of the Himalayas. All the country's climbing heroes began with the mountains on their back doorstep, the peaks of the Eastern Alps, the Karawanken or the Totes Gebirge. Most of them passed their first baptism of fire on difficult sections such as the south wall of the Dachstein. All of them have tackled the king of Austrian mountains, the Grossglockner.

At 12,153 ft (3,798 metres) high the Grossglockner is the most majestic of all the country's peaks. It is notorious above all for its

to gaze at the marmots. The first hour is spent crossing the Pasterze Glacier, passing crevasses up to 80 ft (25 metres) deep. When the surface ice is thawing you will have to wade the last few metres through slushy firn. Then follows an exhausting climb of seven and a half hours through the Leitertal to the Salmhütte refuge. On cloudless summer days the sun beats down unmercifully . The light will already be fading as you reach the hut, which stands at an altitude of 8,460 ft (2,644 metres). At this point you are already 450 ft (140 metres) above the Hochtor, the highest point on the Grossglockner Highway. It is advisable to engage a guide for the next day's climb beyond the Salmhütte.

rapidly changing weather conditions as well as the panoramic road completed during the 1930s, the first of its kind in the world. It enabled the general public to penetrate the very heart of the Austrian Alps.

The Alpine Highway is actually just the approach road to the real world of the Grossglockner. To really explore the area you should park your car at the Franz-Josephs-Höhe near the Pasterze Glacier – at the spot where hordes of tourists in sensible shoes clamber out of their air-conditioned coaches

The remaining 3,200 ft (1,000 metres) include several sections calling for real climbing skills. The terrain to the "Eagle's Nest" (10,880 ft/3,400 metres) becomes progressively steeper, often with a gradient of 50 percent. After one hour you will reach the steep wall below the Eagle's Nest, one of the key sections of the Grossglockner ascent. It takes a good 30 minutes to scale the wall in order to reach the summit ridge, and a further half hour walking along the path – barely 16 inches (40 cm) wide – before you finally reach the lowest of the summits of the Grossglockner. After a short rest you continue towards the Kleiner Glockner. At this

Left, worn fingers. **Above**, rock-climbing in Bad Ischl. **Above right**, bivouac on a glacier.

point you are at an altitude of 9,600 ft (3,000 metres); the terrain becomes steadily more icy from here.

One and a half hours later you will arrive at the "Little Glockner", separated from the summit proper only by the "roof", a relatively flat ridge. To right and left, clefts fall away almost vertically towards Pasterze and Kals down in the valley. From here, much of the remaining way is across patches of snow, stamped down hard and frozen solid. Progress is slow and difficult. The final assault on the summit requires a further half hour. It is perilous, but the incomparable panorama of the Eastern Alps is ample recompense for all the effort. On a clear summer day the visibility is so good that you can see as far as the Silvretta. The path on the approach to the summit cross flattens out a little. At about noon you should finally stand there, at 12,460 ft (3,798 metres) – the highest point in the whole of Austria.

Apart from the Glockner, mountaineers should head for the Grossvenediger, the Silvretta group, the Dachstein, the Ötscher in Lower Austria, the Wilder Kaiser and the precipitous peaks of the Karawanken in Carinthia.

Climbing is taught in Austria's many mountaineering schools. The Alpine School in Kaprun is run by the Austrian Climbing Association. It is directed by mountaineering idol Fritz Morawetz, one of the country's most experienced alpinists, who made climbing history at the end of the 1950s by becoming the first man to scale the 25,600-ft (8,000-metre) Gasherbrum III peak in the Karakorams. The Alpine Centre itself lies in a picturesque high mountain valley by the top reservoir of the Kaprun hydroelectric scheme. The school uses the rock faces of the Glockner as practice walls. Morawetz is famous for his children's courses, which give youngsters a first taste of alpine sports.

Austria's mountaineering schools also offer courses in free climbing, the newest trend in the Alps. Free climbers are not interested in a 9,600-ft (3,000-metre) peak, but in the trickiest rock face in one of Austria's increasing number of climbing parks (one of the best-known is in Bad Ischl in the Salzkammergut). "Pleasure Dome", "Magic Flute", "Albatross", "Gipsy Baron" are the names free climbers give to their climbing routes. Most are in the limestone Alps, in the Gastein Valley or in the Salzkammergut.

Another variation gaining popularity among mountaineers is ice or waterfall climbing. Equipped with two ice picks and exceptionally large crampons, experienced mountaineers make the ascent of frozen waterfalls and ice-covered mountain slopes. Their only grip is by means of the axes embedded in the ice; the crampons only serve to support some of their weight. One false blow, and the fragile ice shatters – and the climber is alone. The ice climbing centre is the Gastein valley. Here, at temperatures many degrees below zero, the frozen waterfalls offer a variety of climbing opportunities. Other popular ice climbing destinations include the Gesäuse in Styria and the upper Enns valley. In winter, some mountaineering schools are prepared to arrange ice climbing courses for experienced alpinists.

Water sports: The most famous sailing regions are Lake Neusiedler, the Attersee and Lake Wolfgang in the Salzkammergut, Lake Constance and the Achensee in the Tyrol. Small, agile sailing dinghies are the most popular as they adapt more quickly to the wind conditions, which often tend to extremes. Lake Neusiedler is the national windsurfing centre; it lies near the resort of Neusiedl in the Burgenland.

Windsurfing has overtaken sailing as regards popularity throughout Austria; many stars of the international windsurfing scene first tacked into the wind across Lake Neusiedler. The most famous of them all was Hari Dorfner from Vienna, who for some years held the world record as the fastest windsurfer. He also invented the first game for windsurfers; today it is employed in many countries as part of the surfers' winter training programme. Apart from Lake Neusiedler, another popular venue for windsurfers is the "New" Danube in the Lobau, whose mirror-calm waters, and stable wind conditions make it ideal for beginners.

For decades now Austria has been one of the European white water centres. The most attractive rivers for kayak and canoe trips are the Enns, the upper reaches of the Salzach, the Isel in East Tyrol, the Drau, the Gail, the Steyr and the Kamp in the Waldviertel of Lower Austria (though the latter is less turbulent and is thus better suited to relaxing

Right, ice-climbing is not for the timid.

canoeing excursions). During the past few years numerous white water schools have been founded along the banks of all these rivers; all offer instruction as well as touring programmes. Adequate training is essential, especially in spring, when the melting snows make the country's mountain torrents highly dangerous and difficult to navigate.

During the past few years rafting has overtaken canoeing in popularity. The formula for what may well be the most exciting adventure on Austria's mountain rivers is a heavy-duty rubber dinghy, nine men, nine wooden paddles, steel safety helmets, life jackets, wet suits and a raging torrent.

Hydrospeed, a combination of white wa-

The lovely, crystal-clear Alpine lakes offer some of Europe's finest diving experiences. A wide variety of freshwater fish, an as yet unspoilt underwater world and the remarkable flora may not compare with the wealth of colour of the tropical waters of the Caribbean, but living in mountain lakes at heights of 6,400–8,000 ft (2,000–2,500 metres) can present a challenge of quite a different sort. Diving centres in Austria include the Hallstätter See, where the Zauner family, who live in the village of Hallstatt itself, run the most famous and certainly the most unusual diving school in Austria (for one thing they organise the annual competition to choose "Miss Underwater"). Further centres

ter and surfing, is one stage more adventurous still. The hydrospeed is nothing more than an inflatable platform in the shape of a board with two handles. Its small size enables you to tackle more extreme rivers than is possible in a normal rubber dinghy. Bumps and bruises are part and parcel of the proceedings. What is more, it is even colder than in a dinghy. Even this, however, is not extreme enough for some. The very latest fad is canyoning, whereby participants swim down the rushing torrent with only a life jacket to keep them afloat – a sort of body surfing . It is a sport which requires considerable courage – or at least foolhardiness.

include the Attersee, the Grundlsee, the Fernsteinsee near the Fernpass in Tyrol and the Erlaufsee in the Ötscherland of Lower Austria, near the pilgrimage village of Mariazell. Diving in the Toplitzsee is forbidden. The legendary treasure which the Nazis supposedly hid beneath its waters during the last days of the war in 1945 turned out to be nothing more than war debris and counterfeit pound notes, but the fathomless, dark and deep waters of the Alpine lake exercise an almost mystic attraction on divers the world over. The low water temperature turns diving in all Austria's mountain lakes into a hazardous undertaking. A good quality neoprene wetsuit or a dry diving suit is essential.

Airy alternatives: The Alps make Austria a glider's heaven. Perfect thermal conditions are created by the steep mountain slopes during the summer months, permitting the motorless machines to hover for hours above the mountain tops. The gliding centres are the Rax-Schneeberg area with its landing fields and small airfields in the Vienna Basin, as well as the Inn Valley in the Tyrol, and Carinthia. Glider pilots require an internationally recognised licence to take off over Austrian airspace; they must also register their flight with the airport authorities.

Paragliding is free climbing for would-be flyers. During the summer, thousands of

Scattered across the country are more than 30 hang-gliding and paragliding schools.

Mountain biking: The Burgenland, Austria's easternmost province, is the ideal setting for a cycling tour. Extending from around Lake Neusiedler as far as the Hungarian border, the region offers a well developed network of cycle tracks with inns and service stations offering special services for cyclists. Well-maintained tracks also run along the Danube, from the Strudengau in Upper Austria, and through the Wachau – Austria's most famous wine-growing area – to Vienna. In Upper Austria special cycling tours are organised whereby luggage is transported to the next overnight stop whilst the holiday-

brightly coloured hang-gliders hurl themselves down the steep rock faces, but when it comes to popularity, paragliding has long overtaken hang-gliding in Austria. The paragliding centres are Kössen in Tyrol, where the 1989 world hang-gliding championships were held, and the Garstner Valley in the Phyrn-Priel region. The sport is practised all over the country, however. Other favourite starting points are the mountains surrounding Hallstatt in the Salzkammergut or the Zettersfeld in Lienz in East Tyrol.

Left, a swift way to descend. **Above**, ice surfing on Lake Neusiedler.

makers cycle unencumbered along the Danube valley.

The mountain-bike boom reached Austria several years ago. In the province of Salzburg many forest tracks and paths have been made available for these off-road machines with their heavy-duty construction. The province has become an El Dorado for supporters of the sport. There are plenty of opportunities for mountain-biking in all regions of Austria, although the owners of some private woods have banned bikes. Their use is permitted, in most woods managed by the Federal Forestry Commission.

Holidaymakers for whom these kinds of

adventure sports are far too terrifying, not to say strenuous, can settle for hiking.

Hiking and gentle strolls: The Austrian passion for hiking began in in 1825, when an official at the Viennese court by the name of Josef Kyselak applied for absence, shouldered his rucksack and set off to walk the length and breadth of the land. Wherever he arrived he wrote his name to prove the point – on walls, on rocks, on towers, churches and bridges. Even in the remotest corners of Austria, hunters and shepherds read the name and talked about the remarkable eccentric. He went on to write up his experiences in a two-volume work. It was the first book to describe the pleasure of walking in Austria

and was published simultaneously in Europe and the United States.

Many people have followed in the footsteps of the eccentric courtier in his role as happy wanderer. The slogan invented a few years ago by the National Tourist Authority – "Austria is wanderbar!" – is not so much a challenge as a statement. During holdays or sunny weekends large numbers of Austrians leave the towns for the coutryside; they are joined in their wanderings by many of their country's numerous visitors.

Any list of suggestions for mountain walks will inevitably lead to disagreement, but particularly recommended are the Bregenser Wald and the Montafon in the Vorarlberg and the Kitzbühel Alps in Tyrol. In Salzburg province, the best hiking areas include the Österhorn Mountains (between the Salzkammergut and the Dachstein), the Pinzgauer Mountains (Saalback, Zell am See, Uttendorf) and the head of the Rauris Valley (Kolm-Saigurn), where gold-mining and glacier trails have been devised. In Carinthia, the gently rolling Nockberg Mountains are worth a mention, as are the Low Tauern, the Hochschwab and the Koralpe in Styria. In Upper Austria, favourite recommendations include the Warscheneck Mountains in the Toes Gebirge, the Salzkammergut and the hills of the Muhlviertel. Popular in Lower Austria are the Otscherland, the Ybbstal Alps and the Waldviertel.

One route which is especially rewarding is the footpath from the Bokstein in Salzburg province (Gastein Valley) across the Korntauern Mountains to Mallnitz in Carinthia. Parts of the pass have existed for 5,000 years. On the north side of the steep, narrow pass the ascent is via steps formed by flat stone slabs which were probably placed there by the Celts. Equally stunning is the Klafferkessel in the Low Tauern south of Schladming. In a high-altitude valley at 8,300 to 7,000 ft (2,600–2,200 metres) lies more than 100 lakes formed by glaciers in the last Ice Age. As the distances involved are relatively great one should allow two days for the trip from the Golling Refuge to the Preintal Shelter; during the descent one has a continuous view of the the lakes.

There are a few precautions to remember before setting out on any walk. Always seek advice in the local tourist office as to a walk's degree of difficulty (staff are well-informed on such matters); some mountain footpaths are steep tracks over rocky terrain requiring surefootedness and a head for heights.

It has to be said that one of the pleasures of walking in Austria are the mountain refuges offering high-altitude refreshment and accommodation. In some regions, however, especially in Styria, the refuges in the medium altitude districts close in mid-September because hunting takes priority. Apart from this, long periods of fine weather make the early autumn an ideal time.

Left, non-walkers can always ride. **Right**, looking towards the Sonnenspitze.

If one feature characterises Austria more than any other it is its towering mountains. "Land of Mountains" is the opening line of the country's national anthem and today the people of Austria have even more reason to eulogise their landscapes. The upland pastures, which once made life so difficult for highland farmers, are now criss-crossed by ski lifts and cable cars, evidence of the booming summer and winter tourist industry that accounts for the largest slice of the national economy.

Nestled amongst the wild Alpine scenery are hundreds of mountain lakes and idyllic watercourses which exercise an attraction of their own, especially in summer. The gentle charms of the Salzkammergut and the Carinthian Lake District are underlined by the majestic backdrop of the mountains.

To the east, the foothills of the Alps gradually peter out in the Vienna Woods, reaching to the very suburbs of the nation's capital. Along the Danube, which for 350 km (220 miles) of its course crosses northeast Austria, stood the outposts of the Roman Empire. It was here, too, that Irish monks brought

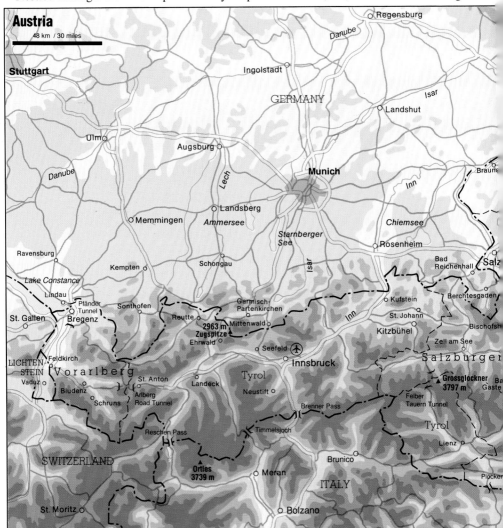

Christianity to Central Europe. Upper Austria, Lower Austria and Eastern Styria have been cultivated by man since time immemorial and have been the scene of many episodes of Central European history.

Vienna, once the seat of the Babenberg dynasty and for over 600 years the centre of the vast Habsburg empire, is today one of the loveliest cities in the world and the repository of a wealth of art treasures.

Every period of European cultural history is also reflected in Austria. Romanesque, Gothic, Renaissance and Baroque buildings are scattered across the land. Statues, frescoes, ceiling and wall paintings document more than 1,000 years of history.

Austrians have the reputation of being an hospitable and amenable race. The tradition stretches back a long way. For centuries Austria has been crossed by foreign peoples and tribes, by soldiers and traders. Many of them made their homes here; the inhabitants of the eastern provinces, in particular, reveal a mixture of Germanic and Slavic characteristics. In Salzburg and Tyrol, by contrast, the people are very like Bavarians. The natives of Vorarlberg are of Alemannic and Rhaetian descent, and are related to the inhabitants of the Engadine and the Upper Rhine.

In spite of these differences they are all proud Austrians. After the fall of the monarchy and the testing period of the Third Reich they found a new identity which distinguishes them from their neighbours.

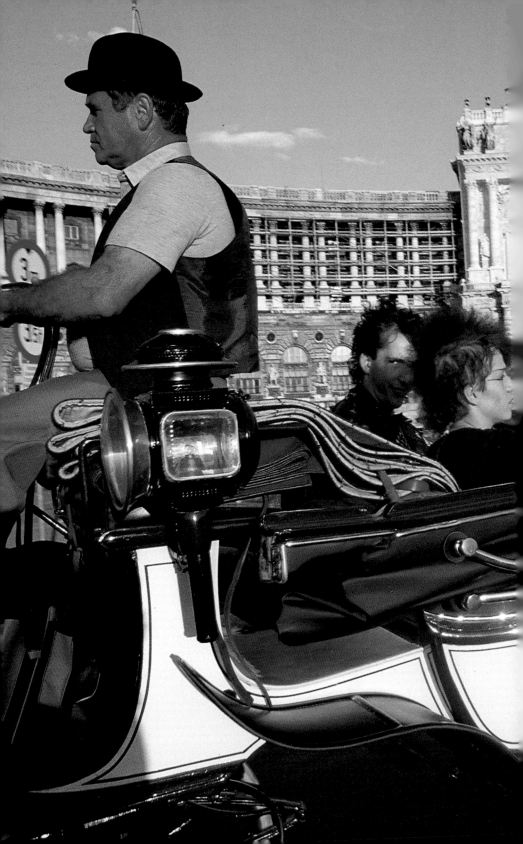

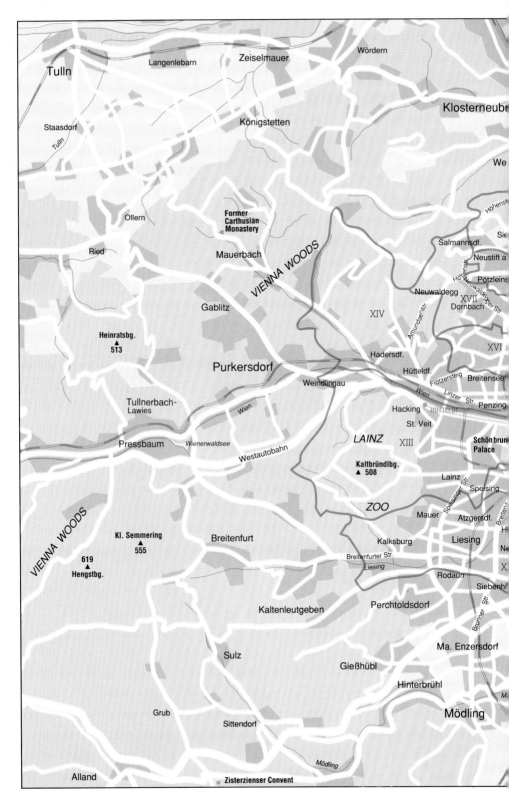

Tulln
Langenlebarn
Zeiselmauer
Wördern
Klosterneubu
Staasdorf
Königstetten
We
Tulln
Ollern
Former Carthusian Monastery
Höhens
Ried
Mauerbach
Salmannsdf.
Sie
Neustift a
VIENNA WOODS
Neuwaldegg
Pötzleins
Gablitz
XIV
XVII
Dornbach
Amundsenstr.
Heinratsbg.
▲
513
XVI
Hadersdf.
Purkersdorf
Hütteldf.
Flötzersteig
Breitensee
Weindlingau
Wien
Linzer Str.
Penzing
Tullnerbach-Lawies
Wien
Hacking
HÜTTELDF
St. Veit
Pressbaum
Wienerwaldsee
Westautobahn
LAINZ
XIII
Schönbrun
Palace
Kaltbründlbg.
▲ 508
Lainz
Spelsing
ZOO
Mauer
Atzgersdf.
VIENNA WOODS
Kl. Semmering
▲
555
Breitenfurt
Kalksburg
Liesing
619
▲
Hengstbg.
Breitenfurter Str.
Liesing
X
Rodaun
Siebenhf
Kaltenleutgeben
Perchtoldsdorf
Ma. Enzersdorf
Börner Str.
Sulz
Gießhübl
Hinterbrühl
M
Grub
Mödling
Sittendorf
Mödling
Alland
Zisterzienser Convent

Vienna and Environs

4 km/2,5 miles

VIENNA

Seven million citizens live within the borders of the Republic of Austria – some 1½ million of them in the capital, Vienna. That is quite a lot of capital for such a small country. In the main postal district, the inner city, the administrative buildings of the defunct monarchy – massive, rambling and commanding respect – still stand. The former Imperial and Royal Ministry of War now houses the Departments of Industry, Agriculture and Forestry, Employment and Social Services. A team of civil servants scarcely reduced in size since the days of the empire fill the hallowed halls with bustling bureaucracy.

The red plush in the fine old coffee houses is showing signs of wear, and some of the old mirrors are clouded. But the Viennese are in no particular hurry to get on with the restoration of the treasures of yesteryear. Outpost of civilisation way back in the mists of time, a centre of power for almost a millennium, and finally relegated to the sidelines at the end of World War II – Vienna's status has run the entire gamut during its long history.

Whenever the present was none too rosy, Vienna's citizens sought refuge in the past. After World War II it almost seemed as if the responsibility of being capital of this small country was too much. Vienna seemed in danger of degenerating into a gigantic open-air museum as it wallowed in a mire of saccharine clichés.

The wind of change: It was not until the 1970s that the city awoke from its somnolence. Since then a fresh new wind has blown across the cobbled streets, sweeping new life through the narrow alleys. The ancient stonework has acquired fresh appeal. "*Wunderbar!*"... "*Magnifique!*"... "Oh, how lovely!" enthuse the droves of tourists visiting the

Preceding pages: the rooftops of Vienna; Café Wilhelmshof; the old and the new. Right, Leopold Hawelka, Vienna's best-known café proprietor.

Michaelerplatz and the Naglergasse, the Opera House and the Cathedral or being transported to Fischer von Erlach's Schönbrunn Palace by one of the city's calash-drivers.

Vienna has woken up at last, and has wholeheartedly taken to marketing its most valuable capital asset – namely its past. The present is accepted somewhat grumpily, and the future, symbolised most obviously by the modern architecture encroaching on the city, is regarded with suspicion. In "Transdanubia",on the other side of the Danube, the new United Nations city soars heavenward like a miniature Manhattan, a bright and shining signpost pointing the way into the next century. The Viennese tend to survey it from a distance and make a careful detour should they need to go beyond it.

No child here has the slightest difficulty comprehending the significance of a millennium. Two millennia ago – as all pupils learn during their first year at school – the Romans introduced vines, which have been cultivated ever since

on the gently rolling hills of the Vienna Woods. It is almost half a millennium since the Turks tried in vain to conquer the city, and ever since the citizens (and others) have eaten croissants – crescent-shaped pastries which an inventive Viennese baker created to poke fun at the withdrawing troops.

A brief history: Vienna is a city whose history stretches back over 2,000 years. In prehistoric times it was an Illyrian and then a Celtic settlement before becoming a part of the Roman Empire – along with the Kingdom of Noricum – in about 15 BC. The famous protective wall, the Limes, built along the Danube to keep out the Germanii, was divided into sections by military forts. One of these was constructed on the site of what is now the city centre of Vienna; it was christened Vindonbona. This was the headquarters of the Tenth Legion, where the soldier-emperor Marcus Aurelius died in AD 180; it was here that he wrote his *Meditations*.

In about AD 395 the Roman legions were forced to withdraw from this

Heads roll: how Vienna's mayor Siebenburger met his end in 1522.

outpost as the migration of the peoples overflowed into the Vienna Basin. The early dawn of Christianity, which had been brought to Vindonbona by some of the Roman soldiers, was to suffer a temporary eclipse. The region was finally converted by the missionaries who travelled west after the so-called Dark Ages of the early medieval period.

The Babenbergs in Vienna: In 1137 Vienna was officially declared a *civitas*, which indicates that by then it was already a well-ordered medieval community. In 1155 Duke Henry II, better known as Jasomirgott (meaning "God help me", his favourite catchphrase), a member of the Babenberg dynasty, established a residence on the site of the square now known as Am Hof. In the same year Irish monks founded the Scottish Monastery on the Freyung. From this point on Vienna developed rapidly as a town. The court of the Babenbergs became the centre of a sophisticated knightly culture, influenced by the civilisations of both Byzantium and the Orient. It attracted merchants and lyric poets; even Walther von der Vogelweide and Ulrich von Liechtenstein lived here for a time. By the beginning of the 13th century Vienna possessed a fully developed town centre already sprouting suburbs; after Cologne, it was the most important city north of the Alps.

After the Babenberg dynasty petered out, the Habsburgs took up the reins. The 14th century saw the consolidation of their powerful position. The most important princely ruler was Duke Rudolf IV, who oversaw the foundation of the tower of St Stephen's Cathedral in 1359, the establishment of the university (in 1365), and a series of economic and social reforms. The Council Decree of 1396 declared that prosperous craftsmen and merchants working in the city should share exactly the same rights as the burghers; this was why Vienna was spared the bloody power struggles which shook many German towns during the Middle Ages.

The position of Mayor of Vienna was not without its inherent dangers, however. Any attempt by him to adopt an

ienna in 609.

independent policy contrary to the interests of the Habsburgs was liable to end in summary execution – as in the cases of Konrad Vorlauf, Konrad Holzer and Dr Martin Siebenbürger. In 1526 Ferdinand I felt secure enough to enact a new town constitution. The medieval byelaws were revised to confer absolute power on the Habsburgs. The traditional constitution was suspended, so that from this point on the mayor's decisions required ratification by the feudal overlord.

Meeting new threats: During the 16th century the whole of central Europe was torn apart by the Protestant doctrines of Martin Luther and the threat of Turkish invasion. In 1529 the Turkish army, under Sultan Suleiman, stood at the gates of Vienna for the first time. For three weeks he bombarded the city, which was only saved by the premature onset of winter. In consequence the old city wall, a legacy of the Babenbergs which was financed by the ransom money raised on Richard the Lionheart when he was unfortunate enough to fall into the hands of the Robber Barons on his way back from a crusade, was replaced by the Bastei, a modern Renaissance fortification system based on Italian models.

The city's character was henceforth increasingly determined by the nobles, the court officials and the clergy; the burghers, deprived of their former power, were driven into obscurity. Their Gothic homes, built in the Middle Ages, were replaced by the Baroque palazzi of the aristocracy. Of considerable significance, too, were the effects of the Catholic wars of religion against Protestantism. So strong was the attraction of the new faith that it is estimated that almost three-quarters of the city's population in 1580 was Protestant. The Jesuits responded by initiating the Counter-Reformation. Under Cardinal Melchior Khlesl they took over Vienna's education system, summoning numerous holy orders to the city, and built a great many new churches.

In 1683 Vienna justified for the second time in its history its role as Bastion

Karl Lueger, Vienna's much-loved mayor, 1904.

of Christianity. For three months the Turks assaulted the city; a defensive army of 17,000 men faced a vastly superior attacking force of 300,000 soldiers. The siege was relieved in the nick of time by the arrival on the Kahlenberg of troops assembled with the help of the Pope and the King of Poland. Against all the odds, the Turks were routed and their threat repelled for ever.

The Golden Age of the Baroque: The following era was one of exuberance, and the imperial city developed into a mecca for the Arts. The nobility built themselves magnificent summer palaces in the devastated suburbs. Lukas von Hildebrandt built the Belvedere for Prince Eugene, the best soldier Austria ever had; Schönbrunn Palace was constructed for the Imperial Family according to the plans drawn up by Fischer von Erlach. Austrian Baroque developed as an independent architectural style.

Under Maria Theresa (1740–80) Vienna became the focal point of an extensive empire. The Empress and Joseph II, her eldest son, wrought far-reaching changes in the social, economic and political structure of capital and country. The education system was reformed, serfdom abolished, the standing of the Jewish population improved. At the request of the Imperial Physician, von Sonnenfels, torture was abolished. Van Swieten laid the basis for the reputation of the "First Viennese School of Medicine". Two parks – the Prater and the Augarten – were opened to the general public, and the first *heurige* (wine taverns) were granted a licence. Vienna became the true centre of the Danube monarchy.

The 19th century began turbulently; Napoleon captured the city twice (in 1805 and 1809), and even took up residence in Schönbrunn. Following the defeat of the French Emperor the Congress of Vienna was held here in 1814–15; it has earned a permanent place in history as frequently emulated mix of conferences and glittering balls. "The Congress dances," spectators observed, but the blithe spirit did not extend to the masses; the populace suffered under poverty, housing shortages and the repressive domestic policies of Chancellor Metternich.

The prosperous middle class retired into the idyll of the Biedermeier period. Genre paintings from this era show a Vienna full of smiling, rosy-cheeked children and curly-headed young women with pastel sunshades. In the revolutionary year 1848, the tense atmosphere in Vienna erupted – as elsewhere – in bloody riots. Citizens, students and workers forced Metternich to resign; the court fled for their lives to the "safe" region of Tyrol. The newly-won freedom was short-lived, however, lasting only from March until October 1848. Then the Imperial army, under Prince Windisch-Graetz, triumphed. The drumhead court-martial took up its bloody task. In December 1848 Franz Josef, then barely 18 years old, was crowned Emperor.

From 1850 Vienna was divided into eight districts; its population already numbered more than 400,000. In 1857, with the often-quoted hand-written note "It is my will...", Emperor Franz Josef

St Stephen's cathedral, destroyed by bombing.

finally gave his permission for the demolition of the old fortifications and for the development of the Glacis, the open area in front. This cleared the way for a *tour de force* of town planning which still enchants visitors the world over; the design of the Ringstrasse. The size of the project attracted architects from all over Europe. Public buildings for court and state were constructed, as were patrician residences and apartment houses for the socially mobile bourgeoisie. The "Ringstrasse" era had dawned. Commerce and art, operetta, poetry and painting flourished throughout the city.

During Cajetan Felder's period as mayor Vienna's first spring water supply system was constructed; the second was added under the popular Karl Lueger. In 1904–05 the city's boundaries were enlarged to include the community of Florisdorf on the far side of the Danube as well as the Vienna Woods, which served as a recreation area for the city. Otto Wagner designed a series of priceless Art Nouveau station buildings for the town and suburban railway lines. When, after a 68-year reign, Emperor Franz Josef was carried to his final resting-place in 1916, in the middle of World War I, the vast funeral cortège travelled from the Hofburg palace to St Stephen's Cathedral. It was the last time the city was to present itself in all its glorious pomp and circumstance as the capital of a great empire.

Red Vienna and Fascism: At the end of World War I universal emancipation was introduced, giving the Social Democrats an absolute majority in the city council. The period until 1934 is known as "Red Vienna". Thousands of new flats were built in the city, along with schools and kindergartens. In the Karl-Marx-Hof alone – over half a mile long – some 1,325 homes were made available. There was a revolution in the city's health policy, with open war declared on infant mortality and tuberculosis. At the same time there was a progressive intensification of the polarisation of attitudes between the Social Democrats and the supporters of Fascism; in 1934 the animosity escalated into violence.

Austrian Fascism, under the leadership of Dollfuss, the Chancellor, gave way without difficulty to the occupation of Austria and the assumption of power by the National Socialist forces. When it happened tens of thousands of jubilant citizens stood waving on the Heldenplatz and the Ringstrasse, determined to offer a fitting welcome to the Führer. During the following night, however, thousands more were arrested and carried off to the concentration camps. On November 9th 1938, during the Viennese Crystal Night, the shop windows of Jewish-owned establishments were smashed, and almost all synagogues and meeting houses burned down. Before the holocaust almost 200,000 Jews lived in Vienna; of these, barely 7,000 survived. The city itself suffered heavy bomb damage during World War II; many of its buildings were destroyed and St Stephen's Cathedral actually went up in flames during the battle for the city's liberation.

Perpetual neutrality: At the end of the occupation of the city by the four victorious powers, the state of Austria ratified a national decree guaranteeing perpetual neutrality. From the balcony of Belvedere Castle, the Foreign Minister, Leopold Figl – flanked by his colleagues from the erstwhile occupying countries – showed the citizens of Vienna the treaty with the precious signatures. On this occasion the grounds for celebration were genuine.

Since then, Vienna and its citizens have been trying to come to terms with their new role. The former powerhouse has been relegated to a subordinate position in the world of politics – a bitter pill for many who have remained faithful to the city's imperial traditions. Since the end of the 1980s, however, a new wind of hope has been blowing in the east, bringing whispered promises: Trieste, Vienna, Prague, Budapest, names which evoke not only memories, but also ambitious dreams of the future. The city of Vienna is preparing to meet an exciting new millennium.

A stroll through Vienna: Vienna's most famous square is also the city's bustling centre. This is where the elegant shop-

Left, rebuilt after the war, the cathedral remains the symbol of Vienna.

ping streets and pedestrian precincts converge, making it a natural magnet for foreign visitors as well as locals and school groups from the provinces. Street performers fiddle tunes or swallow fire, preachers deliver soap-box sermons and lovers of all ages flirt. At the first rays of spring sunshine waiters put out tables and chairs, and the entire square assumes the character of an open-air stage.

Forming a soaring backdrop for the colourful scene is **St Stephen's Cathedral** – affectionately known as the "Steffl" – one of the most outstanding examples of Gothic architecture in Europe. The South Tower rises almost 450 ft (137 metres) above the steeply sloping roof of glazed tiles. During the first building phase, under Babenberg Duke Henry II, a simple parish church was erected on a site which, in the 12th century, still lay outside the city walls. The West front with its vast portal, together with the "Towers of the Pagans", dates from the 13th century. The cathedral received its Gothic countenance during the third building phase,

between 1359 and 1445, at the hands of the Habsburg ruler Rudolf IV. A heady scent of incense invariably fills the interior, which houses such treasures as the 14th-century "Messenger Madonna" and the late Gothic pulpit by Master Pilgram. The famous Prince Eugene is buried in the transept chapel.

Austrians have a highly emotional relationship with their Steffl. At midnight every New Year's Eve the "Pummerin" – one of the biggest bells in the world – rings in the New Year and the entire nation waltzes its way merrily into the future to the strains of the *Blue Danube*. The Cathedral Square has been the subject of controversy on a national scale. Years of animated discussion preceded the construction of the postmodern building diagonally opposite, designed by architect Hans Hollein. Opinions are only now beginning to cool down a bit. Beyond this, is the **Graben**, Vienna's most elegant pedestrian precinct. Mirror-like shop windows and doorways gleaming with brass conspire to make visitors spend their schillings. There are

The Vienna Opera House.

gifts and souvenirs to suit every taste and budget – from finest Augarten porcelain in the form of pirouetting Lippizaner horses, to petit point spectacle cases and "Metres of Love". The latter are sweet dishes, exactly one metre long and filled with minute handmade confectionery. Such sweet novelties are typical of Vienna. At Altmann Kühne, whose spacious sweet shop on the Graben is a long-standing Viennese landmark, miniature chocolates are packed into tiny chests of drawers, suitcases and dolls' hat boxes and exported to destinations all over the world. But the locals, too, cannot resist buying such treats as nougat squares or bitter chocolate wafers.

In the middle of the Graben stands the imposing Baroque **Plague Column**, a reminder of "God's mercy in delivering this town from the justly deserved curse of the plague", a type of monument found all over Austria. Children play and organ-grinders ply their trade in the shadow of the grimly beautiful column.

If you look upwards as you stand before the Plague Column, you may notice the glass dome atop the house on the corner of the junction of Graben and Spiegelgasse. This is the residence of Friedensreich Hundertwasser, the eccentric but business-minded painter and bon-vivant. The conversation-stopping *pièce de résistance* in his flat – distinguished address notwithstanding – is the earth closet in the middle of the jungle-like living room. The artist is also responsible for Hundertwasser House – a crooked, multicoloured housing complex crowned with onion-shaped towers in the third postal district, which during the past years has become a big tourist attraction.

Another Vienna Original, Waluliso, whose name is an abbreviation for "Wood, Air, Light, Sun" died in 1997. Dressed in a white toga and carrying a red apple and an apostle's staff, Waluliso would march through the city centre, blessing tourists and posing for photographs. His quest for world peace and environmental protection took him to Moscow and Washington where he

Arnold Schwarze-negger at the Spanish Riding School.

protested his case at the highest levels. In summer he liked to wander through Lobau, the nudist bathing area, clad only in a laurel wreath.

Other notable shops along Graben include Meinl am Graben, the delicatessen where, on Saturday mornings, gourmets like to meet for a snack, and Thonet where you can buy the famous bentwood furniture created during the last century by Michael Thonet, the Viennese cabinet-maker. His work – the epitome of timeless elegance and good taste in Viennese homes – fetches sky-high prices at auctions today.

Until the turn of the century, the premises of the official suppliers of the Imperial and Royal Court stood cheek by jowl within the short street known as the Kohlmarkt. Still to be found at No. 14 is Demel, confectioners to the Imperial and Royal Court and a magnet for the sweet-toothed from all the corners of the world. The firm was founded 200 years ago; its cakes, sweets and salads are as popular as they ever were. Try the fruity *crème du jour*, served by wait-

resses in demure black uniforms, and watch the crowds round the shop windows gazing admiringly at the miniature fondant statues of Emperor Franz Joseph or Bruno Kreisky.

Just round the corner, at Michaelerplatz no. 3, stands a house whose unadorned facade is completely lacking in garlands and frippery. Built by Adolf Loos in 1910, its unusual secessionist architecture was the object of lively interest and criticism at the time.

The Hofburg: The Imperial Palace complex, a maze of wings and inner courtyards, begins at the Michaelerplatz. An arcaded walk leads through the **Stallburg**, the stables where the Imperial **Spanish Riding School** and the newly opened **Lipizaner Museum** are housed. The Arcade Courtyard, three storeys high, is considered the most important Baroque building in Vienna. Performances by the Spanish Riding School take place in the **Winter Riding School** on the opposite side. You need to order tickets well in advance.

Walking straight across from the

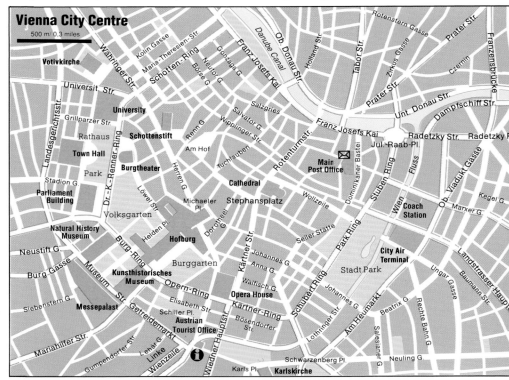

Michaelerplatz, the visitor enters a circular hall topped by a large dome. The entrances to the **Imperial Apartments** and the **Imperial Tableware and Silver Treasury** lie to the left. Above the courtyard one arrives in the **Swiss Court**, the oldest section of the palace. The **Imperial Court Chapel**, where the Vienna Boys' Choir sings Mass from time to time, was mentioned in records for the first time in 1296. Here, too, can be found the world-famous **Liturgical and Secular Treasury** housing the Imperial Jewels. Traversing a wing which used to form part of the Habsburgs' living quarters, one reaches the **Heldenplatz**, with a classicistic Ceremonial Hall and the Neue Burg. The Heroes' Square is laid out on generous lines, inviting visitors to take a leisurely stroll. The **New Château** houses a section of the **National Library** collections of musical instruments, armour and weapons, the **Ephesos Archeological Museum** and the **Ethnological Museum**.

The Ring: The Heldenplatz is separated from the Ringstrasse by the **Imperial Gateway**, site of a monument erected after World War II to commemorate Vienna's Jewish population and the victims in the Austrian Resistance Movement. The view of the Volksgarten nearby, however, carries no such tragic undertones. The park's rose garden is renowned for its pungent scent during the summer months. Pensioners enjoying the Mediterranean atmosphere may even feel moved to hum a few bars of Strauss as they sit, accompanied by their elderly dachshunds, in peaceful harmony between the courting couples on the elegant benches. Johann Strauss once gave evening concerts here; they were always greeted with resounding applause.

Every visitor to the Heldenplatz finds it difficult to decide which direction to take next. To right and left lies the Ringstrasse with its magnificent buildings. On the other side of the road stands the **National Gallery of Art** and the **Natural History Museum**. The collections housed in both museums – today under state control – are among some of

the finest and most important in the world. The National Gallery of Art contains the fourth-largest collection of paintings, among them works by Pieter Brueghel the Elder. In the Natural History Museum, excited children and accompanying adults with strong nerves delight in the displays of prehistoric skeletons, pinned beetles and stuffed, sometimes rather motheaten mammals.

Between the two museums sits a monumental tribute to Empress Maria Theresa; her statue is enthroned on a vast monument almost 65 ft (20 metres) high, and surrounded by her generals, government advisers and 16 worthy personalities of her times.

From the resolute Empress it is only a few hundred steps to the most famous building amongst the wealth of those bordering the Ringstrasse: the **Vienna State Opera**. Built after the plans of Siccardsburg and van der Nüll, it opened on 25 May 1869 with Mozart's *Don Giovanni*. The local citizens lampooned its architects mercilessly: "Siccardsburg and van der Nile (*sic*) have no style,"

A fitting hairdo for the Opera Ball.

they chorused. When the rumour was spread abroad that even the Emperor had criticised the edifice, the sensitive van der Nüll was driven to suicide. Deeply shocked by this event, Franz Joseph thenceforth restricted his speeches at dedications and opening ceremonies to an inoffensive "It is very nice, I am delighted."

Few sections of the old opera house survived the devastating bomb attack of March 1945. Only 10 years later, on 10 November 1955, could the re-opening of the new Opera House be celebrated with a performance of *Fidelio*. Since then, the Opera House has played a prominent role in Vienna's cultural scene, providing an arena for society gossip, glittering first nights with the much-loved "House Tenors", and even occasional whispers of scandal.

Every year, punctually on the the last Thursday in February, the Vienna Ball Season closes with its crowning glory, the Opera Ball, held in the building on the Ring. It is a glamorous event, attracting guests from all over the world.

A private box with a bird's-eye-view of the colourful scene costs the equivalent of a medium-sized car. And every year, too, the debutantes prepare for their moment of glory. Accompanied by their partners and under the eagle eyes of the nation, they execute perfect left turns on the mirror-like surface of the dance floor. The whole evening is one of waltzes

Conveniently close to the Opera House are a number of elegant establishments which can claim almost as much kudos. Here, many a political summit has taken place over a discreet dish of Viennese boiled beef and innumerable crowned heads have settled down to sleep in the plush-walled suites. Traditionally, minor disputes have been settled by cake-throwing contests: Sachertorte versus Demeltorte – international experts have so far been unable to reach a decision as to which makes the best missile.

Baroque Jewel: A congenial post-prandial stroll will take you across the spacious **Karlsplatz** – condemned to traffic chaos by the town planners – to the **Church of St Charles**. Regarded as the

Café Landtmann on the Ring, meeting place for celebrities.

finest ecclesiastical Baroque building in the city, it was pledged by Charles VI during an epidemic of plague in 1713, started by Johann Fischer von Erlach and completed by his son, Joseph Emanuel. With its magnificent green cupola, twin triumphal pillars with notable spiral reliefs and exterior belfries, the church is unique in design and overall effect. When it was built, the church stood beside vineyards beyond the meadows bordering the river Wien. Its silhouette is seen to its best advantage from a distance.

The **Music Association Building** was built in 1867 by Theophil Hansen in classical style to serve as the meeting place of the "Company of Music Lovers", which had been founded in 1812. The famous Golden Room with its imposing decorations is regarded by many experts as the concert hall with the best acoustics in the world. An audience of millions experiences annual proof of this fact on 31 December, when the Vienna Philharmonic Orchestra performs its New Year Concert – a pot-pourri of traditional Viennese favourites transmitted by satellite as a musical greeting to the rest of the world.

Lying slightly further afield is the **Schwarzenbergplatz**, dominated by a memorial to Field-Marshal Prince Karl Philipp Schwarzenberg, the commander who led the allied forces against Napoleon in the Battle of the Nations near Leipzig in 1813.

The Castle of the Turkish Victor: Past the fountain and the Liberation Monument to the Red Army of 1945 is the Belvedere. Prince Eugene of Savoy acquired this plot of land for his summer residence in 1693, when he was still a young field-marshal. The ground rises gently before the city gates. Twenty years later, at the height of his fame as a statesman and general, he set about building his palace. His architect Johann Lukas von Hildebrandt designed a building which was one of the most splendid examples of secular Baroque architecture. The name Belvedere – "Beautiful Outlook" – actually really only applies to the **Upper Belvedere**, built in 1721.

Exhibit in the Vienna Sex Museum.

Designed exclusively for parties and receptions, it affords a breathtaking view of the city. You can walk downhill through a park filled with statues, cascades and fountains to the main palace, the **Lower Belvedere**, built between 1714–16. This is where the legendary general and strategist from Savoy spent his days when he wasn't leading his troops, surrounded by his art treasures. Montesquieu, who was a guest of Prince Eugene after staying at the Imperial Court, remarked: "It is a pleasant feeling to be in a land where the subjects live better than their master."

After its owner's death the palace was acquired by the Royal Family; before World War I it served as the residence of Franz Ferdinand, the heir to the throne. It was from here that he and Princess Sophia embarked upon their fateful journey to Sarajevo. Two world wars later, the Austrian State Treaty was signed in the Marble Hall of the Upper Belvedere. Today the Belvedere contains the **Austrian National Gallery**, the **Museum of Baroque Art** and the **Museum of Medieval Art**.

Returning to the Ringstrasse, you pass the Schanig Gardens, the Opera House and the multilingual throng in the Kärntner Strasse. To the left lie the museums, to the right the Hofburg. The vista focuses on the noble proportions of the complex housing the **Parliament Building**, the **City Hall**, the **National Theatre** and the **University**. Here can be seen the finest and most perfect flowering of historicism. The architectural styles of a variety of historical periods are found here, but the ensemble attains an overall harmony.

Friedrich Schmidt chose the neo-Gothic style for his City Hall because he wanted to recall the Gothic era as the Golden Age of the bourgeoisie. Theophil Hansen, a Dane who arrived in Vienna via Athens, chose the Hellenistic style for the Imperial Council building, which since 1918 has housed the State Parliament. His aim was to express the link between the city states of Greece and the constitutional monarchy – even though universal suffrage had not been introduced in Austria-Hungary. And so it has come about that the parliament building of the Republic of Austria resembles a Greek temple, with a balustrade embellished with 60 marble statues representing famous Greek and Roman figures. In front of it is the Fountain of Pallas Athena, where, in summer, exhausted tourists surreptitiously bathe their feet.

The main tower of the imposing **City Hall** is topped by the celebrated "City Hall Manikin". The spacious arcaded courtyard is the setting for evening concerts between spring and summer. In front of the City Hall lies one of the loveliest public gardens in Vienna, adorned with numerous monuments to worthy Austrian citizens – among them Karl Renner, Chancellor and subsequently President of the Republic, past mayors (Seitz and Körner), artists (Waldmüller) and the unforgettable composer duo, Josef Lanner and Johann Strauss. In winter this is also the site of the Viennese Christmas market, where merchants erect their tents and stalls, stocked with candied apples and grapes, hand-painted baubles, gingerbread and mulled wine, beneath a gigantic Christmas tree, the gift of the states to the national capital.

If you hear a Viennese citizen remark, "I'm going to the Burg tonight", he is referring not to the Imperial Palace, but to the Palace (Burg) Theater. The **Burgtheater** is at the centre of Austria's cultural heritage. It stands on the Ringstrasse, directly opposite the City Hall. What is performed here, and how well, is a subject of intense national interest. The "House on The Ring" is justifiably considered the most significant theatrical stage in the German-speaking world. Built between 1874 and 1888 in accordance with plans drawn up by Semper and Hasenauer, it was intended to replace the theatre on the Michaelerplatz, which Joseph II had elevated to the rank of National Theatre. The convex arch of the central tract is particularly impressive. The spreading wings on either side house the staircases leading to the boxes. The magnificent main staircases still have their original painted ceilings, some sections of which

The Karlskirche.

were the work of Gustav and Ernst Klimt.

Next door to the Burgtheater stands the Landtmann, the largest and most beautiful coffee house in Vienna. With its crystal chandeliers and ceiling-high mirrors, intimate niches with velvet-upholstered benches, the latest newspapers from all over the world, it's a magnet for famous actors, politicians from the nearby City Hall and Parliament engaged in discreet discussions and political journalists trying to eavesdrop on what is being said. The food is excellent; the prices are reasonable.

Around the next bend in the Ringstrasse is the **University**, built between 1873 and 1883 by Heinrich Ferstel. The original building in the town centre was founded as early as 1365 by Rudolf IV, "The Benefactor"; thus Vienna University is the oldest German-speaking centre of higher education in Europe. The lovely arcaded inner courtyard, with its fountain and birdsong is freely accessible. Studious undergraduates leaf through piles of books in an atmosphere of medieval learning. Marble busts of important rectors and professors stand round its perimeter.

Another favourite spot of students is the neighbouring park surrounding the **Votive Church**. In true neo-Gothic style its twin spires soars exactly 324 ft (99 metres). They mark a failed attempt on the life of Emperor Franz Joseph in 1853. Under the energetic guidance of Archduke Maximilian, who was later to become Emperor of Mexico, funds were collected and the church planned. Its official dedication took place on 22 April 1879, the Silver Wedding Anniversary of the Emperor and his wife.

Around the Herrengasse: The square in front of the Votive Church and the university is known in short as the **Scots' Gate**, although the old city gate which once stood on this site has long since disappeared. On both sides of the adjoining Schottengasse lie old monasteries: to the left, the **Schottenhof**, built by Josef Kornhäusel in the first half of the 19th century, and on the right the **Melker Hof**, dating from the 15th century. Ancient cellars lie beneath both these

The Loos Bar on Kärntner Strasse.

establishments – nowadays occupied by cheerful restaurants.

The **Herrengasse** leads from the Freyung directly back to the Imperial Palace. Its course follows the route of an ancient road along the Roman Limes. Its proximity to court encouraged many of the city' aristocratic families to settle here in the 16th century – hence the name: Herrengasse. The right-hand side, in particular, is lined with historic palais from the 16th–19th centuries, including **Palais Porcia** at no. 23 and the **Palais Trauttmansdorff** at no. 21 to the **Palais Batthyany** at no. 19. On the other side of the road lie the back facades of the **Palais Harrach** and the **Palais Ferstel**.

On the corner of the Strauchgasse stands the legendary **Café Central** (now restored to its former glory), a meeting place for Viennese intellectuals at the turn of the century. One of the most enthusiastic chess players in the Central was a certain Mr Bronstein, alias Leo Trotsky. During the 1848 revolution, the street in front of the country house at no. 19 was the scene of dramatic occur-

rences. By crossing the **Square of the Minorites**, dominated by the 14th-century **Church of St Maria Schnee**, you will soon reach the hub of Austrian politics: the **Office of the Federal Chancellor**, on the Ballhausplatz.

The city park: A rest may seem called for after such an extensive walking tour. Fortunately, Vienna possesses a number of lovely parks. The most extensive patch of green in the vicinity of the Ringstrasse is the City Park. It was constructed in 1862 along the lines of a sketch by Joseph Selleny, the landscape painter. The ancient trees are reflected in the ponds and miniature rivers. Old and young alike meet here to feed the ducks or simply to enjoy the sunshine on a secluded bench. A string of architecturally interesting pavilions and staircases and a riverbank promenade adorned with statuary flank the River Wein. In the middle of the park stands the **Pump Room**, resplendent in Maria Theresa Yellow. It has been the setting for many glittering balls and concerts over the past century. On some evenings

Inside the Dorotheum, Austria's equivalent of Sotheby's or Christie's.

the wind transports the melodies far over the Ringstrasse and into the city. During the Biedermeier period, mineral water could be taken here; today it is more likely to be ice cream. Standing above the merry confusion is an inimitably elegant figure with his fiddle tucked nonchalantly under his chin: the statue of Johann Strauss, the most memorable memorial in Vienna.

Maria Theresa's yellow palace: A short distance beyond the confines of the Ringstrasse and the inner city lies the **Schönbrunn**. In 1683, after the glorious victory over the Turks, Leopold I commissioned Johann Fischer von Erlach to design an imperial summer residence. The original sketches provided for an extensive complex overlooking the city, occupying the highest eminence. Because of financial restraints, this scheme, which would have outdone the Court of Louis XIV at Versailles in every respect, was never realised, and the building was begun on its present site in 1700 in modified form. Then, in 1743, Maria Theresa instructed her architect, Nikolaus Pacassi, to design a palace for the summer residence. Pacassi achieved an harmonious ensemble which is one of the most perfect examples of Austrian Rococo architecture. On the eminence, the imperial clients settled for a symbolic ornamental building, the Gloriette – which boasts a magnificent view of the city and the Vienna Woods beyond. In many ways Schönbrunn came to be regarded as a symbol for an entire epoch as well as an attitude to life.

The colour of the palace exterior, the so-called "Schönbrunner Yellow", with the contrasting green of the shutters, evokes an image of the monarchy which is just as enduring as the black and yellow of the Habsburg flag. At any rate it is a colour combination which was repeated on numerous public buildings and private villas, whether they were situated in Merano, Trieste, Chernovtsy, Sopron or Olmütz. Also attributed to Schönbrunn – indeed, named after it – is the manner of speaking known as "Schönbrunnese", which combines a

The baroque facade of Schönbrunn Palace.

cultivated nasal accent with the Viennese dialect, liberally sprinkled with French turns of phrase. It can sometimes still be heard today in the cafés on the Graben; it invariably crops up – on the stage or in the stalls – at the Theatre in the Josefstadt.

For all citizens of Vienna the name Schönbrunn evokes childhood memories of their first visit to the **Zoo** in the palace gardens. Founded in 1752, it is the oldest surviving zoological garden in the world.

A Viennese miscellany: There are still countless squares and alleys to explore in the city – churches and museums, parks and quiet corners. Visitors in search of tranquillity are strongly recommended to take the nearest available local into their confidence. Language barriers present no real problem, for the Viennese are adept at springing over such hurdles with the help of eloquent gestures and a few snatches of broken English. If the worst comes to the worst they will even accompany the lost foreigner as far as the next corner, explaining as they do so not only the way to the Burgtheater but also their opinions on life in general.

Any visitors wishing to get to know the city and its inhabitants more closely – or even understand them – must first fight their way through a mountain of clichés assembled over the centuries: Vienna's Golden Heart, Viennese *gemütlichkeit*, Viennese artfulness.

As in the case of all cliché images, there is a minimal element of truth in all of this. One thing is quite clear; here in Vienna, no-one ever lived only for his work. On the contrary, the Viennese have always worked in order to be able to live well. Workaholics are about as easy to find as the proverbial needle in the haystack. Eating and drinking well is regarded as the basis for any sound approach to life. Fast-food establishments earn the bulk of their living from foreign tourists rather than locals. Taking sustenance in Vienna is invariably linked to communication, and the average day of a Vienesse citizen is punctuated by visits to four different places for

Resting the legs in the tadtpark.

refreshment: the **coffee house**, the **beisl**, the **heurige** and the **sausage stand** – listed in the chronological order in which they will be visited during the course of an average day.

For centuries lovers of Vienna's world-famous coffee houses have indulged in the maxim "Not at home, but not in the fresh air". Salon, smoking room, artists' den, favourite meeting place, the Viennese coffee house is, in the words of the poet Alfred Polgar, "the perfect place for people who want to be alone but who need company for solitude." Only the ignorant are satisfied with ordering just "a coffee, please"; the connoisseur makes his choice between a large or small "brown", an *Einspänner* ("one-horse carriage"), a *Schale Gold* ("dish of gold"), a *Verlängerter* ("long coffee") or simply a *Melange* ("Viennese mixture"); the traditional names indicate not only the volume, but also whether milk or whipped cream is desired . The obligatory glass of water is served simultaneously, on a silver tray, and renewed at regular intervals. You can sit in the warm for hours over a single coffee, leafing through newspapers and watching the world go by.

Only on warm summer evenings can inveterate coffee-house devotees be persuaded to give up their favourite seat. Then they make their way to the hard wooden bench of a *heurige*, preferably in **Sievering**, **Nussdorf**, **Kahlenbergdorf** or **Stammersdorf**, to sample the new wine of the year. When a garland of pine twigs hangs from a pole outside the gates of these establishments, it indicates that the barrel has been breached. The etiquette that prevails in a *heurige* is enough to confuse any outsider, especially one in the relaxed haze that ususally ensues after sampling a few measures. The really good *heurige* is not overcrowded with young people, but quiet and comfortable. You sit at a rough wooden table, helping yourself to a slice of bread and dripping with onion rings from the buffet, with a litre of white in a bulbous glass carafe. It may be a Veltliner or a Neuburger, fruity and dry, and pleasantly acid. Customers sit

Mayer's is a typical *Heuriger*.

for hours in easy-going tranquillity; social barriers fade away in the gathering dusk. A quartet of traditional *schrammelmusik* players may even come by and sing their songs of death and the transience of life, completing the mood of quiet reflection.

The ingredients which together transform a tavern into a *beisl* are also as simple as possible: wood panelling and checked tablecloths, and a long counter known as the *schank* in the front room. The menu is usually hand-written and short, but excellent; the lunch menu changes daily. In a true *beisl* you can still enjoy the traditional Viennese sequence of courses, without any ultra-modern trimmings. First there will be a clear soup enriched with strips of pancake, liver or semolina dumplings. The main course will consist of vegetables with beef, goulash or lungs, with fish on Friday – or maybe home-made poppy seed noodles, or sweet plum or apricot dumplings. Usually the landlord's wife, invariably comfortably proportioned, watches diligently over the well-being

arly morning t the aschmarkt, ienna's old roduce arket.

of guests: office workers, pensioners, students and professors.

The final official engagement in the exhausting daily round of a Viennese *savant-vivre* is usually a visit to the sausage stand. Strategically situated, the network of outlets covers the entire inner city area, providing welcome oases of warmth. Elegantly-dressed opera guests – the men in dinner jackets, the the ladies in plunging décolletage – stand side by side with prostitutes, ne'er-do-wells and tramps. They reflect on everything under the sun, from politics to football, over a hot sausage with sweet mustard and chili – though one is rarely enough. Every true Viennese citizen knows of at least one sausage-stand whose whereabouts he is reluctant to disclose to anyone.

The Viennese love to eat and drink, to chat idly or philosophise. Their attitude to physical fitness is less enthusiastic. Visitors can gain certain advantages from the fact that they tend to show little enthusiasm for sporting activities in general. "In public swimming pools

there is usually plenty of space, in the water at least" is the ironic comment in one guide to the city. Anyone who feels the need for a few hours' relaxation should pay a visit to the **Amalienbad** in Favoriten. Here one can splash around in a beautiful Art Nouveau hall; from the high glass roof a milky light falls on to Turkish tiles. The steam bath, decorated with intricate mosaics, is a wonderful place to flush out toxins produced by over-indulgence in the city's restaurants.

Snobs, fresh-air fanatics or even gambling freaks, on the other hand, cannot resist the Prater. Trotting races are held in the **Krieau**, whilst flat races take place in the **Freudenau** race course. The Freudenau, former meeting point for the chic society under the Imperial and Royal monarchy, is still considered one of the most beautiful race courses in the world. From the white-painted covered stands the spectator has an excellent view of the start and the finishing post. At the end of every race coloured betting slips rain like confetti on to the seats. Traces of a long-vanished world still hang in the air. The green park landscape also serves as Vienna's one and only golf course. There is a second, much-loved recreation area surrounding the **Old Danube** and on the **Donauinsel**. Against the backdrop of the UNO City one can surf, row, swim, or even ice-skate in winter.

The largest and most popular "green lung" in the metropolis is, however, undoubtedly the **Prater**. The Habsburgs were not always as popular as people like to maintain in retrospect. Until the 18th century, for example, it was strictly forbidden for their subjects to enter the forests and meadows extending before the gates of the city. These were reserved exclusively for imperial hunts. It was Joseph II, the liberally-minded son of Maria Theresa, who decreed in 1766 that the Prater should be open to everyone. The local citizens streamed in enthusiastically from the very first day, delighted by the rolling meadows and shady nooks.

Roundabouts, swings and skittles

Theater an der Wien.

alleys were constructed, and variety acts and shooting galleries sprang up. In 1855 the celebrated "Calafatti", a 30-ft (9-metre) wooden figure with a long thin Chinese pigtail, was installed as the centre post of a roundabout. The true mascot of the Prater, however, was Punch, affectionately known in Vienna as "Sausage". The Viennese felt themselves to be the kindred spirits of this tragicomic character: one of life's victims, pursued by the crocodile, the little goblin scrapes through from one adventure to the next, cheekily victorious at the last.

The **Giant Wheel** was erected for the World Exhibition of 1897; its diameter, 220 ft (67 metres), makes it the largest panoramic wheel in the world. The Prater was burned down during the last days of World War II, and the wheel and big dipper were reduced to ashes. Reconstruction commenced in 1948, and in 1949 it was a key prop in the film of Graham Greene's *The Third Man*, one of the first British films to use genuine locations instead of studio sets.

The director, Carol Reed, used the wheel to great dramatic effect in the film. The hero, Holly Martins, meets Harry Lime at the wheel to confront him about his racket in diluted pencillin and feelings for lover Anna. As their car ascends to the highest point, the people beneath diminish in size. Harry justifies the racket that produces deformities and death: "Would you really feel any pity if one of those dots stopped moving for ever? If I said you can have £20,000 for every dot that stops, would you really, old man, tell me to keep my money?" The wheel suddenly stops and their car swings to a standstill at the top. It is a moment of high tension, when the issue hangs in the balance. The moment the wheel starts again is when Martins decides to shop Harry to the authorities.

Today the Prater is in danger of turning into just an American-style amusement park. One-armed bandits and peepshows have taken the place of the old-fashioned roundabouts with their brightly-painted wooden horses, and instead of pickled gherkins the visitors

n the **Kaktus** Café.

now eat fast food. Indeed, there are plans to turn the fairground and adjoining areas into an enormous and anonymous adventure theme park.

Anyone wishing to recapture something of the character of the old days should take a trip on the Lilliput train, a miniature narrow-gauge railway leading into the wilder regions of the park. Or else take a stroll along the **Prater Hauptallee**, an elegant boulevard bordered by enormous trees and for thousands of Viennese a popular destination for a Sunday bicycle ride. Many of these cyclists afterwards repair to the Lusthaus, where they replace the burned-up calories with a piece of *gugelhupf* and coffee with milk.

On the south side of the city, on the edge of the tenth postal district, Favoriten, lies the **Bohemian Prater** – a very remarkable area. On clear autumn days there is a magnificent view of Vienna from the gently rolling hills of the Laaerberg. As late as the 19th century, Bohemian brickmakers laboured under inhuman conditions on this pretty spot as they fired bricks for half the Danube monarchy from the dry clay soil. They slept in the open air with nothing but a brick for a pillow. Bohemian workers, maids and cooks were sought-after employees in the factories and aristocratic households of the Imperial and Royal capital. They were the object of sentimental songs and ruthless exploitation.

The Bohemian Prater is one of the last remaining relics of this period; it stands hidden between allotments and birchwoods, wooden shacks, blown crooked by the wind. The air is heavy with the smell of candyfloss and nougat. Beneath a wooden canopy erected in 1840 revolves the oldest carousel in Europe; it was declared an historic monument in 1985.

Come to the cabaret: Those who find such amusements too tame have only to leaf through the announcements section of the daily papers. The **Vienna Cabaret** is in full swing again. It flourishes in a highly specific form within the "Culture and Cabaret" Beisl, an establishment where entertainment and gourmet food are provided with equal style. While risqué cabaret is being performed on the boards, the audience can enjoy a first-rate dinner.

The most famous establishments of this kind are the **Metropol** and the **Kulisse** in Hernals, the **Spektakel** near the Naschmarkt and the **Kabarett Niedermair** in the Josefstadt. In the **Simpl** in the Wollzeile, you'll find good old gentle satire; even politicians dare to cross the threshold here. Vienna's markets, especially the **Naschmarkt** – flanked by Otto Wagner's fine Art Nouveau houses beside the River Wien – offer excellent improvised theatre, without entrance fees of any kind. The stallholders run the show with military precision, dressed in full regalia from headscarf to apron, and singing the praises of their rosy-cheeked "Crown Prince" (they are referring to their ever-popular "Kronprinz" apples).

Preparing for the worst: All good things must come to an end, however – even the Good Life in Vienna. The Viennese therefore prepare themselves for death with magnificent resignation. It is viewed as the final highlight – in some cases the only one in an uneventful life. Saving and planning for a handsome funeral is a priority of later life for the Viennese.

The city's burial grounds, therefore, are not merely places of mourning, as in other cities but a place of repose, and not just for the dead. The **Central Cemetery** is an excellent place for a walk and a chat or for feeding the squirrels and sparrows. It is particularly attractive in autumn, when the narrow gravel paths are showered with leaves and the last rays of sunshine fall on the statues and inscriptions. Greetings and farewells between the strollers are graded with consummate skill. *Grüsse Gott*; *Küsse die Hand*; *Meine Verehrung*; *Ciao*; *Gschamsterdiener* (God be with you; I kiss your hand; My deepest respect; So long; Your humble servant). Visitors who are unable to find their way throught this jungle of nuances should make do with a broad smile and a straight *"Servus"*, meaning Welcome and Good-day as well as Goodbye.

The Giant Wheel at the Prater.

148

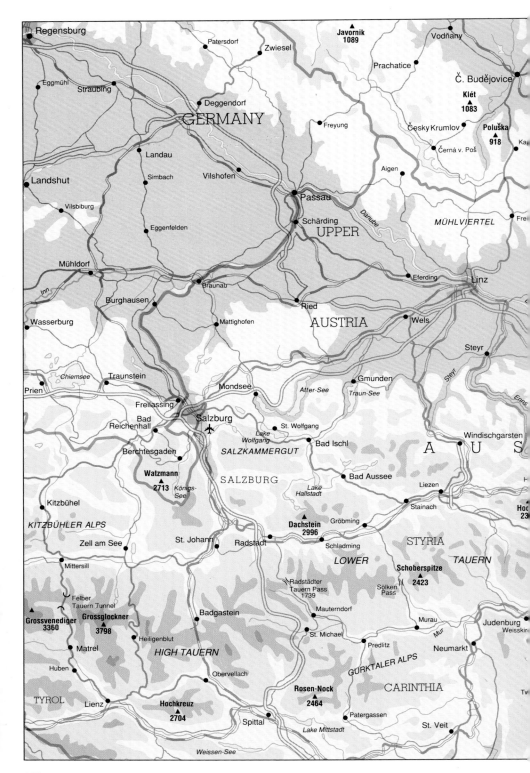

Regensburg
Patersdorf
Zwiesel
Javornik 1089
Vodňany
Prachatice
Č. Budějovice
Eggmühl
Straubing
Klét 1083
Deggendorf
GERMANY
Freyung
Česky Krumlov
Poluška 918
Landau
Černá v. Poš
Ka
Simbach
Vilshofen
Aigen
Landshut
Vilsbiburg
Passau
MÜHLVIERTEL
Fre
Eggenfelden
Schärding
UPPER
Danube
Mühldorf
Eferding
Linz
Inn
Braunau
Burghausen
Ried
Wasserburg
Mattighofen
AUSTRIA
Wels
Steyr
Traunstein
Chiemsee
Mondsee
Gmunden
Steyr
Prien
Atter-See
Traun-See
 Enns
Freilassing
Salzburg
St. Wolfgang
Windischgarsten
Bad Reichenhall
Lake Wolfgang
Bad Ischl
A U S
Berchtesgaden
SALZKAMMERGUT
Watzmann 2713
Königs-See
SALZBURG
Bad Aussee
Liezen
Lake Hallstadt
Ho 23
Kitzbühel
Stainach
KITZBÜHLER ALPS
Dachstein 2996
Gröbming
STYRIA
Zell am See
St. Johann
Radstadt
Schladming
TAUERN
Mittersill
LOWER
Schoberspitze 2423
Felber Tauern Tunnel
Radstädter Tauern Pass 1739
Sölken Pass
Grossvenediger 3360
Grossglockner 3798
Badgastein
Mauterndorf
Murau
Judenburg
Weisskir
Heiligenblut
St. Michael
Mur
Matrel
HIGH TAUERN
Predlitz
Neumarkt
Huben
Obervellach
GURKTALER ALPS
CARINTHIA
TYROL
Lienz
Hochkreuz 2704
Rosen-Nock 2464
Spittal
Patergassen
St. Veit
Tv
Lake Mittstadt
Weissen-See

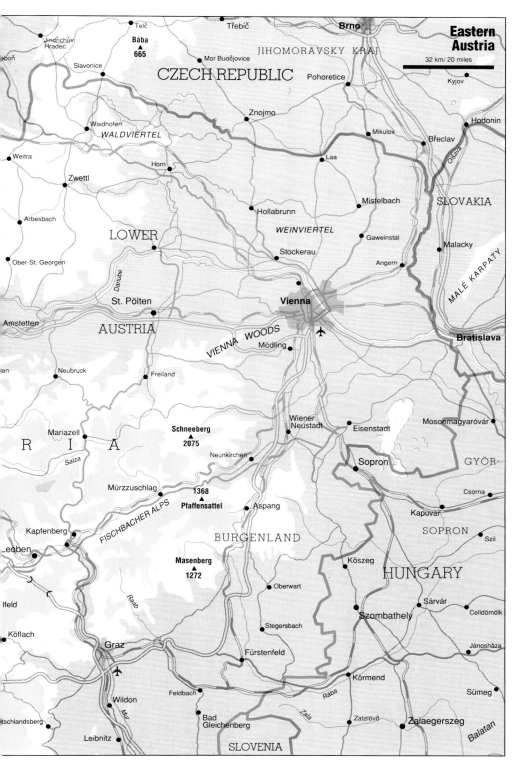

Eastern Austria

32 km/ 20 miles

Jindřichův Hradec
Telč
Třebíč
Brno
JIHOMORAVSKÝ KRAJ
Bába ▲ 665
Mor Budějovice
CZECH REPUBLIC
Pohoretice
Kyjov
Slavonice
Znojmo
Hodonin
Waidhofen
WALDVIERTEL
Mikulov
Břeclav
Weitra
Horn
Laa
Zwettl
Mistelbach
SLOVAKIA
Arbesbach
Hollabrunn
LOWER
WEINVIERTEL
Gaweinstal
Malacky
Ober-St. Georgen
Stockerau
Angern
MALÉ KARPATY
Danube
St. Pölten
Vienna
Amstetten
AUSTRIA
VIENNA WOODS
Bratislava
Mödling
Neubruck
Freiland
Wiener Neustadt
Mariazell
Schneeberg ▲ 2075
Eisenstadt
Mosonmagyaróvár
R I A
Salza
Neunkirchen
Sopron
GYÖR
Mürzzuschlag
1368 ▲ Pfaffensattel
Csorna
Aspang
Kapfenberg
FISCHBACHER ALPS
Kapuvár
eoben
BURGENLAND
SOPRON
Szil
Masenberg ▲ 1272
Köszeg
HUNGARY
Ifeld
Oberwart
Sárvár
Celldömölk
Raab
Köflach
Szombathely
Stegersbach
Graz
Jánosháza
Fürstenfeld
Körmend
Sümeg
Wildon
Feldbach
Rába
schlandsberg
Bad Gleichenberg
Zala
Zatalövö
Zalaegerszeg
Leibnitz
Mur
Balaton
SLOVENIA

151

THE BURGENLAND

It is possible that German-speaking visitors to the Burgenland might be tempted to believe that the region derives its name from the numerous castles (*burgen*) within its boundaries. Their theory, however, is false. Before putting the record straight here, however, it should be pointed out that even the majority of Austrians cannot explain the real origins of the name.

Once upon a time, there was a large area of land called German West Hungary. It consisted of four administrative districts: Pressburg, Wieselburg, Ödenburg and Eisenburg, each with a county town bearing the same name. The inhabitants were predominantly German-speaking. After World War I the victorious and defeated powers sat down together to negotiate the reallocation of national boundaries. Peace conferences were held – among other places, at the Trianon in Paris – which is where Austria's territorial claims with respect to Hungary were debated. In the Venice Protocol the eastern boundary of Austria was finally agreed – with the proviso that the inhabitants of Ödenburg themselves should decide to which country they wished to belong.

Austria's agreement to the plebiscite was, in fact, tantamount to a surrender at the outset, for the area in question was inhabited predominantly by Hungarians. There was no alternative, however, for this was the price Austria had to pay in order to gain the rest of the territory.

After the plebiscite in 1921, most of German West Hungary was ceded to Austria. It was named the "Burgenland" after the suffix "Burg" which formed part of the former names of the constituent districts. Of the former county towns, three now lie in Hungary and one – Pressburg – in Slovakia.

The community of Ödenburg – now called Sopron – forms a "peninsula" which appears to jut into Austria and which, had it not been for the plebiscite, would probably have become the

Preceding pages: the town of Rust above Lake Neusiedler. **Below**, wine-tasting in the cellar.

154

"natural" capital of the Burgenland. And so, since 1925 the province's capital – succeeding Mattersburg – has been Eisenstadt. Five years later the regional government of the Burgenland was also transferred there.

Haydn and the Esterházys: Eisenstadt itself is quite small as provincial capitals go, claiming a population of about 10,000 people. It is unusually attractive. The town is dominated by the names of its most famous inhabitants: Esterházy and Haydn.

It is a town where the visitor is best served by exploring on foot. All notable sights are easily accessible. Instead of merely admiring the facades of the fine old houses, it is worthwhile stealing into the lovely inner courtyards of some of them. Dominating the town is the magnificent **Esterházy Castle**.

Reconstruction of the existing medieval fortress for Paul I, the son of Nikolaus Esterházy von Forchtenstein, began in 1663 under the direction of Carlo Carlone, the Italian master builder. His French successor, Charles Moreau, added pyramid-shaped roofs to the corner towers, previously topped by onion-shaped domes. He also designed a number of porticoed constructions and completely rearranged the garden, even filling in the moat which surrounded the castle. He was also responsible for the **Leopoldine Temple**, built to house a marble statue which had earlier stood in the castle: a likeness, created by Antonio Canova, of Princess Leopoldine of Esterházy, who subsequently married into the Liechtenstein royal family. When the work was complete the complex boasted a total of more than 200 spacious rooms and 6 ballrooms.

Joseph Haydn, the world-famous composer, born in Rohrau (30 miles/50 km from Eisenstadt) lived in what is now **Haydngasse 21** between 1766 and 1778. The building is now a museum commemorating Haydn, Liszt and the dancer Fanny Elssler, who was a daughter of Haydn's valet. For 30 years, from 1761, Haydn was the Esterházys' court composer, initially serving under Gregory Joseph Werner and then, after Werner's death in 1766, taking sole charge of the prince's music. He wrote some of his best symphonies, operas and chamber music at Eisenstadt.

Prince Paul Anton Esterházy finally allowed the maestro to retire in 1792; by this time he had amassed both honour and fortune, and was able to move to Vienna. In 1795, however, Haydn was summoned back to Esterházy Castle once more. He took up his previous position of court music master again before composing two consummate masterpieces: his great oratorios *The Creation* and *The Seasons*. In 1800 Lord Nelson and the Hamiltons visited Haydn at Eisenstadt; Haydn's D minor Mass later became known as the Nelson Mass.

Haydn died in Vienna in 1809. Eleven years later his body was transferred to Eisenstadt by Prince Nikolaus II. During the process it was discovered that the skull was missing. The macabre hunt to find the "real head" continued until 1954. When it was found, it was borne with due ceremony back to Eisenstadt in a formal cortège, before being finally laid to rest with the remains

Right, Karl Eidler, an original from Neusiedl.

of the torso in the **Church of the Calvary** (the Haydn Mausoleum), also built by the Esterházys.

Nowadays the composer is celebrated by a series of top-rate musical performances in the city. An annual highlight, for example, is the **International Haydn Festival**, which is usually held in September in Esterházy Castle.

Lake Neusiedler: The sun shines down in the powerful colours of an oil painting, massive and clear. Above the golden yellow belt of reeds a heron prepares to land, its wings beating ponderously... Images from a strange, exotic world? Not at all. Barely 45 miles (70 km) from Vienna, on the shores of Lake Neusiedler, can be found one of the last major breeding grounds for almost 300 rare species of bird. The lake has no outflow and loses most of its water through evaporation. Only a handful of more celebrated regions in the world, such as the Camargue in France or the Danube Delta, can stand comparison with this region.

The last foothills of the Alps subside to the Pannonian plain, creating a steppe-like climate, the extremes ranging from very hot summers to bitterly cold winters. Low rainfall and a steady breeze are additional characteristics of this specific micro-climate.

Sun-worshippers might like to note that in some of the lakeshore communities the average temperatures in July and August lie only one degree centigrade below those of the French Riviera. This Mediterranean characteristic, combined with the varying saline levels of the ponds and lake (soda, Glauber's salt, Epsom salts and common salt), provide an ideal condition for a unique flora and fauna.

An enthusiastic early-riser armed with binoculars or a camera will find Europe's largest steppe lake (125 sq. miles/ 320 sq. km), containing 15 nature conservation areas, a real paradise. At the "heart of the bird world" in the elbow of the lake, lies **Illmitz** – the largest community of the Burgenland as regards area, and a perfect starting point for excursions into the unspoiled nature area.

Ice-sailing on Lake Neusiedler.

Exploratory trips, guided by knowledgeable ornithologists, can be made by horse-drawn carriage, bicycle or even on foot into the wildlife reserves lying along the shore of the lake. A well-signposted nature trail provides interesting information about the scientific work of the Biological Field Station. **Lange Lacke**, the conservation area near **Apetlon**, is completely closed to the public but you may walk or cycle along a footpath skirting its perimeter.

An exploration of Lake Neusiedler usually begins in the fair weather community of Illmitz (2,000 hours of sunshine per year, they claim). Generally considered the prettiest house in the district is the **Florianihaus**, with its original thatched roof. Almost as old as the narrow rectangular Baroque courtyard is the **Pusztascheune**, a famous heurige and an historic monument often resounding to the impassioned dance rhythms of the Czárdas.

Eight miles to the north lies the tourist centre of **Podersdorf**, the "Pearl of Lake Neusiedler". The largest camp site in

Austria, a yachting marina and a total of 2 miles of reed-free shoreline account for its popularity. An integral part of the charm is one of the last working windmills in the Burgenland whose sails continue to turn in spite of an advanced age of 200 years. Incidentally, it has an exact twin in the wine district of Retz, in Lower Austria.

At the foot of a geological formation known as the **Parndorfer Platte** lies the wine-growing village of **Weiden**, which has retained its true rural character. Everyday in summer the peasant women sit on plain wooden chairs in front of their houses along the main road, offering all sorts of produce for sale: fresh fruit and vegetables from their own gardens, and hand-made items of straw woven during the long evenings of the previous winter.

Before continuing one's journey along the lake shore, a short detour to the village of **Halbturn**, just before the Hungarian border, is recommended. The **Baroque Castle**, situated on the edge of the village, was built at the beginning of

Boathouses in Rust.

the 18th century by Lukas von Hilde-brandt for Count Harrach. Emperor Charles VI joined the hunting parties there; it served his wife Elisabeth as a dower residence. Empress Maria Theresa finally had it rebuilt. It is thanks to her that it contains priceless frescoes by Maulpertsch. Extensive damage was wreaked during World War II, but a major restoration campaign got under way in 1971. Today the building serves as an attractive venue for exhibitions and special shows.

A Burgenland original: Back on the lake shore, our route brings us to **Neusiedl**, a little town of some 4,000 inhabitants. Don't miss the **Karl Eidler Private Museum of Pannonia**. First impressions of Eidler are of his incredibly long snow-white beard and the fiery gleam in his steel-grey eyes. Without outside help, the active sexagenarian has created one of the largest private museums in Austria, all since 1979.

More than 6,000 exhibits document the original character of the Burgenland, and the changes which have taken place over the years. They include such items as an early 19th-century mousetrap, an antediluvian lathe and an ancient fire engine. Karl Eidler has collected everything which others have rejected as "too old-fashioned" and thrown out or confined to the attic.

Karl Eidler has become an institution in the northern Burgenland. Folklore experts, sociologists and teams of radio and television journalists beat a constant path to his door. Since he found a permanent site for his collection, it has been visited by over 80,000 tourists from all over the world. His five outsize guest books have become worthy of study in their own right.

Karl Eidler enjoys sitting with his guests in the remarkable world he has created, chatting with them over a glass of fine local wine. "It's part of the service," he insists – a service which you are unlikely to find in any other museum in Europe. His visitors appreciate it and keep coming back. Genuine originals like "Mr Karl" from Neusiedl-by-the-Lake are becoming all too rare in contemporary Austria, indeed, in the modern world.

At nearby **Jois**, a Roman double grave containing the skeletons of a mother and daughter was discovered in 1982. Another skeleton discovered a few years later, the **Lame woman of Jois**, showed evidence of two badly healed breaks in the lower leg. One of the most gruesome finds, however, is the family grave of a Bronze Age prince. It was flanked on all sides by 12 further graves containing male skeletons. All the skulls had been smashed, indicating unequivocally the barbaric customs of the Scythians, who were wont to dispatch a number of courtiers into the next world to accompany a dead ruler.

In **Breitenbrunn** a friendlier atmosphere greets the visitor. The 105-ft (30-metre) high watchtower known as the **Türkenturm** is a relic of the wars against the Turks. It is the town's principal landmark, and figures prominently on every postcard. From the balcony of the free-standing edifice, nicknamed the "Pranger", there is a fine panoramic view of the lake. Baroque farmhouses

Left, a Burgenland character from Mörbisch. **Right**, a face weathered by the wind and the sun.

and dark, picturesque alleys complete the picture of the pretty village set in the water meadows.

As in all the other lakeside villages of any size, the sports-oriented holiday-maker will find here a yachting marina and a surfing school. One can reach the neighbouring village of **Purbach** by sailing dinghy or even surfboard. It's the site of a 807,400 sq. ft (75,000 sq. metre) camp site as well as a sailing school and a wide range of leisure activities. This community also suffered badly during the Turkish Wars. In 1683 it was virtually razed to the ground. The marks of charring dating from this event explain the origin of the Hungarian name of "Feketevaras", which means "Black Town". Rare relics dating from the Turkish Era and still standing today are parts of the city wall and gates. According to local legend, the stone figure peeping out of the chimney of the Türkenkeller represents a single remaining Turk.

A short distance from the lake lies the wine-growing village of **Donnerskirchen**. Those lucky enough to visit the area between mid-April and the beginning of May will be able to witness a splendid natural spectacle – the cherry blossom. The thousands of cherry trees laden with white blossom on the slopes of the Leitha Mountains surrounding Donnerskirchen are truly spectacular. The sight puts local inhabitants in festive mood, too. The entire village takes to the streets for a high-spirited celebration of the arrival of spring. Donner–skirchen is also famous for its highly successful village restoration project, and well-cared-for appearance.

Since the parish church here is dedicated to St Martin, it seems appropriate to mention a few facts about the patron saint of the Burgenland and an associated custom which is still observed. The local version of the legend has it that St Martin, pursued by a number of persecutors, sought refuge here but was betrayed by the loud gabbling of some geese. However it came about, 11 November is the day of the traditional St Martin's Goose dinner – not only in the Burgenland, but also in Lower Austria and Vienna. And since the Burgenland is one of Austria's foremost wine-growing areas, 11 November is also the day on which the new wine, *heurige*, is broached – to wash down the excellent roast goose dinner.

The "Wine University": There is one more point of interest in Donnerskirchen: the **Wine Forum** in the Leisserhof – a documentation and communication centre devoted to the viticulture of the Burgenland. In the so-called **Wine Vault** there's an exhibition assembled by 42 vineyards offering 126 wines; in the **Wine Exchange** are stored 125,000 bottles of rare vintages. Guests may rent a private wine safe here. And whoever has not lost his eye for a ball in spite of a glass or two can try his handicap on a magnificent 18-hole golf course.

The neighbouring village of **Oggau** has two things in common with Donnerskirchen. It, too, was settled several thousands of years ago, and derives its main livelihood from wine-growing. Judging by the proportions of the parish church, started in 1727 according to the plans of the celebrated Master Pilgram,

The grapes are collected in tubs.

though they were never carried out in their entirety.

The Free Town of **Rust**, next along the route, is world famous as the summer retreat for families of storks. In conjunction with the World Wide Fund for Nature a Stork Post Office (postal code A-7073) has been set up here. It is open all the year round, and the special postmark depicting a stork is much sought-after among philatelists and animal lovers. You can also buy special "stork" envelopes or postcards in the town's shops. With the proceeds, the local inhabitants and the WWF aim to acquire new food sources for the long-legged visitors, and to create additional breeding places on the roofs of the houses in the Old Town, their traditional nesting sites. These measures will, it is hoped, secure stocks of the much-loved bird at their present levels – or possibly even manage to increase them.

Rust is at least as famous for its wine as for its storks. Pleasantly full-bodied, it is well-rounded and easily digestible. No other community has such a large number of special quality wines; every cork bearing the brandmarked "R" guarantees the Rust origins of the wine. Wine buffs can become connoisseurs at the town's **Burgenland Wine Academy**. One should also find time to visit what is – artistically and culturally speaking – the most significant building in the Free Town: the **Fishermen's Church**. Romanesque in origin, it later acquired a Gothic extension. With a bit of luck you may even be able to enjoy a romantic concert by candlelight.

Also worthwhile is an excursion to the **Roman Quarries** in **St Margarethen**, 2 miles (4 km) away. During the summer months artists from all over the world converge here to work on monumental sculptures.

As we return to the lake again, our circumnavigation brings us to **Mörbisch** – almost back to our starting point, in fact. The Hungarian border, only a few miles away now, makes its proximity felt in the appearance of the old Burgenland houses, ablaze with a riot of flowers and displaying the characteris-

e autumn
ape
arvest.

tic dried sheaves of maize. Window-boxes bright with geraniums and large tubs overflowing with blossoming oleander conjure up a Mediterranean atmosphere, redolent of warm sunshine in long alleys and courtyards bordered by gleaming whitewashed houses.

Operetta on the lake: Mörbisch has been famous since 1957 as the site of the **Festival**, which takes place on a pontoon built out over the lake. The themes chosen are those from light music; every year a different operetta is performed during July and August. In order that nothing should spoil the evening's entertainment, here is a tip: it is advisable to smear oneself liberally with insect repellant, for the pesky mosquito also enjoys warm evenings on the water...

All the villages lying directly on the lakeshore share a typical infrastructure, including a bathing area, boat rental, sailing and surfing facilities, a camp site, bicycle rental, etc. There is a simple explanation for the predominance of sailing and surfing; the lake is very shallow – mostly only 3–7 ft (1–2 metres) deep – and on four out of five days you can be sure of finding a Force 6 wind whiping across its surface.

A congenial "frontier experience" is the **Raab-Ödenburg-Eberfurt Railway**, which has been in operation for over a century. It still puffs cheerfully along on its Austro-Hungarian rails, as if nothing had changed since its heyday; its pace is so sedate that one can wave to the farmers working in the adjoining fields. And the latter, too, mostly find time to wave back at the passengers aboard the handsome steam trains.

Forchtenstein Castle is one of the most interesting in Austria. Certainly no other fortress makes such a strong, multi-faceted impression. Nothing remains of the oldest section, dating from the 14th century, apart from the keep with its roof which recalls the keel of a ship. After the rest of the complex was completely destroyed, the construction of the New Castle was begun by Count Nikolaus Esterházy in 1635. On his instructions were built the entrance tract in the inner courtyard, the vaulted

Operetta is performed on the Mörbisch lakeside stage.

162

passage linking it to the higher section of the ramparts, the true castle entrance, the arsenal and the chapel. In the middle of the 17th century his successor, Count Paul, continued the extensions and gave the castle its present form. From this period date many door frames and doors with exquisite hand-wrought locks, some parts of the original window glazing, tiled floors, fireplaces and the 465-ft (142-metre) deep "Turk's Well". Apart from its Baroque rim, the well boasts a fine echo. Forchtenstein itself also has another claim to fame: the **Gourmet Restaurant Reisner**, renowned for its regional specialities.

Further south (half-way to Lockenhaus), lies **Stoob**. The pretty roadside village is a mecca for potters; apart from a traditional potters' guild – the original round-bellied clay pots with thin necks known as "Pluzer" are manufactured here – Stoob is the home of the only specialist ceramics academy in Austria.

The town of **Lockenhaus on the Geschriebenstein**, lying in the Günstal, is first mentioned as a settlement at the

Symbol of the Burgenland.

end of the 9th century. The imposing Romanesque castle – today the scene of chamber music festivals and other cultural events – once belonged to the Order of Templars, officially disbanded in 1311. During the 17th and 18th centuries the present castle housed an Augustinian monastery together with a philosophical and theological college. The Italian master builder Orsolini constructed a Baroque parish church here in 1669. Today it is a place of pilgrimage.

Bernstein is anything but stony broke, for it is the only known source of the gleaming green semi-precious serpentine stone in the world. Interested parties can learn more about Bernstein itself, the history of the village and its mining development from the laboriously executed details with which Otto Potsch, the painter and sculptor, adorned the **Rock Museum**. (The Chinese astronomical sphere on display is also his work.) The castle, which dates from the 13th century, was of great strategic importance in the border skirmishes between Austria and Hungary – in contrast to **Schlaining Castle**, originally in the possession of the Babenbergs, and predominantly involved in local ruses and treachery.

Bad Tatzmannsdorf offers a comprehensive range of treatments for patients suffering from rheumatism or coronary, circulatory, spinal, metabolic or vascular disorders. As long ago as the 17th century the medicinal baths in this spa town – previously a Magyar and before that a Croatian settlement – were popular with the aristocracy.

The most important centre in the southern Burgenland in **Oberwart**. Half of the population of this town at the crossroads where the north-south and east-west axes meet is Hungarian. **Güssing** is famous for its pretty situation and mineral water; the town itself is dominated by a magnificent castle perched high on a hillside. Dating from the 12th century, it contains a museum, an ancestral portrait gallery containing some pictures attributed to Brueghel, and an armoury. The chapel houses the oldest organ in the Burgenland.

LOWER AUSTRIA

The names of many regions conjure up particular sets of expectations. This is, however, rather different in the case of Lower Austria, especially as parts of the province are anything but low. Sometimes, in fact, it is the very opposite; take the majestic Schneeberg, for instance, or the comfortably rounded Ötscher Mountain.

What image, then, should be evoked by the name of this region? Here are a few landmarks to enable you to get your bearings: Lower Austria is Schubert and Blondel the minstrel, moated castles and thermal springs, bustards and slow-worms, streams and rivers, a place for hiding in haystacks and playing tag in the meadows. You will find something of everything here – forests and vineyards, plains and mountains. Provided you don't expect to find it all at the same time, you will be pleasantly surprised.

The Vienna Woods: As you leave Vienna in a north-westerly direction following the National Road No.14, you will see Vienna's twin local mountains: the **Kahlenberg** and the **Leopoldsberg**. The road leads on past them to **Klosterneuburg**, which consists of three distinct parts: **Kierling**, **Weidling** and **Gugging**. The principal sight, visible from far away, is the imposing Klosterneuburg **Augustinian Monastery Church**, topped by a dome in the form of the Imperial Crown. The monastery was founded in 1108 by Margrave Leopold III of Babenberg, also known as Leopold the Pious. The **Collegiate Church** is in Romanesque style and dates from the early 12th century, with a number of later additions. The present interior arrangement, with its high altar and organ, is of 17th-century origin.

The picturesque road between Klosterneuburg and Hüttendorf is known as the **Vienna High Road**; it leads back along the upper slopes of the Kahlenberg and the Leopoldsberg, which we have already seen from below. From the 1,585-ft (485-metre) summit of the former there is a magnificent view of the city of Vienna lying at the foot of the mountain, with the Marchfeld beyond. Visitors never fail to enjoy afternoon coffee on the sunny panoramic terrace of the restaurant, followed by a stroll or drive to the neighbouring Leopoldsberg, with its church dedicated to the patron saint of Lower Austria.

The way leads over the **Sophienalpe**, with its pretty rustic café and picnic meadows (and all only a few minutes' drive from Vienna), through fairy-tale woods to **Mauerbach**, which boasts the remains of a Carthusian monastery founded in 1313. The combination of the Baroque church, added some three centuries later, and the monks' cells built on to the outside presents an interesting architectural ensemble.

Purkersdorf, which is also only a few miles from Vienna, was the site of the first staging post on the old Imperial Road to Linz. The post house, built in 1796 in an early classicistic style, is decorated between the windows with reliefs depicting in symbolic manner the secrecy of the postal service. Recently created near this town, which still retains much of its turn-of-the-century charm, is the **Sandstein-Wienerwald Nature Park**, which includes wildlife enclosures.

The western boundary of the Vienna Woods is marked almost straight away by a reservoir, the **Wienerwaldsee**. It is surrounded by a district which is elegantly discreet as regards both landscape and inhabitants. **Tullnerbach**, **Pressbaum** and **Rekawinkel** are typical of the recreation areas in the vicinity of the capital; they all lie in the direction of **Neulengbach**, the "Pearl of the Vienna Woods". It lies on the western fringe, nestled between the **Buchberg** and the **Kohlreith**, two mountains which are popular excursion destinations. The town centre was built in about 1200 around the castle of the Lords of Lengbach. Its present-day countenance is characterised by well-maintained Renaissance buildings. It is well worth walking from **Altlengbach**, which lies to the south and which is dominated by a 16th-century late Gothic church, as far as the **Schöpfl**. Its 2,930-ft (895-metre)

Preceding pages: sphinx in front of Greillenstein Castle. **Left**, a view from the Sonntagsberg.

summit makes it the highest eminence in the area, hence affording a spectacular panoramic view across the entire Vienna Woods.

Via **Klausenleopoldsdorf**, where the main defile of the Schwechat Brook with its twin wooden attendants' huts provides an attractive scene, one eventually reaches **Alland** and **Mayerling**. Alland was once the home of the Babenbergs and the birthplace of Frederick of Austria. Today its main attraction, apart from a wide range of sporting facilities, is its stalactite cave. Mayerling became a household word when it rocketed to fame as the setting for the tragic suicide of Crown Prince Rudolf, which occurred in the hunting lodge. On the spot where the prince shot first his mistress, Baroness Mary Vetsera, and then himself, there now stands the convent of atonement of the Carmelite nuns, founded by the Emperor Franz Josef.

A stroll through history and nature: From this point it is possible to drive directly along the romantic and much-sung **Helenental** to the neighbouring town of Baden bei Wien; before doing so, however, it would be a pity not to make the acquaintance of some of the other villages in the Vienna Woods which lie on an alternative route – **Heiligenkreuz**, for example. The Cistercian abbey of the same name is an architectural gem. The basilica, begun in 1135, is the oldest example of ribbed vaulting in Austria; the Gothic hall chancel served as a model for many South German hall churches. Beyond the Romanesque cloisters on the south side is the well house, its lead well glinting mysteriously. The chapter house, which has the tombs of 13 rulers – including the last of the Babenbergs – is moving in its simple perfection.

According to local legend it was in the shade of the spreading linden tree just in front of Höldrichs Mill in the **Hinterbrühl** that Franz Schubert composed his much-loved song *Am Brunnen vor dem Tore* (By the well before the gate). Nearby **Mödling**, which has been a settlement for almost 8,000 years, has

The rustic Häuserl am Stoan, a popular destination for the Viennese.

attracted a wide range of interesting personalities over its long history. From Adolf Loos to Oskar Kokoschka, from Anton Wildgans to Johannes Mario Simmel, from Johann Strauss to Arnold Schönberg – countless numbers of artists have painted, written and composed here. Ludwig van Beethoven commented on one occasion to August von Kloeber, the painter: "You must really take a proper look at Mödling, for it is a beautiful place."

Visits to the Romanesque charnel house of St Otmar, the magnificent **Plague Column** and the **Town Hall** on the Schrannenplatz, a stroll to the **Black Tower**, to the mysterious **Lake Grotto** or through the pedestrian area of the **Old Town**, make a visit to Mödling well worthwhile. A tip for avid mountaineers: the almost vertical rock faces – for example, on the way to Hinterbrühl – serve as popular practice crags for climbing schools.

The Lower Austrians are known for their friendliness.

Also recommended is a detour in an easterly direction, to **Laxenburg**, which lies 4 miles (6 km) away. The castle, surrounded by a beautiful park, is resplendent in gleaming "Schönbrunn Yellow". The garden layout is not regular as, for example, that of Versailles; instead, it has been designed to look as natural as possible. A large artificial lake stretching from the central area towards the east invites visitors to take a boat trip or to visit the **Franzensburg** on an islet. Reached by ferry or via the Roman bridge, the castle houses a museum and a café. At the end of a long, straight avenue of poplars, beside the Forester's canal, lies a recreation centre with a restaurant, swimming pool, minigolf course and a camp site.

Following the path to Mödling, one passes through **Gumpoldskirchen**, the most popular wine-growing village to the south of Vienna. The hilly stretch through the vineyards conveys something of the the district's convivial atmosphere and serves as an ideal preparation for the pleasures of the worldfamous Gumpoldskirchner vintages. Wine amateurs may also enjoy visiting villages nearby, such as **Pfaffstätten**.

With its thermal baths, its theatre or casino the spa town of **Baden** has a nostalgic air of a faded Empire. A slightly decadent, turn-of-the-century charm continues to pervade the architecture and the spa park; this impression is underlined by events such as the Operetta Summer.

Sooss, on the other hand, is another classic wine-growing village; it lies on the foothills of the Wienerwald.

After a quick splash in the thermal waters of **Bad Vöslau** – where the spa complex is worth visiting for its architecture alone – the visitor should end this tour of the Vienna Woods in **Berndorf**. The undisputed cultural focal point, not only of the town, but of the entire Triesting valley, is the magnificent **Municipal Theatre**, built in the spirit of Vienna's Ringstrasse architecture and with an interior which resembles the Rococo stage at the court of a minor prince.

But the neo-Baroque Church of St Margaret, whose gleaming green cupola tops the roofs of the town, is also worth attention. The church building is flanked by two apparently unremarkable school buildings constructed in 1808, but their interiors are anything but everyday: the 12 classrooms have been decorated in 12 important architectural styles, ranging from Mauresque to Gothic and from Egyptian to Doric.

An abundance of castles: Any journey through the March-Donauland is an excursion back through history, as the visitor leaps from castle to castle and wends through unspoilt countryside. Most of the little villages in the northern part of the Marchfeld have retained their charming rural character. A favourite first port of call on this excursion is **Grossenzersdorf**, which can be reached via the South-East Tangential Road (Urban Motorway A23). First mentioned in 1158, it is a charming little town which has managed to retain a large proportion of its medieval fortifying wall. The **Town Hall**, a former monastery church and numerous meticulously restored old houses testify to Grossenzersdorf's rich past.

Lower Austria's rivers are teeming with fish.

Gourmets are recommended to visit the **Taverne am Sachsengang**. A few miles further on, in the dark alluvial woodland surrounding Oberhausen, lies the castle of same name, **Schloss Sachsengang**. Originally built in 1120, the castle was reconstructed several times during its long history. Its present owners are the Thavonat family. Worth visiting is the ceramics workshop within the castle itself.

Orth an der Donau is the site of a moated castle straight out of a fairy tale. The forbidding complex was built in the 12th century, but acquired its present-day appearance about 1550. The New Castle, which lies on the western flank, was added in 1784. Orth Castle became the property of the Habsburg family in 1824, subsequently becoming one of the favourite residences of Crown Prince Rudolf (*see pages 56–58*). Today it houses three museums, of which the most interesting and unusual are the **Fishing Museum** and the remarkable **Museum of Apiculture**. To fortify your energy, repair to the "**Uferhaus**", where the speciality – Serbian-style carp – has made the restaurant a great favourite amongst Viennese fish-fanciers.

The hunting lodge **Eckartsau**, reached via **Wagram an der Donau**, was destroyed in 1945 but has since become a fine example of superb restoration. The original 12th-century castle was completely rebuilt in the 18th century; the creation of what was, in effect, a new building, testifies to the consummate skills of such great masters as Fischer von Erlach, Johann Lukas von Hildebrandt, Lorenzo Mattielli and Daniel Gran.

The next stage of our tour should encompass the Danube meadows near **Stopfenreuth**, which have attracted much public attention as the result of citizens' initiatives and WWF campaigns. An observant and careful walker will find a unique biotope which is home to kingfishers, beavers and cormorants as well as herons and freshwater turtles. It is one of the last primeval forests to be found in Europe.

Niederweiden Castle is a magnifi-

cent building which reveals the unmistakable guiding hand of Fischer von Erlach despite its subsequent reconstruction in accordance with the instructions of Empress Maria Theresa. The master builder designed the hunting lodge at the end of the 17th century for Count Ernst Rüdiger Starhemberg, as a replacement for Grafenweiden Castle, which had been destroyed by the Turks.

Two miles (3 km) further on lies **Schlosshof**, the real centre of royal and aristocratic life in the Marchfeld. Prince Eugene once acquired a 17th-century fortress here. In 1729 Johann Lukas von Hildebrandt completed the extensive alterations. With the addition of two wings and the resulting courtyard, the beautiful fountain and the sweeping staircases, the building was intended to be the most lavish and magnificent summer residence far and wide. It was also intended that it should be capable of being defended in an emergency.

After the castle passed into the possession of Maria Theresa in 1755 she immediately embarked upon a pro-gramme of alterations and extensions. The outcome was that the combination of splendour within and a lovely park without rapidly made Schlosshof a favourite residence of the Imperial court. Following extensive damage over the years, a laborious total restoration programme was begun in the 1980s. Today the castle provides an elegant scenario for special exhibitions.

Retracing the route back to the National Road No. 49, you pass Niederweiden and cross the Danube before reaching the well-fortified citadel of **Hainburg**. The erstwhile fortress of the Babenberg empire lies to the left. Situated on the Braunsberg, it is a pretty little town which has retained much of its original character – a fact best appreciated by the present-day visitor arriving from the west, whose approach will be through the attractive **Wienertor**, the 13th-century town gate. There are two other town gates: the Ungartor and the Fischertor.

Apart from sections dating from the 11th century, the forbidding fortress on

The rolling hills of the southern Vienna Woods.

the **Schlossberg** still boasts a massive round-arch gateway and a keep with ribbed vaulting constructed in 1120, and an entrance hall built in 1514. The complex has been uninhabited since the 17th century, but has nevertheless been constantly modernised and restored. The Wienertor, by the way, contains a museum in which documents concerning the Carpathian German Husbandry are displayed. Visitors yearning for wider horizons should continue their journey along the panoramic road on the **Braunsberg**. The view is breathtaking, especially at sunset.

If you now travel in the direction of Vienna you will come to **Bad Deutsch Altenburg**. Even healthy visitors will appreciate a short break in the thermal baths of this spa town. The **Church of St Stephen** (or St Mary), lying on an eminence, is considered to date from about 1000 AD. It was extended during the 13th and 14th centuries.

A few miles further on lies **Petronell-Carnuntum**, the site of the most extensive Roman excavations in Central Europe. During its heyday the town of Carnuntum had a population of 70,000; including the military camp, it covered an area of 4 sq. miles (10 sq. km). The open-air museum includes exhibits showing the floor plans of an entire section of the town, indicating the position of houses, baths, workshops etc. The highlights include the Main Baths, the Palace ruins, an amphitheatre and the Heidentor, once more than 65 ft (20 metres) high and now reduced to 40 ft (12 metres) but still imposing.

Rohrau lies in a southerly direction. It was here that Joseph Haydn was born on 31 May 1732; today his birthplace houses the **Haydn Museum. Harrach Castle** dates from the 16th century but has been rebuilt several times. It now contains the largest private gallery in Austria; its collection represents a complete cross-section through the classical Dutch, Flemish, Italian, Spanish and French schools of painting.

Bruck an der Leitha is the last station on our journey through the Marchfeld/Donauland. On its outskirts lies **Prugg Castle**, a 13th-century moated castle which has been reconstructed several times. Once again it was Johann Lukas von Hildebrandt who supervised the conversion to the Baroque style, including on this occasion a massive Gothic keep known as the Heidenturm, the **Pagans' Tower**. Bruck was an important town in the Middle Ages; even today, as a crossroads for traffic from all the points of the compass, it is a centre of some significance.

Wine country: The village of **Deutsch-Wagram**, 5 miles (20 km) from Vienna in a north-easterly direction, actually lies on the edge of the Marchfeld. It is, however, on the way to the wine country. The little community is first mentioned in records as long ago as 1250, and the church belfry is actually 1,000 years old. The village owes its fame, however, to no less a personage than Napoleon Bonaparte. He established his base camp here in 1809 in the Battle of Deutsch-Wagram. The memorial stone on the relevant spot, as well as numerous mementoes to be seen in the local museum, provide information concern-

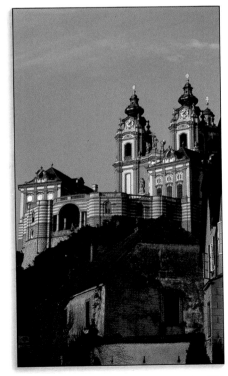

ing this period. Here, too, is the ever-popular **Marchfelderhof**, which provides culinary delights in an opulently rustic environment.

Wolkersdorf is often mentioned as the true gateway to the Wine Country. Here, too, the historic Battle of Deutsch-Wagram left traces: first of all, the Emperor Franz I set up his base camp in the priest's backyard; shortly afterwards, following the victory of his army, Napoleon took up residence in the castle. Nowadays the main building, originally built in 1050 as a moated castle and subsequently converted into a hunting lodge in 1720 by Emperor Charles VI, has become the landmark of this attractive little town.

Gross-Schweinbarth lies hidden in a valley on the edge of the Wine Country. Sloping vineyards and the 2,470-acre (1,000-hectare) Hochleithenwald forest invite the visitor to an extended walk in the fresh air, followed perhaps by a visit to the Museum of Local Culture or the International Shepherds' Museum.

The area even contains an entire museum village in **Niedersulz**. The open-air collection includes almost 30 complete original buildings in representative vernacular style: two chapels, various workshops, a wine-pressing shed, a water mill and the obligatory tavern complete with bowling alley presenting a picture of a Wine Country village before industrialisation.

The market town of **Wilfersdorf**, lying in the midst of a fertile agricultural and wine-growing region, presents a completely different character. As early as the 14th century it was the seat of the local assizes; its history as a thriving trading and business centre is still apparent today. The most eye-catching element is undoubtedly the bright yellow **Liechtenstein Castle**.

The wine market at **Poysdorf**, with its picturesque alleys and fine vintages, is a highlight for winebibbers. Twenty winegrowers from the municipality have joined together to form the Poysdorf Wine-Growers' Syndicate. This permits an expert selection from a total of approximately 100 different wines,

A butcher's opens its doors in Weitra in the Waldviertel.

174

predominantly green Veltliner, Welsch-riesling, Rhine Riesling and white Burgundy, but also several red wines of excellent quality.

Mistelbach is an ideal place in which to relax; it possesses a large sports centre offering a wide range of facilities, open-air swimming pool, a lawn and a minigolf course. A Gothic hall church, a 12th-century charnel house, the College (with frescoes by Maulbertsch) and a small Baroque castle provide cultural interest.

Asparn an der Zaya lies in the foothills of the **Leiser Mountains**. The heart of the old wine-growing and market town is undoubtedly the **Fortress** complex, complete with moat, church, battlement walk and monastery. Housed in sections of the castle, which is one of the most attractive historic monuments in the country, is the Wine Country Museum and a Museum of Prehistory.

Near to **Michelstetten** is the site of a very special museum: the Lower Austria School Museum. It contains one of the most important collections in the country, providing a complete record of the Austrian school system. Michelstetten lies in the middle of the **Leiser Mountains Nature Park**; here one can study, on foot or by bicycle, the habitats of plants and animals which have unfortunately long since vanished from other parts of the country.

Less than 6 miles (10 km) away lies **Fallbach**, together with **Loosdorf**, its castle, and the other communities listed in the district's historic land records. The cultural centre in **Winkelau**, the village square in **Hagenberg** and the romantic pilgrimage town of **Friebitz** give the impression that the area enjoys a broad range of activities; biotope information, creative courses and a music laboratory are just a few examples of the hobbies on offer.

As a settlement with a 5,000-year history, **Laa an der Thaya** was fortified as a bulwark against Bohemia by the Babenbergs in approximately 1200. Sections of the town walls and the town's general appearance both date from this time. So, too, does **Laa Castle** – now

Support and sustenance for walkers.

the home of a **Beer Museum**; also worth more than a cursory glance are the Gothic pillory, the Plague Column on the main square, and the local churches.

Alberndorf im Pulkautal is a European community with long-standing traditions. It received an award from the Council of Europe for the exceptionally hospitable attitude with which it greets its guests, and merits a short visit. The clay builders and master potters always have time for a chat; the unobtrusively nostalgic Kellergasse and the lively bustle of the produce market leave the visitor with pleasant memories.

The ground beneath **Retz** has an important inner life of its own: an extensive cellar complex (the largest historic wine cellar in Austria) criss-crosses beneath the town. The subterranean network actually covers a larger area than the streets and alleys above ground; the tunnels extend two and three storeys deep into the underlying sand. The daily conducted tours only encompass 5 percent of the system of vaults, but still include 2,955 ft (900 metres) of tunnel. The town also possesses a large number of Baroque and Renaissance buildings; its landmark is a windmill which is still in working order.

The Waldviertel: The "Woodland Country" possesses a singular, austere charm of its own. One becomes aware of its northerly latitude (albeit only as far as Austria is concerned) particularly at night, when jackets are automatically buttoned a little higher on account of the persistent cool breeze. One will seldom experience here the riotous outdoor activity which characterises the balmy summer nights of Carinthia, for example; in any case, here the visitor comes in search of peace and quiet.

Hardegg, the smallest town in Austria, is situated right on the Czech border, surrounded by the coniferous forests of the **Thaya Valley**. Perched on a high mountain ridge overlooking the town is a forbidding **Knight's Castle** dating from the 12th century. The Thaya Bridge will make the heart of every competitive angler beat faster, for the waters below are teeming with rainbow and river trout.

A few miles to the west lies the magnificent Baroque **Riegersburg Castle**, which one should not fail to visit on the way to **Geras**. The latter, a peaceful holiday village, owes the abbot of the local monastery a debt of gratitude for reviving the local tourist industry. The courses he runs in painting rustic furniture and glass-blowing techniques have proved very attractive to people who like to combine relaxation with creative activity. **Drosendorf** is popular amongst holidaymakers wishing to take riding lessons; there is a riding arena and covered riding school, where riding teachers and well-schooled mounts make even beginners feel confident.

Raabs an der Thaya has been nicknamed "The Pearl of the Thaya Valley". If you look down on the attractive little town from above, you will certainly agree that the name is justified. The best bird's-eye perspective can be gained from the picturesque 11th-century **Castle** which is perched on a steep cliff high above the confluence of the German and Moravian Thaya rivers.

Krems' romantic old town.

The round trip through the Waldviertel leads via **Gross-Siegharts** and **Diet–manns** to **Waidhofen an der Thaya**, a town with a long history; it developed from a fortified settlement in the 12th century. Today, the attractions include the Town Hall (a 15th-century complex), the assizes and the parish church (1716–23); in addition, one can visit the **Weaving Museum** or the Silo Museum. For the sports-oriented, there are plenty of opportunities for archery, flying model aircraft or angling.

The situation of the market town of **Thaya im Waldviertel** was determined by its sunny climate and healthy, bracing air. Two Renaissance fountains adorn the market place, surrounded by beautifully renovated merchants' houses and a Romanesque parish church. In a wood just beyond the town boundary you will find the excavations of the medieval village of **Hard**. A final visit to nearby **Peigarten Castle** would bring the cultural aspect of the tour to a fitting conclusion.

Animal lovers will be in their element in the **Thaya Valley Nature Park**; this remaining tract of primeval forest, with easily accessible footpaths and facilities, is one of the most attractive stretches of countryside in the land. The **Dobersberg** mountain, lying on the outskirts and dominated by a 16th-century castle, offers a relaxing environment characterised by coniferous forests and little ponds. Our route takes us through **Kautzen** and **Eggern**, two sleepily peaceful villages, to **Litschau**, the most northerly town in Austria. It is a tourist-oriented place, but an ideal destination for a family holiday thanks to its compact 18-hole golf course, tennis, riding and angling facilities, and the southern shore of the **Herrensee**, ablaze with dandelion-dotted meadows.

Many of the small villages in the area, including **Alt-** and **Neu-Nagelberg**, **Angelbach** and **Hirschenwies**, are the home of the famous Waldviertel glass cutters. They are the best places to buy good quality glassware.

A massive moated castle lends a fairy tale aura to the general appearance of

Country folk from the Waldviertel.

the romantic town of **Heidenreichstein**, first mentioned in records in 1205. The fortress is still approached via medieval drawbridges.

Of slightly later date is the castle in **Gmünd**, the main town in the northwest district of the province. With two border crossing points into the Czech republic and its position as administrative and educational centre, Gmünd is an important regional centre. It is also the terminus of the **Waldviertel Narrow Gauge Steam Railway**, which runs from here to **Gross Gerungs**. The principal attraction, however, is the almost mystic charm of the unique **Blockheide Eibenstein Nature Park**. A tip for food-lovers: the gourmet restaurant Hackl, provides fine examples of the region's cuisine.

Passing through **Weitra**, the oldest brewing town with the smallest family brewery, we reach the curative **Mudbaths of Harbach**. The recently completed modern complex lives up to its reputation as a source of youth for young and old alike. Metabolic and rheumatic disorders, and even sensitivity to changes in the weather have been successfully treated here.

The romantic Kuenring town of **Zwettl** is the seat of the largest privately-owned brewery in Austria; the beer is worth sampling. Apart from this, the most important places to see include the medieval town wall and the 11th-century Presbytery Church. On the outskirts lies a magnificent **Cistercian Abbey** built in 1138; a little further out of town is the Baroque **Castle of Rosenau**, where an initiation into the mysteries of Freemasonry awaits the curious visitor. The castle's restaurant serves a selection of good and hearty fare, such as "steamed leg of pork with root vegetables".

At the very heart of the Waldviertel lies **Ottenstein Reservoir**, with its countless fjord-like inlets. Rastenfeld is an ideal starting point for this water sports centre, which attracts anglers, swimmers, sailors and surfers; for landlubbers there are 20 miles (35 km) of signposted footpaths, bicycle rental, a

The courtyard of the old castle in Scheibbs.

fitness circuit, tennis courts and bowling greens. **Ottenstein Castle** – which has a Romanesque chapel adorned with frescoes – as well as the **Lichtenfels Ruins** and **Rastenberg Castle**, will delight anyone interested in ghosts.

Driving through **Krumau am Kamp**, near the Thurnberger and Dobra reservoirs, you reach **Gars am Kamp**. It is a pretty village lying at the foot of a ruined castle once belonging to the Babenbergs; it offers – apart from a comprehensive exhibition documenting the local excavations which reveal that the Gars district has been the site of human settlements for 5,000 years – the Romanesque-Gothic **Church of St Gertrude**, and a number of fine patrician houses. Another local speciality is Willy Dungl's Bio-Training Hotel, with active regeneration programmes of the highest quality.

Further upstream along the Kamp, we soon catch sight of the idyllically situated **Castle of Rosenburg**, near **Mold**. First mentioned in 1175, the magnificent structure possesses a unique jousting yard and houses a large number of works of art, including weapons and items of Renaissance furniture.

Our final choice of places to visit in the Waldviertel must be the historically important town of **Maissau**. It lies on the border between the Wine and Woodland country, on the **Manharts-berg**. The community, its skyline dominated by a romantic castle, has always been an important crossroads. The Manhartsstrasse, one of the principal routes linking the Wachau to the Elbe and the Oder, has passed through Maissau since time immemorial.

The Wachau: Apricot blossoms and Richard the Lionheart, the waves of the Danube, castles, fish and wine are all aspects of the most charming river region in Austria. First impressions are dominated by the magnificent **Abbey of Melk**, its side facade some 1,115 ft (340 metres) long, perched atop a steep cliff with two precipitous faces. Jakob Prandtauer was the masterly builder of the abbey. Originally a fine castle stood on this site; it was the residence of the old

Milk churns drying in the sun.

Austrian family of the Babenbergs. Since the land came into their possession in 1089, the Order of Benedictines have lived and worked on this spot; they had the abbey built in its present form in the 18th century.

About 3 miles (5 km) further downstream lies **Schönbühel**, on National Road 33. The castle, dating from the 12th century, occupies a dominant site on a 130-ft (40-metre) high cliff above the river; it has an interesting relief depicting the Last Supper on one of the exterior walls. It is worth allowing yourself time to explore the next village, **Aggsbachdorf**, at leisure. It contains a Carthusian monastery dating from the 14th–16th centuries as well as the tombs of the founding Maissau family, embellished with coats of arms.

The most interesting excursion, however, is accomplished on foot; to the ruins of **Aggstein Castle**, almost 700 years old. Here it was that the Kuenrings, a lawless tribe of robber barons, barricaded the Danube with chains in order to plunder passing ships. Today the main attraction is undoubtedly the fine panoramic view: upstream towards Melk, it stretches past the foothills of the **Forest of Dunkelstein** and across the highland plateau of the Waldviertel.

On the other side of the Danube lies **Willendorf**, famous for the discovery of the "Venus of Willendorf", a neolithic limestone statue. The soil here is a repository of many a fascinating historical detail; it reveals, for instance, that a camp of mammoth hunters was situated here during the Ice Age.

Arnsdorf offers the next opportunity to cross to the other bank of the river; but preferably not before one has studied the delightful interior of its parish church. There is a ferry link with **Spitz**, the famous wine-growing town that sprawls around the **Tausendeimerberg**. The mountain's name refers to the claim that, during a good year, the yield from its vineyards will total one thousand buckets of wine. Romantic souls among the town's visitors are bound to fall heavily in love with **Erlahof Castle** and the ruined **Fortress of Hinterhaus**. The

The countryside near Waidhofen a der Ybbs.

late-Gothic church boasts a triple nave and a baroque high altar with an oil painting by the artist Kremser Schmidt.

It is well worth planning a stopover in **Joching**, and in particular at Josef Jamek's wine cellars. His wines are featured on the menus of the best gourmet restaurants in the land; no visitor should fail to take advantage of this chance to taste them on home territory. **Weissenkirchen** is a very picturesque village, with narrow alleys, historic houses and ancient gleaning yards. The entire community is dominated by an imposing fortified church which dates from 1190.

Dürnstein is probably the most popular village in the whole of the Wachau. It also enjoys what must be one of the most beautiful situations. People all over the world have heard the legend of King Richard the Lionheart and Blondel, his minstrel. At the end of the 12th century, the King of England, captured by the Robber Barons on his return from a crusade, languished as a prisoner in the dungeons of the impregnable fortress.

Only one faithful follower, his minstrel Blondel, refused to believe that his beloved master was no longer alive; he took his lute and set off to find him. Eventually, striking up the first bars of Richard's favourite song beneath Dürnstein Castle, he was answered by the familiar voice of his master; soon afterwards, Richard the Lionheart was released upon payment of a large ransom by the English. (The money was used to finance the construction of Vienna's first city wall.)

Further sights to attract the visitor in Dürnstein include a 17th-century Renaissance castle built to a square ground plan, a 15th-century former canonical church, and **St Clare's Convent**, dating from the year 1300. The entire village is pervaded by an unusual charm which it is easy to succumb to.

Across the bridge lie two of the best restaurants in Austria. Chef Liesl Wagner-Bacher wields her wooden spoon in **Mautern**, fully justifying her three "chef's hat" symbols in the *Gault-Millau* guide. In Klein-Wien at the foot of the **Göttweig Abbey**, is the restaurant of her sister, Gerda Schickh, whose apricot dumplings seem to capture the unique taste of the Wachau.

Crossing to the other bank again, we pass through **Stein** and soon reach the hamlet of **Und** ("And"). This tiny community, with its odd name, includes a former monastery housing a wine-growers' college with enormous cellars containing the choicest vintages from Austria's wine-growing valleys; visitors are able to taste and purchase them to their heart's content.

And so, continuing along the route, you soon arrive in **Krems**, the "Model Town for the Preservation of Historical Monuments". A considerable proportion of the buildings are beautiful old houses. The town itself lies nestled among terraced vineyards, clinging to the bank of the Danube. Every visitor to the Wachau should taste the region's fine wines and in particular, its apricot brandy. The entire valley is full of apricot trees. During a visit in spring, the blossom turns the countryside into a spectacle of great beauty.

ttenstein astle.

UPPER AUSTRIA

From the Dachstein in the South to the Bohemian woods in the North, from the Inn to the Enns – these are the boundaries of Upper Austria. To facilitate orientation the province has been further sub-divided into regions: the Mühlviertel, the Innviertel and the Hausruck Forest, the Salzkammergut and Pyhrn-Eisenwurzen.

Upper Austria, rich in scenic landscapes and historic sights, offers its visitors a wide range of holiday facilities: adventurous souls, for example, will get their money's worth hang-gliding (Windisch-Garsten), potholing (Dachstein Caves), wild-water canoeing (on the Steyr) or by scaling one of the region's many mountain peaks. Those whose interests lie more on the cultural side will find much to explore in the countless monasteries and convents (above all in the Innviertel and Linz areas), as well as in the countless pretty villages with their quaint houses. More than 70 lakes in the Salzkammergut cater to every type of water sport. If you prefer a more tranquil atmosphere, the Mühlviertel will prove a paradise for extended cycle tours and walking holidays. Whatever your choice, you will soon fall prey to the comfortable rural charms of Upper Austria.

Linz: A popular rhyme, claiming that "It all begins in Linz", arouses the new arrival's curiosity about the provincial capital of Upper Austria. It proves to be a city which at once invites the visitor to stroll through its streets, to watch the world go by, to eat, drink, shop. The third-largest city in the land has been the capital of the "Land around the Enns" since 1490.

The town's landmark, the white marble **Plague Column**, was dedicated in 1723. It dominates the **Hauptplatz**, whose dimensions – 720 by 195 ft (220 by 60 metres) – make it the largest enclosed square in Austria. Between the stately patrician houses with their Baroque and Biedermeier facades stands

Preceding pages: a steelworker at the giant VOEST plant. **Below,** industrial landscape near Linz.

the imposing Gothic **Old Town Hall**.

The fact that Linz was long the seat of the local bishop and hence a town of considerable importance explains the presence of the numerous churches. Worthy of special mention is the Jesuit church known as the **Old Cathedral**, where the composer Anton Bruckner was once organist. Anton Bruckner, "God's musician", as he was dubbed is a great favourite among Austrian people. The citizens of Linz honoured him by naming the **Brucknerhaus** after him; opened in 1974, this has since become one of the most famous and most modern concert halls in Europe. It is the stage for the annual optical-acoustic cultural and social event known as **Ars Electronica**, which combines art and technology.

The city's roots stretch far back into history, long before the time of the Romans, whose records mention "Lentia" for the first time in 410 AD. The name is of Celtic origin, and it is even claimed that the site was settled in Neolithic times. In approximately 700 Linz became the eastern base of the Bavarian kingdom.

At the beginning of the 13th century it came into the possession of the Babenbergs and received its town charter soon afterwards; at the end of the 15th century Linz even became the royal seat for a short while. In 1672 the "wool textile factory" (which later employed as many as 50,000 home workers) was constructed. In 1832 Austria's first (horse-drawn) railway commenced operations between Linz and Budweis, and 1842 saw the foundation of the shipyard, which manufactured the first iron ships in Europe. Thanks to the nitrogen works and the VOEST steelworks, during this century Linz has become the principal industrial city in Austria.

Within the city, the attractive **Old Town** has preserved its predominantly Baroque countenance, inviting the visitor to a leisurely stroll followed by a "small brown" in one of the many cafés – perhaps with a piece of *Linzer torte*, the traditional local cake. By way of a change there are the town's renowned

Below left, arcades in Linz. Below right, Steyr.

galleries, such as the **Ursulinenhof**, or the world-famous cactus collection in the **Botanical Gardens** on the Freinberg. An essential component of any tour of Linz is a trip up the **Pöstlingberg** on the steepest tramway in Europe. Those who enjoy shopping are recommended to visit the sophisticated pedestrian zone in the Landstrasse.

There is plenty to do in the evening. Linz offers a wide range of restaurants, from fine gourmet temples to refreshing beer gardens or *beisl* which, with their welcoming atmosphere, cater to both body and soul.

The Upper Austrian Iron Road: Following the course of the "Eisenstrasse", you can make an interesting and informative tour through Upper Austria. This ancient trading route links the towns of **Eisenerz**, **Leoben** and **Steyr**. Its significance as a cultural-historic monument and as a scenic road have only recently been acknowledged. For many years the region slumbered peacefully, minding its own business and largely forgotten by the rest of the world. The small metalworking companies have long since lost their economic significance and even the larger steel manufacturing centres of Leoben and Steyr suffered badly as a result of the Europe-wide steel crisis. Recently, however, new life has been injected into this once-important trading route.

A local initiative group dedicated to the Styrian Iron Road is revitalising important historical sights associated with the iron and steel industry in and around Eisenherz. Nature conservationists and alpinists are responsible for the meticulous preservation of the **Reichraminger Hinterland** mountain nature reserve.

Any exploration of the Iron Road is best begun in the old iron town of **Steyr**, situated where the river of the same name flows into the Enns. The medieval Old Town, in particular, offers an impressively harmonious countenance. The **Bummerlhaus**, completed in 1497, and the **Parish Church** (15th–17th centuries) are real jewels of Gothic architecture. Between 1886 and 1894

Rural idylls near Burgstall...

Anton Bruckner put his finishing touches to his last great compositions in the Priest's House next door. Only a few yards away from the Stadtplatz across the Grünmarkt is the **Innerberger Getreidestadel** (1612). The former granary now contains the Municipal Museum and the **Steyrer Kripperl**, a world-famous mechanical puppet theatre (performances held only in December and January).

The **Wehrgraben** district has retained all its fine 16th–18th century architecture, making it an enchanting setting for a leisurely stroll. It also contains a remarkable museum, the "World of Work", which displays industrial history in a particularly lively manner.

A worthwhile short excursion into the surrounding countryside would be to the pilgrimage **Church of Christkindl**, situated only 2 miles (3 km) from Steyr and constructed during the 18th century by the Baroque master builders C. Carlone and J. Prandtauer. The special post office set up every year at Christmas in the town sends letters bearing the coveted special stamp to all the corners of the earth.

Only a few miles south of Steyr rise the densely wooded Alpine foothills, already amidst a number of quite considerable mountains. **Losenstein**, the highlight of the Enns valley, lies on the Enns beneath the peak of the Schieferstein. Perched on a cliff above the village itself stand the ruins of a castle. Worth seeing are the Gothic parish church (*circa* 1400), the Castle Tavern and the Klausgraben ravine.

Two miles further on, the Iron Road brings the traveller to **Laussa**, one of the prettiest and neatest villages in Austria. The village still supports a flourishing scythe maker's forge.

The next town, **Reichraming**, was once an industrial centre with hammer mills and a brass factory; today it is above all the gateway to the tourist region of the **Reichraminger Mountains**. From here, for example, it is possible to undertake a 12-mile cycle tour through unspoiled countryside – without encountering any steep inclines

…and near Schwalsödt in the Mühlviertel.

– or to swim in the Reichramingbach, one of the loveliest natural bathing spots in the country. By way of a contrast to such demanding sporting activities, a visit to the **Holzknechtmuseum** is highly recommended.

Grossraming lies some 7 miles further along the road; **Brunnbach**, on the outskirts, is also an ideal starting point for mountain walks through the hinterland. Since it lies on the Enns and just above the **Ascha**, Petri disciples should be in their element here.

The former "golden market" of **Weyer** was reputedly founded in the 13th century, receiving its charter as a market town as early as 1460. In the 18th century Weyer, in league with Weidhofen, was locked in bitter confrontation with Steyr over the iron trade. In 1781 the iron merchants of Steyr brought into operation trade barriers against the two towns; the Turkish threat and the plague also prevented any ideas of extensive expansion. Nowadays the resort area is a perfect base for extensive walking tours, riding holidays, herb-gathering walks, fishing, and in winter both Alpine and cross-country skiing as well as ice-skating. Visitors who are interested in the town's past should view the impeccably restored market place with pretty townhouses, the late Gothic **Church of St John** and **Egerer Castle**.

Also of interest is **Kastenreith**. Formerly known as "Kasten" and today the site of the **Enns Museum**, it was an important resting place and trade centre when the rafting and boat traffic on the Enns was in its heyday. Apart from the museum, one can visit Katzenstein Mill and a hammer forge.

The Iron Road continues via **Kleinreifling** – today an important rail junction between Amstetten and Selzthal – to **Altenmarkt**, by which time it has crossed the provincial border into Styria.

The Mühlviertel: This remarkable region lies within the boundaries of Upper Austria, in the north. The Mühlviertel's name derives from its two principal rivers, the **Greater** and **Lesser Mühl**. It stretches out to the north and north-west of Linz, between the Danube and the

Pausing on a walk in the forest.

Czech border. It consists of a hilly granite plateau whose densely wooded slopes remain largely untouched, even by tourism – a welcome, if increasingly rare phenomenon. For visitors in search of rest and recreation the Mühlviertel can still offer inexpensive accommodation. Extended walking or cycle tours lead through large areas of woodland alternating with pastures and cultivated fields. The rural scene is interspersed with the occasional castle or ruined fortress and little market towns and villages which look as though they have been nestling between the hills since time immemorial.

Freistadt, in the north-east, lies 25 miles (40 km) from Linz and is regarded as the capital of the lower Mühlviertel. It is considered to be one of the most interesting sights in Austria. Founded by free merchants in 1200, today the town retains its medieval fortifications: the double defensive wall, moats, circular towers and the late Gothic town gates – the **Linzer Tor** and the **Böhmer Tor**. The former merchants' houses surrounding the main square still boast their original Gothic interiors behind magnificent Renaissance and Baroque façades. Also of note is the parish church, the so-called **St Catherine's Cathedral** with two world-famous masterpieces of late Gothic architecture: the chancel and the baptism chapel (1483–1501). To the north-east lies the **Castle**, the former residence of the local rulers; the medieval keep is well preserved (14th century). It contains, among other interesting things, the **Mühlviertel Museum** which contains an extensive collection of stained-glass pictures. The 15th-century **Church of Our Lady** stands outside the Böhmer Tor.

Sandl, some 10 miles (15 km) north-east of Freistadt, is a destination which is still a closely-kept secret amongst winter sportsmen. The **Viehberg** (3,645 ft/1,110 metres) offers some very acceptable Alpine ski pistes, whilst the extensive network of cross-country ski runs has made the town a centre for Nordic skiing.

Kefermarkt, 7 miles (11 km) south

The young continue the traditions of their elders.

of Freistadt, is famous for the **Gothic Altarpiece** in the parish and pilgrimage church of St Wolfgang. Carved by an unknown master from limewood, it measures 44 by 20 ft (14 by 6 metres). The village is dominated by **Weinberg Castle** (17th-century) to the north, which boasts a remarkable collection of hunting trophies and an apothecary dating from 1680. Not to be missed are the Ancestral Hall (1604), the Knights' Hall, the Imperial Hall, the falconry and the castle chapel which has an interior by Bartolomeo Carlone, one of the great Baroque stuccoists.

If we continue to use Freistadt as our base for our explorations of the Mühlviertel, there are a number of worthwhile destinations in the west as well. **Bad Leonfelden** is a peat and Kneipp spa about 12 miles (20 km) away. The Sternstein (winter sports facilities) is, at 3,690 ft (1,125 metres), the highest peak in the entire Mühlviertel. By continuing through **Rohrbach**, which lies 12 miles to the west encircled by the dense pine and spruce forests of the **Bohemian Woods**, our tour brings us to **Aigen-Schlägl**. Here special mention must be made of the Postulants' Foundation in Schlägl, rebuilt in the Baroque style during the 17th century.

South of Rohrbach lies another of the Mühlviertel's special attractions: the **Altenfelden-Mühltal Nature Park**. Its 200 acres (80 hectares) house over 700 animals, including ibexes, wild horses, aurochs, antelopes and sambar, sika, David's and axis deer. The park is crisscrossed by a network of paths, some of them suitable for pushchairs.

The Mühlviertel, although a prime example of hilly walking country, is also perfect for a cycling tour. With its alternating uphill and downhill tracks it is ideal territory for mountain bikes, and with the growth of mountain biking in Austria in recent years it has become a major centre for the sport's enthusiasts. There is an extensive network of cycle paths without steep slopes in the southern Machland district by the Danube.

Keen long-distance walkers may like to tackle the route from Aigen to Sandl.

Splashing around in Wolfgangsee.

It can be covered in seven or more stages from April to June or from September–October without the necessity of carrying one's luggage. A scheme has been arranged whereby your landlords will transport it to your next overnight stop on your behalf.

The Innviertel: If you cross the border from Germany into Austria at Passau and continue in a southerly direction for about 10 miles (17 km), you will come to **Schärding**, a little town perched high above the River Inn. Famous today as the home of the largest Kneipp cure clinic in Austria, its appearance is characterised by its medieval silhouette, which is dominated by a ruined castle (15th century), the town ramparts and gates.

In **Reichersberg**, 11 miles (18 km) further on, stands an imposing Augustinian seminary. Founded in 1084, the buildings were badly damaged by fire in 1624 and rebuilt over the course of the rest of the century. During summer months a variety of craft courses and cultural events are held in Reichersberg.

The National Road 143 will finally bring us to **Ried im Innkreis**, the economic focal point of the Innviertel. The Schwanthalergasse was named after the celebrated family of sculptors (1632–1838) whose former home is at no.11.

A number of scenic roads thread through the **Hausruck** forest to **Frankenburg**. The town was the setting for a macabre spectacle in 1625; citizens and peasants alike were forced to throw dice to decide which of them would die and which would live. As a reminder of this gruesome event dating from the Peasant Wars, the **Frankenburg Game of Dice** is staged every year.

Ampflwang, which lies slightly further to the east, has earned a reputation during the past few years as a significant equestrian centre. The entire village has dedicated itself to the sport; novices and professionals alike will find a wide range of activities and classes to suit their abilities. It is also worth remembering that horseriding is available here not just in the summer months but all the year round.

Imsee in ｅ Salz-ammergut.

THE SALZKAMMERGUT

The Salzkammergut is famous for its lakes, which provide unequalled possibilities for summertime recreation. There are 76 of them altogether, strung out like a necklace of pearls, each one of them possessing its own inimitable charm. There are lakes for bathing in, like the Mondsee and the Wolfgangsee; yachting centres (the Attersee or the Traunsee), apparently bottomless gleaming "emeralds" (the Grundlsee and the Hallstättersee), and romantic retreats like the Gosausee and the Altausseer See. The area is also known for its numerous salt-mines (the word Salzkammergut means "salt chamber estate"), at one time an important source of revenue for the crown.

It is difficult to encompass the Salz–kammergut within a single geographical term, but it extends from Lake Wolfgang and Lake Fuschl in the Salzburger Land in the west to the Ausseer Land in Styria in the east. If Salzburg is your point of departure, the quickest route to the Salzkammergut Lake District is the motorway leading via **Thalgau** to **Mondsee**. If you have sufficient time at your disposal, however, a short detour to the south is recommended. **Lake Fuschl** lies only minutes away from the busy main road, its dark, cold waters nestling between the forested slopes.

Not far from the road stands the **Fuschl Hunting Lodge**, with a museum containing a number of rare trophies. **Schlosshotel Fuschl** stands on a promontory overlooking the lake. It was built in 1450 as a hunting lodge for the archbishops, and in the 20th century it became the property of the Nazi politician Ribbentrop. It is now a luxury hotel offering guests every imaginable facility: beach, fishing jetties, indoor swimming pool, tennis court and one of the most scenic golf courses in Austria. Walking through the castle's magnificent grounds, the visitor follows in the illustrious footsteps of monarchs, film

Preceding pages: boathouses o Lake Hallstatt. Below, Hallstatt gav its name to the first European Iro Age (8th–4th centuries BC)

stars and politicians (Nixon, Ford and Khrushchev), all of whom have slept or conferred here.

Skirting along the south side of Lake Fuschl we soon reach **St Gilgen** on **Lake Wolfgang**. Of particular interest is the birthplace of Mozart's mother, Ann Maria Pertl (1720–78); today, the building houses the local assizes. Nor should one miss a boat trip on the lake itself, which extends over an area of 5 sq. miles (13 sq. km).

The excursion to the village of **St Wolfgang** itself is strongly recommended. The landing stage is near the **Weisses Rössl**, the "White Horse Inn", made famous by Ralph Benatzky's operetta. Strolling through picturesque alleys, the visitor arrives before the **Pilgrimage Church**, which is one of the most remarkable architectural monuments in Europe. It houses a magnificent Gothic high altar created by Michael Pacher between 1471 and 1481.

St Wolfgang can also be the starting point for a unique highlight. A steam-driven train (commissioned in 1893!) chugs along unhurriedly to the summit of the 5,850-ft (1,785-metre) **Schafberg**. From here there is a breathtaking panorama of the Lake District, a stunning view of 12 lakes: Wolfgang, Fuschl, Attersee, Mondsee, Irrsee, Wallersee, Obertru-mersee, Niedertrumersee, Grabensee, Absdorfer See, Chiemsee and Waginger See.

Lake Wolfgang, with an average water temperature of 73°F (23°C), is a many-faceted paradise for those who like watersports: with fishing jetties, diving schools, boat rental (rowing, sailing, pedal and motor boats), surfing and sailing schools, it offers a range of water-borne activities for every taste. Moreover, the former Emperor Franz Joseph and his beloved wife Sisi were regular visitor to the natural beach at **Strobl**, a pretty lakeside village on the warmest part of the lake.

Those who choose **St Gilgen** as their base for further exploration of the Salzkammergut can take the National Road 154 to the **Mondsee**. The lake lies in the shadow of the dominant silhouettes of the Drachenwand and the Schafberg; 7 miles (11 km) long and over 1 mile (2 km) wide, its waters are among the warmest in the region. Lakeside bathing beaches and sailing schools lend the lake a carefree holiday atmosphere.

The village of Mondsee, founded in 748 by Odilio, a Bavarian count, when the Benedictine monastery was established, offers a number of historical sights. The local museum, for example, has a display of finds dating from the Mondsee's prehistoric culture, whilst the market place is surrounded by well-preserved houses dating from the 16th–18th centuries. The 12th-century **Parish Church** was rebuilt at the end of the 14th century; it is considered a particularly fine example of Gothic ecclesiastical architecture.

The villages surrounding the Mondsee offer yet another attraction: gourmets will discover more illustrious restaurants here than in almost any other region of Austria. Creative nouvelle cuisine of the highest quality, with strong local influences, will be found on the lovely terrace of the **Seehof**, in the Francophile **La Farandole**, in Karl Eschlböck's pretty **Landhaus Plomberg** and in the no less renowned **Weisses Kreuz** of Gustav Lugerbauer.

Those continuing their lakes tour from Mondsee will find themselves spoilt for choice between the vast eastern waters of the **Attersee** and the **Traunsee** and the untamed romanticism of the south – the **Hallstätter See**, **Grundlsee** et al – quite apart from the enchanting lakes of the Alpine foothills to the north. To get a better perspective you would do well to make a detour into the neighbouring flatlands and the Salzkammergut catchment area.

The National Road 154 leads off in a northerly direction from Mondsee, reaching **Zell am Moos** some 4 miles (6 km) later. The village lies on the eastern shores of the **Zeller See** (or Irrsee), a nature conservation area. The lake's waters reach temperatures of 80°F (27°C) during the summer months, allowing bathing between May and September. There are easily accessible bathing areas all round its perimeter. Zell am

Moos is a particularly attractive holiday destination for families with children. Playgrounds, activity programmes and a children's bathing area on the lake ensure variety.

Returning to our original starting point, the Mondsee, you can then take the National Road 151 to **Unterach**, on the Attersee. Its dimensions (12 by almost 2 miles/20 by almost 3 km) – make it the largest lake in the Austrian Lake District. It is an El Dorado for sailors and is encircled by a succession of picturesque villages ideal for holiday-making: **Unterach**, **Nussdorf** and **Attersee** on the western shore, **Seewalchen** and **Kammer** to the north and **Weyregg**, **Steinbach** and **Weissenbach** to the east. Most have excellent campsites, sailing and surfing schools and boat rental. The Attersee is the only lake in the Salzkammergut which never freezes in winter. Its waters are also considered to be particularly unpolluted; its underwater topography makes it ideal for divers (3- and 4-star courses).

Those wishing to explore the **Traun-see**, yet another jewel of the Salzkammergut, should follow the road round the southern tip of the Attersee before continuing via **Neukirchen** to **Gmunden**.

Lying in a picture-postcard setting on the northern shore of the Traunsee and offering a wide variety of water sports facilities as well as traditional cures (salt-water baths), Gmunden (population 12,000) is a typical summer resort. Architecturally, it also has much to offer: there is the Renaissance-style **Town Hall** with its porcelain-tiled glockenspiel, as well as a number of fine town-houses and numerous castles (Cumberland, Württemberg, Freisitz-Roith). The **Landschloss of Orth** on the mainland, is linked by a 425-ft (130-metre) long wooden bridge to the **Seeschloss** ("Lake Château"), built in the 17th century on an artificial island.

One should also make a point of visiting the town's famous porcelain factory, with its characteristic green-glazed china. Gmunden, once the salt capital and residence of the local prince,

In the Dachstein Mountains.

documents to this day its close links with the "white gold" in the Kammerhof, which was for centuries the seat of the Salt Authority. The museum contains displays tracing not only the development of the history of salt, but also that of the local pottery. In addition there is a collection of original manuscripts by the town's most famous sons Friedrich Hebbel and Johannes Brahms.

A particular attraction is a trip on the oldest coal-fired paddle steamer in the world. The *Gisela* has been ploughing through the waters of the Traunsee since 1872; she even transported the Emperor Franz Joseph to his cool summer retreat in the heart of the Salzkammergut. It seemed in 1980 that the *Gisela* was doomed to an ignoble death as, dilapidated and rusting, she appeared in imminent danger of breakup. Only an initiative of the Association of Friends of Gmunden saved her from the scrap heap. First of all the ship – the only one of its kind in Austria – was declared an historic monument; later, when the necessary funds had been raised, she was restored to her original splendour. And so today the *Gisela* can puff merrily across the Traunsee once more.

The famous salt town of **Ebensee** lies on the southern shore of the Traunsee. As early as 1607, its townfolk were refining brine from the salt mined in the area. Ebensee is a good starting point from which to make excursions into the nearby **Totes Gebirge** and **Höllenge–birge** mountains. Particularly recommended is a visit to the romantic **Lang-bathseen lakes** (4 miles/6 km).

Following the course of the Traun from Ebensee, the visitor will duly arrive in **Bad Ischl**. The spa town, where the Emperor used to come for a cure, is still well worth a visit today. Its inimitable turn-of-the-century aura greets the traveller everywhere, not only in the **Imperial Villa** and the **Lehàr Museum**. The oldest saline baths in Austria now boast ultra-modern therapeutic equipment; even a short cure will prove relaxing. It is pleasant to follow such a session by a stroll along the Esplanade bordering the Traun and then to sample coffee and cakes at **Zauner's**, the legendary pâtisserie.

Thus fortified, the 7-mile (11-km) journey to **Bad Goisern** will prove child's play. A resort with sulphur and brine baths, the town is also the shopping centre of the Salzkammergut. Manufactured here and nowhere else are the "Original Goiserer" mountain boots – possibly the best of their kind in the world.

If there is a single village which fully deserves to be the subject of a picture postcard, then it must be **Hallstatt**. Predominantly Baroque in style, the pastel-coloured houses cling precariously to the steep mountain slopes. The historic part of the town looks as if, by some superhuman effort, it has reclaimed a narrow strip of land – scarcely wide enough to allow room for cars – from the mountains and the lake.

The past 4,500 years have left their mark here; salt was the basis of wealth in the town even for the Celtic and Illyrian tribes. An entire epoch, marking the first phase of the European Iron Age between 800 and 400 BC, has been

Carnival time in Altausee.

christened the "Hallstatt Period". Highly sophisticated artefacts were produced by this ancient culture.

But the village achieved world fame when a 2,500-year-old burial site was discovered. Visitors with an interest in the macabre should take a look inside the charnel house; since space is at a premium here, the bones have to be removed from the tiny cemetery after 10 years. They are stacked up, but not before the skull has been artistically labelled and painted. Those who prefer to find out where the salt in their soup comes from can visit the salt mine.

Obertraun, at the southeastern tip of the **Hallstätter See**, is regarded by winter sports enthusiasts as a place where snow is assured. A funicular leads up the **Krippenstein** (6,920 ft/2,110 metres), providing an impressive view of the **Dachstein Massif**.

From **Schönbergalm**, the intermediate station, one can visit the famous **Dachstein Ice Caves**. Imposing vaults and corridors lead into the interior of the mountain; the highlight of this chilly excursion is undoubtedly the **Mammoth's Cave** (several storeys with a total combined height of 985 ft/300 metres!). Equally impressive is the **Koppenbrüller Cave**, with its fantastically-shaped stalactite sculptures.

The Hallstatter See is an El Dorado for all those who are interested in freshwater diving, shipwrecks and the recovery of sunken treasure. Gerhard Zauner, proprietor of the diving school and Divers' Inn in Hallstatt, spends almost more time underwater than above it. Even experts can learn something from his classes. He offers more than 20 courses, from a basic introduction to diving to such esoteric topics as "Fish Language" and "Cutting and Welding Under Water".

When Zauner – bearded and with the physique of a Viking – addresses you with "Search, Recover, Salvage," he knows what he is talking about. He has rescued large quantities of treasure which was buried in the **Toplitzsee** during World War II, earning himself a mention in the international press. His

Orth Castle, one of the delights of Traunsee.

activities have also contributed to the fame of the lake itself; the visitor surveying its dark waters, secluded shores, steep rocky cliffs and roaring waterfalls will understand why he chose this lake rather than any other one.

A 10-minute walk through the forest, including a steep track with 71 steps, leads to the tiny, idyllic **Kammersee**. Eerie reflections, utter peace and a sense of seclusion engender a delusion of having escaped from the world.

Before the Toplitzsee lies the **Grundlsee**, its emerald-green waters shimmering like a jewel. It is 4 miles (6 km) long and is popular among sailors and surfers; anglers, too, like to try their luck from its shores. In summer, an official horse-drawn post coach plies the route between **Gössl** (at the far end) and the Toplitzsee – much to the delight of holidaymakers of all ages. The Grundlsee is the largest lake within the Styrian Salzkammergut.

Although the lake boasts a village of the same name, the regional capital is **Bad Aussee**, which lies between the Dachstein foothills and the Totes Gebirge. It is a lively little town boasting a number of architectural jewels: the 15th-century **Parish Church of St Paul,** the **Spital Church** (14th-century), with a very fine altarpiece (1449), and the Gothic **Kammerhof,** once the office of the salt-works in the region, and now housing the local museum. An aura of sleepy enchantment hangs over the entire place; some houses give the impression that time really has stood still here. The town's recently completed spa complex, with its brine baths, contrasts starkly. The salty water is said to work miracles in the case of gynaecological complaints, digestive problems and rheumatic illnesses.

It is well worth seeking a panoramic view of the **Altausser See**. The best one is reached by leaving Altaussee itself on the Salzkammergut road up the **Loser**. The brilliantly-engineered toll road requires 15 hairpin bends to reach an altitude of 5,250 ft (1,600 metres) above sea level. From this height one has a magnificent eagle's-eye view of the entire lake and its fairy tale surroundings. If you are lucky, you will see a hang-glider or parasailing enthusiast launching himself from the platform into the depths below.

In World War II the Germans stored several important works of art in the salt-mines of the Altausser region.

Opinions are divided, but the **Gosausee** can certainly lay claim to be the loveliest lake in the Salzkammergut. Whether you are visiting it for the first or the fifth time, you will not fail to be captured by an indescribable emotion as you gaze upon the view of the lake in the foreground against the slopes and glaciers of the Dachstein massif.

It's best to stay until the late afternoon, taking the last funicular to **Zwieselalpe**. The benches in front of the shelter are perfectly placed for watching the Alpine pyrotechnics at sunset. After supper and a glass of schnapps the invigorating mountain air will guarantee a deep, refreshing sleep – at least until the overpowering spectacle of sunrise over the mist-cloaked valleys lure you from your bed.

Gosau Lake at the foot of the Dachstein Mountains.

Southern Austria

32 km/20 miles

Munich

Vilsbiburg
Taufkirchen
Eggenfelden
Schärding
Mühldorf
Inn
Braunau
Ried
UPPER
AUSTR
Ebersberg
Burghausen
Wasserburg
Mattighofen
GERMANY
Rosenheim
Chiemsee
Traunstein
Mondsee
Atter-See
G
Trau
Prien
Freilassing
Bad Tölz
Bad
Reichenhall
Salzburg
St. Wolfgang
Tegernsee
Bad Ischl
Lake
Wolfgang
Berchtesgaden
SALZKAMMERGUT
Bad
Kufstein
Watzmann
2713
Königs-
See
SALZBURG
Lake
Hallstadt
Wörgl
Kitzbühel
Dachstein
2996
Gröbming
Fügen
KITZBÜHLER ALPS
Schladming
Schwaz
Zell am See
St. Johann
Radstadt
LOWE
Gerlos
Pass 1507
Mittersill
Zell
am Ziller
Mayrhofen
Radstädter
Tauern Pass
1739
Mauterndorf
Hintertux
Gross Venediger
3360
Felber
Tauern Tunnel
ZILLERTALER ALPS
St. Michael
Hochfeiler
3523
Grossglockner
3798
Badgastein
HIGH TAUERN
GURK
Matrei
Heiligenblut
Huben
Obervellach
Rosen-Nock
2464
Brunico
TYROL
Lienz
Hochkreuz
2704
Pate
Dobbiaco
Spittal
Lake Mittstadt
Ortisei
Cortina
d'Ampezzo
S. Stefano
di Cad.
Weissen-See
Villach
Pordoi
Hermagor
3342
Marmolada
ITALY
Timau
Jeser
DOLOMITES
Pieve di
Cadore
Arta
Triglav
2864
Agordo
S. Martino
Tolmezzo
FRIULI-VENEZIA GIULIA
Belluno
Maniago
Artegna
Kobarid
Feltre
M. Cavallo
2250
Tagliamento
Udine
Cividale
Tolmin

200

MÜHLVIERTEL
Freistadt
Arbesbach
Hollabrunn
WEINVIERTEL
Stockerau
ding
Linz
Ober-St. Georgen
LOWER
Danube
Danube
Grein
St. Pölten
Vienna
ls
AUSTRIA
VIENNA WOODS
Amstetten
Mödling
Steyr
Waidhofen
Neubruck
Freiland
Wiener
Neustadt
Enns
Windischgarsten
Mariazell
Schneeberg
2075
Neunkirchen
A U S   T R I A
Salza
Hieflau
Mürzzuschlag
1368
Pfaffensattel
Aspang
iezen
nach
Hochtor
2373
FISCHBACHER ALPS
Kapfenberg
BURGENLAND
STYRIA
Leoben
TAUERN
Masenberg
1272
Schoberspitze
2423
Knittelfeld
Oberwart
Murau
Judenburg
Weisskirchen
Köflach
Raab
Stegersbach
Neumarkt
Graz
Fürstenfeld
RINTHIA
Twimberg
Wildon
Feldbach
Raba
St. Veit
Deutschlandsberg
Mur
Bad
Gleichenberg
Leibnitz
Zala
Klagenfurt
Völkermarkt
Radkersburg
oibl
Dravogard
Maribor
Mura
Lendava
Hoch Obir
2141
1696
SLOVENSKE GORICE
Ljutomer
Loibl-Pass
1366
Pleši vec
Sp. Dolič
Drava
Ptuj
Čakovec
SLOVENIA
2558
Velenje
Varaždin
Grintavec
Celje
Rogatec
CROATIA
ranj
Kamnik
Durmanec
Trbovlje
N. Marof

STYRIA

The "green heart of Austria" is an appropriate slogan for Styria. This second-largest Austrian province includes high Alpine topographical forms – perpetual ice and deeply cut ravines – as well as extensive expanses of forest which slowly give way to gently rolling ranges of hills skirting the lower Hungarian plains.

For some the Steiermark may at first seem exotic: dark pumpkin-seed oil, ruby-red Schilcher wine, and dialect which may be unintelligible to unpractised ears. But, in fact, here Austria shows itself at its best: pithy and natural. Two factors – a genuinely hospitable attitude to visitors and affordable prices – unite the mountainous north, with its countless opportunities for active and adventure holidays, and the gently rolling hills of the romantic south (which have often been compared, not without justification, to the landscape of Tuscany). These favourable conditions are underlined by the fact that the Austrians themselves regard the "Green Province" as their favourite holiday region within their own borders.

It is a well-known fact that people in Austria feel most at home where creature comforts and spiritual welfare are given priority. For those unconvinced by all the aforementioned attractions, this information may prove a deciding factor.

So take a deep breath and gather your strength; Styria is even better if you have plenty of energy.

Around the Dachstein: If you decide to take the area surrounding the **Dachstein Massif** as your springboard for exploration of Styria, you could choose no better starting place than **Schladming**. If you approach via the Munich-Salzburg motorway and Tauern motorways (which are toll-free as far as **Radstadt**) you should continue your journey along the National Road 146, and you will soon reach the little town itself (population 4,000). It has the largest Protestant church in Styria, built in 1862 but

Preceding pages: the Austria Hut on the Dachstein. **Below,** a bellowing stag near Mautern.

containing a much older altarpiece dating from approximately 1570. Today, it is a textile manufacturing town, specialising in loden, the heavy green wool of the ubiquitous green overcoats beloved by Germans and Austrians.

In 1982, Schladming and the neighbouring village of **Haus im Ennstal** were the venue for the Alpine Skiing World Championships. The wintersports infrastructure is correspondingly well developed. Linking the ski centres of **Reiteralm, Planai-Hochwurzen** and **Hauser Kaibling** are 55 miles (90 km) of avalanche-free pistes, a cable car network and chair and drag lifts. For those wishing to sample these snowy pleasures in summer – in a bathing costume – ample opportunities are available on the Dachstein glacier (*see pages 103–104*).

Ramsau, a neighbouring village, has in the meantime developed into an El Dorado for Nordic skiers. And in the warmer months the entire region is ideal for mountain and walking tours.

Ramsau-Rössing is the site of the oldest loden-dyeing factory in Austria; Germany's and Austria's loden coats (green with a short pile) are famous for their warmth and hard-wearing qualities all over the world. Holidaymakers spending any length of time in the area should certainly order a tailor-made "Janker", or loden jacket.

If you follow the B 146 (along the course of the Enns) in a north-easterly direction, you will quickly arrive in **Gröbming**. The village is a popular holiday resort because of its sunny climate; the late Gothic parish church (15th century) contains the largest altarpiece in Styria, with representations from the New Testament. Families with small children are particularly welcome in Gröbming. Childcare facilities and babysitting services have been set up to relieve parents of some of the strain of holidaymaking.

A romantic destination for an excursion is the 13th-century **Trautenfels Castle**, only a few miles away. It was built to defend the Enns valley and acquired its present-day appearance in 1670. Some sections of the colossal structure date from around 1520. Frescoes, a two-storey **"Knights' Hall"** and the **Ennstal Local Museum** are all on view here.

Popular holiday destinations in the area, which are also ideal centres for winter sports of all types, are **Tauplitz, Irdning, Donnersbach** and **Aigen**. **Stainach** is the most important railway junction, with an express train link and connections to Bad Mitterndorf, Bad Aussee, Wörschach, Liezen, Leoben, Schladming, Salzburg, Vienna, Graz etc. The neighbouring town of **Bad Wörschach** has famous sulphur springs, beneficial for gout, rheumatism, sciatica and gynaecological complaints. The **Wörschach Gorge** is considered one of the most striking in the land. There is a fine panorama from the ruins of **Wolkenstein Castle** (1186), which overlooks the town.

The capital of the Styrian section of the Enns valley is **Liezen**, a town with over 7,000 inhabitants. It is a winter paradise for skiers thanks to the nearby **Wurzeralm**; in summer, Liezen is the

The Dachstein Mountains viewed from the south.

stepping stone to mountain experiences of every description.

One of the highlights of any tour of Upper Styria is a visit to the **Admont** community. Mentioned in records as long ago as AD 859, a **Benedictine Abbey** was founded here in 1074. For centuries it had the reputation of being the artistic and cultural centre of the Enns valley.

Many of the foundation buildings were destroyed by a devastating fire in 1865, after which they were rebuilt in the neo-Gothic style. Connoisseurs of architecture will be interested to know that the renovation of the church was directed by the Wiesbaden architect Wilhelm Bücher, who vented his anger at the unification of his native Hessen-Nassau with Prussia by using the heads of Wilhelm I and Bismarck as models for gargoyles. Fortunately the abbey library escaped the ravages of the fire. It is housed in a two-storey monumental hall approximately 235 ft (72 metres) long, and is beautifully decorated with frescoes by Bartholomeo Altomonte.

The abbey library is considered one of the finest examples of Rococo architecture in the world; it contains more than 150,000 volumes, 1,600 manuscripts, 900 early printed works and 123 12th-century codices, making it the largest and most valuable monastery library in the world. The foundation buildings also house a museum of the history of art, an exhibition of curiosities and, perhaps not for the squeamish, an insect collection comprising no less than 252,000 exhibits.

Through the Gesäuse to the Styrian Iron Road: The "eastern approach" to the **Gesäuse Ravine** is marked by **Hieflau.** Between mountains which rise up to 7,875 ft (2,400 metres) high, the River Enns laboriously carves its way through precipitous rock faces. The rushing torrents and majestic mountains make this countryside some of the most bizarre and fascinating in Austria. Hieflau, only 9 miles (15 km) north of **Eisenerz,** is the principal traffic intersection in the Gesäuse region: here the B 115 (the Iron League Road) meets the B 112 (the

In the Klein Sölktal Valley.

Gesäuse Road), and the Amstetten-Selzthal railway line meets the Erzberg line to Leoben.

A few miles further on we are in the middle of a wildly romantic mountain world. **Gstatterboden** deserves its epithet of "Capital of the Gesäuse". It is a suburb of Weng bei Admont and lies exactly in the middle of the Enns corridor between the **Hochtour Range** in the south and the **Buchstein Group** and the **Tamischbachturm** in the north. Gstatterboden is another good starting point for a variety of Alpine pursuits. Walkers, mountaineers, climbers, ski touring enthusiasts, wild water canoeists and fishermen are all well catered for here.

Johnsbach is regarded as the second most important climbing centre for the Gesäuse. It is linked with the Enns valley by a 4-mile (6-km) long, wildly romantic gorge, lying in an idyllic high-altitude valley between the Hochtor and the **Jahrlingmauer** ranges in the north and the gentler **Eisenerz Alps** and the **Admonter Reichenstein** to the south

and west. Many visitors to Johnsbach consider it to be the prettiest of all Alpine villages. Not to be missed are the **Mountain Church** (14th-century), with its world-famous cemetery for climbers, the **Wolfbauer Waterfall** and the **Odelstein Stalactite Caves**. Tours of all grades of difficulty are available here for outdoor types.

Up the legendary Erzberg: The **Leopoldsteiner See**, 4,920 ft (1,500 metres) long by 1,640 ft (500 metres) wide, recalls the fjords of Scandinavia. A mountain lake impressively surrounded by craggy rock walls, it lies south-east of Hieflau. According to local legend a malevolent water sprite is supposed to have brought bad luck to the lake's fishermen. Eventually they gathered up their courage and caught the wicked fellow, but the sprite, somewhat subdued, made his henchmen a proposal: "A golden river, a silver heart or an iron hat" in exchange for his release. His captors wisely chose the iron hat, whereupon the sprite pointed at the Erzberg mountain which rises nearby. It is said

Sun and snow: Austria guarantees both.

that this incident marked the beginning of the history of ore mining in Upper Styria, a fact which accounts for the term **Styrian Iron Road** to describe the main route through the region.

The town of **Eisenerz** lies in a wild, romantic valley basin directly at the foot of the Erzberg, at the mouth of the **Krumpental** and the **Trofeng** valleys. In view of its historical development, Eisenerz can justifiably claim to be the beginning and the centre of the so-called Iron Road.

The town's present-day appearance owes much to the period in the 15th and 16th centuries and the economic heyday of the 19 wheelwrights who worked here. Eisenerz is ideal as the starting point for expeditions up the Erzberg (guided tours daily between 1 May and 31 October, at 10 a.m. and 2.30 p.m.). There are also a number of other sights worth visiting: the **Schichtturm** bell-tower (1581), the **Bergmannsplatz** with its fine miners' union houses, the remains of the Rupprechta furnace, the treasury buildings (now containing the fascinating Styrian Iron Museum), the Kaiser-Franz-Stollen, where the ore was prepared for smelting, remains of the ore consignments at the railway station and the enormous slag heaps in **Münichtal**.

In addition Eisenerz has a well-developed infrastructure for tourists: campsite, climbing school, fitness circuit, footpaths and a lake for bathing (with boat rental and surfing opportunities too). The area as a whole is ideal for a restful holiday.

The Erzberg (4,810 ft/1,470 metres) rises more than 2,300 ft (700 metres) above the valley floor. It is divided from base to summit into sections. The opencast mining consists at present of 23 quarries (stages), each on average 80 ft (25 metres) high and 2,820 ft (860 metres) long. Once or twice each day an explosive charge is laid, and for the rest of the day the miners are then occupied clearing away and processing the 60,000 tons of loosened ore. Blind stone ("rock") is taken straight to the tips, whilst the pure ore ("ready ore") is bro-

A girl from the Ausseerland.

208

ken up and sieved. It is then ready for transport. Approximately two-thirds of the ore is produced from "intermediate material", adhesions between the rock and the ore, by means of an ore preparation complex consisting of breaking and sieving belts and a heavy liquid separation unit, in which the ore is mechanically separated.

The multiple transport requirements have led to the development of an extensive transportation system. On the mountain itself, 50 miles (80 km) of roads must be maintained to permit more than 20 extra-large lorries to cart away the annual yield of 15 million tons of rubble. A works railway brings the ore from the tip shafts to the breaking machine and the ore loading bays. One hundred years ago there were 150 miles (240 km) of track within the mining works alone.

The Erzberg is the largest consumer of explosives in the whole of Austria (6 tons a day). It is also the oldest mining concern in the country to be in constant use, and the largest opencast iron ore mining concern in Central Europe (underground mining ceased here in 1986). It is estimated that the mighty mountain still contains some 180 million tons of ore – in other words, as much as has been mined to date since excavations began here almost 1,500 years ago.

If it were not for the continuing rise in production since the beginning of the 19th century, when the amount of ore excavated was approximately 40,000 tons each year, the reserves would have been adequate for at least another 8,500 years. Technical progress, however, has led to undreamed-of increases in production with the result that the ore available will only last for another 50 years or so.

It seems certain that the Slavs who lived here in the 6th century were already able to smelt the ore, using techniques developed in Roman times. The procedure required the ore which came to the surface below the mountain peak to be heated on the spot in 6-ft high kilns until a lump of iron formed. This lump was withdrawn from the kiln before it

The Eisenerz Alps from the Präbichl.

became completely hard, and was then hammered into a workable material. This work was undertaken by the so-called "iron farmers", who ran the mine as a sideline to their seasonal agricultural work.

It was not until the harnessing of water power, some 700 years later, that industrial forms of iron production were developed. New jobs were created; mining, smelting, ironworking, charcoal burning and transport needed increasing numbers of labourers. The sudden boom brought its own problems, however: there was a sudden shortage of charcoal, and production came to a swift halt.

In 1448 Frederick III issued his Mining Edict which brought the industry under state control. Iron and charcoal prices were regulated, as were wage levels, and the charcoal was earmarked exclusively for the iron mines. The area was further subdivided into districts from which food was to be supplied, where the iron was to be delivered, and those in which it could be worked. Only the

merchants who delivered the precious metal to the countless manufacturers of wire, nails, lead, axes, sickles, scythes and knives actually made much of a profit from the iron. The results of the wealth arising from the iron industry can be seen in the beautifully preserved townhouses in Leoben, Weyer and Steyr.

The **Präbichl Pass** (4025 ft/1,230 metres) links Eisenerz and **Vordernberg**. The Erzberg railway, which traverses the pass and the Erzberg through a series of tunnels, was not completed until 1892. As recently as 1978 steam engines puffed up the steep rack railway track over the pass. Nowadays the Präbichl is held in high regard as a first-class ski resort.

The Vordernberg, which lies south of the Erzberg, was once a centre for iron production; Archduke Johann was largely responsible for the development of the Vordernberg coal and steel industry, the history of which can still be traced in numerous places, along with other relics of the area's cultural past. Vordernberg is certainly one of the most interesting towns in the history of European iron manufacture. Apart from numerous old mineworkers' houses and the **Meran House** (Archduke Johann's house), there are several wheelwrights' shops, a rack railway museum, the route of the former ore transport railway, an iron roasting plant and an old blacksmiths to see.

Trofaiach, which lies 6 miles (9 km) from Leoben, is an archetypal summer resort. It was once the main resting place along the iron ore route to Leoben. Today, thanks to its castles – **Möll**, **Stibischofen** and **Oberndorf** – it is an attractive goal for excursions.

Leoben, the second-largest town in Styria (37,000 inhabitants) is not only the seat of an iron and coal university with a worldwide reputation, but also offers much to appeal to the culturally-interested traveller.

On the **Toll Tower**, the town landmark, you can read the following inscription (in German, of course):

"In 1280 I was built here, in 1794 I was on the verge of collapse. I am therefore in any case very old, much

Left, a miniature painting in the library of the Benedictine Abbey in Admont. **Right**, bread, apple wine and fruit schnapps, essentials of rural life.

older than all of you. I saw many enemies pass through me, and yet I remained standing here. I even saw the Franks four times, but the emperor's throne remained safe."

Visitors passing through the "Mushroom Tower" – as the local populace lovingly calls the tower in reference to its toadstool-shaped roof – emerge into the Kärntner Strasse, which winds through the entire town centre. A little further on, on the right-hand side, is the **Municipal Theatre** (founded in 1791). It is the oldest public theatre in Austria, but no longer has a resident troupe of players. Apart from productions from the stages of Vienna and Graz, it hosts touring groups from Germany and Switzerland.

The nearby **Kirchplatz**, dominated by the **Church of St Xavier** (built in around 1660 by the Jesuits) was the setting for a dramatic event on 16–17 July 1949: *Jedermann* (Everyman), an annual highlight of the Salzburg Festival, was performed here.

The Kirchgasse leads to the **Municipal Museum**, housed in what was formerly the castle of the local prince and the seat of the von Dümmerstorffs, a baronial family. One section of the museum is devoted to exceptionally fine examples of wrought-ironwork of past centuries; another commemorates the "French period" in Leoben.

The Mur Valley: If you continue your tour of Styria in a southwesterly direction, you should include an excursion through the **Upper Mur Valley**. The countryside here is still mountainous, but becomes slightly gentler, housing idyllic little villages where old traditions are still cultivated. The setting is ideal for a more restful holiday. Protected by the **Schladminger** and **Rottenmanner Tauern**, many of the village resorts here are renowned for their healthy climate. Walking enthusiasts will find excellent conditions at any season of the year.

Approaching from Leoben, a visit to the famous **Benedictine Abbey** in Seckau is recommended. It was founded in 1140 and, following a fire, rebuilt in the original style in 1259. The abbey is considered one of the finest Romanesque buildings in Central Europe. A cloister courtyard with Tuscan-style pillars, a basilica which retains its Romanesque character, the Imperial Hall, the Homage Hall and the so-called Black Hall are all worth seeing.

Some distance to the west lies the village of Zeltweg, internationally known as the site of the **Österreichring**, the national motor racing circuit. **Judenburg**, **St Peter** and **Unzmarkt-Frauenburg** are all good starting points for walking tours through the **Seetaler Alps** or the **Lower Tauern**.

Castle fanatics should not fail to visit **Teufenbach**. The village has a population of barely 600, but houses a whole series of castles: **Alt-Teufenbach** (12th century), **Neu-Teufenbach** (16th century), the ruins of **Stein Castle** (12th century) and **Pux Castle** (12–14th centuries), and two particularly spectacular rarities: the only two remaining medieval **Underground Castles**. Find them in the caves at Pux.

Murau, a few miles further west, is a centre for Nordic sports. The village itself contains a number of ancient trees dating from medieval times; the **Mur Valley Railway**, which runs between Murau and **Tamsweg**, offers pleasure trips – even for amateur train drivers. In the neighbouring village of **St Georgen** stands the **Styrian Wood Museum**, documenting the close links between the province's inhabitants and their lush green forests.

Those wishing to continue their journey towards Carinthia – or rather, towards Klagenfurt – should turn left on to National Road 95 near **Predlitz**. It leads steadily uphill through the romantic **Turracher Graben** between the **Gurktaler Alps**. The summit – literally – is the **Turrach Heights** (5,850 ft/1,780 metres), which forms the natural boundary between Styria and Carinthia. A trio of lakes, the **Turracher See**, the **Grünsee** and the **Schwarzsee**, invite the visitor to explore the district on foot. In winter the area is a favoured ski centre; in summer, the mountain pastures and forests attract almost as many visitors. Care is recommended on the

Left, Graz is dominated by its clocktower.

downhill stretch into Carinthia, for the road is winding and the inclines fairly steep, with gradients reaching 1 in 4.

In Rosegger's forest home: If, however, you continue your exploration of Styria in a northeasterly direction from Leoben, you will soon enter the **Hochschwab** region. Of note is the resort village of **Aflenz**, often referred to as "the Davos of Styria". Those wishing to recuperate here can either take a Kneipp cure or simply enjoy the healthy, bracing air by taking a long walk – the Hochschwab has now been designated a conservation area. The region also provides the headwaters for the freshwater supply network of Vienna.

A detour to the east, to **Krieglach**, is strongly recommended. Here stands the house where Peter Rosegger, the celebrated Styrian poet, lived and died. It is now a museum. A memorial recalls the famous local son, whose grave you'll find in the village cemetery. Krieglach is also the starting point for walking tours through "Rosegger's native country". A side road on the **Alpl** will

transport the visitor into a woodland landscape that could have come straight out of a Grimm's fairy tale. The **Austrian Walkers' Museum**, Peter Rosegger's birthplace and the famous woodlands make the village an attractive stopping point.

Place of pilgrimage: After crossing over the **Seebergsattel** (4,115 ft/1,255 metres) and taking a drive through romantically wooded countryside, we arrive in the village of **Mariazell**, which lies almost on the provincial boundary between Styria and Lower Austria. The church, Romanesque in origin, was rebuilt in the 14th century as a Gothic-style hall church before being transformed into a baroque edifice between 1644 and 1683. The goal of all pilgrims is the late Romanesque carved wooden **Statue of the Virgin Mary**. Fischer von Erlach created the magnificent high altar of various coloured marbles dominated by a larger-than-life silver Crucifixion group.

Mariazell also offers a variety of attractions making it suitable for a longer

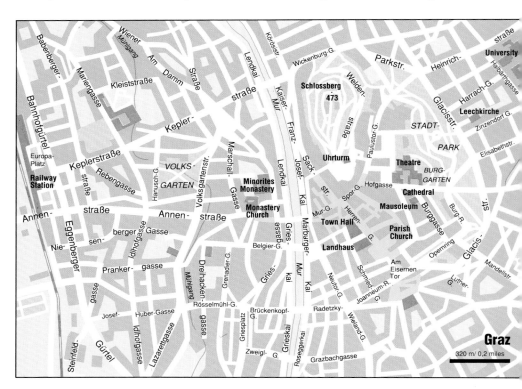

stay: a Kneipp cure complex, tennis courts, fishing facilities, canoeing, riding, and excursions to **Lake Erlauf**, to the **Grünau-Maria Waterfall**, to **Lake Hubertus**, up to the **Bürgeralpe** or into the Hochschwab mountains.

Graz: With its population of 240,000, **Graz** is the second-largest city in Austria. Situated on the Mur, it is an economic and cultural centre settled as long ago as AD 800, but first mentioned in records in 1128. The town was awarded special privileges under the Habsburg King Rudolf I, who managed to seize it from his archrival Ottokar, and from 1379 it became the chief residence of the Leopoldine line. A bastion against the Osmanic threat, Graz was fortified between the 15th and 17th centuries and subsequently withstood a succession of Turkish sieges. The Italian influence on the architecture is unmistakable.

The starting point for a walking tour should be the **Old Town**. Its appearance is characterised by numerous gabled houses dating from the 17th and 18th centuries, some of which still display fine stucco decorations. A favourite meeting place is the **Archduke Johann Fountain**. The four female figures on the bronze fountain are allegorical depictions of the Enns, Mur, Drau and Sann – the four principal rivers of Styria before the partition. The **Town Hall** is a classic example of historicism; not to be missed is the late-Gothic **Franciscan Church** (1520).

Of particular architectural interest is the **Landhaus** (built in the style of the Renaissance by Domenico dell'Allio between 1557 and 1565). It is considered one of the finest intact Renaissance buildings in the south German-speaking area. The arcaded courtyard with its bronze Renaissance well, and the **Knights' Hall**, with its magnificent stucco ceiling depicting the four elements and the signs of the zodiac, should not be missed.

Armour for a medieval army: On the south side of the Landhaus stands the **Arsenal** (1642–44). Its armory contains a unique collection of weapons. In the 17th century it could easily have

A cherub in the old city.

equipped a 28,000-man army of mercenaries. Experts consider this historic arsenal to be the finest in the world; 15th-century suits of armour, old guns, warhorses, two-handed swords, chain mail, shields, muskets and rifles are all on view here. (Opening times: 30 March–31 October, Monday–Friday 9 a.m.–5 p.m, Saturday, Sunday and public holidays 9 a.m.–1 p.m.).

The social focal point of the Old Town is the **Herrengasse**, a fashionable shopping street with a number of noteworthy townhouses. The Herrengasse eventually leads to the square **Am Eisernen Tor**, with the **Türkensäule**, the Turks' Column (also known as the Virgin's Column) in the middle. Graz also contains a number of architectural jewels: the **Castle**, the **Old University**, the **Cathedral**, numerous Baroque palazzi (**Palais Attems**, **Palais Khuenburg**, **Palais Herberstein**) as well as the **Freemasons' House** in the Paulustorgasse.

Not to be missed by any visitor to Graz is the **Schlossberg**. The dolomite rock is 1,550 ft (470 metres) high and can be ascended by funicular in three minutes or by foot in 20–25 minutes. It is crowned by the **Clocktower** (90-ft/28-metres high, with a clock dating from 1712). Visible for miles around, it has become the city landmark.

Graz is also a university town (the **Karl-Franzens University** and the **Technical University** as well as the **Conservatory for Music and the Performing Arts**). It has an active cultural life. Every autumn it is the setting for the avant-garde arts festival *Steirischer Herbst*, and in summer, the *Styriarte*, devoted to classical music.

As expected, Graz can offer the visitor a wide range of gastronomic pleasures. Those in need of refreshment after an extended exploration of the city on foot will find it in one of its many fine restaurants: Gambrinuskeller, Gösserbräu, Krebsenkeller, Pichlmaier's, the Goldene Pastete, Landhaus-Keller, Milchmariandl or Steirerhof. In recent years the Old Town has also become an attractive rendezvous for night owls. There should be something to suit all

Evening time near Schileiten.

tastes among the numerous "in" places, many of which boast live music. A stroll through Graz after dark is in any case a worthwhile affair. Expert opinion claims that the local girls are among the prettiest in the land.

The environs of the Styrian capital are also worth exploring. Approximately one mile west of the main station stands **Eggenberg Château**, (1625–35) with its characteristic four towers. The public rooms are decorated with magnificent stucco and ceiling paintings. Apart from housing a museum of prehistory and antiquity, the castle contains a hunting collection and a coin collection belonging to the provincial museum, the Johanneum.

Ten miles (15 km) north of Graz, on the right bank of the Mur near **Stübing**, is the **Austrian Open Air Museum**. It boasts a collection of old farmhouses, barns and mills from the nine provinces. There are more than 70 exhibits, ranging from cattle troughs to a vast four-square farmyard.

Some 25 miles (40 km) west of Graz, 2 miles (3 km) north-east of **Köflach**, lies the **Piber Stud Farm**. This is the home where the Lipizzaner stallions for the Spanish Riding School in Vienna are bred (daily tours are available). Of Spanish origin, the horses were brought here from Lipica in the republic of Slovenia in Yugoslavia. One should not be surprised to see young foals with black coats; Lipizzaners do not acquire their characteristic grey colour until they are grown.

More wine Country: "I could not tear myself away from the window; I was overcome by a strange emotion; and, as I write, the picture appears living before my eyes. A beautiful day, the peace which ruled everywhere. 'O God!' I thought, 'protect this lovely land; it lies in Thy hand to grant it peace and prosperity. You have stamped it with beauty and peopled it with good men.'"

It was thus that the "Styrian Prince", Archduke Johann, saw and described the **South Styrian Wine Country** in the autumn of 1811 – and thus it has remained, at least in its essentials. It is a land of hills, a land which radiates peace,

calm and a salubrious air. The slopes are clad with vines, interspersed with farmyards with little farmhouses and poplar trees. No eye-catching gimmicks are necessary – the charm of the countryside speaks for itself.

"The Styrian Tuscany" is the nickname given to this corner of the Green Province. Visitors approaching from the north of Graz via **Leibnitz** and passing through **Ehrenhausen**, the Gateway to the South Styrian Wine Country, will find themselves making this comparison. The vineyards cascade steeply down the hillsides to the valley floors; flat-roofed farmhouses are scattered as if by some caprice across the scene; and the graceful poplars recall the similarly-shaped cypresses so familiar in the Tuscan landscape.

Maize, another important component of the local economy, is also much in evidence; only the olive trees are missing. In their place in the South Styrian Wine Country grow sweet chestnuts, known here as *maroni* and roasted over the countless stoves that proliferate

The Admont Abbey library.

beside woodland and roadway when they are harvested. The chestnuts are especially good accompanied by grape juice, which can be sampled at the long tables usually placed near the chestnut stoves or in the kitchens of the neighbouring farmhouses. Musicians perform on accordion and dulcimer by some chestnut stands until well into October.

The **Klapotetz**, a kind of windmill, is an important landmark. Six or eight slanting wings, fixed to a powerful shaft, each carry small hammers positioned to hit an anvil – either furiously if a strong wind is blowing or intermittently if only a breeze is stirring. The actual purpose of this contraption is to scare away the birds, especially starlings, which may have designs on the grapes. Each of the bird-scarers, which are of varying size, power and wood type, produces its own individual sound. The vintners start up their klapotetz each year on St Jacob's Day, 25 July, and shut them down on St Martin's Day, 11 November.

Where the Schilcher grows: The restaurants in the Styrian Wine Country are,

by and large, dedicated to nouvelle cuisine. Old Styrian recipes are imaginatively transformed; the wines with which they are served are in the main piquant Rhine Riesling and Welschriesling varieties. The **Schilcher**, the Styrian speciality produced in the western region of the province, is not so much a wine as a staple of life.

It claims to be the oldest and most original Styrian wine; it was probably first cultivated from a wild vine stock by the Celts. Pope Pius VI reported on the occasion of his journey to Vienna in 1782, that he had been served at the foot of the Koralpe mountain a "light-red sharp-tasting wine, agreeable and refreshing". In the 16th and 17th centuries the Wildbach grape was widely grown in Styria. Archduke Johann, an enthusiastic supporter of Styrian wine-growing, had the Wildbach grape bred in his own vine nurseries in Western Styria. At the end of the 19th century, however, the vine louse destroyed most of the Schilcher stocks; the continuation of the strain could only be assured by means of

Tobacco harvest in Styria.

the grafting of the Wildbach grape on to an American stock. In the middle of the 1960s this ancient Styrian grape species was rediscovered and cultivation along modern lines was begun.

The Schilcher, whose name derives from its colour – it shimmers light to dark red – is one of the rarer Austrian wine varieties. Its production is the only one to be protected by law and restricted to a specific area. Light yellow to ruby-red in colour, it is characterised by a pleasantly fruity yet lively sharpness, a mild yet distinctive bouquet and a balanced, slightly acid taste. It is not an acquired taste. You will either enjoy Schilcher or dislike it intensely from your first mouthful.

The central village in the **Schilcher District** is **Deutschlandsberg**. Dominated by the fortified **Landsberg Castle**, it is an excellent place for resting awhile in one of the numerous rustic taverns. Those who prefer to live more healthily should pay a visit to the neighbouring spas, **Bad Gams** or the mudbaths at **Schwanberg**. Castles and country houses are scattered across the whole of Western Styria: the Renaissance **Palace Hollenegg**, **Frauental Castle**, **Limberg Castle** and the magnificent **Stainz Castle**, ancestral home of the Counts of Merano. Another castle in the area which should not be overlooked is **Wildbach Castle**; Franz Schubert stayed here in 1827. Schilcher is pressed here too, from the Blue Wildbacher Grape. The wine lends its name to the panoramic **Schilcher Road**. It leads across charming ranges of hills, bordered by the pretty wooden vintner houses, winding from **Ligist** via **Greisdorf** to **Stainz**, **Bad Gams**, **Deutschlandsberg** and thence to **Eibiswald**, almost to the Yugoslavian border, where it joins the South Styrian Wine Road.

Way down south, where the Wine Road runs along the national frontier, the traveller should not be surprised to suddenly notice men in Yugoslavian uniforms. It does not mean that he has unknowingly strayed across the border in a region where there are no fences and

Styrian autumn.

watchtowers; they are neighbouring frontier guards who cross over to sample the local wine.

At present, more than 7,400 acres (3,000 hectares) of land are devoted to viticulture in Styria. This means that the province only contributes approximately 5 percent of the national total wine production; the 4,000 wine-growing concerns, however, produce predominantly high-quality vintages.

The South Styrian Wine Country stretches from the **Frauenberg** near Leibnitz to the Slovenian border. **Eichberg**, **Leutschach**, **Glanz**, **Gamlitz**, **Berghausen**, **Ratsch** and many other famous wine-growing villages all lie on the South Styrian Wine Road. Gamlitz, with a total of 870 acres (350 hectares) under cultivation, is regarded as the largest wine-growing village in the province.

The Land of Spas: The southeastern corner of Styria is one of the healthiest regions in Austria. A total of four thermal spa resorts invite the visitor to undertake a health tour. **Bad Radkersburg** lies in the southeast corner of the German-speaking area; the River Mur, flowing along the southern side of the town, also serves to mark the border with Slovenia.

Bad Radkersburg is an attractive town, characterised by well-preserved merchants' and noblemen's houses from the Gothic, Renaissance, Baroque and Art Nouveau periods; in 1978 it was the recipient of the European Gold Medal for Historic Preservation. Today the town is devoted to the cause of health and fitness. The spa buildings, which lie a short distance from the town itself, contain warm spring waters which are considered beneficial for renal complaints of all kinds.

One of the loveliest and largest thermal baths in Austria is **Loipersdorf Therme**. The mineral spring, with a temperature of 145°F (60°C), was only discovered in 1972. The treatment clinic is equipped in accordance with the most up-to-date findings of the medical profession. Primarily rheumatic and other joint disorders are treated here, together

An estate in southern Styria.

with circulatory problems of all major and minor blood vessels.

Apart from this, Bad Loipersdorf boasts a water fun bath for the entire family, with waterfall, wild water stream and a 230-ft (70-metre) water slide. An 18-hole golf course provides alternative outdoor activity for those not on their last legs yet.

The Styrian spa with the longest tradition retains its elegant mid-19th century Biedermeier character. **Bad Gleichenberg** was highly esteemed during Imperial times for its efficacy in the treatment of circulatory and pulmonary disorders.

In recent years cure programmes for children suffering from respiratory disorders have been available here. The village is surrounded by a 50-acres (20-hectare) nature park in which no motor traffic is permitted. Bad Gleichenberg also offers an excellent golf course.

Waltersdorf Therme specialises exclusively in relaxation and fitness. In addition to the wide range of cure facilities on offer, there are walks and well-tended footpaths through peaceful woods, past vineyards, fishponds and fairy tale castles.

The centre of the south Styrian spa district is **Fürstenfeld** (6,000 inhabitants). It contains the largest swimming pool in the country (215,300 sq. ft/20,000 sq. metre). Fürstenfeld is above all a paradise for cyclists, where an excursion to the mighty **Riegersburg** is highly recommended.

The monumental castle, standing majestically on a basalt cliff, was built in 1170 on the site of a Roman fort. It received its present appearance in the 17th century. Riegersburg Castle became the country's main bulwark against Turkish invasion and is today one of the best-preserved medieval castles in Europe. Since the Provincial Exhibition in 1987 (Witches and Sorcerers) it has housed a number of the special displays.

To explore the country south of Graz one should allow plenty of time. All the places that are listed here are easily reached from the provincial capital.

Morning mist over the Hartberger Land.

CARINTHIA

Warm lakes and clear rivers, majestic mountains and secluded valleys, gently rolling meadows and dense woodlands have given the people of Carinthia a happy disposition which often expresses itself in song. An above-average amount of sunshine makes the snow-clad slopes glisten in winter, melts the ice in spring, warms lake waters – and hearts – in summer, and illuminates golden landscapes in autumn.

Klagenfurt and Lake Wörther: Today it is hard to imagine that this region was once rough marshland. Legend tells of a winged dragon which once struck terror into the hearts of the local inhabitants. Its statue is immortalised as the emblem of **Klagenfurt**. It stands in the middle of the **Neuer Platz**, which is actually anything but new; most of the lovely old houses around its perimeter date from the 17th century, as do the **Palais Porcia** and the **Town Hall**. A number of picturesque inner courtyards can be glimpsed off **Kramergasse** and the **Alter Platz**, the adjoining streets. In the vicinity are the **Trinity Column** (1680), the **Palais Goess** (18th-century) and the **Landhaus**, dating from the 16th century, which contains the **Great Blazon Hall** displaying 665 coats of arms.

The house **Zur Goldenen Gans** (the golden Goose), listed in records of 1489, was originally planned as an imperial residence. In return, the emperor handed over his former castle and its park to the estates for the erection of a country house. The estates of the realm was an influential body in Klagenfurt, and at their request, in 1518, the Emperor Maximilian I formally handed over the town to them, a situation unique in German constitutional history. Naturally they cherished their jewel with all their combined strength, creating a chequerboard street layout which was unique at the time, and which characterises the town plan to this day.

Klagenfurt has also retained its traditional function as a shopping centre. Whether you seek traditional costumes or jewellery, gourmet delicacies, fine china, books or exquisite linen, shopping or just browsing through the town's elegant shops is always a delight. There are plenty of cultural attractions too: the **Cathedral Church**, the **Church of the Holy Ghost** (14th-century), the **Town Parish Church** on the Pfarrplatz and the 9th-century **Carolingian Church** in **St Peter am Bichl**. There are also no fewer than 22 castles within a radius of a few miles. On the **Magdalensberg** lies the site of the largest archaeological excavations in Austria – a Noric-Roman town, with an open-air museum and display rooms.

No-one should fail to visit **Minimundus**, the miniature world by Lake Wörther. Many thousands of enthusiastic guests, large and small, visit the exhibition annually between the end of April and the beginning of October. There are more than 150 replicas of famous buildings, all constructed to a scale of 1:25, as well as a miniature railway and a harbour with model ships.

There is no shortage of restaurants in the Carinthian capital. Visitors with a sweet tooth, gourmets, wine buffs and beer drinkers, devotees of spaghetti and chop suey, will all find establishments to suit their tastes. Worthy of particular mention are the café and restaurant in the romantic **Hotel Musil**.

Klagenfurt's advertising campaign claims that "A town by a lake has twice as much feeling for life". Surveying **Lake Wörther**, it's difficult not to agree. The town is justifiably proud of the largest lakeside bathing area in Europe. One of the most modern camp sites in the country is a further example of the town's exemplary infrastructure. In spite of its depth of 275 ft (85 metres) in places, the water temperature can reach 83°F (28°C) – a fact which makes it irresistible for swimmers.

The five ships of the **Wörthersee Fleet** are available for pleasure cruises from the beginning of May until the beginning of October. One of them, the *Thalia*, is the last propeller-driven steamer in Austria. The *Muse of Grace* has had a very varied life since she was launched in 1909. After being destroyed

Preceding pages: high up the Karawanken Mountains. Left, a detail from the crypt of Gurk's Romanesque cathedral.

by an explosion in 1945, she was rescued several years later by high-level politics. Restored by the governement, she hosted the US and Soviet ambassadors for the preparatory discussions leading to the SALT-1 agreement.

The first landing jetty on the north shore is **Krumpendorf**. The atmosphere of this resort community with 4 miles (7 km) of sunny beaches can best be described as informal. Lakeside promenades, bathing beaches, shady avenues and green parks provide the setting for a restful holiday; the requisite amenities are also all here: water skiing, surfing, diving and an 18-hole golf course at nearby Moosburg.

The bronzed Adonises of the area can be found at the bathing areas, boulevard cafés or tennis courts in **Pörtschach**. A peninsula of land with old trees, flower-bordered paths and little bays juts far out into the lake. Nowadays it seems hardly possible that until the middle of the 19th century this was just a sleepy fishing village.

It was the Southern Railway that brought the wealthy citizens of the Habsburg monarchy and it was here that they built their summer residences in order to escape the bustle of the cities. Johannes Brahms was a summer visitor; inspired by the beauty of the lake, he composed a number of songs, sonatas, rhapsodies and a symphony. Those wishing to follow in the great composer's footsteps are advised to visit the **Weisses Rössl** – the White Horse Inn. The parlour with his favourite table has not changed since his time.

Velden is the local high-life arena, for it is the resort favoured by the rich and the beautiful, the sailors and the golfers; this is the home of the surfboard and the convertible. Playground of the jet set, Velden's yacht marina, golf course and casino attract the rich and sporty from all the corners of the globe.

The Illyrians, and later the Baron von Khevenhüller, had quite different reasons for settling in Velden. The **Renaissance Castle** he built here in 1590 was a favoured rendezvous for the upper aristocracy at the end of the 16th cen-

Waterski show on Lake Wörther.

226

tury; in 1920 it was converted into a luxury hotel. Present-day visitors can sleep in the royal chambers. If you can't afford that, a stroll through the castle park must suffice.

Maria Wörth, on the south shore of the lake, is an idyllic spot. The character of the village stems from the church, which dominates the promontory (an island until the water level sank because of the ford on the river Glan); it was built in AD 890 by Bishop Waldo of Freising (in Bavaria) and later extended. The former presbytery church stands on the highest spot; it was rebuilt in the Gothic style following a fire and houses a number of art treasures: a Baroque likeness of St Christopher on the exterior wall, a Baroque high altar, an exquisite statue of the Madonna and Baroque carved wooden altars. Maria Wörth has enjoyed considerable political and economic importance over the years; for this reason, the lake was named after it.

Warm bathing lakes: Since there is insufficient space in this guide to describe individually all 1,270 lakes in the province, details are restricted to those with an average summer temperature of 77°F (25°C) or more. At the top of the list lie **Lake Klopeiner** and **Lake Turner**, where the thermometer registers up to 83°F (28°C). The warmth encourages outdoor activities: sports facilities include 40 tennis courts, three surfing schools and two riding schools. A variety of attractions provides additional interest in the environs; apart from the wooded heights of the **Kolm** and the 170-ft (55-metre) high **Wildenstein Waterfall**, there is the largest Austrian bird reserve in **St Primus am Turnersee**. More than 1,000 feathered creatures, some very rare, live and breed there.

The National Road no. 82 leads through **Brückl** to **St Veit an der Glan**. Three miles (5 km) before reaching the latter, there is a fork to the left leading to **St Georgen am Längsee**. The waters of the lake, nestling between densely wooded mountain slopes, reach summer temperatures of 80°F (27°C). Here are all the ingredients for a varied holiday: sailing, rowing, riding, cycling and

Villach's "Thermal Adventure Pool".

fishing (thanks to careful stock management), not only for pike and carp, but also zander. Highlight of any stay is an excursion to **Hochosterwitz Castle**, a Carinthian landmark. The path up the 525-ft (160-metre) cone-shaped rock passes through no fewer than 14 gateways; next to the eighth stands the castle chapel, with an unusual bronze altar. The castle museum houses an imposing collection of weapons.

The **Keutschach Valley**, south of Lake Wörther, is the setting for four large lakes. Camp sites and bathing areas fringe the shores of **Lake Hafner** and **Lake Rauschel**; the idyllically situated **Bassgeigensee** is shaped like its namesake (*Geige* means violin). And then there is **Lake Keutschach** itself; its 0.5 sq. mile (1.4 sq. km) expanse and water temperatures which reach 80°F (26°C) in summer entice visitors to swim or to hire a rowing, sailing or pedal boat. Its shores are ringed by bathing areas, camp sites, tennis courts, minigolf ranges and even football pitches. The Lake Keutschach Children's Summer is always popular, featuring play festivals, do-it-yourself workshops and "children's gastronomy".

Keutschach itself is the focal point of the valley and possesses two cultural attractions in the form of its 17th-century Baroque castle and the late Romanesque **Church of St George**. Remains of pile dwellings, Neolithic implements and Stone-Age caves bear witness to the region's long history of settlement.

Lake Ossiach offers sports enthusiasts in particular a wide choice of activities. There are 13 schools of sailing, surfing and water-skiing. Exceptionally bold spirits can even attempt parasailing from a motorboat with Sigi Nindler in **Steindorf**. Overcoming initial fears will be rewarded by an extraterrestrial floating sensation and a bird's-eye view of the surrounding countryside. Even the inevitable soft, wet landing is no hardship, for here, too, the water attains a temperature of 80°F (26°C).

Culture addicts can enjoy the events of the Carinthian Summer in the monastery of **Ossiach**; anglers are in their element catching the catfish, pike, tench,

trout, eel and many other fish which abound in the lake; for others there is the attraction of a summer sledging run; an attractive diversion for the young at heart is the remarkable **Elli Riehl Museum** in **Treffen**.

Lake Millstatt is idyllically situated amid gentle countryside, offering – in addition to its exceptional beauty – excellent facilities. Its unspoilt southern shore, densely wooded, is a nature reserve with free access for the public. The sandy beaches and warm, clear waters make the lake ideal for bathing. Parasailing and diving, illustrated lectures and fashion shows, evenings of traditional music and piano recitals are typical of the region's leisure activities. Rounding out the palette is the Kneipp circuit and footpath in **Kaning**, where six flour mills dating from around 1800 can be seen clattering away within a stretch of 2 miles, inviting passersby to a bread-baking session or to a tot of *Mühlengeist*, the local schnapps.

There is another, somewhat longer, excursion which all visitors are urged to

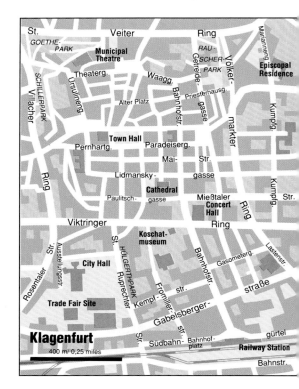

Klagenfurt

undertake. Taking the E 55 route from **Spittal** to **Gmünd**, the traveller should make a point of pausing for long enough to visit the **Porsche Museum**. Between 1944 and 1950 the revolutionary car designer's workshop was situated here; and in 1948 the legendary Porsche 356 was born on this very spot. A road branches off to the northwest towards **Malta**. Six miles (10 km) beyond the village, the tollbooth marks the beginning of the remarkable section of road between Malta and **Hochalm**, which passes through the **"Valley of Falling Waters"**. A new panorama opens up after every hairpin bend – another waterfall, or a glimpse of the 655-ft (200-metre) high wall of the **Kölnbrein Barrage**, the highest dam wall in Austria. Soon we reach the reservoir, which lies amidst mountain peaks at an altitude of almost 6,560 ft (2,000 metres). The **Sporthotel Malta** stands directly next to the dam. A night spent here, with an evening and morning walk, is an unforgettable experience; walkers can set off after breakfast to the **Osnabrück Hut**

A view of Maria Wörth.

or even go on a wild-animal safari.

The **Weissensee** also possesses its own distinctive charm. The fact that at each end it can only be approached from one side makes of it a quiet and peaceful holiday destination. The crystal-clear waters are a shimmering turquoise hue due to the white sandy shores – which also gave the lake its name. In the shallow sections near the bank one can see the stems of the water lilies right down to the lake bed – an unusual sight, also due to the white sand. Lying at an altitude of 3,050 ft (930 metres) above sea level, the Weissensee is the highest Alpine lake in which bathing is still possible; the waters reach temperatures of 77°F (25°C) in summer.

The best amenities are available on the western approaches, on the **Techendorf** shore. Apart from fishing, sailing and water-skiing there are also archery and canoeing facilities. A local speciality is *schlurfen*, a sort of waterborne cross-country skiing on polystyrene boards. There are also golf in summer and curling in winter. The coun-

tryside is a scenario world-famous since it was used as a location in the James Bond film *Licence to Kill*.

The B 87 leads through the lovely **Gitsch Valley** via **Weissbriach** (with a Kneipp cure centre) and **Hermagor** to **Lake Pressegger**. The latter is small but very attractive – and its waters can reach 83°F (28°C) in summer. Flanked to the north by the **Gailtaler Mountains** and to the south by the **Carnic Alps** (with a number of fascinating geological trails), the lake lies in the pretty **Lower Gail Valley**.

There is a 240-ft (72-metre) waterchute providing an exhilarating way of entering the water; for those who prefer to remain above the surface, there are rafting excursions on the nearby River Gail. A delight to both eye and palate is an excursion into the **Upper Gail Valley** as far as **Kötschach-Mauthen**. Not without reason is the gourmet restaurant **Kellerwand** listed among the best eating establishments in the land; in 1990 its proprietor, Sissy Sonnleitner, was elected Chef of the Year.

The Valley of the Möll: If you start from **Spittal**, the best place to start any exploration of the **Möll Valley** is close to **Möllbrücke**, at the confluence of the Möll and the Drava. The first "diversion" lies in store in **Kolbnitz**. It is possible to climb from 2,625 to 6,560 ft (800 to 2,000 metres) without exerting oneself unduly and in a short space of time; or when the weather is fine, take the trip by funicular and underground railway up to the **Reisseck-Lake Plateau**. You are bound to want to prolong your stay here, so go prepared; the invigorating mountain air, good range of accommodation and signposted walks of all grades of difficulty make Reisseck ideal for a short holiday.

Alternatively, or additionally, tackle the next range of mountains: the **Kreuzeck Group**. The funicular runs as far as the **Rosswiese Reservoir**. There are peaks to suit all levels of experience; but those who prefer to take it easy can just sit on the Alpine meadow and enjoy the all-round panorama. The road through the Möll Valley leads on past

Some of the nicest models at a car rally in Velden.

the ruins of **Falkenstein Castle**, arriving next in **Obervellach** with its pretty townhouses and 16th- century tower. Art connoisseurs will enjoy the 400-year-old parish church with its early Dutch altar paintings and Gothic carvings. Also worth visiting is the Baroque **Trabuschgen Castle**.

The National Road 105 branches off here northwards towards **Mallnitz**, a high-altitude resort lying at 3,905 ft (1,190 metres) and marking the southern end of the Tauern Tunnel. Day by day, a car-ferry train system passes on a 10-minute journey through the 28,870-ft (8,800-metre) long tunnel, carrying thousands of cars between Carinthia and the Salzburger Land each year.

Castles, glaciers, waterfalls: Castle addicts will be in seventh heaven when they visit **Groppenstein Castle**. Its roots reach back to the 13th century. It stands majestically over the countryside, next to the waterfall of the same name.

We soon reach **Flattach** – a small village, but one of the most important centres in the Möll Valley. It is the starting point of the magnificent panoramic road leading up to the **Möll Valley Glacier**. Every bend opens up new perspectives, each more breathtaking than the last, until, at 7,215 ft (2,200 metres), the road reaches the valley station of the mountain railway. This takes you across the glacier itself up to the mountain station, situated at 9,185 ft (2,800 metres). If you don't feel inclined to jump on your skis (forgetting them is no problem, for all equipment can be rented here) nor to climb a 9,845-ft (3,000-metre) peak, you may prefer to enjoy the intoxicating mountain air, the blue sky and glittering snow from the sun terrace of the mountain restaurant.

Also near Flattach lies the counterpart to the panoramic view of the Möll Valley Glacier: the wildly romantic **Ragga Gorge**, carved over the millennia. A meticulously constructed system of bridges and steps permits the visitor to traverse the remarkable site without difficulty, admiring the eight thundering waterfalls formed by the Ragga torrent as it plunges downhill.

Traditional baking in the Carinthian mountains.

Typical of the resorts of the central Möll Valley is the village of **Rangersdorf**, which boasts the ruins of a castle first mentioned in records in 1278. **Lainach**, too, with its miniature iron and sulphur spring, is a good choice for a restful holiday. **Winklern**, nestling between meadows and fields, lies in a conservation area. The village's landmark, the **Toll Tower**, was built in about 1500 on foundations which probably date back to Roman times.

From this point onwards the course of the cheerfully babbling Möll (the name is of Celtic origin) turns northwards, passing through pretty villages on the way to **Döllach-Grosskirchheim**. The settlement – known even in Roman times – was the gold mining centre of the Tauern in the 15th and 16th centuries. As many as 3,000 miners extracted the precious metal from 800 different sites. The Museum of Gold Mining, housed in **Kirchheim Castle**, contains interesting displays on the subject. A mountain walk through the nearby **Zirknitz Valley** affords views of two magnificent waterfalls, the "Neunbrunnen" (Nine Springs Falls) and the "Gucklöcher des Lindwurms" (Dragon's Peepholes).

The **Upper Möll Valley Mountain Road** leads on from here via **Mitten, Apriach** and **Ober-** and **Unterschachern** to Heiligenblut, where it joins the Grossglockner Road.

Long and winding road: The discussions are endless as to which high-altitude mountain road is the most beautiful in the world. Definitely deserving of a place on the short list in any case is the **Grossglockner Alpine Road**, a curvaceous beauty which is inaccessible for long periods each year, and only open to traffic between May and October. Even in summer there may be times when the road is impassable. But visitors who make allowances for its unpredictable conditions – a course strongly recommended in the interests of safety – will be rewarded with a succession of truly unforgettable vistas.

This major project, planned by civil engineer Hofrat Franz Wallack, employed more than 3,000 workers

Mountain pastures near Weissensee.

between 1930 and 1935. The impressive result was the "Dream Road of the Alps", 30 miles (50 km) long and 25 ft (7.5 metres) wide and with a maximum gradient of 12 percent. Before venturing up the mountain, however, there are two sights worth visiting in **Heiligenblut**, our starting point.

The first is the Gothic **Parish church of St Vincent**, dating from the 15th century. It contains the most important winged altarpiece in Carinthia and an equally renowned, elaborately decorated sacramental shrine. The second recommendation is to join the local gold and silver panning society. This entitles you to search for the precious metals at three different places using the traditional hand washing method.

All equipment is provided, all finds may be kept, and the goldrush atmosphere even extends to an evening campfire. There is no doubt about your chances of striking it rich; the mountains behind the Fleisstal are called the **Goldberge** – the Golden Mountains.

Back on our route, the first spectacular view is of the **Hoher Sonnblick** (10,190 ft/3,105 metres), with the highest weather station in Austria. About 4 miles (6 km) further on, the route forks off to the left on to the glacier road leading to **Franz-Josephs-Höhe**. From the plateau, which at an altitude of 7,750 ft (2,360 metres) lies above the tree line, you can see across the **Pasterze Glacier** to the summit of the Grossglockner (12,460 ft/3,800 metres) beyond. (You may feed the marmots which sometimes appear here when visitors arrive.)

The Pasterze, the biggest glacier in Austria, was recently surveyed by scientists, who came to the conclusion that it was 720 ft (220 metres) thick. With a surface area of 70 sq. miles (190 sq. km), that represents a vast amount of water. A funicular transports visitors directly to the edge of the ice sheet; if you are wearing suitable shoes, you can venture on to the slippery surface.

Another worthwhile excursion is the **Gamsberg Nature Path**, which can be tackled with ease and which leads alongside the Pasterze to an idyllic waterfall.

The Fuscher Törl on the Grossglockner Alpine Road.

Noticeboards provide information about the glacier, the marmots and the ecological state of the biotope.

Returning to the Guttal fork along our main route, take the left-hand road leading towards the **Hochtor**. Here, at 8,450 ft (2,575 metres) above sea level, lies the boundary between Carinthia and the Province of Salzburg. The Grossglockner Road continues through the unique **Hohe Tauern National Park**, the largest continuous stretch of unspoiled countryside in Austria. Passing the picturesquely situated **Fuscher Lake**, we reach one of the most impressive stages of our journey: a pause at the **Edelweissspitze** (8,455 ft/2,580 metres). The spectacular panorama includes no fewer than 37 mountain peaks over 9,840 ft (3,000 metres).

In Carinthia, the **Lavant Valley** is a paradise. It begins in **Reichenfeld**, at the foot of the **Seetaler Alps**. Enclosed by the **Packalpe**, the **Zirbitzkogel** and the **Hohenwarth** peaks, this pretty village marks the upper end of the valley. It is an ideal resort for a varied holiday thanks to its well-developed sports infrastructure for both summer and winter, and a healing spring, the "Kölzer Sauerbrunn".

Bad St Leonhard can also offer excellent spa facilities, for its sulphur springs provide rejuvenation and relaxation from mid-May to mid-October. In addition to the numerous folklore festivals there is a fine Gothic parish church and 60 miles (100 km) of signposted footpaths leading up to an altitude of 5,905 ft (1,800 metres). There is also an excellent network of mountain refuges.

It was in **Waldenstein Castle** in **Preitenegg** (3,525 ft/1,075 metres) that the Carinthian anthem was composed in the 19th century. This little community on the **Packsattel Mountain Road** boasts a late Gothic parish church with a Baroque interior and a small colection of notable paintings.

In all senses of the word, **Wolfsberg** is the centre of the Lavant Valley. Its mountain parks, the **Saualpe** and the **Koralpe**, invite the visitor to wander at **Isolation.**

234

leisure, to tarry awhile, or to fly – by motorised aircraft, glider or hang-glider.

The ancient diocesan town of **St Andrä**, which grew up around the pilgrimage church of **St Mary of Loreto**, enchants the traveller with its lovely setting amidst verdant meadows, encircled by castles and palaces. Gourmets flock here in May and June for the "Asparagus Sundays"; in autumn, fruits are pressed amidst scenes of great merriment, and a culinary walking tour covering local specialities takes place. The Lavant Valley local museum, in **St Ulrich**, is also worth visiting; it provides a well-displayed insight into the life and traditions of the region.

St Paul im Lavanttal is often referred to by locals as "Carinthia's treasure chest", a name it owes to its **Benedictine Abbey**, founded in 1091. The museum displays collections featuring remarkable masterpieces from a wide variety of cultures. The exhibitions are open to the public during the summer months when guided tours are conducted round the abbey.

Lavamünd marks the end of the Lavant Valley, and the end of Austrian territory. The **River Drava**, which flows into the Lavant at this point, forms for several miles the border with Yugoslavia. The little town itself lies far from the madding crowd, its picturesque scenery attracting large numbers of anglers and walkers. But the wine-growing regions of Styria and Yugoslavia are also close enough to encourage a detour in search of a fine vintage.

The Gurk Valley: Standing sentinel over the entrance to the Gurk Valley at **Zwischenwässern** is **Pöckstein Castle**, a late Baroque bishop's residence. Its magnificent audience rooms make it a much-visited architectural curiosity. This is also the starting point of the **Gurk Valley Museum Railway**, which puffs along to **Glödnitz** from early June to late September – a unique experience for railway fanatics, romantics and keen photographers. You can even apply for an amateur engine-driver's certificate .

Strassburg is dominated by the castle of the same name, which is visible

The *Garden of Eden* in the Bischofskapelle in Gurk Cathedral.

for miles around. The original building dates from the year 1131; between the 14th and 17th centuries it was constantly altered and added to, and served as the summer residence of the Bishops of Gurk until 1780. Apart from viewing the exquisite arcaded courtyard and the castle chapel, the visitor should not miss the **Church of Lieding**, an architectural gem with a 1,000-year history.

Countess Emma, the consort of the ruler of Carinthia and the region's patron saint, founded the **Romanesque Cathedral** in Gurk during the 12th century. The priory courtyard was built in the 15th century; the crypt, supported by 100 pillars, the Gothic paintings and the most important Romanesque series of murals in the German-speaking world give it architectural and artistic significance. The celebrated Raphael Donner immortalised his memory with the transept altar and a set of lead reliefs on the pulpit. When the sun is shining brightly, the 13th-century stained-glass windows in the West Porch transform the light into cascades of colour as it enters.

Weitensfeld is a village which appeals to the visitor on second sight. It is a centre in which ancient Carinthian customs, such as the "Kranzlreiten", are still observed. The district also possesses a rich artistic heritage. Austria's oldest item of worked glass, the **Magdalene Windowpane**, originated in a church in Weitensfeld. The church in the neighbouring village of Zweinitz houses frescoes in the apse which are real jewels of sacred art.

The road soon forks off to the right towards **Flattnitz**, a resort village situated at an altitude of 4,590 ft (1,400 metres). Here, where once the Roman legions crossed the Alps, the walkers gather in summer and the skiers in winter. The **Spitzeralm** and the **Pfandlhütte** are popular goals. The Pass Church contains magnificent frescoes which provide a moving reminder of the faith of early Christians.

Deutsch Griffen is the site of one of the few remaining medieval fortified churches in the entire Alpine region. A flight of 200 steps leads up to the sacred

Canoeing down the Isel.

edifice, picturesquely situated on a hillside and housing a collection of 15th-century frescoes.

Standing at the point where the Gurk Valley becomes increasingly wild and romantic is **Sirnitz**. **Albeck Fortress**, today a romantic ruin, experienced its Golden Age at the time of Barbarossa, later becoming the administrative seat of the Bishops of Gurk. Visitors are captivated by the octagonal form of the late Gothic charnel house attached to the medieval parish church. After a detour via **Hochrindl**, which lies at 5,250 ft (1,600 metres) in the middle of the Gurktaler Alps, the road crosses the Gurk once more near **Ebene Reichenau** before climbing a gradient of 1 in 4 up to the **Turracher Höhe** (5,850 ft/1,785 metres). The spectacular panorama is enlivened by the emerald-green waters of the mountain lakes; even the air tastes of pine woods. There are plenty of choices for a mountain walk; for those preferring not to exert themselves too much, there are two chair lifts climbing to 6,590 and 7,350 ft (2,010 and 2,240

metres) respectively. A **Mineral Museum** (closed on Wednesday), a summer toboggan run and a total of 800 hotel beds also tempt visitors to stay a day or so.

The Drava Valley: Villach, a chic and historically important town, lies at the heart of the Carinthian Lake District. The Romans built a fort and a bridge over the Drava here during the first century, constructing paved roads as they did so. It was not until 1759 that the town and its surrounding area were ceded to Austria from the Bishopric of Bamberg; they were purchased by Maria Theresa. In the 16th century, when Paracelsus spent his youth here, the town was already the economic and cultural centre of Carinthia. He later described the healing power of the springs which were to move Napoleon to rapturous enthusiasm. Even today, the warm waters offer relaxation and healing to guests from all over the world in a number of well-planned cure and bathing centres.

The National Road no. 100 leads on

Starting young.

through the gradually widening lower valley of the Drava via **Kellerberg** to **Feistritz**. Numerous finds bear witness to the fact that not only Villach but also the entire surrounding area was settled in the 1st century. Even the high-altitude plateau on which the Celtic town of Görz originally lay bears traces of its historic past in the fortifications on the **Duel Hill** and the excavations of an early Christian basilica.

Paternion nestles between sunny mountain slopes and shady woodland, offering a range of amenities for the holidaymaker. Between swimming, fishing and walking and skating, curling and cross-country skiing there is the opportunity to witness the lovely altars of the **Pilgrimage Church of St Paternianus** as well as, on an eminence, a castle complex dating from the 16th century.

Another rewarding detour is the trip to **Stockenboi am Weissensee** to see the remarkable architecture of the farmhouses. **Spittal an der Drau** is also an exceptionally pretty little town. It lies on the boundary between the upper and lower Drava valleys; its fine houses, historic monuments and elegant shops make it worth visiting whether one's interests lie in sightseeing or shopping. Stately **Porcia Castle** unites the civilisations of past and present: not only does it house a fascinating museum of local history, but its pretty arcaded courtyard serves as setting for the drama festival held in August and September each year.

Continuing through **Lendorf** – a fine-weather community in the main, consisting of eight little farming hamlets – the road B 100 leads on towards **Sachsenburg**. The Drava Valley becomes very narrow here, and is therefore also known as the Sachsenburg Defile. Ruins of several castles and fortresses dating from the 13th century testify to the valley's strategic importance in those days, and hence to the necessity to defend it.

Greifenburg is often known as the "Heart of the Upper Drava Valley". As early as the 2nd century, this market

The Gothic church of Magdalensberg.

238

town in the shadow of its castle was an important staging post on the Roman road to Gurina. Today, there is a newly constructed artificial lake for bathing with a 1,310-ft (400-metre) long beach. **Berg im Drautal** appeals to even the most discriminating traveller, offering a good choice of hotels with indoor and outdoor swimming pools and a wide variety of restaurants. For walking enthusiasts there are the **Gaisloch** and **Ochsenschluchtklamm**, two unspoiled, romantic gorges; adventurous souls might enjoy a boat trip on the Drava in an inflatable raft.

Crystal-clear air and plenty of sunshine are the hallmarks of **Dellach im Drautal**, nestling in pretty countryside and the location of one of the most attractive camp sites in the Alps.

Further to the north lies the **Drassnitz Rift**, setting for the picturesque **Weit Valley Waterfall**; to the south, perched on a high rock overlooking the Drava on the other side of the valley, stands **Stein Castle**, whose existence was first recorded in 1190.

A short distance further on, a road branches off to the right towards **Irschen**, an attractive resort village on the southern slopes of the **Kreuzeck Range**. The local **Parish Church of St Dionysius**, originally Romanesque in style, was rebuilt in the 15th century. It contains an exceptionally fine winged altarpiece and murals dating from the 14th century.

Oberdrauburg is the last bastion of the Carinthian section of the Drava Valley before the border with East Tyrol. A market town lying at the foot of the Lienzer Dolomites, Oberdrauburg was first settled in the 13th century; today it offers the traveller a number of historical sights as well as a full range of tourist amenities. The castle on the eastern side of the town dates from the 16th century; it was badly damaged during World War II and subsequently rebuilt, losing much of its original character in the process. The **Church of St Leonhart**, however, housing a winged altarpiece and 15th-century murals, has retained its aura of historical charm.

he dark
rags of the
ienzer
olomites.

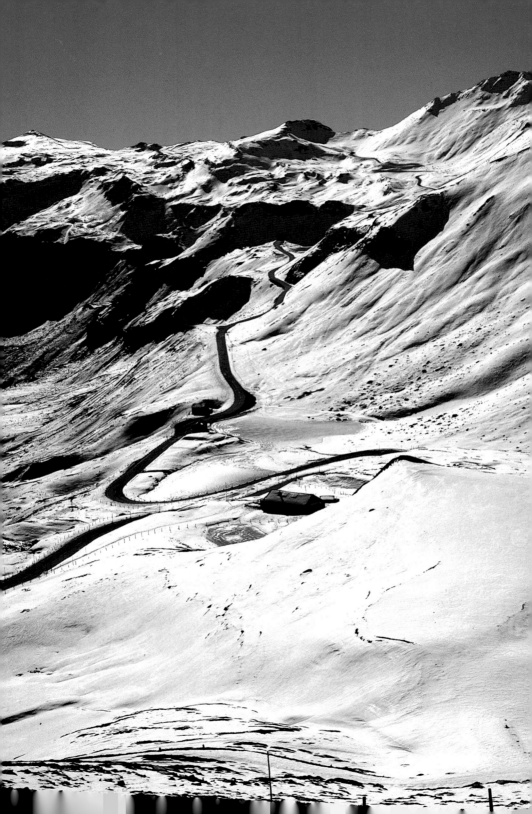

EAST TYROL

Nikolsdorf marks the beginning of the East Tyrolean section of the Drava Valley on the way to Lienz. There is a woodland swimming pool in which you can splash and sunbathe in glorious surroundings. Not far beyond, **Lavant** appears on the left-hand side, recognisable from a distance by its pretty **Pilgrimage Church of St Peter and St Paul**. Since 1948, the foundations of settlements dating from various different eras have been discovered. A mile or so further on lies *Aguntum*, an excavated Roman town and a diocesan city until 622 AD. Many rare and interesting exhibits are on display here.

Not far away is **Dölsach,** a resort village at 2,420 ft (740 metres) above sea level. Like the villages of **Amlach** and **Tristach** – situated on a pretty little lake – Dölsach lies in the **Lienzer Dolomites** resort area, the starting point in summer for delightful mountain walks

eft, the
rossglockner
lpine Road.
elow,
vaterfall in
ie Virgental
alley in the
ast Tyrol.

and in winter for skiing trips, curling and cross-country skiing.

Lienz is the capital of East Tyrol. It was an Illyrian settlement as long ago as 500–1000 BC; in fact, the region surrounding Lienz at several points in history acquired considerable importance; between 1250 and 1500, the Counts of Görz resided at **Bruck Castle** near Lienz. At this time the town was subject to planned development; later, it passed to the Counts of Wolkenstein and finally to the Convent of Halle. In 1798 the town centre was destroyed by a major fire; only on the right bank of the Isel did there remain traces of the old city defences. The Soldiers' Memorial Chapel, built by Clemens Holzmeister, also contains the tomb of the painter Albin Egger-Lienz, as well as that of Franz Defregger – a native of East Tyrol.

The Puster Valley: Southwest of Lienz, behind the Lienz defile, begins the **Puster Valley**. One way of getting a preview of this breathtaking countryside, is to climb the **Sternalm** – the first half of the ascent as far as **Hochstein** is accessible by twin chair lift – from which you will have a magnificent panoramic view. Shortly after **Leisach** the mountain road forks off to **Bannberg**; from here, a toll road leads almost as far as the Hochstein refuge. **Assling**, too, lies on the "sun terrace" on the mountain road; it is the largest village in the area. It boasts a **Game Park** with rare native animals; in winter, Assling can offer a newly-created ski area including a 4,265 ft (1,300 metres) lift.

Down in the valley again, on the National Road 100, lies **Thal**. The Gothic parish church of St Korbinian, dedicated in 1486, contains a late Gothic Crucifixion group dating from 1490, three altars of considerable artistic merit and and two paintings by Pacher (ca. 1500). **Mittewald**, situated directly at the mouth of the **Burger Valley**, is the starting point for an enjoyable excursion, lasting several hours, to the **Sichelsee** (8,195 ft/2,500 metres above sea level). On the sunny north slopes of the valley nestle four idyllic little villages: **Unterried**, **Wiesen**, **Anras** and **Asch**. Accessible by means of a narrow road, they all lie at altitudes of 3,280 ft (1,000 metres) or more.

Running parallel to the B 100 through the entire Puster Valley is a Roman road. **Abfaltersbach** is popular for its sulphur springs; the mineral baths provide relief for a variety of ailments. **Abfaltern**, on the sunny northern slope, has a church dedicated in 1441 which is worth a brief visit. Traversing **Strassen**, with its late Gothic church of St James, the road next passes through **Heinfels** and **Panzendorf**. The name of **Heinfels Castle**, the valley landmark and the property of the ancient Görz Family, is derived from the Hunnenfels – Huns' Rock. During the Venetian Wars, Emperor Maximilian I surrounded it with a defensive wall to protect the arsenal.

Silian is a sports resort dominating the end of the Austrian section of the Puster Valley. Only a short distance beyond lies the Italian border, which already makes its presence felt here in the mild climate. Each season has its own particular charms: the magnificent colours of the blossom in spring, the luxuriant green of the mountain pastures in summer, the riot of rusts and golds in autumn and the picture-postcard whiteness of the snow in winter. The village itself, with a population of 2,000, presents a broad range of leisure amenities: indoor swimming pool and sauna, tennis courts, hang-gliding school, shooting range, fitness circuit, library and reading room, cycling paths, toboggan run, skating and curling rinks, Alpine and cross-country ski schools and a number of facilities for children. The most romantic way of exploring the countryside – and falling in love with this part of East Tyrol – is by a horse-drawn sleigh.

Matrei: In a spectacular setting against the background of the **High Tauern** lies the little town of **Matrei**. Majestically dominating the scene from a high crag is the landmark **Weissenstein Castle**, dating from the 12th century. Standing in solitary splendour is the **Church of St Nicholas**; 800 years old, it houses some remarkable Romanesque wall paintings. *The Healing* evokes memo-

Hydrospeeding through a gorge.

ries of the frescoes in the cathedral of Gurk. In the tower are three stone sculptures dating from the first half of the 15th century. The impressive **Parish Church** originally dates from the 14th century, but acquired its present form between 1768 and 1784, when it was rebuilt by Wolfgang Hagenauer.

Every year in September the charming **St Matthew's Market** takes place in Matrei, but most visitors actually come for the mountains. Over 100 with peaks above 9,845 ft (3,000 metres) can be tackled from here. The **Mountain Climbing Advisory Office** on the Rauterplatz was opened in the summer of 1989; it offers guided tours of the entire region and provides information, touring tips and meteorological information. The mountaineering tradition is an important part of life here; on 11 August 1865 an expedition starting in Matrei conquered the **Grossvenediger** (12,055 ft/3,675 metres) from its most attractive side – via the **Innergschlöss-Alm**. Nowadays the "Grossvenediger Adventure" is offered as part of a package in a number of variations by the Mountaineers' Office.

Matrei has more to offer than just mountain walks: trekking to the isolated **High Tauern** miners' huts, mountain biking, paragliding and kite flying, climbing and the flying of model aeroplanes are just some of the attractions in this pretty village community. Alpine rafting on the Isel is a classic adventure for lovers of water sports. Fly-fishing enthusiasts can also indulge in their hobby here; information can be obtained at the Hotel Rauter.

Visitors who would like to try one of the many sports available here, but who have left their equipment at home, will be delighted to discover that the Mountain and Sports Gear Rental Service can supply most needs. Another pleasant surprise is the Kindergarten for visitors' children situated in Goldried Castle.

Even after night falls, there is no excuse for boredom, for concerts, theatrical performances and multi-media lectures provide entertainment even in this remote corner of the mountains.

Winter fodder for the animals.

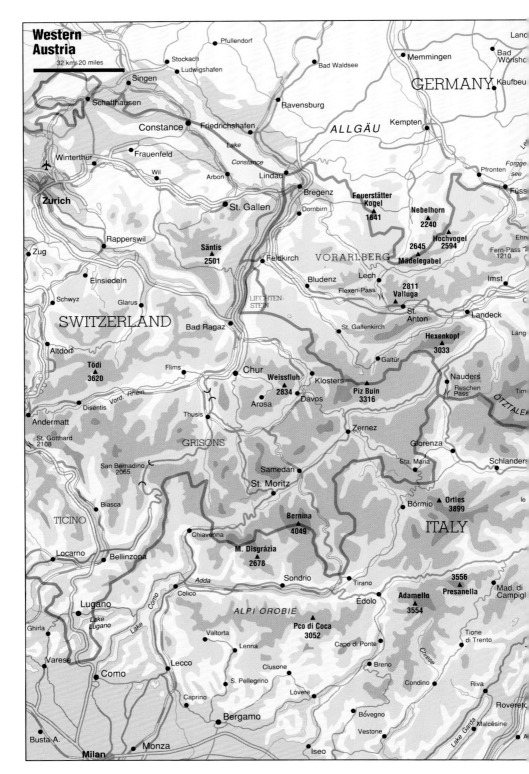

Western Austria

32 km/20 miles

Pfullendorf
Stockach
Ludwigshafen
Bad Waldsee
Memmingen
Land
Bad Wörlsho
Singen
Kaufbeu

GERMANY

Schaffhausen
Ravensburg

Constance
Friedrichshafen
ALLGÄU
Kempten

Winterthur
Frauenfeld
Lake
Constance
Pfronten
Forgge
see

Wil
Arbon
Lindau
Füss

Zurich
Bregenz
Feuerstätter Kogel
1641
Nebelhorn
2240

St. Gallen
Dornbirn
Hochvogel
2594

Rapperswil
Säntis
2501
Feldkirch
VORARLBERG
2645
Mädelegabel
Fern-Pass
1210
Ehn

Zug
Bludenz
Lech
2811
Valluga
Imst

Einsiedeln
LIECHTEN-
STEIN
Flexen-Pass
St.
Anton
Landeck

Schwyz
Glarus
St. Gallenkirch
Hexenkopf
3033
Läng

SWITZERLAND
Bad Ragaz
Galtür
Nauders
Reschen
Pass

Altdorf
Flims
Chur
Weissfluh
2834
Klosters
Piz Buin
3316
ÖTZTALE
Tim

Tödi
3620
Davos
Zernez

Vord. Rhein
Arosa
Samedan

Disentis
Thusis
GRISONS
Glorenza
Schlanders

Andermatt
San Bernadino
2065
Samedan
Sta. Maria

St. Gotthard
2108
St. Moritz
Bórmio
Ortles
3899

Biasca
Bernina
4049

TICINO
Chiavenna
M. Disgrázia
2678
ITALY

Locarno
Bellinzona
Adda
Colico
Sondrio
Tirano
3556
Presanella
Mad. di
Campigl

Lugano
ALPI OROBIE
Édolo
Adamello
3554

Ghirla
Lake
Lugano
Valtorta
Lenna
Pco di Coca
3052
Capo di Ponte
Tione
di Trento

Varese
Lecco
Clusone
Breno
Condino
Riva

Como
S. Pellegrino
Lóvere
Bóvegno
Malcésine

Caprino
Roveret

Busta-A.
Bergamo
Iseo
Vestone
Lake Garda

Milan
Monza

Munich

Ebersberg
Wasserburg
Burghausen
Braunau
Mattighofen

ersee
Starnberger See
Weilheim
Rosenheim
Chiemsee
Traunstein
Mondsee
Prien
Freilassing
Salzburg
St. Wolfgang
Wolfgang-See

Bad Tölz
Bad Reichenhall
Berchtesgaden
SALZKAMMERGUT

Kochel
Tegernsee
BAVARIAN
ALPS
Watzmann
2713
Königs-See
SALZBURG

Garmisch-Partenkirchen
Walchensee
Kufstein

KARWENDEL
Wörgl
Kitzbühel
Zell am See
St. Johann
Radstadt

spitze
64
ERSTEIN
Grubenkaar
2662
Schwaz
Fügen
KITZBÜHLER ALPS

Innsbruck
Gerlos Pass 1507
Mittersill

2248
Patscherkofl
Zell am Ziller
AUSTRIA

UBAIER
ALPS
Rosenjoch
2798
Mayrhofen
Hintertux
Gross Venediger
3360
Felber Tauern Tunnel
Grossglockner
3798
Badgastein

erhütl
511
Brenner Pass
Brennero
ZILLERTALER ALPS
Hochfeiler
3523
Matrei
Heiligenblut
HIGH TAUERN

St. Leonhard
Mezzaselva
Brunico
Huben
Obervellach

Merano
Bressanone
Brixen
TYROL
Dobbiaco
Lienz
Hochkreuz
2704
Spittal

Ortisei
Cortina d'Ampezzo
S. Stefano di Cad.
Timau
Weissen-See
Hermagor

Bolzano
Pordoi
3342
Marmolada
Arta

Cavalese
DOLOMITES
Pieve di Cadore
Tolmezzo
FRIULI-VENEZIA GIULIA

Sover
Cima d'Asta
2847
S. Martino
Agordo

Belluno
Maniago
Artegna
Kobarid

Feltre
M. Cavallo
2250
Cividale

Primolano
Udine

Asiago
Vittório Véneto
Pordenone
Codróipo
Cormons

Valstagna
Conegliano
VENETO

Bassano

SALZBURG

Many towns in Austria are blessed with splendid churches, squares and ornamental fountains; in none but Salzburg, however, do they enjoy such a vibrant, cosmopolitan atmosphere and such magnificent surrounding scenery. Home of Wolfgang Amadeus Mozart (1756–91), Salzburg is one of the most visited towns in Austria, especially during its annual tribute to the composer, the Festival, when Mozart lovers stream here from all corners of the globe.

The **Mönchsberg** and the **Burgberg** – the two mountains within the city boundaries – still stand sentinel over the narrow alleys of the **Old Town,** with their tall, narrow merchants' houses, hidden arcaded courtyards, baroque-domed churches, palaces and spacious squares of the prince-bishops' quarter. Clinging to the side of Mönchsberg, and dominating the old town is the fortress of **Hohensalzburg**, a symbol of the powerbase which shaped so many chapters in the city's history .

Princes and archbishops: The Celts were the first to recognise the region's attractions; and it was here that the Romans built Juvavum ("the seat of the god of heaven"), their administrative centre. Over the course of a few hundred years, the see founded by St Rupert shortly before AD 700 grew into the mightiest spiritual principate in South Germany. In the 13th century its archbishops were given the title of Princes of the Holy Roman Empire of German Peoples. Thanks to their considerable income from the salt and silver mines of the area they were able to express their power in fine buildings. Three bishops in particular, all possessing an awareness of aesthetics as well as of their own might, stamped the town with the characteristics it still bears today.

Wolf Dietrich von Raitenau (Archbishop from 1587) was a typical Renaissance prince, who dreamed of creating a "Rome of the North". He charged the Italian architect Scamozzi with the task of constructing a cathedral larger than St Peter's in Rome. At the same time he commissioned Mirabell Palace for his mistress Salome von Alt, by whom he had 12 children. His successor, Marcus Sitticus von Hohenems (Archbishop from 1612), reduced the cathedral to a more modest scale, but commissioned a summer residence, Hellbrunn Palace, set in an extensive park and surrounded by an elaborate system of fountains. Paris Lodron (Archbishop from 1619) was finally able to dedicate the cathedral in 1628; it was during his term of office that the new Bishop's Palace was also completed.

In Renaissance and Baroque times, the starting point for the building activity of the prince-bishops was the **Residenzplatz**, an excellent place to begin a tour of the town. In the square stands the 50-ft (15-metre) baroque fountain (1661). Grouped around this focal point – partly following the dictates of history and partly the whims of the prince-bishops – stand the most important episcopal buildings. On the south side is the **Cathedral**, begun according to Renaissance precepts in 1614 and completed in the baroque style in 1655. If you walk across from the Residenzplatz to the **Domplatz**, you will gain a view of the West Front, built of light-coloured Salzburg marble and framed by twin towers capped by cupolas surmounted by lanterns.

As a result of the performances of Hofmannsthal's *Everyman*, the three arcaded porticos with their four statues have achieved world fame. The latter depict the apostles St Peter and St Paul flanked by two local saints, St Rupert and St Virgil. Watchfully surveying the scene are statues of the four evangelists, Moses and Elijah, whilst a statue of Christ dominates the ensemble. The contemporary bronze doors are dedicated to the themes of Faith, Hope and Charity. The baptismal font in the left aisle, dating from 1321, is a relic from the previous Romanesque church. So, too, is the crypt, in which traces of the original walls have been exposed. The mosaic-tiled floor shows the ground plans of the three cathedrals built in succession upon this site. The priceless treas-

Preceding pages: Salzburg by night. **Left,** Austria's brilliant actor Klaus Maria Brandauer as *Jedermann*.

ures assembled by the bishops across the centuries can be seen in the **Cathedral Museum**.

Forming the western boundary of the Residenzplatz is the **Bishop's Palace**. Archbishop Wolf Dietrich von Raitenau had it constructed from 1595 to replace the previous 12th-century building. The state apartments of the Residenz are predominantly decorated in late baroque and Classicistic style. A total of 15 rooms are lavishly appointed with murals, stucco, paintings, tapestries and statues. The young Mozart frequently performed for the Prince-Bishop and his guests in the Conference Hall. The **Gallery of Paintings** contains works from the 16th–19th centuries. Opposite the Bishop's Palace, on the east side of the square, stands the **Glockenspiel**, erected in 1705 and comprising 35 bells cast in Antwerp.

To the west of the Domplatz stands the **Franciscan Church**, dedicated in 1221 and demonstrating an interesting transition between the Romanesque and Gothic styles. The nave is still completely Romanesque and creates a rather austere impression due to the massive columns and capitals decorated with stylized foliage and animal figures. The light, late Gothic chancel dates from the 15th century and features stellar vaulting supported by cylindrical pillars with palm-tree capitals. Of the late Gothic winged altarpiece created by Michael Pacher in 1496, only the Madonna remains; it is integrated in the baroque high altar.

The first Christians: Tucked away on the north side of the Burgberg are the **Collegiate Church of St Peter** and its churchyard. The church itself is a Romanesque triple-aisled basilica; during the 17th and 18th centuries it was completely redesigned and as a result acquired elaborate frescoes and ornate stucco. The nave vaulting contains frescoes depicting scenes of the life of St Peter; the walls above the great arches are decorated with a Passion and a Crucifixion scene. Beneath the clerestory are scenes of the life of St Benedict on the left and St Rupert on the right. St

City skyline with the baroque catherdal.

Peter's Churchyard is surrounded on three sides by arcades housing family tombs; hewn from the rock face above are the catacombs, in which the first Christians celebrated Mass during the 3rd century.

Wealth and power: The fortress of **Hohensalzburg** is a symbol of the worldly power of the prince-bishops. Archbishop Gebhard began the construction of the stronghold, on the site of a Roman castrum, in 1077, during the Investiture Dispute. The castle was continuously extended until the 17th century. Bishop Leonhard von Keutschach had the royal apartments furnished. Conducted tours around the state apartments, dungeons and torture chamber take place throughout the day. One particularly interesting item is a monumental porcelain tile stove dating from 1501 in the so-called Golden Room; it portrays Biblical scenes and the princes of the time.

To the east of the fortress lies the Benedictine convent of **Nonnberg**. It was founded at the beginning of the 8th

century by St Rupert, which makes it one of the oldest convents still in existence. Its late Gothic church dates from the end of the 15th century. Its greatest treasures are a Gothic winged altarpiece, created by Veit Stoss in 1498, and remarkable 12th-century frescoes to the rear of the nave.

The **Getreidegasse** was one of the principal thoroughfares of Old Salzburg. The houses lining the street were built between the 15th and 18th centuries; they are characterised by lovely arcaded courtyards, wrought-iron signs and carved stucco window frames. Passageways occur at regular intervals; the people of Salzburg call them "Durchhäuser" ("Through-houses"). The house at Getreidegasse no. 9 is **Mozart's Birthplace**, where the child prodigy Wolfgang Amadeus was born on the third floor on 27 January 1756. It was while living here that Mozart composed almost all his juvenile works; today the house contains many mementoes of the composer's life. The Getreidegasse leads on in an easterly direction towards the

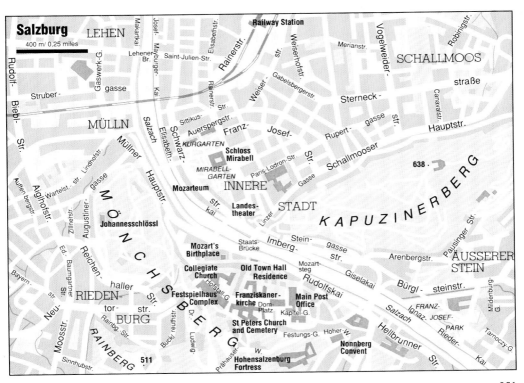

Town Hall and the **Old Market**, with the **St Florian's Fountain**. The rococo interior of the **Hofapotheke**, founded in 1591, retains the fittings of the original chemist's shop.

Shortly after this, the Getreidegasse joins the **Judengasse**, once the centre of Salzburg's thriving Jewish quarter; it, too, is characterised by numerous elaborate wrought-iron shop signs.

Lying on the opposite bank of the Salzach, the **Mirabell Gardens** form the most attractive park in Salzburg. Designed by Fischer von Erlach at the beginning of the 18th century, they enchant visitors with their statues, fountains and well-tended flowerbeds. One of the loveliest views is towards Hohensalzburg fortress from the terrace of the former palace, now housing administrative buildings. The original palace built on this spot was the Altenau, in 1606, commissioned by Wolf Dietrich to accommodate his celebrated Jewish mistress, Salome von Alt. Between 1721 and 1727 it was rebuilt by J. Lukas von Hildebrandt, but this structure was destroyed by a catastrophic fire in 1818. The present palace is a reconstruction of that building by Peter von Noble.

The **Pilgrimage Church of Maria Plain** stands on a hilltop on the northern side of the town. Built between 1671 and 1674, it possesses a facade framed by two towers. The interior is exceptionally attractive, representing the transition from baroque to rococo.

Hellbrunn Castle, to the south of Salzburg proper, symbolises pleasures of a primarily worldly nature – even though the complex, surrounded by a spacious park, was the summer residence of Archbishop Marcus Sitticus. It was designed by Santino Solari, the architect that was also responsible for Salzburg's cathedral (an unfinished sketch of this is kept in the castle's dining-room). The most interesting aspect of the interior appointments are the ball-room's *trompe-l'oeil* paintings by Donato (Arsensio) Mascagni; the main attraction of Hellbrunn, however, is undoubtedly the collection of fountains in the park. Elaborate fountains and **The Pferde-schwemme.**

grottoes with countless figures, scenic representations and a mechanical theatre in which no fewer than 113 marionettes are set in motion by water power, were designed for the prince-bishop's private amusement.

The German Corner: Southwest of Salzburg, obscured from view by the Undersberg, the German Corner juts into Austrian territory. There is a concrete historical explanation for this anomaly: on the site of what is now Berchtesgaden there was once an Augustinian priory which served as one of the bastions of the Bavarian House of Wittelsbach against the predations of the Archbishops of Salzburg. The Wittelsbachs themselves appointed three powerful Prince-Provosts to the priory between the 16th and 18th centuries. The entire region was finally ceded to the Kingdom of Bavaria in 1809.

Apart from the **Foundation Church**, **Berchtesgaden** today contains the former Priory, with 13th-century cloisters and a Gothic dormitory. The former monastery **Salt Mine** is still in opera-

tion and can also be viewed. The main attractions are the **Königssee** – with the **Pilgrimage Church of St Bartholomew** and the panoramic drive via the Rossfeld-Ringstrasse to the Obersalzberg – and the ascent to the Kehlstein House (6000 ft/1,834 metres). All these destinations afford views of spectacular countryside.

Salt and water: Hallein, which lies a short distance south of Salzburg, was one of the most prized possessions of the archbishops of Salzburg. From the 13th century onward they had salt refined from the brine extracted from the Dürrnberg, a practice that had been carried out at various points in history. Even the Celts had exploited this source of "white gold"; traces of their civilisation can be seen in the Museum of Celtic History in Hallein.

The salt mine is still in operation today, and is open to visitors. Part of the tour includes riding on a toboggan down the salt miners' wooden slide, a trip in a punt across an illuminated salt lake and a thundering journey on the underground train. It is strongly recommended; children and adults thoroughly enjoy it.

Opposite the parish church in the picturesque Old Town is the house where the organist Franz Xaver Gruber (1778–1863) lived. He it was who in 1818 composed the world-famous carol *Silent Night, Holy Night* for the Christmas Mass in Oberndorf (14 miles/22 km north of Salzburg).

South of Hallein, the **Salzach Valley** is increasingly dominated by flowing water. The karst water from the **Hoher Göll** (8,280 ft/2,523 metres) plunges in an awe-inspiring curtain of water, foam and mist known as the **Gollinger Waterfalls**. Schwarzenberg, a prince-archbishop of Salzburg, commissioned the construction of the footpath to the top of the falls.

The **Salzachöfen** and **Lammeröfen** are two narrow gorges carved over many millions of years through the limestone rock by the rivers Salzach and Lammer. In the case of the Lammer, the walls of the gorge, known locally as "Öfen" ("ovens"), are only one metre apart in some places. The Salzachöfen is a vast jumble

Perfect setting for Mozart's Magic Flute.

of rocks, crevices, caves and erosions. The Salzach Gorge is accessible from the Pass Lueg.

Tennengebirge to the High Tauern: Beyond Golling, the Salzach is forced into narrow, forbidding ravines by the mountain ranges of the **Hagengebirge** in the west and the **Tennengebirge** in the east. Near **Werfen** the naturally impregnable countryside gives way to defences of a man-made nature: here, dominating the scene from a rocky eminence, stands **Hohenwerfen Castle**. As in the case of the fortress of Hohensalzburg, the stronghold was begun by the archbishops of Salzburg at the beginning of the Investiture Dispute. It was enlarged to its present form towards the end of the 16th century by the addition of an extensive system of outer defences after the Italian manner. For the present-day visitor the fortress provides an excellent impression of medieval defences.

Opposite Hohenwerfen, hidden away between the cliffs of the Tennengebirge, lie the **Eisriesenwelt Caves**. They form one of the most extensive cave complexes in the world; to date, only about 30 miles (50 km) of galleries, subterranean halls and labyrinths have been systematically explored. Since the entrance to the caves lies at an altitude of 5,385 ft (1,641 metres), the approach by bus and cable car is an experience in itself. The cave is illuminated only by the carbide lamps of the visitors and the magnesium lamps of the guides; the effect of this is magical. Some of the individual ice structures are as much as 65 ft (20 metres) thick; they all bear names taken from the *Norse Edda* legends. From the cave entrance there is an exceptionally fine view westwards to the névé fields of the **Hochkönig** (9,650 ft/2,941 metres).

The parish church of **Bischofshofen** is one of the finest examples of Gothic architecture in the Austrian Alps. The transept dates from the 11th century and the chancel from the 14th century, whilst the nave was built in the hall style with groined vaulting in the 15th century. On the left wall are 16th and 17th-century frescoes depicting the Passion of Christ.

Archbishop Wolf Dietrich von Raitenau, 1578.

ÆTAT SVÆ XXX

The north transept contains the marble tomb of Sylvester, Bishop of Chiemsee, completed in 1462. It is the only example of a Gothic standing tomb in the Salzburg region.

Radstadt is a medieval town situated at the foot of the pass through the Radstätter Tauern which lost much of its importance following the construction of the motorway. As a result, its protected position behind moats and turrets enhances its charm for the visitor. Once upon a time, however, the ancient walls had a more crucial role to fulfil: they were built between 1270 and 1286 on the orders of the prince-bishops of Salzburg as a border defence against the by no means always friendly neighbouring province of Styria. Furthermore, Radstadt served as control point over the access to the northern approach to the Radstädter Tauern Pass.

Thanks to the construction of the motorway, the **Radstädter Tauern Pass** (5,700 ft/1738 metres), which marks the boundary between the Low and the High Tauern ranges, has become a quiet country road once more. Encouraged by the excellent walking possibilities in summer and the reliable snow conditions in winter, a holiday village has grown up along the combe. On both sides of the pass there are cable cars for the journey to the summit and the ridge.

The southern approach to the Radstätter Tauern Pass was once controlled from **Mauterndorf**. King Henry II gave Archbishop Hartwik not only possession of the area, but also the right to levy customs duties. Thus the first occupied tollbooth in the Eastern Alps was founded. As a result, the castle was built at the beginning of the 14th century; it was extended in about 1500 by Archbishop Leonhard von Keutschach. The residential apartments, the chapel and the frescoes on the wall of the triumphal arch are of particular interest.

Moosham Castle, just south of Mauterndorf, was also once a stronghold of the prince-bishops of Salzburg. It served as a bastion of local defence in the Lungau, a remote but strategically important region. As the seat of the

Mozartkugeln (Mozart balls) are a delicious Salzburg confection.

ordinary court in the 17th and 18th centuries, the fortress achieved a degree of notoriety through numerous trials of witches, sorcerers, beggars and other "miscreants". The judicial procedure was usually extremely brief, thanks to the intervention of the executioner (on the instructions of the bishop). Today Moosham Castle functions as a local history museum.

The principal town in the Lungau is **Tamsweg**, first mentioned in records as Tamswick in 1160. The most famous monument is the ancient pilgrimage **Church of St Leonard**, situated on one of the foothills of the Schwarzenberg. Its turretted surrounding wall lends it the appearance of a fortified church. It houses a number of notable treasures, including stained-glass windows, manufactured between 1430 and 1450. Most famous of all is the church's "gold window", composed almost entirely of blue and gold pieces. Hardly less precious is a choir stall dating from around 1415 and decorated with intricate carvings and inlaid woodwork.

It is only upon reaching **St Johann im Pongau** that the Salzach, which in its upper reaches flows in a precise west-easterly direction, finally decides to change its course towards the north. Characteristic of the entire upper stretch are the tributaries, some of which flow through deeply cut north-south valleys. They all descend from the main Alpine crest and were previously the cause of frequent flooding. The area surrounding the elbow of the Salzach was once the domain of the Lords of the Pongau, who also gave it their name.

In the immediate vicinity of St Johann, the **Grossarl Valley** branches off before opening into the remarkable **Liechtensteinklamm**. The gorge is reached by a path which in many places has been blasted through solid rock; after passing through the first section of the gorge, it opens out into a basin enclosed by 980-ft (300-metre) high walls of rock. Then the gorge narrows down again, becoming sometimes no more than 6 feet wide; finally, in order to reach the 20-ft (60-metre) high waterfall at the end of the gorge, one must

pass through a tunnel which is a good 165 ft (50 metres) long.

Perched up high above the left bank of the Salzach stands **Goldegg Castle**, built in the 12th century by the Lords of the Pongau in the centre of their area of feudal jurisdiction, in their capacity as ministers of the prince-bishops of Salzburg. The present-day fortress and its outer wards both date from the years 1320–23. In 1527 the Goldegg Castle passed into the possession of Graf Christoph von Schernberg; he had it decorated with frescoes and tempera paintings on wood and canvas. Today the castle houses the Pongau Museum of Local History.

Healthy radioactivity: The largest and also the wealthiest of the side valleys of the Salzach is the **Gastein Valley**. It is a district which has always possessed the right basis for wealth at the right moment in time. First of all, gold and silver mined in the area brought the local princes riches and prestige. Later, the healing powers of the local hot springs made the valley famous, and in 1434, when Emperor Friedrich III became the first prominent visitor of his time to take a cure here, its reputation as a spa flourished. In recent years, the snow itself has become a marketable commodity, and the population has put their efforts into the skiing industry. Consequently, the fact that mining is no longer lucrative is unimportant.

The "Court at Gastein", as **Bad Hofgastein** was originally called, belonged first of all to the Dukes of Bavaria, subsequently to the Counts of Pongau and finally to the Diocese of Salzburg. Even in the 16th century the bishops were able to have gold and silver extracted here. Hofgastein first became known as a spa town in 1828, following the laying of water mains to divert some of the thermal waters from Badgastein itself.

Nonetheless, Badgastein remains pre-eminent as the centre of the spa facilities in Austria. Its thermal springs contain radon; the therapeutic waters are drunk and used for bathing, and the steam is inhaled. Particularly favoured are the steam baths in the radioactive thermal

The sun clock on Mozartplatz.

tunnels, where the waters climb to temperatures as high as 106°F (41.5°C). A little train transports patients and visitors down into the tunnels, where they inhale the rare radon gas.

In spite of its position at an altitude of more than 3,280 ft (1,000 metres), Badgastein seems in many respects to have many of the characteristics of a miniature international metropolis, with its tall hotel buildings, elegant shops and bustling atmosphere. The spa and congress complex, situated near the upper waterfall, is the centre of activity; it contains the congress centre, pump room, spa pool and museum. The **Kaiser-Wilhelm-Promenade** is the most attractive place for a stroll, affording fine views of the valley basin and up to Bad Hofgastein.

The numerous chair lifts providing access to the mountains around Badgastein were erected primarily to serve skiing enthusiasts. They also provide an easily-reached starting point for delightful mountain walks. In **Böckstein** cars are loaded on to the train for transport through the 27,960-ft (8,522-metre) Tauern Tunnel, the shortest link between Salzburg and northwest Carinthia or East Tyrol. In winter, **Sportgastein** attracts mountain sports enthusiasts with its facilities for ski-touring, downhill and cross-country skiing.

Zell am See and the Saalach Valley: Along the entire length of the Upper Salzach Valley there is only one fork which is open at both the northern and southern ends. During the Ice Age this was the only place where the Salzach glacier managed to carve out an exit to the north – a course which the river itself did not follow, however. The build-up of moraine deposits at this spot prevents the waters of the **Zeller See** from flowing away to the south-east into the Salzach or northwards into the Saalach. Even today, no meltwater flows into the lake; for this reason, in summer the temperature of the water rises exceptionally quickly for an Alpine lake.

Perched on a small alluvial hill in a pretty setting on the western lake shore stands **Zell am See**, the principal town

Autumn time in Zell am See.

258

in the Pinzgau. As the central of the "**European Sports Region Kaprun-Zell-Saalbach**" it has plenty of attractions to offer – although admittedly most of them are in Saalbach or Kaprun. Within Zell itself there is only the cable car to the **Schmittenhöhe** (6,447 ft/ 1,964 metres), which nonetheless affords an excellent view of the Pinzgau, and the mighty snow peaks of the High Tauern and the Grossglockner.

The Salzburg monks soon discovered the picturesque lakeside setting and founded a "Cella in Bisontio" (Pinzgau) in AD 743. This expanded to become an Augustinian priory, whose church – dedicated to St Hippolytus – has been the **Parish Church** since 1217. Its squat fortified tower, dating from the middle of the 15th century, can still be seen for miles around. The interior contains frescoes from the 13th, 14th and 16th centuries, the most impressive of which include a Madonna in Glory (13th century) in the apse of the north aisle, and the Martyrdom of St Catherine (14th century) in the porch. The delicate trac-

The typical Salzburger.

ery on the balustrade of the West Gallery dates from 1514, and the fine representations of St George and St Florian on the west gallery wall from 1520.

In the winter months, Zell am See belongs first and foremost to ski enthusiasts. In summer – apart from the walkers and climbers – it is gliding fans who find optimum conditions here. Thanks to the east-west orientation of the Pinzgau, the southernmost chain of the **Kitzbühel Alps** provide more than 30 miles (50 km) of south-facing slopes producing the thermals gliders need to attain height. What is more, the pilots of the Alpine Gliding School are willing to take guests up with them.

A footpath across 11 peaks: A few miles north of the Zellam See, the road meets the Saalach as it flows westwards from the Kitzbühel Alps. If you follow the course of the river you will arrive in the skiing community of **Saalbach-Hinterglemm**. The local tourist managers take pride in their 41 tree-free ski slopes, more than 50 lifts and approximately 93 miles (150 km) of pistes.

From the **Schattberg** (7,220 ft/2,200 metres), the intrepid and fit can trek across no fewer than 11 mountain peaks to the **Schmittenhöhe**, with stunning views across to the summits of the High Tauern Range.

Lying immediately to the south of the "German Corner" and the Berchtes–gadnerland, **Saalfelden** has developed at the point where the Saalach Valley is at its widest. It was once an important market town where horses and cattle were traded; today it is above all a good starting point for climbing expeditions up to the **Hochkönig** (9,648 ft/2,941 metres) and the vast limestone plateau of the **Steinernes Meer**. It is a beautiful trek across to the **Königsee**, dominated by the mighty **Watzmann** (8,900 ft/2,713 metres) rising almost vertically from its western shore.

East of Saalfelden lies the **Urslau Valley**, which extends as far as the western slopes of the Hochkönig. The prettiest village in the valley is undoubtedly **Maria Alm**. Its Gothic pilgrimage church houses not only a Madonna dat-ing from 1480 but also a graceful spire which at 275 ft (84 metres) rises one metre higher than the towers of Salzburg's Cathedral.

Further to the north, the Saalach Valley becomes narrower, closed in as it is on the western side by the **Leoganger Steinberge** and to the east by the precipices of the **Hochkalter**. Near **Weissbach** it is worthwhile climbing up to the **Seisenbergklamm** or visiting the **Lamprechtsofenloch**.

St Martin, near Lofer, is a village of historical interest. Until 1803 its **Parish Church** belonged to the Augustinian Priory of St Zeno in Reichenhall. The church, a late conversion to the baroque style, contains fine 17th and 18th-century altar paintings, the work of Wilhelm Faistenberger, Johann Friedrich Pereth and Jakob Zanusi.

West of St Martin, hidden away at the top of a high-altitude valley, nestles the pilgrimage **Church of Maria Kirchental**. It was built between 1694 and 1701 according to the plans of no less a celebrity than Johann Bernhard **Pongau scenery.**

Fischer von Erlach. It is interesting above all for the two marble side altars, completed in 1700. The pulpit, too, dates from 1709. An early 15th-century Madonna in Glory is venerated as possessing miraculous powers. Of interest to the visitor are the numerous votive gifts. They are collected in an *ex voto* chapel.

In **Lofer** the Saalach Valley crosses the trunk road leading from the Inn valley via the German Corner to Salzburg. Some 7 miles (12 km) further along, the **Steinpass** (2,000 ft/615 metres) marks the frontier of the German Corner and the Bad Reichenhall-Berchtesgaden area.

Zell am See to the Grossglockner: The valley of the **Fuscher Ache**, branching off southwards near **Bruck an der Salzach**, is both lonely and wild, but from earliest times it attracted travellers seeking a mountain pass to the South. Even the Romans knew of this particular pass: a 7-inch (17-cm) bronze figure dating from the 1st century AD was found at an altitude of 8,430 (2,570) metres near the Hochtor during the con-

struction of the Grossglockner Road. The south side of the pass was also of interest to the Romans, for they mined gold in the region of Heiligenblut. In the Middle Ages the "Blood Pilgrimage" to Heiligenblut drove the faithful from the Pinzgau into these hostile mountains.

Where the demons reside: One old chronicle describes the perils of the district surrounding the Grossglockner as they were perceived in medieval times: "There is a region up there where the demons reside, threatening with rattling falling rocks and avalanches every mortal who ventures into the vicinity."

That in earlier times it really was perilous up here, and that even today it can be dangerous to leave the road, is proved by the "Cairn of bones" near the Hochtor. A group of Pinzgauer pilgrims met a tragic end in a summer snowstorm on this spot. For many years, a pile of their bleached bones were left there as a salutary reminder of the tragedy.

The metre-high walls of snow which border the road until well into the summer relay an unequivocal message. In

Hohenwerfen Castle.

winter, the snow here lies an average of more than 16 ft (5 metres) deep. On approximately 99 days every year a stormy wind blows with gusts of up to 93 miles per hour (150 km/h); on 250 days of the year it snows. The climate along the comb of the Grossglockner Road is equivalent to that of Siberia.

The summit of the panoramic road is marked by the **Edelweissspitze** (8,450 ft/2,577 metres), which naturally also offers the best view. Despite the fascination of the Edelweissspitze, this observation post does not mark the southern pass proper. Instead, our journey continues downhill again to the **Fuscher Törl** (7,890 ft/2,405 metres), down again to the Fuscher Lake, and then along the eastern sides of the Brennkogel and uphill again past a long section of scree slopes to the **Hochtor Tunnel** (8,220 ft/ 2,505 metres).

From the car park by the southern tunnel entrance there is a quite splendid view far into the south, towards Carinthia and East Tyrol: across to the Schober Range and down into the Möll Valley.

In the Upper Pinzgau: The star attraction of the "European Sports Region" is the largest year-round ski slope in Austria – the **Schmiedinger Kees**, which lies beneath the jagged peak of the **Kitzsteinhorn** (10,508 ft/3,203 metres). It has brought fame (at least in the skiing world) to the little Alpine village of **Kaprun**, which lies a few miles south of Zell am See, at the entrance to the valley of the same name. In order to provide access to this sporting paradise it was necessary to build a glacier cable car in three sections; it leads via the intermediate stations at the Salzburger Hütte (6,223 ft/1,897 metres) and the Alpine Centre (8,044 ft/2,452 metres) to the Mountain Station (9,937 ft/3,029 metres) on the ridge of the Kitzsteinhorn. Since the cable car soon proved inadequate to cope with the traffic, a second fixed cable car lift was constructed parallel to the two lower sections; it is 13,287 ft (4,050) metres long and climbs directly to the Alpine Centre.

The best view of the Grossglockner: The excellent access to the Pinzgau's most

Climbing the High Tauern.

famous mountain provides even visitors without mountaineering aspirations with a spectacular experience of the Alps; from the Mountain Station of the cable car there is a safe footpath to the summit of the Kitzsteinhorn. Its exposed position affords an outstanding view of the Glockner massif, the Wiesbachhorn and the Grossvenediger. Lined up to the north stand the Kitzbühel Alps, the Steinernes Meer with the Hochkönig, the Tennengebirge and the Dachstein ranges. Far down below gleam the vast green reservoirs of the **Tauern Hydro-Electric Power Station**.

The Glockner-Kaprun power complex is considered one of the boldest and most successful in Austria. Construction began before World War II; today, it is one of the biggest hydraulic power stations in the Alps. The main power plant can generate 220,000 kW; the catchment area extends as far as the Möll on the south side of the Glockner Massif, thanks to the bulk water transfer tunnel from the Margaritze Reservoir by the Grossglockner Road. A total of almost 200 million cubic metres of water are stored in two vast reservoirs. The **Wasserfallboden** (5,485 ft/1,672 metres) is dammed by the 393-ft (120-metre) high Limberg Barrage; to form the **Mooserboden Reservoir**, two dams were necessary: the Mooser Barrage and the Drossen Barrage, each 360-ft (110-metres) high and situated to the east and west of the Höhenburg (6,916 ft/2,108 metres).

Visitors can tour the entire power station complex – an undertaking which also includes a trip up the mountain to an altitude of 3,937 ft (2,036) metres. Private cars cannot be used all the way; the only means of transport is by funicular and bus. The first stage is the ascent by the Lärchenwald funicular from 3,937 to 5,380 ft (1,200–1,640 metres).

From here the bus skirts the Wasserfallboden reservoir, climbing another 1,300 ft (400 metres) to the Mooserboden reservoir, where the road peters out by the so-called **Heathen Church**, claimed by archaeologists to be a Celtic religious site. The high spot – literally – of this impressive mountain tour is the 6,916 ft (2,108-metre) Höhenburg, between the twin barrages damming the Mooserboden reservoir. From here one can see both lakes at the same time; there is a breathtaking panorama of the mountain peaks and glaciers flanking the Karlinger Kees.

The **Stubachtal**, which forks off southwards near **Uttendorf**, has also been exploited by the construction of a power station and cable cars. On this occasion one can drive right down to the floor of the valley and up to the first stage: the **Enzingerboden** (4,816 ft/ 1,468 metres), which is set in spectacularly forested scenery. The Stubach-Weisssee cable car climbs from here to the **Weisssee**, at an altitude of 7,621 ft (2,323 metres). The best view can be obtained from the **Rudolph's Shelter**, the Austrian Alpine Association's Centre on the **Hinterer Schafbühel** (7,716 ft/2,352 metres). **Mittersill** is a town of historic importance, for it marks the intersection of the great north-south route via the Thurn Pass and the Felber Tauern Tunnel with the Salzach Valley.

Looking towards the Grossvenediger.

An ancient mountain pass: The route across the **Felber Tauern** was an important one for Austrians long before the construction of the 3.2 mile (5.2 km) long tunnel. Back in the Middle Ages it was a much-used trade route, crossing the Alpine crest at an altitude of 8,139 ft (2,481 metres) at precisely the point where the St Poltner refuge is situated today. In those days packhorses carried velvets and silks, barrels of wine and loads of citrus fruits northwards and copper, iron, leather and salt in the opposite direction.

Of corresponding significance was Mittersill, marking the start of the climb. The town itself came into the possession of the Counts of Matrei in the 12th century as a Bavarian fief. They called themselves the Counts of Mittersill from 1180; in 1228 they became subject to the archdiocese of Salzburg. The Castle has been rebuilt complete with massive corner towers and battlements.

The triple-bayed Gothic castle chapel was rebuilt in its present form in 1553; it houses a winged altarpiece dating from the middle of the 15th century. The **Deanery Church** was completed in 1749; dedicated to St Leonard, it contains interesting stained-glass windows designed by Hans Hauer and Franz Sträussenberger.

Even from afar, the Church of St Anne stands out from the usual Salzburg baroque by virtue of its curved gable facade. This is hardly surprising, since the architect was Jakob Singer, from Schwaz in Tyrol, who completed the church in 1751. Also a native of Schwaz was Christoph Anton Mayr, who, in 1753, painted the frescoes adorning the interior. Nor should the visitor omit a visit to the Gothic daughter Church of **St Nicholas in Felben**, which houses a High Altar dating from 1631 depicting a series of highly expressive late Gothic figures of the 14 auxiliary saints.

Behind Mittersill, the Salzach Valley gradually becomes narrower and more typically Alpine. The peaks fringing the horizon are dominated by the 12,053-ft (3,674-metre) **Grossvenediger**. There are two ways of approaching this majestic giant. The first is to make the ascent through the **Obersulzbach Valley** to the **Kürsinger Refuge**, which lies at 8,362 ft/2,549 metres. This involves a journey on foot of several hours. An easier route is by chair lift from **Neukirchen**. By this means one is transported to the Alpine Ridge west of the **Wildkogel** (7,306 ft/2,227 metres), at a height of 6,866 ft (2,093 metres). From this point one has a perfect view across the Salzach Valley towards the Alpine Ridge, dominated by the Grossvenediger.

The waterfall of the 12 glaciers: A unique natural phenomenon awaits the traveller in the upmost reaches of the Salzach Valley, near **Krimml**. The **Krimml Waterfalls** are the most spectacular in the entire Alps, deserving superlatives on several counts: firstly, there is the sheer volume of water of the Krimmler Ache, which is fed by no fewer than 12 glaciers. Then there is the total height of the falls, which, divided among the three great cascades, totals 1,295 ft (395 metres). And finally there is the variety of settings and wealth of natural features which the thundering water passes through on its path.

Amazingly, so far the engineers employed in Austria's electricity supply industry have not worked out a way of persuading these magnificent waterfalls to give up their lifeblood for a power station.

The entire site is marked by well-signposted footpaths which make exploration of the area by foot surprisingly easy. Starting at Krimml, the new **Gerlos Pass Toll Road** leads up and across the 4,944 ft (1,507 m) high Gerlos Pass. It describes a large loop around the Tratenköpfl, thereby offering an excellent view of the cascading waterfalls.

Shortly after the top of the pass, virtually on the Salzburg border, the traveller can expect to see another remarkable sight. Immediately below the road lies the dammed Wildgerlossee, and dominating the scene, towering proudly above the rather less lofty Alpine peaks, are the summits of the Gerlosspitze and the Reichenspitze.

Fine stained-glass in the pilgrimage Church of St Leonard in Tamsweg.

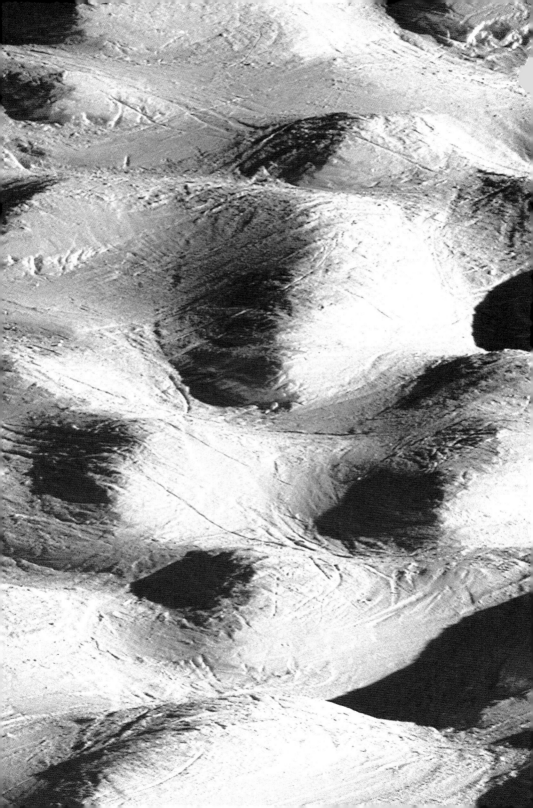

THE TYROL

According to a popular song, Innsbruck is a "beautiful Alpine town". As long as one restricts one's observations to its breathtaking location surrounded by mountains and to the medieval Old Town itself, the description holds true. Now, as during the reigns of the Emperor Maximilian and Maria Theresa, the encircling chain of unspoiled peaks ensure that nothing changes too much: the town is contained by the **Karwendel Range** to the north, towering more than 6,560 ft (2,000 metres) above the town itself, and the twin landmarks in the south, the **Patscherkofel** and the **Nockspitze**. Only in the east and to a lesser extent in the west has Innsbruck been able to expand to any degree during the past 100 years.

It was no less a personage than Emperor Maximilian I who first recognised the many-faceted charms of this town in the mountains. Although the residence of the Tyrolean branch of the Habsburgs was transferred from Merano to the River Inn as early as 1420, Maximilian was the first monarch really to hold court here. Maria Theresa also brought the splendour of court life to Innsbruck. She had the ancient royal residence extended and had the Triumphal Arch erected to mark the marriage of her son. Because Emperor Franz suddenly died in 1765 in the middle of the festivities, the arch is decorated on one side with motives of earthly glory and on the other with symbols of mourning.

Tyrolean idol: The year 1805 marked the beginning of a dark but heroic period of history, after the Habsburgs had been forced to cede Tyrol to Bavaria in the Treaty of Bratislava. The Tyrolese, under Andreas Hofer, rebelled and in 1809 made Innsbruck the seat of a civilian government following their victory in the battle of Bergisel. Andreas Hofer ruled Tyrol "in the name of the Emperor". The resistance was broken in November 1809; one year later, the Tyrolean popular hero was betrayed and shot in Mantua. Since then the Bergisel Mountain on the southern boundary of the town has symbolised the Tyrolese love of freedom.

Innbruck's late Gothic centre has been preserved largely intact. Pedestrians can easily explore the compact area between the **River Inn** and the beginning of Maria-Theresien-Strasse. **Herzog Friedrichstrasse**, enclosed by arcades, fans out in front of the famous **Goldenes Dachl** (Golden Roof), providing an insight into the intimacy which must have characterised life at court.

This magnificent balcony was built to provide a fitting stage for the ruling family to see and be seen. It was erected on the orders of Emperor Maximilian I and completed in 1500. The balustrade of the upper section, which juts out slightly, is decorated on the front and sides with carved reliefs. The two middle sections represent Maximilian with his two wives, Maria of Burgundy and Maria Bianca Sforza, and Maximilian with his chancellor and his court jester. The remaining panels portray Morris dancers. The structure was the work of Nikolaus Türing the Elder, the Innsbruck court builder. It is to him that the balcony owes its roof, which was covered with gold-plated copper tiles.

Diagonally opposite the Golden Roof stands the **Helblinghaus**, a late Gothic building to which a rococo façade was added in the 18th century. The window frames, oriels and tympana are painted in pastel colours and lavishly decorated. A little further on, near the River Inn, stands the **Goldener Adler** (Golden Eagle) – the oldest inn in the town – dating from the 16th century. Goethe stayed here twice. The **Ottoburg**, diagonally opposite, was originally built as a residential tower in 1495; still furnished in period style, it serves today as a wine bar.

The **Cathedral**, dedicated to St James, is hidden away to the north of the Golden Roof. It was completed in the baroque style in 1722 in accordance with plans drawn up by Johann Jakob Herkommer. The interior space is enclosed by a series of domes: three domed vaults spanning the nave and a dome with lantern above the chancel. The frescoes adorning the vaulting – dedicated to St James

Preceding pages: the Tyrol is a skier's paradise; horses graze in the Lechtaler Alps. **Right,** Innsbruck is dominated by the Karwendel Mountains.

the Intercessor – are the work of Cosmas Damian Asam, whilst the stucco was decorated by his brother, Egid Quirin. Above the high altar is a painting of Our Lady of Succour by Lukas Cranach the Elder. In the left transept stands the tomb of Archduke Maximilian, a Grand Master of the Teutonic Order, who died in 1618.

The **Hofburg**, extended during the reign of Maria Theresa, adjoins the cathedral on the north side. The **Giant's Hall**, over 100 ft (30 metres) long, is one of the main attractions. Its walls are clad with magnificent stucco panels with a marble finish; the ceiling was painted in 1776 by Franz Anton Maulbertsch. The subject he chose – the Triumph of the House of Habsburg-Lorraine – is symbolised by two women holding out their hands to one another. The walls are decorated with portraits of Maria Theresa's children and relatives from other ruling houses.

Austria's greatest Renaissance building: Situated at the south-east corner of the Hofburg, the **Hofkirche** was completed in 1563. It was built in the late Gothic style with a Renaissance porch, and was designed to house the Tomb of Emperor Maximilian I, the Habsburg whose talents as a matchmaker ensured that there was a member of the Imperial family in every House in Europe at his death. In 1502, 17 years before he finally expired, the emperor commissioned his own mausoleum. It was to become the most outstanding work of art in the Tyrol, and the most moving imperial monument in the Western world.

Gilg Sesselschreiber, a Munich artist, was asked to produce sketches for the tomb. He proposed a bronze edifice with 40 larger-than-life statues of the most important ancestors and kinsmen of the Emperor. They were to bear candles and thus represent the participants at his funeral procession. The ensemble was to be completed by two rows of statuettes and busts of patron saints of the Habsburgs and Roman emperors. Of the 40 statues originally planned 28 were actually cast, between 1509 and 1550. The two most famous represent

The *Letztes Aufgebot* (1872), by Tyrolean artist Franz Defregger.

King Arthur and Theodoric; they were cast in 1513 in Nuremberg by Peter Vischer. It was not until 1550 that the idea arose of erecting a cenotaph bearing the statue of Maximilian as the focal point of the monument. Its construction, in accordance with the design of Alexander Colin, was completed in 1583.

South of the Old Town runs **Maria-Theresienstrasse**. It is dominated by St Anne's Column, erected in 1706 in memory of the retreat of the Bavarian troops from the Tyrol during the War of the Spanish Succession. Surmounting the slender pedestal is a statue of the Virgin Mary; St Anne stands next to St George (the patron saint of the Tyrol), and St Vigilius and St Cassianus (the patron saints of the dioceses of Trent and Bressanone), symbolising the political unity of the Tyrol. The southern end of the street is marked by the **Triumphal Arch**.

The **Tyrol Museum of Popular Art** contains an important collection of local costumes, tools and peasant furniture from all parts of the province. The **"Ferdinandeum" Tyrol Museum** attempts to record the development of painting and sculpture in the Tyrol. The **Bergisel Panorama**, situated near the Hungerberg funicular station, depicts the famous battle of Bergisel as a moment of glory for the freedom fighters of the province. The Imperial Light Infantry Memorial at Bergisel commemorates the elite Tyrolean corps, which was disbanded in 1919.

Wilten, the district of Innsbruck at the foot of the Bergisel itself, was once the site of the Roman town of *Veldidena*. The **Abbey of Wilten** was founded in 1128 under the jurisdiction of the Premonstratensians. Until 1180 they controlled the entire area as far as the Inn. Only after this date, following an agreement with the Counts of Andechs, did the Order permit settlers to leave the northern bank of the Inn and to make their homes in what is now the Old Town. The present Abbey Church is a baroque edifice dating from the 17th century, with an imposing facade completed in 1716. The church vestibule is

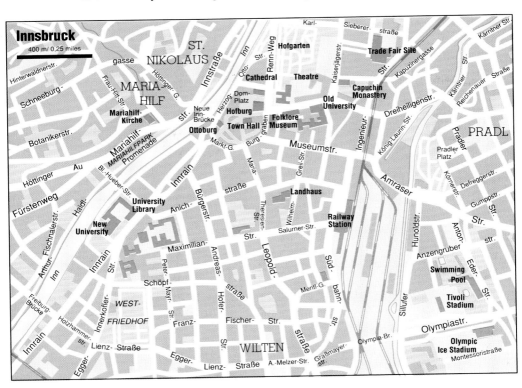

adorned with a Gothic wood carving of the giant Haymon, according to legend one of the founders of the abbey.

Wilten Basilica was completed in 1756 in accordance with the plans of the Tyrolean priest-architect Franz de Paula Penz. Its rococo interior was the work of Franz Xaver Feichtmayr, the stuccomoulder of the Wessobrunn school, and Matthäus Günther, the Augsburg painter. The high altar is adorned with a statue of the Virgin under a baldachin supported by marble columns. "Our Lady of the Four Pillars" has been venerated as a source of miraculous powers since the Middle Ages.

The Bergisel, a hill that featured in many episodes in Tyrolean history, is surmounted today by a ski jump erected for the 1964 Winter Olympics.

Sporting Kitzbühel: The reputation of **Kitzbühel** as a chic winter sports centre dates at least from the triple Olympic victory of local boy Toni Sailer – the "Kitz Comet" – in the 1956 Winter Games in Cortina. Apart from that, the famous Hahnenkamm Races ensure that the Kitzbühel skiing area attracts top enthusiasts from all over the world. It can boast more than 50 slopes and countless first-rate descents in every imaginable permutation.

The mountains surrounding Kitzbühel have contributed most to the town's sporting reputation, especially the **Kitzbüheler Horn** to the east and the **Hahnenkamm** to the west. In summer, the relatively tame Kitzbühel Alps afford an extensive range of mountain walks; for those who prefer it steeper, rockier and more challenging, there are the vast limestone peaks of the **Wilder Kaiser** over to the west.

The charms of the broad Kitzbühel Basin can best be experienced when the wall of mountains are lit by the setting sun and reflected in the dark waters of the moorland **Schwarzsee**.

The **Parish Church** (1435) is a relic of Kitzbühel's earlier period of prosperity. The triple-naved Gothic structure with its slender tower and overhanging single roof blends in well in its Alpine setting. The church was built under **Townhouses on the Inn.**

274

Stefan Krumenauer; the high altar was created during the second half of the 17th century by Benedikt Faistenberger. Restoration work has exposed the original Gothic splendour of the columns and chancel arch, as well as 15th-century frescoes in the choir.

The **Church of Our Lady** has an unusual two-storey design. The lower church is mentioned in records dating from 1373, in which year a prosperous family had a burial chapel built. The upper storey was adorned in the baroque manner in 1735; its most attractive feature is the series of frescoes by Simon Benedikt Faistenberger, regarded as representing his finest work. The painting adorning the high altar is a copy of *Our Lady of Succour*, the Lukas Cranach masterpiece in Innsbruck Cathedral. The rose grille in front of the high altar was created in 1781.

Barely 5 miles (8 km) south of Kitzbühel, the parish church of **Jochberg** also contains frescoes by Faistenberger. The apostles St Peter and St Paul, fathers of the church, and St Wolfgang are portrayed as vividly as in a Rubens painting.

Works by the same artist can also be seen in the parish church of **St Johann**, the scattered village lying in the valley between the Kitzbüheler Horn and the sheer face of the Wilder Kaiser. The church's most notable feature, however, is actually the protruding west front, completed by Abraham Miller in 1728 and flanked by twin towers capped by baroque cupolas.

St Johann is first and foremost the central starting point for walking and mountaineering in the Wilder Kaiser. Those who wish to have a grandstand view of the region can take the route from Griesenau into the **Kaiserbach Valley**, and from thence up to the **Griesner Alm**. From here one has only to climb a further 1,905 ft (580 metres) to the legendary **Stripsenjoch**. Those who prefer more prettily romantic scenery can travel from Scheffau to the picturesque **Lake Hintersteiner**.

More art and culture in **Brixen Valley**, west of Kitzbühel. In **Kirchberg**,

Kitzbühel, for the chic.

the first village in the valley, the baroque parish church – decorated in 1737 by Jakob Singer – houses some fine ceiling frescoes by Simon Benedikt Faistenberger. That **Brixen im Thale** was once a prosperous place can be gathered from the twin-towered **Parish Church of the Assumption**, which has a nave roofed by three domes. It was constructed by the Kitzbühel master-builder Andrä Hueber between 1789–95. Josef Schöpf painted the brightly coloured *Coronation of the Virgin* on the main dome.

The third important church in the Brixen Valley is in **Hopfgarten**. Begun in 1758 by Kassian Singer, it was completed by Andrä Hueber. Once more we see a twin-towered facade with an extravagantly curved gable. The ceiling frescoes here are the work of Johann Weiss. Ensuring that mountaineering addicts are not left in the lurch in the Brixen Valley is the **Hohe Salve**, accessible by cable car and providing the best views of the Wilder Kaiser.

Along the Green Inn: Kufstein For-tress lies just on the Austrian side of the border with Bavaria. The town itself changed hands between the Tyrolese and the Bavarians on numerous occasions. Maximilian was the first to fortify the stronghold, first mentioned in 1205, to any great extent. At his behest the Emperor's Tower acquired walls which were up to 25 ft (7.5 metres) thick. Today the castle houses a museum of local history and the Heroes' Organ, built in 1931 in memory of the Tyrolese freedom fighters.

The busy little village of **Wörgl** is the centre of the Tyrolean Lowlands. The baroque parish church houses the Virgin of Wörgl, dating from about 1500; perched up on a terrace overlooking the Inn stands the medieval castle and **Chapel of Mariastein.** The keep, with its pentagonal ground plan, was built in around 1350 to defend the Inn Valley route, which in those days ran past its door. The Chapel of Miracles containing the venerated image of the Virgin is tucked away on the upper floor.

The little hamlet of **Kundl** boasted a church as long ago as 788. Nonetheless the most interesting religious building here is not really the Parish Church of the Assumption itself – in spite of its stucco decorations and frescoes – but rather the pilgrimage **Church of St Leonhard in the Meadows**, lying just outside the village proper; reputedly founded by Emperor Henry II in 1012, it was dedicated in 1020 by Pope Benedict VIII. The present building dates from 1512. The fresco depicting the Crucifixion on the north wall also dates from the 16th century, whilst the rest of the decorations, which are baroque in style, were completed in the 17th century. Walkers will enjoy the wild and romantic footpath through the **Kundlerklamm**, which affords direct access to the Wildschönau.

Family fortune: The smallest town in Tyrol, **Rattenburg**, owes its prosperity to the mining rights which Maximilian awarded to the Fugger family. From here they controlled all silver mining operations in the entire province. The town itself has managed to retain almost intact its medieval splendour. The late

Left, snowboarding is an exhilarating sport. Below, powder-snow skiing on the Arlberg.

Gothic Parish **Church of St Virgil**, which boasts a magnificent baroque interior, testifies to the great wealth Rattenburg once enjoyed.

Kramsach lies on the opposite bank of the Inn, a village surrounded by a trio of lakes which are all ideal for bathing: the **Buchsee**, the **Krummsee** and the **Reintaler See**. The **Brandenberg Valley** is delightful walking country, and can include a visit to the Kaiserklamm Gorge and the Archduke Johann Hermitage. A chair lift provides access to the **Rofan Mountains**. Beyond Brixlegg the traveller is reminded that the Inn Valley was once a land of castles; the fortresses of **Matzen** and **Lichtwer** recall the era of medieval chivalry. Unfortunately today they are closed to the public.

Tratzberg Castle, however, is open for viewing. It was built in 1296 as a stronghold on what was in those days the Bavarian frontier. The complex extends over a wide area and consists of four main wings; it received its present form during the 16th and 17th centuries at the instigation of the Fugger family.

At the beginning of the 16th century there were 20,000 miners working underground in **Schwaz**. The town's parish church dates from this period; it was begun in 1460 and was completed after 1492 by Erasmus Grasser, the Munich architect. The largest Gothic hall church in the Tyrol has a roof covered in 15,000 hammered copper tiles; it is known as the "Mountain Blessing".

The prosperity of the salt-water spa of **Hall** comes from its salt deposits. The latter are guarded by **Hasegg Castle**, in which Archduke Ferdinand II set up the first mechanical mint in 1567. For this reason the fortress's distinctive tower is known to this day as the Mint Tower. The parish church of St Nicholas was completed in 1437 and remodelled in the baroque style in 1752.

Ambras Castle, perched on the mountainside southeast of Innsbruck, was the favourite residence of Archduke Ferdinand and his lovely wife Philippine Welser. Ferdinand had the castle extended to its present size from 1564;

Taking in the sights.

today visitors can admire a comprehensive arms collection, an exhibition of paintings and curios and the **Spanish Hall**, with a magnificent Renaissance coffered ceiling.

The Karwendel and the Wetterstein: Its gigantic cirques and grey limestone walls gave the **Karwendel Range** – which lies between Achensee in the east and the Seefeld Ridge in the west – its name. To the north, the foothills gradually peter out into the Bavarian uplands; to the south, the 6,560-ft (2,000-metre) peaks plunge steeply down towards the Inn Valley. The highest mountain in the range is the **Birkkarspitze** (9,045 ft/2,756 metres); the most convenient cable car access is via the Northern Cable Car from Innsbruck, which climbs to the summit of the **Hafelekar** (7,660 ft/2,330 metres). The Karwendel covers an area of 350 sq. miles (900 sq. km) all told, two-thirds of which lie within the boundaries of the Tyrol.

The mountainous region is subdivided by four long mountain ranges running from west to east. Correspondingly long are the valleys in between, some deeply eroded and all inaccessible to traffic. For this reason the Karwendel has remained as it always was: a remote and lonely mountain region with precipitous limestone cliffs, silent high-altitude cirques and pine-fringed Alpine meadows. The threat to the ecology of the area has been averted by plans for a national park covering the entire area.

The sick Alps: Many of the trees in the Alps look perfectly healthy, and herds of chamois give the impression that there are no real dangers. Appearances are deceiving, however. Even here, every other tree suffers from a fatal disease; the pine trees no longer give off their characteristic scent and the crystal-clear streams are not infrequently as acid as dilute car battery fluid. And yet, the Karwendel remains an apparently unspoilt mountain wilderness offering walkers, mountaineers and climbers a high-altitude experience which is second to none.

Despite the almost 9,845 ft (3,000 metres) attained by the **Zugspitze**, its

Après-ski in an Arlberg discotheque.

highest peak, the **Wetterstein Range** has less to offer the visitor. It consists of a single vast mountain ridge, of which only the south side lies in the Tyrol. This is actually no real disadvantage, for the **Mieminger Mountains**, with the prominent **Hohe Munde** (8,510 ft/2,595 metres), rise up parallel to the Wetterstein Range to the south. This, in conjunction with the western slopes of the Karwendel, creates a high-altitude triangle in which the austerity of the mountain scenery is interspersed by rolling hills, idyllic lakes and vast tracts of unspoilt natural beauty.

The centre of the plateau is marked above all by **Seefeld**, famous as a winter sports resort and the Tyrolese centre for Nordic skiing. During the summer months, mountain walkers will find extensive touring routes of all grades.

The Lech Valley: The main "landgrabber" in the Tyrolese stretch of the Lech valley is the untamed **Lech** itself. The torrent acquired its nickname from the local inhabitants, for long stretches of the valley have frequently been flooded by detritus which centuries of carefully tended meadowland have only been able to cover after a fashion.

At first glance, this region, the Ausserfern, may not look interesting. In fact, geologically-speaking, it is fascinating. To the north the valley is hemmed in by the **Allgäu Alps**; to the south lie the **Lechtal Alps**. Whilst only the southern and southeastern slopes of the Allgäu mountains belong to the Tyrol – and the northern section disperses into Bavaria – the Lechtal Range forms the longest independent mountain ridge in the northern limestone Alps. The summits form a single ridge of countless 6,560-ft (2,000-metre) peaks, except for one single 9,845-ft (3,000-metre) mountain – the **Parseier Spitze** (9,960 ft/3,035 metres).

The best view of this unique mountain ridge can be gained from the summit of the **Valluga** (9,225 ft/2,810 metres), accessible by cable car. From this vantage point one can begin to comprehend the forces which once pushed the layers of rock across each other and into a vertical position, and how the subse-

Cross-country skiing, hard work but rewarding.

quent weathering gouged out cracks and clefts, thus forming the jagged mountain peaks. This is ideal countryside for a high-level walk across the peaks and ridges since the latter are uninterrupted by deep valley clefts, and the shelters lie at convenient distances from each other.

The position on the north side of the Lech Valley is quite different. Here the terrain is dominated by the tertiary rock known as flysch, consisting of alternating layers of clay, slate, marl and limestone, which, lightly weathered, acquire a less jagged profile. Soft forms, verdant meadows, dense forests, marshy water meadows and highland moors are the external characteristics of this "soft", easily weathered stone. Rising up above this geological region are the peaks and ridges of dolomite, characterised by desolate cirques and sheer rock faces and vast gravel beds.

Limestone also contributes to the appearance of the mountain world of the **Allgäu**. The variety of rocks explains the wealth of flora, for different plants flourish on different geological founda-tions. Only here in the Allgäu, where the mountains are clothed right up to their summits in a thick carpet of grass and the alpine meadow flora blooms in such a riot of colours, can such myriad species be found.

Meadows and lakes: The most attractive part of the Tyrolean section of the Allgäu Alps lies tucked away behind the **Gaicht Pass** (3,585 ft/1,095 metres), accessible via **Weissenbach** on the Lech. On the other side unfolds a valley revealing a gentle mountain landscape of meadows where turquoise lakes contrast with grass-green pastures and ochre-coloured dolomite rock. Two lakes, the **Haldensee** and the **Vilsalpsee**, are as yet virtually unknown but offer an ideal starting point for an expedition into the **Tannheim Mountains** or along the Allgäu Jubilee Path.

The focal point of the Ausserfern region is **Reutte**, which lies at the junction of the Fernpass road. The village grew up as a typical ribbon development along the valley road; even today, it is dominated by the squat, low-lying houses

Left, ice speed-skating in the Innsbruck stadium. Right, a two-person bob makes its descent.

with overhanging gables. Particularly noteworthy are the elaborately painted outside walls, dating from the 18th century and the work of the Zeillers, a family of local artists. The most original murals are those of the two inns, the Goldene Krone and the Schwarzer Adler. The highly decorative and figurative murals on the Zeiller family house were painted by Franz Anton Zeiller. Johann Jakob Zeiller executed the vast ceiling fresco in the **Parish church of St Nicholas** in Elbingenalp, the oldest parish in the entire Lech Valley.

South of Reutte, the landscape changes once more. Tucked away between the mountains of the Lech Valley in the west, the Mieminger Range in the south and the Zugspitze in the east, lie Lake **Heiterwanger** and the **Plansee**, surrounded by a region of dense mountain forest. A unique high-altitude basin opens up around **Lermoos**, at a height of 3,280 ft (1,000 metres).

A completely flat meadow unfolds like a single bright-green clover leaf between the rock walls of the Mieminger Range, the Zugspitze, the Daniel and the Grubigstein.

Dark forested slopes rise up continuously on all sides, surmounted by 3,280-ft (1,000-metre) high limestone cliff faces: the western escarpments of the Schneefernerkopf and the Zugspitze massif. On the periphery of the basin lie a succession of resorts: **Biberweier**, **Lermoos** and **Ehrwald** – all three are excellent starting points for extended mountain tours. From Ehrwald it is possible to reach the Tyrol side of the Zugspitze by cable car.

Ziller Valley contrasts: There is no other region that has become so associated with the Tyrol than the Ziller Valley, and this despite the fact that the area has only been part of the Tyrol since 1816. Previously it had belonged to the Duchy of Salzburg; at the end of the 17th century Archbishop Johann Ernst of Salzburg erected a hunting lodge in Floitengrund. Today the valley's one of the best-known in the entire Alps. But while Mayerhofen offers more hotel beds than Salzburg, the valley as a whole

The Tyrolean riflemen recall the liberation struggles of the Napoleonic era.

still contains many remote nooks which remain largely unspoilt. The glaciers, the precipitous mountain faces and the razor-edge ridges, combined with the considerable height of the mountains have ensured that the beauty of this pristine landscape has remained intact.

The valley extends for some 20 miles (30 km) in a north-south direction, from **Strass** to **Mayrhofen**. Over this distance, however, it only rises some 330 ft (100 metres). This gentle incline made it possible to open up the valley by means of a narrow gauge railway, sometimes served by a steam train. Mayrhofen stands at the head of the four "Gründe", as the highest mountain valleys are known. The **Zillergrund** stretches from Mayrhofen for 10 miles (15 km) in a south-easterly direction as far as the Bärenbart Inn (4,760 ft/1,450 metres); the **Stilluppgrund** is the most deeply eroded and sparsely inhabited of the four mountain valleys.

The **Tuxer Grund** is the most accessible of the four valleys. It has the most inhabitants and is particularly popular among skiers because the **Hintertux Glacier** affords fine opportunities for skiing until well into the summer months. The last valley, the **Zemmgrund**, leads right into the heart of the Zillertal Alps. The construction of the Schlegis reservoir means that there is now a good road leading up to the Dominikus Refuge in the Zamser Valley. The latter branches off from the Zemmgrund near the Breitlahner Inn, thus enabling the traveller to drive right up to the reservoir, which lies at 5,850 ft (1,780 metres).

The **Zillertal Mountain Road** affords the best panoramic view of the valley and the main ridge of the Zillertal Alps and its remarkable glaciers, jutting out to the south and weaving its way along at a height of 5,580–6,560 ft (1,700–2,000 metres) along the western side of the valley. Access points are from **Ried**, **Aschau**, **Zellberg** and Hippach, so that visitors can plan their ascent and descent via different routes if they so wish. The highest point on the road (6,725 ft/2,050 metres) lies just below the summit of the **Arbiskopf**

The village of Eilmau beneath the crags of the Wilder Kaiser.

(7,000 ft/2,130 metres); from here you will experience the best view of the main Alpine ridge.

If, however, you follow the valley itself, you will be able to view the remains of the early 14th-century frescoes in the late Gothic parish church of **Fügen**, and the **Pilgrimage Church of St Pancratius**, built above the village at the end of the 15th century, whose altars date from the 17th century; a bonus point is the view of the valley.

Zell, the principal village in the Ziller Valley, lies at the junction with the Gerlos Pass. Its name is derived from the monk's cell which was reputedly founded here in the 8th century by St Rupert. The present parish church was finished in 1782 by the master-builder from Kitzbühel, Andrä Hueber.

The main construction is rococo in style although the pointed tower was retained from the original Gothic building. Franz Anton Zeiller from Reutte painted the vast dome over the main area with a single enormous fresco. He was also responsible for all the other frescoes as well as the altar painting.

The summer ski area: Whilst the Ziller, Stillupp and Zemm high-altitude valleys have remained virtually untouched, the Tuxer Grund has become a lively tourist centre. **Tux, Lanersbach** and **Hintertux** have developed rapidly since the construction of the Hintertux Glacier Railway. The cable car opens up good skiing opportunities until well into the summer, and after that it provides access to an extensive high-altitude region for mountain tours, including the Hoher Riffler (10,600 ft/3,230 metres), the Olperer (11,405 ft/3,475 metres) and the Hoher Wand (10,040 ft/3,060 metres). Those who prefer rather warmer temperatures than these heights afford will enjoy the radioactive thermal spring.

From the Wipp Valley to the Stubai: Between the Tux Alps in the east and the Stubai Alps in the west lies the **Brenner Pass** (4,510 ft/1,375 metres), the lowest-lying cleft in the entire Alpine Ridge and as such the easiest and also the oldest Alpine pass. The Illyrians used a mule track here; the Romans had a chariot road. In the Middle Ages the pass was the route used by emperors and kings on pleasure journeys or with their armies. Today, the old main road, the motorway and the railway attempt to cope with the route's ever-increasing passage of traffic.

A brilliant example of modern technology is the **Europa Bridge**, which crosses the valley of the Sill near Schönberg. It is over 2,625 ft (800 metres) long and 625 ft (190 metres) high, which makes it the highest motorway bridge in Europe.

The first village in the Wipp Valley, **Matrei**, is also the oldest. Oriel-windowed houses with overhanging roofs, Gothic entrances and ground-floor vaulted ceilings characterise the appearance of this typical linear village. The parish church, which dates from the 12th century, was refurbished in the 18th century with brightly coloured baroque frescoes.

The **Navis Valley** branching off to the left, contains the **Chapel of St Kathrin**, built on the remains of Aufenstein Castle. The chapel houses the two oldest

Left, a street in Kitzbühel. **Right**, Hasegg Castle.

known wooden statues in North Tyrol, dating from the early 14th century.

Following a major fire in **Steinach** in 1853, only the chancel remained of the old parish church but it was integrated into the new construction. Its most impressive feature is the magnificent altar by the South Tyrol artist Johann Perger. The Gschnitz Valley leads off westwards from Steinach.

Tyrol's Flower Mountain: North of Trins, the first village in the valley, the road starts to climb towards the **Blaser** (7,360 ft/2,245 metres), the Tyrolese mountain with the richest carpet of flowers in spring. The **Stubai Valley** is the largest subsidiary valley leading off the Wipp Valley. It leads into the very heart of the massive Stubai glaciers. By taking the Stubai Glacier Railway visitors can even venture on to the icy surface.

Mieders, **Telfes**, **Fulpmes** and **Neustift** are not merely lively tourist villages. They all boast parish churches built during the 18th century by Franz de Paula Penze, the parish priest of Telfes. The loveliest of his churches stands in Neustift. Josef Anton Zoller, Josef Keller and Josef Haller were the craftsmen responsible for its splendid baroque frescoes.

Fulpmes was in former times the home of the most famous iron workers in North Tyrol. Their hammers were driven by hydraulic power derived from the Plövenbach stream; even today, a few riverside workshops continue to ply their trade. Ice axes and crampons from Fulpmes are famous the world over.

The northern exit of the Wipp Valley is marked on the eastern side by the **Patscherkofel** and to the west by the **Nockspitze**. At their feet extends a broad upland plateau with sleepy villages like Mutters and lively ones like **Axams**. Between the two, in **Götzens**, stands what rates as perhaps the loveliest baroque parish church in Tyrol. It was completed in 1780 by Franz Singer. Colourful late rococo frescoes by Matthäus Günther enhance the master builder's fine stucco.

The **Ötztal** is the longest and most imposing side valley of the Inn.

Wintertime in the Lermooser Valley, with the Zugspitze in the background.

Obergurgl itself is at least 30 miles (50 km) from the valley mouth; the difference in altitude, 4,050 ft (1,235 metres), corresponds to that of quite a considerable mountain ascent. The valley opens up like a staircase in distinct steps which mark the stages of the retreating glaciers. Steep narrow sections with a deeply cut river bed alternate with broad, almost level fertile valley areas, on which the district's villages and agricultural lands are located.

In the upper reaches of the valley, in **Zwieselstein**, the Ötztal divides into two; the **Gurgltal** and the **Ventertal**. Here lie the two highest villages in the eastern Alps: **Obergurgl** (6,300 ft/1,920 metres) and **Vent** (6,220 ft/1,895 metres). Both valleys continue upwards until they reach the glaciers of the main Alpine ridge. It was here, by the Italian border, that the famous "Ötzi", a Celt who died in this icy region 5,000 years ago, was discovered in 1993.

Apart from the approaches to the villages of Obergurgl and Vent, the Ötztal has two high points that are, unusually,

accessible by car: the **Timmelsjoch** (8,120 ft/2,474 metres) and the car park (9,200 ft/2,805 metres) on the glacier road to the **Rettenbachferner**.

Before turning into the Ötz valley, however, make a short detour to the **Cistercian Abbey of Stams**, which lies a little further to the east in the Inn Valley. Together with Göttweig and Melk, it is one of the finest monastery complexes in Austria. Founded in 1268 to mark the death of Konradin, the last of the Hohenstaufen, the monastery became so important within the next century that in 1362 Charles VI had the Imperial jewels deposited here for safekeeping. The abbey church, 265 ft (80 metres) long, had a flat roof until 1615, when a vaulted roof was added.

The appearance of the village of **Ötz** is dominated by the silhouette of the parish church, which overshadows the historic houses with their painted façades. The most attractive of the latter is the **Gasthof Stern**, whose frescoes date from 1573.

High above the valley **Lake Piburger**

The snowboard can be taken just about anywhere.

lies hidden; it's a popular spot for bathing. The most important spa in the Ötztal – thanks to its sulphur springs – is **Langenfeld**. Here, too, is the highest church tower in the valley (245 ft/75 metres). The late Gothic parish church was completed in 1518. On the other side of the valley stands a votive chapel erected in 1661 to commemorate the community's plague victims.

Sölden, which lies at an altitude of 4,520 ft (1,380 metres), is primarily a winter sports resort. Skiers are attracted in hordes to Hochsölden, which lies 2,300 ft (700 metres) higher still, and to the glacier road to the Rettenbachferner, where skiing is possible well into the summer months. Mountaineers, on the other hand, set out from Zwieselstein into the valley of the Venter Ache and to Vent itself. From here they can easily reach many of the 9,840-ft (3,000-metre) peaks surrounding the Ötztal.

Obergurgl and **Hochgurgl** are also ski resorts. From here cable cars fan out in all directions towards the surrounding peaks: the toll road to the

Timmelsjoch begins in Hochgurgl, the pass connecting the valley with the South Tyrol. The best view can be had from **Windegg** (6,825 ft/2,080 metres), which affords a panorama extending over the entire Gurgl Valley and part of the Gurgler Ferner. To the north one can see extensive sections of the Ötz Valley.

Since the Ötz Valley merely marks the eastern boundary of the Ötztal Alps, the **Pitz Valley** – which branches off from the upper Inn Valley some 5 miles (8 km) further to the west – provides the first route into the heart of the mountains themselves. For long stretches it is merely a forbiddingly narrow gorge, only occasionally opening out into a sunny basin. The villages of **Wenns**, **Jerzens** and **St Leonhard** owe their new prosperity to skiing enthusiasts and the Glacier Road, constructed to provide access to the Mittelbergferner. The principle sight in the valley is the **Platzhaus** in Wenns, which is adorned from top to bottom with fine Renaissance murals.

The **Kauner Valley** in the west runs in a north-south direction through the Ötztal Alps. It branches off from the Inn Valley in an easterly direction south of Landegg near Prutz, turns briefly towards the south, and offers at its far end – near the Gepatsch reservoir – another glacier with skiing facilities beneath the slopes of the **Hochvernagt Spitze** (11,610 ft/3,540 metres).

The parish church in **Kaltenbrunn** was a place of pilgrimage and site of miracles as long ago as 1285. The Gothic chancel, completed in 1502, was commissioned by Archduke Sigmund; the nave contains the domed Chapel of Miracles with the carved votive statue of a Madonna with Child (1400).

From Landeck to Arlberg: Even in pre-Roman times there was a settlement at the confluence of the Sanna and the Inn. During the 13th century, Duke Meinhard II of Tyrol had the existing fortress here rebuilt in its present form with a defensive wall, circular keep and ward. The chapel, which dates from the same period, was adorned with frescoes during the first half of the 16th century. Today the castle houses a museum of

Left, the Zugspitze seen from the Tyrol side. **Right**, a Tyrolean in his rifleman's uniform.

local history. The most important architectural monument in **Landeck** is the parish church, in the Angedair district. The elaborate tracery of its windows and the network vaulting make this the most harmonious Gothic church in Tyrol. Inside there is a remarkable late Gothic work of art, the **Schrofenstein Altarpiece**.

Behind **Pians** the valley forks again; to the left opens up the **Paznaun Valley** with the **Trisanna Valley**, whilst the **Rosanna Valley** leads straight ahead, climbing towards the Arlberg. Near Wiesberg Castle the railway crosses the valley at a height of 280 ft (85 metres) by means of the famous **Trisanna Bridge**. In former times the Paznaun Valley was virtually cut off from the rest of the world; nowadays, thanks to the tourism within the region, it has been completely opened up. The construction of the **Silvretta Alpine Road** (with a pass at an altitude of 6,665 ft/ 2,035 metres), and the development of the skiing area around Ischgl, are the principal reasons for this expansion.

Skiers have also brought world fame to the **Arlberg**. What was once just a mountain whose slopes were covered with pine trees ("arlen") is today a vast winter sports paradise, including **St Anton**, **Zürs** or **Lech**. The area surrounding the Valluga forms a part of this region, as does the eastern section of the Lech catchment area.

The Arlberg: One hundred years ago the rural existence centred on farming, which for centuries had functioned satisfactorily on the Arlberg, was on the verge of extinction. Only modern technology and the development of skiing as a sport brought about the region's renaissance. First came the construction of the railway through the Arlberg itself (on 20 September 1884 Emperor Franz Josef officially opened the tunnel by travelling along the route in his Imperial train), followed by the building of the Flexen Road (which reached Lech in 1900). But it was really the invention of skiing which led to the boom. A priest named Müller, from the village of Warth in the Lech Valley, was the first to try out the new sport.

Progress in the footsteps of the daring priest was rapid. The Arlberg Ski Club in St Christoph was founded in 1901, and Hannes Schneider from Stuben started to adapt techniques imported from Scandinavia to suit Alpine conditions. Stefan Kruckenhauser developed the parallel turn – today practised all over the world – and wedeling, which makes skiing seem like child's play.

The skier's delight was until recently the bane of the car driver. The Arlberg is still the only link between Tyrol and its western neighbour, the Vorarlberg. In winter the pass, which lies at 5,885 ft (1,795 metres), was frequently closed due to snowdrifts or the danger of avalanches. Only since the end of 1978 has the road tunnel, almost 9 miles (14 km) long, provided a year-round link.

So now the motor traveller too can enjoy, in peace, the broad alpine meadows as well as the tunnels and avalanche galleries on the Flexen Road. He can also enjoy breathtaking views down into the **Kloster Valley** and towards the pretty village of **Stuben**.

Left, hunting in the mountains. **Right**, frescos on a house wall in Holzgau.

VORARLBERG

For the Irish missionary Columba, who came to **Bregenz** on Lake Constance in AD 610 to convert the region to Christianity, the town of *Brigantium* lay "as in a golden dish". What he described so vividly in words is the impression gained by a modern-day traveller approaching Bregenz in one of the ships of the lake Constance Line, or surveying the town, lake, Rhine Valley and Swiss Alps from the summit of the Pfänder.

The town lies on a gently rising terrace on the shores of a wide bay on Lake Constance. To the east the shell-shaped intrusion is sheltered by the slopes of the Pfänder; to the west lies the Rhine, which once provided the necessary protection against enemy attack from the plains behind.

It was precisely this protected position which encouraged the Celts to settle on the site. Their village, *Brigantioi*, later became under Roman occupation *Brigantium*, complete with forum, basilica, baths and temple. The Romans were the first to build a fortified harbour. Following attacks by the Alemanni in the 3rd century the Romans withdrew up the hillside to the strategically more easily defensible site of what is now the Upper Town; here they built themselves a new fort.

After the retreat of the Romans in the middle of the 5th century, the Alemanni captured the town and with it the main and subsidiary valleys of the Rhine. The new conquerors did not, however, establish their rule from the town itself but chose Feldkirch, where – as the Counts of Montfort – they built a fortress, the Schattenburg. In 1860 Bregenz became the nominal capital of the Vorarlberg, by virtue of the creation of the first local parliament for the region, which at that time was still a part of the Tyrol. Only in 1918, however, did Bregenz become the official capital of the province.

The **Lower Town** huddles on a mound of land deposited by the lake. Apart from the railway station, it is characterised by a series of neo-classical local government buildings, the regional military headquarters and the museum of the Vorarlberg. In the Middle Ages the lake waters actually reached as far as the foundation walls of the **Lake Chapel of St George**. In 1445 the first memorial to the fallen soldiers of the Appenzell Civil War was erected here. The present church was built in 1698 according to the plans drawn up by Christian Thumb. Externally its most remarkable feature is an octagonal tower with an onion dome; inside, its high altar is an unusual example of late Renaissance craftsmanship. The work, completed in 1615, has a central shrine decorated with a Crucifixion group; on the upper section you can see the figures of St John the Baptist and St John the Evangelist.

A granary was built on to the north side of the chapel in 1686 by Hans Kuen. The chapel was then converted into the **Town Hall**, completed in 1810. Only in 1898 did the broad front acquire its present-day neo-Renaissance facade. The latter is decorated with mosaic portraits of the Emperor Augustus, Duke Sigmund of Austria, Empress Maria Theresa and Emperor Franz Josef.

The most impressive building in the Lower Town is without doubt the **Sacred Heart Church**. It stands at the foot of the Pfänder, characterised by twin pointed spires. The largest neo-Renaissance building in the Vorarlberg, it was built under the supervision of the Stuttgart architect Joseph Cades, and was completed in 1908. The harmonious design of the west front reveals the inspiration of the medieval brick churches of north Germany. Within, too, the architect has followed these examples, constructing a basilica with ribbed vaulting in accordance with the strict rules laid down by the church designers of the past. The overall impression of the interior is enhanced by the stained-glass windows inserted in the aisles and transepts in 1958. The series of 24 pictures was produced from sketches made by Martin Häusle, the Feldkirch painter; they illustrate the theme of the Christian Promise.

If you stroll from the Leutbühel crossroads through the Maurachgasse towards

Preceding pages: enjoying the great outdoors. Right, making cheese in the Forest of Bregenz.

the **Upper Town**, you will pass the site of the former Roman port. Passing through the **Unteres Tor** gateway, you will enter the medieval town centre. Hugo von Tübingen, later known as Hugo von Montfort, had this area laid out in a regular pattern on the ruins of the Roman fortress. Sections of the town wall which formed part of medieval Bregenz have survived to this day.

The most notable building in the Upper Town – **St Martin's Tower** – also serves as the local landmark. The first Count of Bregenz used it as a tithe barn – in other words, as his tax office. During the 14th century two storeys were converted into a double chapel. Finally, by 1601, Benedetto Prato from Roveredo had added the flamboyant canopy to the tower and topped it with its lantern-festooned onion dome.

In 1360 a Swabian artist decorated the chapel with cycles of frescoes. Apart from various scenes from the Life of Christ there is a large portrait of St Christopher on the north wall and one of St Ursula in a ship on the east wall.

Equally moving is a representation on the south wall of a fully-clothed Christ on the Cross; at his feet sits a violin player. The portrait of St Ursula seems to indicate that the saint may have passed through Bregenz on her way from Cologne to Rome. The picture of Christ with the violinist points towards trading links with Italy, since it is modelled on one in the cathedral of Lucca.

Passing along the Meissnersteige, we come down to the Thalbachgrund, opposite which stands the **Parish Church of St Gall**. Its origins date from an early church founded here by the missionaries St Gall and St Columba; the present building was completed by 1737 under the supervision of Franz Anton Beer, using some structural elements from the older edifice. The West Tower, constructed in 1480, acquired its baroque gable in 1673. The single-naved interior seems exceptionally wide because of its relatively low ceiling; it was elaborately decorated in the rococo style by Abraham Bader. Ignaz Wegscheider added the painted ceiling. The imposing high

Bregenz in 1882.

altar, of reddish-brown marble stucco, is also the work of Abraham Bader. As Maria Theresa donated 1,500 guilders to pay for the altar, one of the shepherdesses on the altarpiece bears a striking resemblance to her.

The location of the Upper Town betrays the fact that, at least in early times, the citizens of Bregenz had no strong links to the lake in spite of the town's picturesque situation on the eastern bay. None of the important buildings was erected on the lake shore, and at the end of the last century not many protests were voiced when the railway and a jungle of tracks wormed their way on to the land between the town and the lake. Since that time, those wishing to visit the lakeside or board one of the white ships of the Lake Constance Line must use the only railway crossing. A 5-mile (9-km) path along the lakeshore from Lochau in the north to the mouth of the Bregenzer Ache in the west has proved little compensation.

A Corpus Christi procession in Höbranz.

Bregenz's greatest claim to fame – and one for which the town is now known all over the world – is the **Bregenz Festival**. In 1946 the director of the Vorarlberg State Theatre constructed a stage on a raft anchored in one of the old harbour basins. Mozart's lyrical drama *Bastien and Bastienne* was performed here, as well as a ballet to the music of Mozart's *Eine Kleine Nachtmusik*. The little raft has since been replaced by a floating stage 200 ft (60 metres) wide and 130 ft (40 metres) deep, situated some 85 ft (25 metres) from the shore. The tiers of seats have room for as many as 4,400 spectators.

It's well worth catching a concert here. A performance of Mozart's *Magic Flute* on the lake is unforgettable. The rural setting, the lapping water, the reflections of the night sky all contribute to its power.

Nestled in the meadowland to the west of the floating theatre lies the Cistercian **Abbey of Mehrerau**. It was founded in 1097 by Count Ulrich X of Bregenz, and served as a bastion of the Counter-Reformation. The new abbey church, completed in 1743 by Franz

Anton Beer, was sold for demolition in 1808. Some of the stones were used in the construction of the mole protecting Lindau harbour. In 1854 the Swiss branch of the Cistercian order erected a neo-Romanesque church on the medieval ruins. It was restructured in 1964 and the remains of the Romanesque basilica built in 1200 were exposed and made accessible.

The church itself is a high-ceilinged hall with a transept and a semicircular chancel, impressive in its simplicity. The right aisle wall is broken up by three chapels, each containing an important work of art: a triple portrait of St Anne (*circa* 1515), an Annunciation (second half of the 15th century) and a triptych with Crucifixion scenes from the end of the 15th century. Under the gallery is a votive picture of a Madonna with Child (*circa* 1490).

In the Bregenzerwald: In AD 830 the abbot of Reichenau Abbey, Wahlafried Strabo, described the Bregenz hinterland and the primeval forests along the Bregenzer Ache as far as the Hoch-

tannberg Pass as a "wilderness devoid of human habitation". It was not until the middle of the 10th century that the Counts of Bregenz started to use the forests as hunting grounds and permitted settlers to clear the trees and make their homes there.

Life in the valley of the Bregenzer Ache did not develop exactly along the lines foreseen by the ruling Counts. The settlers decided to form a free commune – in other words, an independent Peasants' Republic. The leader was an official elected for a period of seven years, who governed with the assistance of 24 councillors and a parliament with 48 members. The commune's constitution was known as the "Customs of the Country"; it contained not only its own set of laws by which everyone in the community had to abide, but the right to pass new ones.

The region's autonomy, which it was able to preserve for many years, was not the result of chance. It was not until the first half of the 19th century that a systematic network of footpaths was cre-

A regatta on Lake Constance.

ated, and proper access was not guaranteed until 1912, when the Bregenzerwald Railway finally reached as far as Bezau. The present-day road network was not built until after World War II. Today it is possible to drive from Dornbirn across the Bödele to Schwarzenberg, across the Furka Ridge or the Faschina Ridge to Damüls or from the Lech Valley across the Hochtannberg into the Valley of the Bregenzer Ache. From Bregenz there is a direct link across the gorge of the Schwarzbach Torrent to **Alberschwende,** sitting at the bottom of the Brüggelekopf. The village square in front of the church is adorned by a linden-tree which is reputedly 1,000 years old. It is a memento of a courtyard which Count Rudolf of Bregenz donated to the Abbey of Mehrerau.

Hittisau, which possesses more than 100 privately-owned meadows, and **Sibratsgfäll** – the youngest community in the Bregenzerwald – are ideal destinations for holidaymakers in search of a relaxing atmosphere. **Langenegg** has an exceptionally fine church. Built in 1775, the interior was decorated during the following year by Johann Michael Koneberg. The nave contains murals depicting the Nativity, the Marriage and the Assumption of the Virgin Mary. The fresco under the balcony, depicting Christ expelling the money-changers from the temple, includes (somewhat incongruously) the figure of a woman carrying a basket of eggs, dressed in the unmistakable traditional costume of the Bregenzerwald.

In the village of **Schwarzenberg,** on the road to the Bödele, stands the house where the artist Angelika Kaufmann lived as a child. In 1757, when she was 16 years old, she painted the pictures of the apostles on the walls of the nave of the Parish Church of the Trinity. In 1802 she presented the church of her native village with the picture which adorns the high altar to this day – the *Coronation of the Virgin by the Holy Trinity.*

The market town of **Bezau** is one of the principal communities of the Bregenzerwald. Its **Museum of Local History** is worth visiting for its exhibition of folklore. The terminus of the Bregenzerwald Railway, long since axed, is marked today only by an old steam locomotive. **Mellau,** which lies a little further up the valley, is overshadowed by the lofty summit of the Kanisfluh. Its five rock faces, with a total length of 4 miles (6 km), fall precipitously down to the valley from a height of 4,265 ft (1,300 metres).

Damüls, at the foot of the Glatthorn, was first and foremost a Walser settlement. According to a document dated 1313, the Walser received the mountain valley in fief from the Counts of Montfort. In 1484 they had the massive stone **Parish Church of St Nicholas** built by Rolle Maiger from Röthis. The flat wooden coffered ceiling was decorated in 1693 by Johann Purtscher with scenes from the Life of the Virgin. The walls are a poor man's bible: arranged in four columns on the north wall is the Passion of Christ; the apse portrays Christ at the Last Judgment with the Sword of Justice; scenes on the south wall depict Miracles of Compassion.

The Adoration of the Magi, a priceless

A girl in Montafon costume.

fresco, was painted around the year 1500 by an unknown master.

The early baroque elements in the parish church of Damüls date from 1630 onwards. Erasmus Kern created the high altar and its figures and the Plague Altar in the north wall. The plague statue of Christ, carved in about 1635, stands on the left side altar. By contrast, the statue of St Theodulus on the right-hand side altar dates from as early as 1400. The tabernacle in the chancel is engraved with the year 1485; it bears the mark of the master builder Rolle Maiger.

The last village of any size in the valley of the Bregenzer Ache is **Schoppernau**. The desolate nature of this upland valley is reflected in the name, which means "naked meadows". Even in early times its inhabitants were forced to seek their living elsewhere. Nonetheless, the woodland dwellers had a magnificent church built during the second half of the 18th century; its frescoes and stucco date from 1796.

The last hamlet within the valley proper of the Bregenzer Ache is **Schröcken**, which is also an old Walser settlement dating from the 14th century. In 1863 all the buildings were destroyed in a fire; even the church did not remain unscathed. Behind Schröcken the road winds uphill to the **Hochtannberg Pass**; on the other side lies Warth on the Lech, the last village before the Vorarlberg border. Providing there is no danger of avalanches when you arrive, you can drive across into the bustling world of the Arlberg.

Through the Vorarlberg section of the Rhine Valley: The first town upriver from Bregenz is also the biggest and youngest in the Vorarlberg. **Dornbirn** was formed in 1901 by the amalgamation of four villages. For this reason, between townhouses and factories you will repeatedly come across single farms, large gardens and open fields. The name Dornbirn was first mentioned as long ago as AD 815, when it was known as Torrinpuirron. The present centre is dominated by the **Parish Church of St Martin**, completed in the neo-classicial style in 1840. It has a temple-like porch

The Bregenzer Ache river.

with six Ionic columns. The glass mosaic in the tympanum shows Christ's Entry into Jerusalem. The fresco in the nave portrays the Last Judgment. Near St Martin's stands the **Red House**, the town landmark. Built in 1634, it is a typical Rhine valley dwelling with a brick-built base surmounted by an ornate log cabin construction.

For nature-lovers Dorbirn can offer two attractions: firstly, the Vorarlberg **Exhibition of Natural History** – a remarkable collection explaining the area's geology as well as its wealth of fascinating flora and fauna of the region – and secondly the **Rappenloch Gorge**, a 200-ft (60-metre) deep ravine that was gouged out by the Dornbirner Ache when the Rhine glacier melted.

During the early Middle Ages, the Alemanni advanced as far as **Hohenems** in their struggles against the Rhaeto-Romanic tribes. As early as the 9th century a fortress was built here to guard the frontier. The Emperor Barbarossa gave it to the Knight of Ems, who extended it into a mighty Imperial Castle.

As the castle itself grew in importance, so too did the Ems Family, until Marcus Sitticus became Prince-Archbishop of Salzburg in 1612. As Bishop of Konstanz, long before he was summoned to the Salzach, he began to build a new palace in the valley.

The centre section of the present **Palace** was completed in 1576; the two side wings and the curtain wall on the rock side were finished in 1610. The magnificent main façade is divided into 11 sections; the doorway in the centre bears the arms of Marcus Sitticus. During the warm summer months, a series of concerts is performed in the lovely Renaissance inner courtyard.

Connected by a passageway to the palace is the **Parish Church**, completed in 1581. The most important element in its interior is a Renaissance high altar with a late medieval Coronation of the Virgin in the central shrine. **Glopper Castle** is what is left of the former fortress on the mountainside. The late Gothic complex consists of an inner fortress protected by an outer castle,

The gentle contours of the Grosse Walsertal Valley.

moat and ramparts. The **Town Hall**, too, owes its origins to Marcus Sitticus. He commissioned its construction in 1567 as a guesthouse on the occasion of a synod in Konstanz.

Götzis, first mentioned in AD 842 as *Cazzeses*, owed its early economic importance to its trading rights, dispensed by the Montforts. What is known today as the **Old Parish Church** was thus dedicated in 1514. It enchants the visitor even now with its richly decorated frescoed walls. The left wall of the nave displays scenes from the Life of Christ; the choir arch has a rather grim Last Judgment, and the right wall of the nave shows the Virgin, Saints and the Donor Family. The tabernacle is the work of Esaias Gruber from Lindau and dates from 1597. The Daughter **Church of St Arbogast** has a wooden porch containing a cycle of pictures by Leonhard Werder, painted in 1659 and portraying scenes from the legendary life of St Arbogast, who became Bishop of Strasbourg and died in 1550.

The market community of **Rankweil**

has grown up around a picturesque isolated hill, which was a holy place for the Rhaetians as long ago as 1500 BC and which was subsequently a Celtic and then a Roman fort. At the beginning of the 9th century the bishops of Chur had the first chapel built here; from then until the end of the 15th century, it was extended to form the present **Castle Church**. Two towers and a cemetery, surrounded by the former bailey wall with its wooden surround, betray the original defensive nature of the complex. The most valuable treasure in the interior is the silver cross in the chancel apse. The 13th-century wooden cross, found, according to legend, quite by chance by a shepherd wandering near Sulz, is today housed in a silver sheath decorated with reliefs by Johann Caspar Lutz in 1728.

From Feldkirch to Bludenz: It was Louis, King of the East Franks, who gave **Feldkirch** its name. In the year 909 he gave *"ad Veldkirichum"* – the settlement at the forking of the roads to the Arlberg and the Alpine passes to the canton of Grisons – to the monastery of St Gallen. The village only began to prosper, however, when Count Hugo I of Montfort moved his residence from Bregenz to Schattenburg Castle in Feldkirch, and then, around the year 1200, had a brand-new town built in the shadow of his fortress.

In spite of a colourful political past, Feldkirch has been able to retain its regular medieval plan as well as the picturesque squares enclosed by ancient houses with creeper-clad arbours. The town wall has suffered from the passage of time since the Middle Ages, but its course can still be made out everywhere by virtue of the numerous towers. The Chur Gate, the Water Tower, the Thieves' Tower (which contained the gaol), the Powder Tower and the Mill Tower mark the limits of the former urban area. The finest example of the old fortifications is the **Cats' Tower**, built in 1500. It is 130 ft (40 metres) high and has a circumference of 125 ft (38 metres). It was originally crowned by battlements, which gave way to a belfry during the 17th century. The bell,

Giving the old uniform an airing.

weighing 7.5 tonnes, is the largest in the whole province.

The square in front of the cathedral – now one of the busiest centres of life in the town – was until 1380 the site of the local cemetery. The **Cathedral Church of St Nicholas** is a double-naved late Gothic construction with an asymmetrically placed tower at the end of the north aisle. The church was completed in 1487 by Hans Sturn, the master builder from Göfis. The chancel as we know it today has a number of Renaissance features; it was added to the church in about 1520. The most notable treasure contained within is the picture adorning the right side altar, which shows the Descent from the Cross painted in 1521 by Wolf Huber.

Nowhere else in Vorarlberg are traditions so strongly maintained as in Montafon.

The pulpit is particularly interesting. It is supported on a stone base in the form of a six-pointed star. The chancel itself is hexagonal in form and is elaborately decorated with foliage; it stands on an iron pedestal with round metal bars. The canopy is also of wrought iron, divided into five sections and also richly decorated with carved window arches, pinnacles, ogee arches and finials. Integrated into the structure are 10 coloured wooden figures. This remarkable work of art, completed in 1520, was originally designed as a tabernacle.

Schattenburg Castle was built by Count Haug of Tübingen in 1185. In 1200, in line with his new place of residence, he changed his name to Hugo von Montfort. He was responsible for the 75-ft (25-metre) high keep which forms the heart of the complex as it stands today. In 1436, after the Montfort family died out, the castle came into the possession of the Habsburgs. Emperor Maximilian I had it extended to its present shape and size in about 1500. The castle now houses a **Museum of Local History**.

Where the Walser once lived: Behind the Ill gorge lies the **Walgau**, the basin-shaped section of the Ill Valley between Feldkirch and Bludenz. Hemmed in to the south by the **Rätikon Massif** and to the north by the **Walser Ridge** and the foothills of the **Lechtaler Alps**, the

valley's name recalls the Rhaeto-Romanic tribes who were the first settlers, for they were known to the Alemanni as the Walser. They built their homesteads on the cones of scree deposited by the gushing mountain streams, or on the mountain terraces formed by the glaciers.

The best example of one such settlement is **Göfis**, mentioned in a document of 850 as *Segavio*. Even in those days it had its own church and was part of the king's property. In 1450 local son Hans Sturn, who built the cathedral in Feldkirch, was allowed to build a new church for his fellow-citizens. In 1972, however, the ediface, with the exception of the chancel, was demolished to make way for a new building. This is a particularly good example of a successful symbiosis between ancient and modern building styles.

More typical of the historical aspects of the Walgau is the **Church of St Martin in Ludesch**. This small-scale religious building, completed in 1480 in the Gothic style, has a fascinating collection of valuable treasures which make it one of the most interesting examples of sacred architecture in the Vorarlberg. The high altar was created in 1629 and combines various Gothic elements with Renaissance details. The side altars date from 1487 and 1488. The frescoes on the nave walls and ceiling vaulting were painted in about 1600. They depict saints, scenes from the life of the Virgin, and the Passion.

Bludenz lies at the end of the Walgau, a short distance before the **Kloster Valley** branches off from the Ill. It was founded by Count Rudolf von Werdenberg, who gained lands in the Grosswalsertal, in the Kloster Valley and the Montafon when the Montfort family heritage was divided up. To protect his domain he built a fortress in Bludenz and – in the manner established by his relatives in Feldkirch – started to lay out a town according to a regular grid pattern. His goal was obviously to extract certain advantages from the traffic passing through the Arlberg. In 1394 the last of the Werdenbergs was

The streams fo Montafon are a paradise for white-water enthusiasts.

forced to sell his seigneurial rights to the Habsburgs.

The Werdenbergs' fortress stood on the rock which is crowned today by the baroque-style **Gayenhofen Castle**. It was completed in 1752 by an Austrian governor on the site of the earlier stronghold. Today it houses the district officers' quarters. The prominent position on the castle rock was also chosen as the site of the **Parish Church of St Laurence**. Since the church was mentioned as early as AD 830, it seems to have an even earlier claim to the place than the castle. The present building was completed in 1514; the tower dates from 1670. The interior is almost entirely 18th-century.

The Walsers' Valleys: The high-lying valleys to the west of the Arlberg were inhabited at the beginning of our millennium by Rhaeto-Romanic farmers and hunters. Their settlements, however, did not extend beyond the valley floors. The situation did not change until about 1400, when Germanic Walser tribes from the Upper Rhône Valley

Buggy-riding in Lech am Arlberg.

drove out the Rhaetians, taking possession of their lands and building their own settlements not only in the valleys but also on the upland slopes. Most of their villages were situated in the **Grosswalsertal** and **Kleinwalsertal**, to which they gave their names, and the **Montafon** and the **Brandner Valley**.

The Grosswalsertal, some 15 miles (25 km) long, extends in a northeasterly direction as a branch of the Ill Valley. It is demarcated on its sunny side by the Walser Ridge, and on the shadow side by the Lechtaler Alps. The valley gradually climbs from the depths of the Walgau to the **Schadona Pass** (6,070 ft/ 1,850 metres), through which one can reach Schröcken on the Hochtannberg Pass. Two roads provide access to the Grosswalsertal. One winds along the shadow side of the valley from Ludesch to Ragall; the other opens up the sunny side from Thüringen to the Faschina Ridge and the way to Damüls on the edge of the Bregenzer Wald.

The Land of the Walser and the Rhaetians: The hamlet of **Ragall** is one of the

Rhaetian settlements which was taken over by the Walser. Its **Parish Church** has its origins in a Rhaetian chapel dating from the 12th century; the Gothic chancel is the result of an extension added in 1460. The stucco ceiling, elaborately decorated with painted creepers, was completed in 1899.

The remote **Priory on St Gerold** is worth a detour. It marks the site of a hermitage to which a nobleman once retired. In the year 949 he was pardoned by the abbot of the Abbey of Einsiedeln. As a counter-gesture the hermit gave his cell to the abbey, which founded a monastic settlement on the site. The priory experienced its Golden Age in the 18th century when it was even able to purchase the High Court from the Emperor in Vienna. Today, **Einsiedeln Abbey** arranges seminars, concerts and theatrical productions here.

The principal village in the valley is **Sonntag**, which consists of a number of districts, hamlets and isolated settlements. House 17 in the Flecken district contains the Grosswalsertal **Museum of Local History**. The furnished rooms and workshops provide an excellent insight into the rural life of the Walser as well as their customs and costumes. **Buchburg** is the best starting point for mountain walks in all directions. The surrounding area is regarded with good reason as the largest nature conservation area in the Vorarlberg.

The flora and fauna of the Alps: Here you will still find flower-covered mountain meadows, where gentians of every variety and edelweiss still grow, and where you may even find wild orchids in bloom. Here, on the rocky slopes above, are the homes of the golden eagle and the chamois; all talk of a threatened ecology seems far away.

The highest settlement in the Grosswalsertal is the scattered village of **Fontanella**. Until 1806 it formed a part of the parish of Damüls, on the other side of the Faschina Ridge. Until the middle of the 17th century its inhabitants had to attend the larger village's church. In 1673, however, they were allowed to build their own place of

Skiing is also an exciting spectator sport.

worship. In recent years the district of Faschina has become a ski centre with an international reputation.

An Austrian valley in Bavaria: The **Kleines Walsertal**, situated behind the Hochtannberg Pass, is accessible from Austria only by foot. By road it can be reached through the Bavarian section of the Allgäu, via Oberstdorf. Because of its location, in 1871 Hungary and the German Reich agreed that the Kleines Walsertal should become part of the German Customs union. Today the valley appears more German than Austrian in character, although it remains officially part of Austrian territory.

The largest village in the Kleines Walsertal is **Riezlern**, which contains a Museum of Walser History, a casino and various mountain lifts. **Hirschegg** and **Mittelberg** are also both primarily tourist centres. The oldest parish church in the valley can be found in Mittelberg. Dedicated in 1390, it was extended in 1463 and 1694. Its 15th-century frescoes depict the Creation of the World and scenes from the Life of Christ. The

high altar dates from the 17th century.

The **Brandner Valley**, which lies to the south opposite the Grosses Walsertal, was formerly colonised by the Walser. A community of 12 families received the valley in hereditary feoff in 1347. They built the hamlet of **Brand**, lying at the three-country point near the intersection of the Austrian, Liechtenstein and Swiss borders. It has become a popular tourist centre thanks to the neighbouring **Lüner See**, which lies at an altitude of almost 660 ft (200 metres), and the **Schesaplana** (9,730 ft/2,965 metres), the highest mountain in the Rätikon range.

The Kloster Valley and Montafon: From Bludenz it seems as if the main valley continues in a straight line in a southeasterly direction. This is only strictly true geographically, for the River Ill does indeed spring from this extension of the valley. It is the shorter **Klostertal**, which runs from east to west, however, which is the route taken by the railway, the main road and the motorway heading for the **Arlberg Pass**. Only 5,885 ft

A real expert.

(1,795 metres) high, it has provided the only east-west link between Rhine and Inn, and the only route from the Austria motherland to its westernmost outpost, the Vorarlberg.

The hospices at the pass: It is clear that the traffic to the pass dominated life in the Klostertal from earliest times. Since the way was difficult and dangerous, Hugo I von Montfort instructed the Knights of St John of Jerusalem, who had a base in Feldkirch, to establish and maintain a hospice near the pass to provide travellers with accommodation and assistance. This hospice was called **Klösterle**, and soon gave its name to the entire valley and the village which sprang up in its shadow. Heinrich Findelkind followed this good example in 1386 with the foundation of the St Christopher Brotherhood, which organised searches to find exhausted travellers who had strayed from the path. The Brethren also built a hospice, a short distance east of the pass. The village which grew up there, **St Christoph**, is famous today for winter sports.

The link to the modern world really came in 1884, when the **Arlberg Railway** from Bludenz to Landeck was inaugurated. The section between Langen and St Anton required a 6-mile (10-km) long tunnel; it provided the first all-weather link between the Tyrol and the Vorarlberg. The road followed the trail blazed by the Iron Way with the opening of the **Arlberg Road Tunnel** in 1978; its length of almost 9 miles (15 km) makes it the longest road tunnel in all Austria.

Since the approach road to the Arlberg Road Tunnel is a type of motorway bypassing the villages of the Klostertal, the latter have returned to their former tranquillity once more, affording sufficient leisure to enjoy the sights they have to offer. The first of these can be found in **Braz**, the oldest permanent settlement in the valley. The name comes from the Rhaetian *Prats*, which means "a broad meadow". The **Parish Church of Innerbraz** was rebuilt in the baroque style at the end of the 18th century by Tyrolean artists. The frescoes adorning the vaulting were the work of the artist Carl Klausner from the Paznauntal.

As long ago as the 9th century, **Dalaas** was the centre of the Rhaetian iron mining industry. The Walser took over the excavations, but decided to dig for silver instead. They smelted their finds in **Danöfen**, a little further up the valley. The village's name is directly derived from the location "by the ovens". As already mentioned, the building which until the 17th century housed a hospice founded by the Knights of St John of Jerusalem can still be seen in the village of Klösterle.

In Langen both the railway and the road disappear into the mountain, leaving **Stuben**, an attractive, sleepy place, a little further up the valley. The village's name stems from the room maintained by the Knights of St John as a place where travellers could warm themselves. The little church has a Gothic chancel, a baroque nave and an exceptionally lovely Madonna crowned with a halo and dating from about 1630. Above Stuben, the road finally wends its way to the combe of the Arlberg; to the north, the Flexenpass – long sections of which have been blasted from the solid rock – provides access to Zürs and Lech am Arlberg across almost vertical rock faces.

The Montafon: Hydraulic power stations are as important to the Montafon, as the upper section of the Ill Valley is known, as road traffic is to the Klostertal. In 1953 the Montafon and the Tyrolean village of Paznaun were linked by the **Silvretta Reservoir**, lying at an altitude of 6,680 ft (2,036 metres).

It is located exactly on the watershed between the two valleys. Here the River Ill, fed by the Silvretta glaciers, runs precisely along the European watershed between the Rhine and the Danube; as it seemed unable to make up its mind in which direction to flow at this point, it was necessary to construct dams on both sides. The road, originally built to serve the station, has become a real attraction. It is constructed to a very high standard and leads into a magnificent section of the High Alps, where rocks and névés form a harmonious unity seldom encountered elsewhere in

Right, steep pistes on the Arlberg.

the Alps. Precipitous reddish-brown or grey-green ridges of rock are broken up by gentle névé fields; some mountain peaks which initially look less imposing than the others acquire grandeur from the presence of mighty glaciers. South of the reservoir no fewer than 74 mountain peaks rise above the 9,845-ft (3,000-metre) mark.

The combe section of the Silvretta High Alpine Road is a toll road maintained by the Vorarlberg Ill Power Authority. It begins in the little village of **St Anton** in the Montafon – a region which the commercially-minded Vorarlberg community claims, with some justification, to have made into an Alpine Park. **Schruns-Tschagguns, St Gallenkirch; Gaschurn** and **Partenen** sport pretty Montafon-style houses, lifts of all descriptions – and, at every season of the year, an assortment of Austrian and foreign holidaymakers.

The Montafon lies directly in front of the impassable barrier formed by the giants of the Silvretta Range. In former times the region was poverty-stricken despite the existence of iron ore and silver deposits in the mountains. The profits from the mining industry filled the coffers of the local feudal lords, the Bishops of Chur and the Fugger clan of Augsburg. For this reason the area can boast few major architectural masterpieces or works of art.

The exception is the community of **Batholomäberg**. Not only is it the oldest village in the region; it also possesses the most important church in the valley. The **Parish Church of St Bartholomew** existed even in Roman times; its 12th-century processional cross is the most valuable Romanesque work of art in the Vorarlberg. The folding altarpiece on the right-hand side of the nave, dedicated to St Anne, is Gothic and dates from 1525. The present church is baroque in style and was completed in 1743. Its most valuable treasure is the coffered ceiling dating from 1742 and portraying the 14 auxiliary saints, as well as the magnificent altars, which were completed between 1737 and 1746.

Schruns was the seat of the local court during Maria Theresa's reign; it was also once the terminus of the railway line. Today this is unused except on special occasions when trips are arranged on old steam engines. There are, however, plenty of cable cars and hotels in the town. The Montafon **Museum of Local History** provides an interesting insight into the natural history and the past of the valley.

Mule tracks across to Switzerland and the Tyrol: The highest permanently inhabited village in the Montafon today is **Gargellen**. Its name, derived from the Romance language, means mountain torrent. What was once a miners' summer encampment has become a popular holiday village, bearing not the slightest sign of its former poverty. In any case, the path up to the **Schlappinerjoch** (7,230 ft/2,200 metres) follows an ancient shepherds' trail across the Swiss border to Klosters in the Prättigau. The valley and ridge represent the geographical boundary between the Rätikon and Silvretta.

There were also once ancient footpaths leading from **Partenen**. One mule track led across the Zeinisjoch to the Tyrol; a second, via the Vermuntpass, into the Engadine. The Romans are known to have used the Zeinisjoch, whilst the farmers from the Lower Engadine drove their cattle across the Vermuntpass to the summer pastures in the meadows of the Montafon. Mountain ramblers follow in their tracks to this day.

Some of the scenic highlights of the Montafon are also accessible to non-mountaineers: the various reservoirs of the Ill power station network can be reached to some extent via toll roads (the Silvretta Reservoir and the Kops Reservoir), or via cable car (Vermunt Reservoir). The best view is from the **Bielerhöhe** by the **Silvretta Reservoir**. The entire expanse of water can be seen from the "Veesenmeyerstein". The greater and lesser **Piz Buin** (10,895 ft/3,320 metres) can be seen from here, as can the Ochsental Glacier. And anyone who prefers to travel by water rather than by land can cross the reservoir by motor boat, or sail round its perimeter in a little under two hours.

Right, into orbit on the Arlberg.

INSIGHT GUIDES
TRAVEL TIPS

Insight Guides portray destinations in depth, providing the complete picture and the top photography

INSIGHT POCKET GUIDES PLUS PULLOUT MAP

INSIGHT GUIDE austraLia

BaLi

Insight Pocket Guides focus on the best choices for places to see and things to do and include large fold-out maps

INSIGHT COMPACT GUIDES London

Insight Compact Guides' portability makes them the perfect books to carry with you for on-the-spot reference

Three types of guide for all types of travel

INSIGHT GUIDES Different people need different kinds of information. Some want *background information* to help them prepare for the trip. Others seek *personal recommendations* from someone who knows the destination well. And others look for *compactly presented data* for on-the-spot reference. With three carefully designed series, Insight Guides offer readers the perfect choice. Insight Guides will turn your visit into an experience.

The world's largest collection of visual travel guides

Getting Acquainted

The Place 314
Topography 314
Climate 314
The Economy 314
Government.......................... 314
Historical Overview 314

Planning the Trip

What to Wear........................ 315
Entry Regulations 315
Currency 315
Public Holidays 315
Getting There 316
Maps 317
Tourist Offices 317
Embassies Abroad 317

Practical Tips

Business Hours 317
Tipping 317
Religious Services 317
Media 317
Postal Services 318
Telephone 318
Tourist Offices 318
Consulates 318
Emergencies 318

Getting Around

Public Transport.................... 318
Vienna Rail Map 319
Private Transport 320
Mountain Railways 321

Where to Stay

Private Accommodation 321
Hotels 321
Campgrounds 324
Youth Hostels 325

Eating Out

What to Eat 325
Where to Eat 326
Drinking Notes 327

Attractions

Culture 328
On the Baroque Trail 329
Museums 329
Festival Performances........... 331
Nightlife 332

Sports & Leisure

Participant 332

Further Reading

General 336
Other Insight Guides 336

Art/Photo Credits 337
Index 338

Getting Acquainted

The Place

Area: 83,838 sq. km (32,370 sq. miles).
Capital: Vienna.
Highest Mountain: Grossglockner 3,797 metres (12,657 feet).
Population: 7,898,000.
Language: German.
Religion: 89 percent Roman Catholic.
Time zone: Central European Time (GMT plus one hour).
Currency: Austrian Schilling.
Weights & Measures: Metric.
Electricity: AC220 volts.
International dialling code: 00 43.

Austria borders Germany and the Czech Republic in the north, Hungary in the east, Slovenia and Italy in the south, and Switzerland and Liechtenstein in the west. It has a total surface area of 83,838 sq. km (32,370 sq. miles) and extends over 525 km (330 miles) from east to west, and from north to south between 46 km (30 miles) at its narrowest point and 265 km (165 miles) at its widest.

Vienna, the federal capital, has a population of around 1½ million which means that approximately every 5th Austrian is from this city.

Topography

The Eastern Alps cover as much as two-thirds of the country, tapering off in the east into foothills, the granite and gneiss plateau of Upper and Lower Austria, and the Panonian lowland plains of Burgenland. The economic centre is situated in the flat, eastern part of the country.

The Alps, of which the Grossglockner at 3,797 metres (12,657 ft) is the highest peak, constitute a stunning display of the country's natural beauty, not to mention the lovely lakes in Salzkammergut and Carinthia.

The Eastern Alps consist of three mountain ranges extending from east to west: the Northern Limestone Alps, the Central Alps and the Southern Limestone Alps. The highest ridge, the Central Alps, can be further divided into its best-known ranges: the Rätikon, Ötz and Ziller Valley Alps, the Upper and Lower Tauern Mountains and the Eisenerz Alps.

The Northern Limestone Alps constitute the border to Germany and end in the Wienerwald (Vienna Forest) in the east. The Southern Limestone Alps, which prior to 1919 belonged entirely to Austria, are situated for the most part in what is today recognised as Italy, in the area known as South Tyrol. The Karnisch Alps, on the border to Italy, and Karawanken Range in Northern Yugoslavia are part of this mountain chain. Eastern Austria consists of plains, hills and forests.

On its way to the east the Danube River is fed by a multitude of both big and small tributaries originating in the Alps. It courses through Austria for 350 km (220 miles), draining the land all the way to the Black Sea. Only in Vorarlberg is Austria's water drained by the Rhine, and in the northeast of the country by the Moldau and Elbe.

Climate

The Alps cover most of the land in Austria and play a decisive role in determining the country's different climatic conditions. The weather on the northern edge of the Alps is Central-European for the most part, which means that even during the usually lovely summers you can expect quite a bit of precipitation. South of the Alps, in Carinthia, the climate is almost Mediterranean – warmer temperatures and less rainfall. In the Alps themselves summers are hot and winters are cold and snowy. The eastern part of the country has a continental climate – Burgenland is under the influence of the Panonian Plain, which causes hot summers and freezing winters.

The Economy

Austria has a modern and well-developed industry which is on a par with Western technological standards. The electronic, chemical and textile industries are flourishing. The food and forestry industries are also important. On the Styrian Erz Mountain near Leoben, iron ore is mined, which is then processed into iron and steel in the VOEST-Alpine, Austria's largest industrial complex.

The tourist trade is extremely important for the economic well-being of the country. Without its income, the balance of trade would certainly show a deficit.

Although oil has been found north of Vienna, the majority of the country's energy is produced by hydroelectric power stations. The abundance of power has turned Austria into an electricity exporting country.

Government

Austria is divided into 9 provinces which are as follows: Vienna, Lower Austria, Burgenland, Upper Austria, Styria, Carinthia, Salzburg, Tyrol and Vorarlberg. It is a democratic republic made up of two houses: the National Assembly, composed of 185 members and the Upper House with 58 members. Together, these two houses constitute the Federal Assembly. The voting system is based on proportional representation and every four years the government is elected into office by secret ballot.

Austrian provinces enjoy a large amount of autonomy and are presided over by a top official who is voted in by the provincial parliament. The president is the head of state and the government itself is lead by the federal chancellor.

Historical Overview

30,000 BC: The last interglacial period. Venus of Willendorf. Hallstatt Period. Salt mines. La-Tene Period. The Kingdom of Noricum.
113 BC: The Battle of Noreia.
15 BC: The Romans come to the Danube.
AD 167–180: The Marcomanni Wars.
3rd–6th centuries: The Migration of Peoples. Romans depart. Immigration of Slavs and Bavarians.
791: Avar Wars; Charlemagne establishes the Eastern March.
798: Salzburg becomes an archbishopric.
907: Magyars conquer the Eastern March.
955: Battle of Lechfeld; victory over the Magyars.

996: The first official record of the name *Ostarrichi*.

1150: Vienna becomes the seat of the Babenburgs.

13th century: The transition from Romanesque to Gothic.

1246: Duke Friedrich II succumbs in battle to Hungary, marking the end of the Babenburg Dynasty.

1273: Rudolf of Habsburg is made the German Emperor.

1365: The University of Vienna is founded.

1453: Recognition of primogeniture.

1471: Beginning of the Turkish invasions.

1519: The death of Maximilian I.

1521: Edict of Worms denouncing Martin Luther.

1526: The death of Ludwig II of Hungary. Hungary and Bohemia fall to the House of Habsburg; peasants' wars.

1529: The first siege of Vienna by the Turks under Sultan Suleiman.

1579: Austria becomes Catholic again.

1587: Salzburg goes baroque.

1648: The Treaty of Westphalia.

1683: Siege of Vienna by Kara Mustapha and the liberation of Vienna.

1697: Prince Eugene becomes supreme commander of the army.

1713: Pragmatic Sanction introduced, providing legitimacy for a female succession.

1718: Period of the most extensive expansion of the Habsburg Empire.

1740: Maria Theresa becomes Empress.

1741: Beginning of the War of Succession .

1756: The beginning of the Seven-Year War; the birth of Mozart.

1765: Joseph II becomes co-regent.

1804: Franz II becomes Austrian Emperor.

1806: Abdication of the Roman Imperial Crown.

1813: Beginning of the War of Liberation.

1814: The Congress of Vienna.

1815: Founding of the German Federation.

1848: March Revolution; Franz Joseph becomes emperor.

1858: The beginning of the construction of the Viennese Ringstrasse.

1866: The Austro-Prussian War.

1883: Social welfare legislation.

1898: Assassination of Empress Elizabeth.

1914: Assassination of heir to the throne, Franz Ferdinand; beginning of World War I.

1916: Emperor Franz Joseph dies.

1918: Emperor Karl abdicates; the fall of the Habsburgs.

1919: The March Constitution.

1934: Dollfuss Assassination; proclamation of a people's constitution.

1938: Annexation by Germany.

1939: Beginning of World War II.

1945: Vienna is conquered by the Red Army; a republic is proclaimed.

1955: Conclusion of the International Treaty.

1960: Austria becomes a member of the EFTA.

1971: Kurt Waldheim becomes the UN Secretary-General.

1990: Death of Bruno Kreisky. Chancellor of socialist government elected in March 1970.

1994: Austrians vote to join European Union.

1996: Celebrations for the 1000th anniversary of the first official mention of the name Östaarichi.

Planning the Trip

What to Wear

Comfortable clothes with sensible shoes for walking round the towns. More formal wear is expected at concerts. Those walking in the mountains should be well prepared with proper footwear and equipment.

Entry Regulations

Citizens of most European nations are not required to have a visa in order to enter Austria, but must be in possession of a valid passport. For some, for instance Germans, a valid identification card is sufficient (exemptions apply to all EU members). Visitors entering Austria by car are not required to obtain any special customs documents for their vehicles. However, drivers must have in their possession proof of liability insurance; a Green Insurance Card is advisable.

Animal Quarantine

Cat and dog owners must be prepared to present a valid inoculation against rabies certificate for their pets at the border. The innoculation must have happened between 1 year and 30 days before entering the country.

Customs Regulations

The same customs regulations as in other European Union member countries apply. The following free import allowances are for persons over 17 years old:

Either entering from an EU country where the goods were bought tax free, or entering from another country:

200 cigarettes or 50 cigars or 100 cigarillos or 250 grs tobacco.

2 litres of alcohol max. 22 vol. percent, or 1 litre of more than 22 vol. percent, and 2 litres of wine.

50gr of perfume and 0.25 litres of toilet water.

Other goods (gifts, souvenirs etc.) up to a value of 800 Schillings.

Entering from an EU country where the goods were bought with tax paid:

300 cigarettes of 150 cigarillos or 400 gr of tobacco.

3 litres of alcohol of max. 22 vol percent and 2 litres of wine.

50 grams of perfume and 0.375 litres of toilet water.

Currency

The Austrian unit of currency is the Schilling, with 100 Groschen to a Schilling. There are 1,000, 500, 100, 50 and 20 Schilling notes and 100, 50, 25, 20, 10, 5 and 1 Schilling coins. Groschen come in units of 50, 10, 5 and 2.

Banks and exchange offices will change foreign currency at the current rate of the Viennese stock market exchange. Currencies which are not listed here are exchanged at the free market rate.

There is no limit regarding how much local or foreign money visitors may bring into or take out of Austria.

Public Holidays

1 January: New Year's Day
6 January: Epiphany
April: Easter Monday
1 May: May Day

May: Ascension Day
May/June: Whit Monday
May/June: The Feast of Corpus Christi
15 August: Day of Assumption
26 October: National Holiday
1 November: All Saints' Day
8 December: Day of the Immaculate Conception
25 December: Christmas Day
26 December: St Stephen's Day
Holidays determined by the lunar calendar. The Chamber of Commerce of Austria publishes a current calendar of festivals each year.

Getting There

By Air

Austria's national carrier, Austrian Airlines, operates direct services to most European capital cities on a daily basis from Vienna's Schwechat airport, and less frequently from the other principal international gateways of Salzburg, Graz, Linz, Klagenfurt and Innsbruck. Thirty-six different carriers, including most major European airlines, fly between Vienna and national capitals. From London Heathrow, British Airways has three London–Vienna flights a day, with less frequency to Klagenfurt and Graz. Lauda Air and Garuda Indonesian Airlines connect between London Gatwick and Vienna. The main charter airline from the UK is Britannia; seats on charter flights are sold through travel agents only.

Austrian Airlines' route network is principally within Europe and the Middle East, but it has direct daily flights to New York's JFK airport and less frequently to Tokyo. TWA also flies daily to New York, although the flight involves a change of aircraft at Frankfurt. Other US destinations are best served through JFK, and South America is served by connecting Iberia flights via Madrid. Lauda Air operates from Vienna to Miami, Asia and Australia, with flights to Bangkok, Hong Kong, Phuket and Sydney. Austrian Airlines' internal sister airline, Austrian Air Services, also operates international flights to Frankfurt. Tyrolean, an independent airline based at Innsbruck, operates international flights between that airport and Frankfurt, Düsseldorf, Stuttgart, Zurich, Amsterdam and Paris.

Schwechat airport is located 15 km (9 miles) to the East of the city (25 minutes' drive on the motorway). Its terminals were modernised in 1988, and it has an information booth – tel: (0222) 700 72233 – in the arrival hall which is open from 9am–10pm daily. An express bus service which operates every 20 minutes between 6am–7pm and every 30 minutes from 8am–9pm, links the airport with Vienna's two main railway stations and the City Air Terminal next to the Hilton Hotel. For information tel: (0222) 5800 2300. A train service operates between the central station and the airport every hour on the hour from 7.30am–8.30pm.

Airline offices in Vienna:
Aeroflot, 1, Parkring 10, tel: (0222) 512-1501.
Air Canada, 1, Schubertring 9 tel: (0222) 712-4608.
Air France, 1, Kärntner Str. 49, tel: (0222) 514-1818.
Alitalia, 1, Kärntner Ring 2, tel: (0222) 505 1707.
Austrian Airlines, Sabena, Swiss Air, 1, Kärtner Ring 18, tel: (0222) 505-5757.
British Airways, 1, Kärntner Ring 10, tel: (0222) 795-67567.
Delta Airlines, 1, Kärntner Ring 17, tel: (0222) 512-6646.
Deutsche Lufthansa, 1, Kärtner Str. 42, tel: (0222) 589-140.
El Al, 1 Kärntner Str. 25/2, tel: (0222) 512-4561.
Japan Airlines, 1, Kärntner Str. 11 tel: (0222) 512-7522.
KLM 1, Kärntner Str. 25/2, tel: (0222) 589-245090.
Lauda Air, Opernring 6, tel: (0222) 514-770
Quantas, 1, Opernring 1/E, tel: (0222) 587-7771.
Singapore Airlines, 1, Kärntner Ring 11, tel: (0222) 513 4656.
Thai Airways, 1, Opernring 1/R/10, tel: (0222) 586-8308.
Tyrolean Airways, 1 Opernring 1/R/7, tel: (0222) 586-3674.

By Rail

For travellers from the UK and Northern Europe, the *Austrian Night Express* departs Ostende at 8.30pm every evening, arriving in Vienna at 10.58am the following morning. Bookings from London are made through DER, tel: (0171) 408 0111. There are two main stations in Vienna: the Westbanhof serves Germany, France, Belgium and Switzerland and the Südbanhof serves Italy, the Balkans, Greece and Hungary. Other major international trains are the *Prinz Eugen* (Hanover–Vienna), the *Arlberg Express* (Paris–Vienna via Switzerland) and the *Holland-Vienna Express* (Amsterdam–Vienna). Anybody wanting to arrive in style could catch the *Orient Express* on its weekly run to Budapest with stops at Innsbruck, Salzburg and Vienna.

For passenger information in Vienna tel: (0222) 1717.

By Road

BY BUS

There are no direct bus services from Northern Europe. Would-be bus travellers are advised to travel to Munich and change to the rail network.

BY CAR

Travelling to Austria by car from Northern Europe is a long and arduous journey, best achieved by routing through Germany to take advantage of the toll-free and excellent motorway network. Beware of attempting to enter the country via the less busy alpine passes, which can be closed at night and in the winter. Motorways are also free in Austria itself. Petrol and diesel prices in Austria are similar to those in the rest of Europe.

A Green Card for insurance purposes is not mandatory although it is advised; red accident triangle, seatbelts and first aid kit are mandatory, however, for all vehicles travelling on Austrian roads.

DRIVING IN AUSTRIA

Traffic regulations in Austria correspond to those of other European countries. In snowy conditions (15 November–10 April) winter tyres, chains or studded tyres are required. ARBÖ (Austrian Motoring Association) and ÖAMTC (Austrian Automobile, Motorbike and Touring Club) operate over 100 rental agencies throughout Austria where you can lease chains for your vehicle.

On main roads the maximum speed limit is 100 kph (about 60 mph), on motorways 130 kph (80 mph), and in populated areas 50 kph (30 mph).

The maximum blood alcohol level still within the legal limit is 0.8 parts per thousand; a driver caught exceeding this limit can expect to have his or her licence suspended and be fined at least 8,000 Schillings. It is illegal for children under the age of 12 to sit in the front seat, and wearing a seat-belt is mandatory.

In many cities where you are required to pay a fee for short-term parking, it is first necessary to obtain a parking certificate, available at tobacco shops, banks and petrol stations.

BREAKDOWNS & ACCIDENTS

The police must be called to the scene of all car accidents in which any persons are injured. Foreigners should fill out the accident form entitled *Comité Européen des Assurances*. ÖAMTC and ARBÖ maintain automobile breakdown services along the most important thoroughfares; non-members may also take advantage of these services for a somewhat higher price than members.

ÖAMTC Breakdown Service, tel: 120.
ARBÖ Breakdown Service, tel: 123.
Fire Brigade, tel: 122.
Police, tel: 133.
Ambulance, tel: 144.

TRAFFIC REPORTS

Traffic reports are broadcast on Channel 3 (Ö3) every hour following the regular news edition. Programmes may be interrupted to announce especially nasty traffic conditions. In and around the city of Vienna the radio station Radio Blue Danube broadcasts regular traffic reports in both English and French between 7am–10am, 12 noon–2pm, and again between 6pm–8pm.

Maps

Freytag & Berndt offer a wide selection of Austrian maps, including hiking maps with scales of either 1:50,000 or 1:100,000. In addition to these, you can get a map of postal codes, an "organisational map" (1:500,000) containing over 6,000 registered names and an index of places. Also available are a variety of relief maps and maps for various sporting activities, for example bicycle touring maps, white-water river guides, canoeing maps, different hiking and auto atlases. There are city maps with scales of 1:10,000 to 1:25,000 for the provincial capital cities; for Vienna you'll find both a map booklet (1:20,000) and a city atlas.

Tourist Offices

Austria: Österreich Werbung 1040 Vienna, Margaretenstr. 1, tel: (222) 587-2000
Australia: Austrian National Tourist Office, 1st Floor, 36 Carrington Street, Sydney NSW 2000, tel: (2) 299-3621.
Belgium: Office National Autrichien du Tourisme/Ostenrijkse Dienst voor Toerisme, Avenue Louise 106/Louizalaan 106, B-1050 Bruxelles, tel: (02) 6460-610.
France: Office National Autrichien du Tourisme, 47 Avenue de' Opéra, 75002 Paris, tel: (01) 4742-7857.
Germany: Österreich Information, Postfach 1231, 82019 Taufkirchen, tel: (089) 6667-0100. Fax: (089) 6667-0200.
Great Britain: Austrian National Tourist Office, 30 St George Street, London W1R 0AL, tel: (0171) 629-0461. Fax: (0171) 499-6038.
Italy: Ente Nazionale Austriaco per il Turismo, Via Larga 23, 20122 Milano, tel: (02)5830-7220. Via Barberini 29, 00187 Roma, tel: (06) 481-4658.
Netherlands: Oostenrijks Toeristenburo, Stadhouderskade 2, 1054 ES Amsterdam, tel: (20) 612-9682.
Switzerland: Österreich Information, CH 8036 Zürich, Zweierstr. 146, tel: (1) 451-1551.
USA: Austrian National Tourist Office, PO Box 1142, New York NY10108-1142, tel: (212) 944-6880. Fax: (310) 477-5141 and PO Box 491938 Los Angeles CA 90049, tel: (310) 477-3332. Fax: (310) 477-5141.

Embassies Abroad

Australia: 12 Talbot St, ACT2603, Canberra, tel: (06) 951-376.
Belgium: Rue de l'Abbaye 47, Brussels, tel: (02) 649-3850.
Canada: 445 Wilbrod St, KIN 6M7, Ottawa, tel: (613)789-1444.
Denmark: Gronningen 5, 1270 Copenhagen, tel: (33) 124-623.
France: 6 Rue Fabert, F 75007, Paris, tel: (00331) 195-559-566.
Germany: Johanniterstr. 2, 53 Bonn, tel: (0228) 530-060.
Great Britain: 18 Belgrave Mews West London SW1X 8HU, tel: (0171) 235-3731.
Italy: Via Pergolesi 3, 00198, Rome, tel: (6) 855-8241.
Netherlands: Van Alkemadelaan 342

2597 AS, The Hague, tel: (070) 324-5470.
Switzerland: Kirchenfeldstr. 28, 3006 Bern, tel: (031) 351-0111.
USA: 3524 International Court N.W., Washington, DC 20008, tel: (202) 895-6700.

Practical Tips

Business Hours

In general, shops and businesses are open Monday–Friday from 8am–6pm and on Saturday from 8am–12 noon.

Banks are open on Monday, Tuesday, Wednesday and Friday from 8am–12.30pm and again from 1.30pm–3pm.

Tipping

It is customary to leave a 10–15 percent tip when the service has been good.

Religious Services

Catholic Mass, beginning at 6.30am; for information, tel: (0222) 51552.
Protestant service, for information, tel: (0222) 587-3141.
Israeli service, Temple Vienna, 1, Seitenstättengasse 4, tel: (0222) 531-040.
Old Catholic Church, 1, Wipplingerstr. 6, tel: (0222) 533-7133.
Viennese Islamic Centre, 21, Am Hubertusdamm 17-19, tel: (0222) 270-5574.
Anglican service, 3, Jaurésgasse 17–19, tel: (0222) 714-8900.
Mormons, tel: (0222) 370-32570.
Methodists, tel: (0222) 893-6989.

Media

Foreign Language Radio Broadcasts: Channel 1 (Ö1) from 8.05am–8.15am daily the Austrian Radio Network broadcasts a brief news report in both English and French. In Vienna you can tune into programmes in English on Radio Blue Danube, broadcast parallel to the popular Channel 3 (Ö3).

Postal Services

Post offices are open between 8am and noon and from 2–6pm. Railway post offices in the main cities are open 24 hours.

Telephone

Dialling codes to Austria, from:
Belgium, Germany, Italy and Switzerland: 00 43
Holland: 00 43
France: 00 43
Great Britain: 00 43
United States: 011 43
Dialling codes from Austria:
for operator-assisted long-distance calls: 1616

Tourist Offices

In Vienna:
Österreich Information 4, Margaretenstr. 1, tel: (0222) 587-2000.
Wiener-Tourismusverband 2, Obere Augartenstr. 40, tel: (0222) 211-40; fax: (0222) 216-8492.
In the provinces:
Landesverband Burgenland Tourismus Schloss Esterhazy, 7000 Eisenstadt, tel: (02682) 63384.
Niederösterreich-Information (Lower Austria) Heidenschuss 2, 1010 Vienna, tel: (0222) 533-311-434.
Landesverband für Tourismus in Oberösterreich (Upper Austria) Schillerstr. 50, 4010 Linz, tel: (0732) 600-2210.
Graz Tourismus, Kaiserfeldgasse 15 Graz. Tel: (0316) 80750.
Kärntner Tourismus GmbH (Carinthia) Casinoplatz 1, 9220-Velden, tel: (04274) 52 100.
Salzburger Land - Tourismus G.m.b.H. Alpenstr. 96, 5033 Salzburg, tel: (0662) 6688.
Tirol Werbung Bozner Platz 6, 6010 Innsbruck.Tel: (0512) 5320-170.
Vorarlberg Tourismus Römerstr. 7/I, 6901 Bregenz, tel: (05574) 425-250.

Consulates

Australia, tel: (0222) 512-8580.
Belgium, tel: (0222) 50207.
Canada, tel: (0222) 531-3830.
France, tel: (0222) 502-750.
Germany, 3 Metternichgasse 3, tel: (0222) 71154.
Great Britain, Jauresgasse 12, tel:

(0222) 713-1575.
Ireland, tel: (0222) 715-4246.
Italy, tel: (0222) 712-5121.
New Zealand, (in Germany) tel: (0228) 228-070.
Switzerland, 3 Prinz-Eugen-Str. 7, tel: (0222) 79505.
USA, 9 Bolzmanngasse 16, tel: (0222) 31339.

Emergencies

Lost & Found

Central Lost & Found Office, 9, Wasagasse 22., Vienna. Open: 8am–1pm, tel: (0222) 316-440 (general); 9205 (for items left on trams); 9202 (for lost documents).

Lost & found in railway stations:
Vienna West Railway Station, tel: (0222) 580-032996.
Vienna South Railway Station, tel: (0222) 580-035656.
Innsbruck Main Railway Station, tel: (0512) 503-5388.
Villach Main Railway Station, tel: (04242) 2020.

Useful Telephone Numbers

Police, tel: 133.
Emergency medical service, tel: 141.
Fire brigade, tel: 122.
Rescue service (ambulance), tel: 144
Directory enquiries, tel: 1611.
Telephone services, tel: 1621.
Telegram service, tel: 190.
Vienna flight information, tel: 7007-2233.
Complete Railway Service Office, tel: 1700.
Railway information, tel: 1717.
ARBÖ Breakdown Service, tel: 123.
ÖAMTC Breakdown Service, tel: 120.
ÖAMTC European Emergency Service, tel: 982-8282.
Crisis Intervention Hot-line, tel: 1770.
International Aircraft Rescue Service, tel: (02732) 70007.

Getting Around

Public Transport

By Train

The Austrian Federal Railway System maintains approximately 5,800 km (3,625 miles) of track and is connected with both the Eastern and Western European railway networks. Seat reservation tickets cost 30 Schillings. Passengers are required to pay a surcharge on TEE and IC trains; the price of reserved seating is within this additional charge.

Trains travelling between Vienna and Graz, and between Vienna and Salzburg depart at 1-hour intervals; between Vienna and Innsbruck, and Vienna and Villach they leave at 2-hour intervals.

There are a number of ways to obtain regular fare price reductions, for instance in the form of national and regional network tickets and what are referred to as "Rabbit Cards". Eurorail Passes, Inter-Rail and commuter tickets, senior citizens', group and children's discount fares are all ways to help you save on ticket costs. Children up to the age of seven years ride for free if they do not occupy a seat to themselves. Nearly all trains travelling during the daytime have dining cars; night trains have sleeping compartments and *couchettes*.

For train information, contact:
Vienna, tel: (0222) 1717.
Graz, tel: (0316) 1717.
Klagenfurt, tel: (0463) 1717.
Linz, tel: (0732) 1717.
Salzburg, tel: (0662) 1717.
Villach, tel: (04242) 1717.

RAILWAY NOSTALGIA

There are a number of narrow-gauge railway lines in Austria which are still – or once again – in operation and have recently evolved into tourist attractions. Some of these are serviced by steam engines. The **Steyr Valley Railway** makes its way from Steyr along the Steyr River Valley into Grünburg.

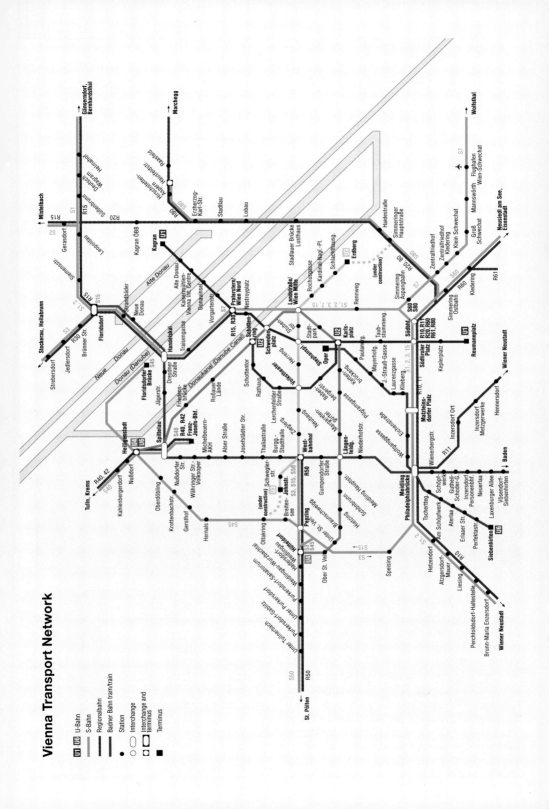

Vienna Transport Network

U1 U6 U-Bahn
S-Bahn
Regionalbahn
Badner Bahn tram/train
● Station
○ Interchange
□ Interchange and terminus
■ Terminus

The **Gurk Valley Railway** plies its way through the Nock area in Carinthia, from Treibach-Althofen to Pöckstein-Zwischenwässern.

The **Feistritz Valley Railway** chugs from Weiz to Birkfeld in Eastern Styria.

Payerbach-Hirschwang, a local train, operates south of Vienna. From here you can also take the **Schneeberg Railway**, which transports passengers to the highest railway station in Austria at 1,795 metres (5,985 ft).

The **Mariazeller Railway** connects St Pölten with Mariazell, a Styrian place of pilgrimage.

In Vorarlberg the **Montafon Railway** runs from Bludenz to Schruns-Tschagguns and in Tyrol you'll find the world-famous **Ziller Valley Train**.

In the area along the border of Upper Styria and Salzburg the **Mur Valley Railway** makes its way from Unzmarkt to Tamsweg.

In addition to these, there is also the privately-operated railway **Vöklamarkt-Attersee** in Salzkammergut, and the **Stainzer Flascher Train**, which runs from Preding-Wieseldorf to the Stainz Palace.

By Boat

From the beginning of April until the end of October there are boats operating on regular schedules along the Danube River. Vienna is connected to Budapest and Passau.

There are also boats running on a regular basis on all larger lakes in Austria. Along the stretch from Vienna to Budapest, the Donau-Dampfschiffahrts-Gesellschaft Blue Danube (the Danube Steamship Company, Handelskai 265, operates the hydrofoil to Budapest. The hydrofoil makes three trips form Vienna to Budapest and three return trips from Budapest to Vienna daily. For timetable information tel: 0222 588-800.

The Tschechoslowakische Donauschiffahrt CSPD offers a hydrofoil service between Vienna and Bratislava. Boats depart Vienna at Reichsbrücke from Wednesday to Sunday at 9pm and 9.30pm and arrive in Bratislava at 10.30am and 11pm. The hydrofoil leaves Bratislava at 5pm and 5.40pm arriving in Vienna at 6.45pm and 7.25pm.

By Bus

There are approximately 70 international bus lines connecting Austria to other foreign countries. The Austrian public bus service primarily links places not served by the railway network. Nearly all tourist areas offer bus excursions into the surrounding countryside.

Private Transport

Taxis & Car Rentals

All taxis are equipped with calibrated taximeters. They park at special taxi stands and cannot be hailed from the street.

Most international car rental agencies maintain offices in Austria. In addition to these, there are also a number of local rental businesses. You'll find offices located in larger cities, at airports and in main railway stations.

Avis, 1, Opernring 1 and airport, tel. 587-6241.

Budget-Rent-a-Car, 3, Vienna Hilton and airport, tel. 714-6565.

Europcar, 3, Erdberg Str. 202, tel. 799-6176.

Hertz, 1, Kärntner Ring 17, tel. 512-8677.

Reisemobil-Vermietung Benkö, (camper rental) 4, Rechte Wienzeile 21, tel. 571-199-93.

Rent a Bus, 12, Assmayergasse 60, tel. 813-3223.

Blecha, Exclusive Rent a Car (Rolls Royce, Bentley, Mercedes 600), 16, Lienfeldgasse 35, tel. 486-13210.

By Car

TOUR SUGGESTIONS

A tour across the Alps:
Away from major thoroughfares, along the main ridge of the Alps from Bergenz to Vienna a trip across Austria may be organised as follows:
Bregenz – Bregenzer Wald – Schröcken – Hochtannenbergpass – Lechtal – Holzgau – Reutte – Leermos – Ehrwald – Fernpass – Nassereith – Mieminger Plateau – Innsbruck – Hall – Schwaz – Zillertal – Gerlos-Pass Strasse – Krimml – Zell am See – Saalfelden – Mühlbach am Hochkönig – St Johann im Pongau – Radstadt – Schladming – Gröbming – Admont – Hieflau – Mariazell – Lilienfeld – Vienna.

A tour around Grossglockner:
Zell am See – Bruck – Fusch – Grossglockner-Hochalpenstrasse (30 miles/48 km, 12 percent gradient maximum, 39 hairpin bends) – Heiligenblut – Winklern – Lienz – Matrei – Felbertauern Tunnel – Mittersill – Zell am See.

From Salzburg to Salzkammergut:
Salzburg – Hof – Fuschl – Wolfgangsee – St Gilgen – Strobl – Bad Ischl – Bad Goisern – Hallstatt – Obertraun – Gosau – Pass Gschütt – Abtenau – Golling – Hallein – Salzburg.

Carinthian Lakes Tour:
Klagenfurt – Pörtschach – Moosburg – Feldkirchen – Gerlitzer Strasse – Ossiach – Treffen – Millstatt – Villach – Maria Gail – Velden – Maria Wörth – Pyramidenkogel Strasse – Klagenfurt. Scenic Roads

The following routes will afford breath-taking views of the Austrian countryside:

VIENNA

Höhenstrasse: This road runs between Vienna and Klosterneuburg, presenting magnificent views of the city along the way.

BURGENLAND

Burgenländischen Rotweinstrasse: Between Siegendorf and Mattersburg.

LOWER AUSTRIA

Hochkar-Strasse: This road takes you from Gösting to Hochkar and has a view of the Hochschwab area.

UPPER AUSTRIA

Cumberland Kasbergalm-Strasse: The road from Grünberg to Kasbergalm affords magnificent views of the Ötscher and Dachstein Mountains.

STYRIA

Südsteirische Weinstrasse: Runs from Bad Radkersburg to Lavamünd (Carinthia) with a view of the Kor Alps.

CARINTHIA

Malta-Hochalm-Strasse: From Gmünd to Kölnbreinsperre.

Nockalmstrasse: From Reichenau all the way to Innerkrems which has a view of the Gurk Valley Alps.

Villacher Alpenstrasse: This road goes

from Villach to Rosstratte and presents a view of the Dachstein and the Grossglockner.

SALZBURG

Gerlos-Strasse: From Krimml to Zell am Ziller (Tyrol) affords a view of the Grossvenediger, Wildkar and the Dreiherren Peaks.

Felbertauern-Strasse: The road going from Mittersill to Matrei (East Tyrol), presenting a fine view of the Grossvenediger and Grossglockner.

Grossglockner-Hochalpenstrasse: This is the road from Bruck to Heiligenblut (Carinthia) with a view of the Grossglockner and Edelweiss Peaks.

TYROL

Achenseestrasse: This road runs from Wiesing to Maurach.

Aussichtsstrasse over the Piller: Runs from Wenns in the Pitz Valley to Kauns in the Kauner Valley.

Fernpass Strasse: From Nassereith to Erwald, affording a view of the Mieminger Mountains.

Hahntennjochstrasse: This road leads from Imst into the Lech valley.

Timmelsjoch-Hochalpenstrasse: This high-alpine road lies between Sölden and Meran (Italy) and presents a view of the Ötz Valley Alps.

Zirlerbergstrasse: From Seefeld to Innsbruck affords the traveller a magnificent view of the Karwendel Mountains.

VORARLBERG

Arlberg-Pass-Strasse: The road from Langen to St Anton (Tyrol).

Flexenstrasse: This road runs between Schröcken and Warth with a view towards the Allgäuer Alps.

Silvretta-Hochalpenstrasse: From Montafon into the Paznaun Valley (Tyrol), affording a view of the Piz Buin.

ALPINE PASSES

Achenpass: Glashütte – Achenwald
Arlberg: St Anton – Arlberg-Stuben
Bieler Höhe: Partenen – Galtür
Brenner: Innsbruck – Sterzing
Felbertauern: Mittersill – Matrei.
Fernpass: Nassereith – Erwald
Flexenpass: Stuben – Lech/Arlb.
Furka Joch: Laterns – Damüls
Gerlospass: Krimml – Gerlos
Grossglockner-Hochalpenstr: Ferleiten – Heiligenblut
Pass Gschütt: Abtenau – Gosau

Hochtannbergpass: Schröcken – Warth
Iselsberg: Lienz – Winklern
Katschberg: St Michael – Spittal.
Nassfeld: Hermagor – Pontebba
Packsattel: Wolfsberg – Köflach
Plöckenpass: Kötschach – Paluzza
Präbichl: Leoben – Eisenerz
Pyhrnpass: Windischgarsten – Liezen
Radstädter Tauern: Radstadt – Mauterndorf
Reschenpass: Nauders – Mals
Pass Thurn: Mittersill – Kitzbühel
Timmelsjoch: Obergurgl – St Leonhard
Turracher Höhe: Predlitz – Reichenau
Wurzenpass: Villach – Kranjska Gora

Mountain Railways

There are about 3,500 funiculars, chair lifts and ski tows operating in Austria which open up the world of the Alps all the way to a height of 3,000 meters (10,000 ft).

View Points

The following viewing points are all accessible either by funicular or rackrailway.

From/To	Meters	Feet
Ankogel/ Mallnitz	2,722	8,930
Bell Alpin-Wesssee/ Uttendorf	2.352	7,717
Bürgeralpe/ Mariazell	1,267	4,157
Dachstein/ Ramsau	2,700	8,858
Eisriesenwelt/ Werfen	1,586	5,203
Gaislacher Kogel/ Sölden	3,058	10,033
Goldeck/ Spital a.d. D.es	2,142	7,028
Hafelekar/ Innsbruck	2,334	7,657
Hoadl/ Innsbruck	2,340	7,677
Kitzbüheler Horn/ Kitzbühel	1,996	6,549
Kitzsteinhorn/ Kaprun	3,029	9,938
Krippenstein/ Obertraun	2,109	6,919
Patscherkofel/ Igls	2,248	7,375
Rüfikopf/ Lech	2,360	7,743
Schattberg/ Saalbach	2,020	6,627
Schmittenhöhe/ Zell a.S.	1,965	6,447
Stubnerkogel/ Badgastein	2,225	7,365
Valluga/ St Anton	2,811	9,222
Zehnerkar/ Obertauern	2,357	7,733
Zugspitze/ Ehrwald	2,966	9,731

Where to Stay

Private Accommodation

On just about every street in tourist-orientated towns you'll find at least one "Zimmer frei", Tourist Information, sign. Staff can give you a listing of local, privately-run accommodation. These constitute the most reasonably-priced lodgings you'll probably find anywhere in Austria.

Hotels

Austrian hospitality enjoys worldwide recognition (many hotels throughout the world are under Austrian management). Even their smallest inns offer excellent service.

Hotels in Austria are divided into five different categories, each distinguished by a number of stars. In the following list you'll find hotels belonging to the first three categories, plus *pensions* in Vienna.

☆☆☆☆☆ = Luxury-class hotels
☆☆☆☆ = First-class hotels
☆☆☆ = High standard hotels

In the ☆☆☆☆☆ hotel category rates including breakfast range from 1,600–4,000 Schillings per night, in the ☆☆☆☆ category from 600 to 1,900 Schillings, and in the ☆☆☆ category between about 350 and 1,000 per night. Prices vary during the year in places affected by seasonal business.

During the height of the tourist season (in July and August, as well as over Christmas and Easter), it is strongly recommended that you make your hotel reservations in advance because at these times most hotels and inns are booked solid. Reservations can be cancelled up to three months before the stipulated date of arrival. On shorter notice a cancellation fee will apply.

Besides the excellent hotel industry Austria is known for inexpensive family vacations. These are offered through a system of vacation on farms and in villages and through the many pensions, guest houses and private accommodations throughout the country. The Austrian National Tourist office has two brochures *Dorfurlaub in Österreich* and *Preisgünstiger Urlaub in Österreich* which list the many possibilities.

Vienna

☆☆☆☆☆
Hotel Ambassador, 1, Neuer Markt 6, tel: (0222) 51466.
Hotel Bristol, 1, Kärntner Ring 1, tel: (0222) 515160.
Hotel Hilton, 3, Landstrasser Hauptstrasse 2, tel: (0222) 717-000.
Hotel im Palais Schwarzenberg, 3, Rennweg 2, tel: (0222) 784-5150.
Hotel Imperial, 1, Kärntner Ring 16, tel: (0222) 501-10410.
Hotel Intercontinental, 3, Johannesgasse 28, tel: (0222) 711-220.
Hotel Sacher, 1, Philharmonikerstr. 4, tel: (0222) 514-57810.

☆☆☆☆
Hotel am Parkring, 1, Parkring 12, tel: (0222) 514-800.
Hotel am Stephansplatz, 1, Stephansplatz 9, tel: (0222) 534-050.
Hotel Amadeus, 1, Wildpretmarkt 5, tel: (0222) 5338-738.
Hotel Astoria, 1, Kärntner Str. 32, tel: (0222) 515-770.
Hotel Erzherzog Rainer, Hauptstr. 27, tel: (0222) 501-110.
Hotel Kaiserin Elisabeth, 1, Weihburggasse 3, tel: (0222) 515-260.
Parkhotel Schönbrunn, 13, Hietzinger Hauptstr. 10-20, tel: (0222) 822-676.

☆☆☆
Hotel Alpha, 9, Boltzmanngasse 8, tel: (0222) 319-1646.
Hotel Austria, 1, Wolfengasse 3, tel: (0222) 51523.
Hotel Casino, 19, Döblinger Hauptstrasse 76-78, tel: (0222) 368-4100.
Hotel Graf Stadion, 8, Buchfeldg. 5, tel: (0222) 405-5284.

PENSIONS

Apartement-Pension, 1, Riemergasse 8, tel: (0222) 512-7220.
Pension Elite, 1, Wipplingerstrasse 32, tel: (0222) 533-2518.
Pension Neuer Markt, 1, Seilergasse 9, tel: (0222) 512-2316.
Pension Am Operneck, 1, Kärntner Str. 47, tel: (0222) 512-9310.
Pension Haydn, 6, Mariahilfer Str. 57-59, tel: (0222) 587-44140.

Burgenland

● **7000 Eisenstadt**
☆☆☆☆ Hotel Burgenland, tel: (02682) 696.
☆☆☆ Gasthof Ohr, tel: (02682) 62460.
● **7072 Moerbisch**
☆☆☆☆ Schmidt Hotel, tel: (02685) 8294.
● **7100 Neusiedl am See**
☆☆☆☆ Wende Hotel, tel: (02167) 8111.
● **7071 Rust am See**
☆☆☆☆ Seehotel Rust, tel: (02685) 381.

Lower Austria

● **2500 Baden bei Vienna**
☆☆☆☆ Parkhotel Baden, tel: (02252) 44386.
☆☆☆☆ Grand Hotel Sauerhof, Weilburgstr. 11-13, tel: (02252) 412-510.
● **3571 Gars am Kamp**
☆☆☆☆ Gars Hotel, Bio-Training Centre, tel: (02985) 2666.
● **2352 Gumpholdskirchen**
☆☆☆☆ Benediktinerhof, tel: (02252) 62185.
● **3400 Klosterneuburg**
☆☆☆ Hotel Schrannenhof, tel: (02243) 320720.
● **2340 Mödling**
☆☆☆☆ Babenbergerhof, tel: (02236) 22246.
● **2380 Perchtoldsdorf**
☆☆☆ Hotel Central, tel: (0222) 8690-2230.
● **2680 Semmering**
☆☆☆☆ Panhans, tel: (02664) 8181.
● **3910 Zwettl**
☆☆☆☆ Schwarz Alm, tel: (02822) 53173.

Upper Austria

● **4864 Attersee**
☆☆☆☆ Seegasthof Oberndorfer, tel: (07666) 78640.
● **4822 Bad Goisern**
☆☆☆☆ Kurhotel, tel: (06135) 8305.

● **4820 Bad Ischl**
☆☆☆☆ Zum Goldenen Schiff, tel: (06132) 24241.
☆☆☆ Hotel Schenner, tel: (06132) 24650.
● **4810 Gmunden**
☆☆☆☆ Parkhotel am See, tel: (07612) 64230.
☆☆☆☆ Seehotel Schwan, tel: (07612) 63391.
● **4830 Hallstatt**
☆☆☆ Seehotel Grüner Baum, tel: (06134) 82630.
● **4573 Hinterstoder**
☆☆☆☆ Berghotel Hinterstoder, tel: (07564) 5421.
● **4020 Linz**
☆☆☆☆ Hotel Schillerpark, tel: (0732) 6950.
☆☆☆☆ City Hotel, tel: (0732) 652621.
☆☆☆☆ Domhotel, tel: (0732) 778-441.
☆☆☆ Goldener Adler, tel: (0732) 731147.
● **5310 Mondsee**
☆☆☆☆ Hotel Seehof, tel: (06232) 5031-0.
☆☆☆ Seehotel Lackner, tel: (06232) 2359.
● **4831 Obertraun**
☆☆☆ Hotel Haus am See, tel: (06131) 371.
● **4780 Schärding am Inn**
☆☆☆☆ Romantik Hotel Forstinger, tel: (07712) 2302.
● **4490 St Florian**
☆☆☆ Erzherzog Franz Ferdinand, tel: (07224) 42540.
● **5360 St Wolfgang**
☆☆☆☆ Weisses Rössl, tel: (06138) 23060.
☆☆☆☆ Hotel Post, tel: (06138) 23460.
● **4400 Steyr**
☆☆☆☆ Hotel Mader, tel: (07252) 533-580.

Styria

● **8922 Altaussee**
☆☆☆ Kohlbacherhof, tel: (03622) 71645.
● **8990 Bad Aussee**
☆☆☆☆ Hotel Erzherzog Johann, tel: (03622) 525070.
☆☆☆ Hotel Post, tel: (06152) 2539.
● **8344 Bad Gleichenberg**
☆☆☆☆ Hotel Austria am Kurpark, tel: (03159) 2205.
☆☆☆ Hotel Pension Allmer, tel: (03159) 2367.

● 8010 Graz
✩✩✩✩ City-Hotel Erzherzog Johann, tel: (0316) 811-616.
✩✩✩✩ Top Hotel Europa, tel: (0316) 70760.
✩✩✩✩ Schlossberghotel, tel: (0316) 80700.
✩✩✩ Grazerhof, tel: (0316) 824-358.
● 8700 Leoben
✩✩✩✩ Brücklwirt, tel: (03842) 81727.
● 8630 Mariazell
✩✩✩✩ Mariazellerhof, tel: (03882) 2179.
● 8972 Ramsau am Dachstein
✩✩✩✩ Hotel Berghof, tel: (03687) 81848.
✩✩✩✩ Gasthof Edelweiss, tel: (03687) 81988.
● 8970 Schladming
✩✩✩✩✩ Sporthotel Royer, tel: (03687) 2000.
✩✩✩ Breilerhof, tel: (03687) 22671.
● 8982 Tauplitzalm
✩✩✩ Sporthotel Tauplitzalm, tel: (03688) 2306.
● 8864 Turrach
✩✩✩ Seehotel Jägerwirt, tel: (03533) 82570.

Carinthia
● 9546 Bad Kleinkirchheim
✩✩✩✩ Ronacher, tel: (04240) 282.
✩✩✩✩ Hotel Die Post, tel: (04240) 212.
✩✩✩ Weisses Rössl, tel: (04240) 568.
● 9583 Faak am See
✩✩✩ Inselhotel Faakersee, tel: (04254) 2145.
● 9844 Heiligenblut
✩✩✩ Hotel Glocknerhof, tel: (04824) 2244.
● 9200 Klagenfurt
✩✩✩✩ Romantikhotel Musil, tel: (0463) 511-660.
✩✩✩✩ Hotel Palais Porcia, tel: (0463) 511-590.
✩✩✩✩ Hotel Wörthersee, tel: (0463) 211-610.
✩✩✩ Hotel Aragia, tel: (0463) 31222.
● 9082 Maria Wörth
✩✩✩✩ Hotel Astoria, tel: (04273) 2279.
✩✩✩✩ Seehotel Wörth, tel: (04273) 2276.
● 9872 Millstatt
✩✩✩✩ Hotel-Gasthof Seewirt, tel: (04766) 2110.
✩✩✩ Postillion am See, tel: (04766) 2552.

● 9821 Obervellach
✩✩✩ Semslacherhof, tel: (04782) 2188.
● 9570 Ossiach
✩✩✩ Schlosswirt, tel: (04243) 347.
● 9210 Pörtschach
✩✩✩✩ Hotel Pörtschacherhof, tel: (04272) 2335.
✩✩✩✩ Hotel Schloss Leonstain, tel: (04272) 28160.
✩✩✩ Gasthof Seerose, tel: (04272) 2502.
✩✩✩ Hotel Wörthersee, tel: (04272) 3721.
● 9220 Velden
✩✩✩✩ Das Park, tel: (04274) 22980.
✩✩✩✩ Casino Hotel Mösslacher, tel: (04274) 51234.
✩✩✩✩ Hotel Schönblick, tel: (04274) 2435.
● 9500 Villach
✩✩✩✩ Hotel Europa, tel: (04242) 26766.
✩✩✩ Hotel Goldenes Lamm, tel: (04242) 24105.
✩✩✩ Pension Karawankenblick, tel: (04242) 217-333.

Salzburg
● 5441 Abtenau
✩✩✩✩ Hotel Moisl, tel: (06243) 21630.
● 5630 Bad Hofgastein
✩✩✩✩ Grand-Parkhotel, tel: (06432) 63560.
✩✩✩✩ Hotel Astoria, tel: (06432) 62770.
✩✩✩ Hotel Christopherus, tel: (06432) 8223.
● 5640 Badgastein
✩✩✩✩ Hotel Elisabethpark, tel: (06434) 25510.
✩✩✩✩ Europäischer Hof, tel: (06434) 25260.
✩✩✩✩ Hotel Salzburgerhof, tel: (06434) 2037.
✩✩✩ Kurhaus Alpenblick, tel: (06434) 2062.
● 5532 Filzmoos
✩✩✩✩ Hotel Dachstein, tel: (06453) 82180.
✩✩✩ Hotel Alpenkrone, tel: (06453) 82800.
● 5330 Fuschl am See
✩✩✩✩ Hotel Mohrenwirt, tel: (06226) 8228.
✩✩✩ Hotel Seewinkl, tel: (06226) 344.
● 5710 Kaprun
✩✩✩✩ Hotel Kaprunerhof, tel: (06547) 7234.

✩✩✩ Alpengasthof Wüstlau, tel: (06547) 8461.
● 5730 Mittersill
✩✩✩ Schlosshotel Mittersill, tel: (06562) 4523.
● 5741 Neukirchen am Grossvenediger
✩✩✩ Romantik Jagdhotel Wald, tel: (06565) 6417.
● 5550 Radstadt
✩✩✩ Alpengasthof Seitenalm, tel: (06452) 490.
● 5753 Saalbach-Hinterglemm
✩✩✩✩ Hotel Bauer, tel: (06541) 62130.
✩✩✩✩ Hotel Kendler, tel: (06541) 62250.
✩✩✩ Gollingerhof, tel: (06541) 7292.
● 5020 Salzburg-City
✩✩✩✩✩ Hotel Bristol, Makartplatz 3, tel: (0662) 873-557.
✩✩✩✩✩ Hotel Goldener Hirsch, Getreidegasse 35, tel: (0662) 808-40.
✩✩✩✩✩ Hotel Österreichischer Hof, Schwarzstr. 5, tel: (0662) 889-770.
✩✩✩✩ Austrotel, Mirabellplatz 8, tel: (0662) 881-6880.
✩✩✩✩ Hotel Bayrischer Hof, Elisabethstr. 12, tel: (0662) 469-700.
✩✩✩✩ Hotel Stieglbräu, Rainerstr. 14, tel: (0662) 88992.
✩✩✩ Hotel Stern, Maxglaner Hauptstr. 68, tel: (0662) 832-414.
✩✩✩ Hotelgasthof Kamml, Wals bei Salzburg, tel: (0662) 850-267.
✩✩✩ Pension Herbert, Nonntaler Hauptstr. 85, tel: (0662) 820-308.
● 5340 St Gilgen
✩✩✩✩ Hotel Hollweger, tel: (06227) 22260.
✩✩✩✩ Parkhotel Billroth, tel: (06227) 2217.
● 5600 St Johann im Pongau
✩✩✩✩ Hotel Alpenland, tel: (06412) 70210.
✩✩✩ Gasthof Alpenhof, tel: (06412) 6040.
● 5700 Zell am See
✩✩✩✩ Hotel Salzburgerhof, Tel: (06542) 765.
✩✩✩✩ Clima Seehotel, tel: (06542) 72504.
✩✩✩ Hotel Bellevue, tel: (06542) 731040.

Tyrol
● 6094 Axams
✩✩✩✩ Neuwirth-Hotel, tel: (05234) 68141.
● 6230 Brixlegg

☆☆☆ Brixleggerhof, tel: (05337) 62630.

● **6166 Fulpmes**
☆☆☆ Alte Post Hotel, tel: (05225) 62358.

● **6563 Galtür**
☆☆☆☆ Fluchthorn-Hotel, tel: (05443) 8202.

☆☆☆☆ Paznauner Hof, tel: (05443) 8234.

● **6294 Hintertux**
☆☆☆☆ Badhotel, tel: (05287) 85700.

☆☆☆☆ Hintertuxerhof, tel: (05287) 85300.

● **6020 Innsbruck**
☆☆☆☆ Alpin-Park-Hotel, Pradler Str. 28, tel: (0512) 348600.

☆☆☆☆ Goldener Adler, Herzog Friedrich Str. 8, tel: (0512) 571-111.

☆☆☆☆ Maria Theresien Hotel, Maria Theresien Str. 31, tel: (0512) 5933.

☆☆☆ Bellevue-Hotel, Höhenstr. 141, tel: (05222) 892-336.

☆☆☆ Berg Isel-Hotel, Bergisel, tel: (05222) 581-912.

☆☆☆ Dollinger Gasthof, Haller Str. 7, tel: (0512) 267506.

● **6365 Kirchberg in Tyrol**
☆☆☆☆ Hotel Alexander, tel: (05357) 2222.

☆☆☆ Tyroler Hof-Hotel, tel: (05357) 2666.

● **6370 Kitzbühel**
☆☆☆☆ Ehrenbachhöhe-Hotel, tel: (05356) 62151.

☆☆☆☆ Goldener Greif-Hotel, tel: (05356) 6431.

☆☆☆☆ Reisch-Sporthotel, tel: (05356) 633660.

☆☆☆☆ Zur Tenne-Hotel, tel: (05356) 64444.

☆☆☆ Hotel Bellevue, tel: (05356) 62766.

☆☆☆ Eggerwirt-Gasthof, tel: (05356) 2455.

● **6631 Lermoos**
☆☆☆☆ Sporthotel Loisach, tel: (05673) 2394.

☆☆☆ Drei Mohren-Hotel, tel: (05673) 2362.

● **990 Lienz**
☆☆☆☆ Sonne-Hotel, tel: (04852) 633110.

☆☆☆☆ Dolomiten-Hotel, tel: (04852) 629620.

☆☆☆ Glocknerhof, tel: (04852) 62167.

● **9971 Matrei**
☆☆☆ Parkhotel Matrei, tel: (04875) 6269.

● **6290 Mayrhofen**
☆☆☆☆☆ Elisabeth-Hotel, tel: (05285) 6767.

☆☆☆☆ Kramerwirt-Hotel, tel: (05285) 6700.

● **6162 Mutters**
☆☆☆☆ Altenburg-Hotel, tel: (05222) 548-524.

☆☆☆☆ Berghof-Hotel, tel: (05222) 585-021.

● **6456 Obergurgl**
☆☆☆☆ Bergwelt-Hotel, tel: (05256) 274.

☆☆☆☆ Hotel Austria, tel: (05256) 282.

● **6433 Oetz**
☆☆☆ Posthotel Kassel, tel: (05252) 6303.

● **6213 Pertisau**
☆☆☆☆ Furtners Sporthotel, tel: (05243) 5501.

● **6351 Scheffau am Wilden Kaiser**
☆☆☆ Wilder Kaiser-Gasthaus, tel: (05358) 8118.

● **6100 Seefeld**
☆☆☆☆ Astoria Hotel, tel: (05212) 22720.

☆☆☆☆☆ Lärchenhof-Hotel, tel: (05212) 2383.

☆☆☆ Alpengasthof-Hotel, tel: (05212) 2249.

● **6450 Sölden**
☆☆☆☆ Central-Hotel, tel: (05254) 2260.

☆☆☆ Alphof-Hotel, tel: (05254) 2559.

● **6580 St Anton am Arlberg**
☆☆☆☆☆ Hospitz-Hotel, tel: (05446) 2611.

☆☆☆☆ Neue Post, tel: (05446) 22130.

☆☆☆ Hotel Grischuna, tel: (05446) 2304.

● **6280 Zell am Ziller**
☆☆☆☆ Theresia-Sporthotel, tel: (05282) 22860.

☆☆☆☆ Zellerhof-Hotel, tel: (05282) 2612.

Vorarlberg

● **6700 Bludenz**
☆☆☆☆ Schlosshotel, tel: (05552) 630168.

● **6900 Bregenz**
☆☆☆☆ Mercure Hotel, tel: (05574) 46100.

● **6850 Dornbirn**
☆☆☆☆ Alpenhotel Bödele, tel: (05572) 7250.

☆☆☆ Hotel Krone, tel: (05572) 22720.

● **6800 Feldkirch**
☆☆☆☆ Hotel Montfort, tel: (05522) 72189.

☆☆☆☆ Hotel Weisses Kreuz, tel: (05522) 3456.

● **6787 Gargellen**
☆☆☆☆ Bachmann-Hotel, tel: (05557) 6316.

☆☆☆ Alpenrose Hotel, tel: (05557) 63140.

● **6764 Lech am Arlberg**
☆☆☆☆☆ Arlberg Hotel, tel: (05583) 21340.

☆☆☆☆☆ Post Hotel-Gasthof, tel: (05583) 22060.

☆☆☆☆ Berghof Hotel, tel: (05583) 2635.

☆☆☆☆ Burg Hotel, tel: (05583) 2291.

● **6780 Schruns**
☆☆☆☆ Alpenhof-Messmer, tel: (05556) 726-640.

☆☆☆☆ Löwen Hotel, tel: (05556) 7141.

● **6762 Stuben am Arlberg**
☆☆☆ Arlberg Hotel, tel: (05582) 719521.

● **6774 Tschagguns**
☆☆☆☆ Hotel Montafoner Hof, tel: (05556) 44000.

● **6763 Zürs am Arlberg**
☆☆☆☆☆ Albona-Hotel, tel: (05583) 2341.

☆☆☆☆☆ Zürserhof Hotel, tel: (05583) 2513

☆☆☆ Hotel Mara, tel: (05583) 2644.

Campgrounds

The Austrian Tourist Office Publicity Department (tel: 0222 -587-2000) will send you a detailed map of all camping sites located in Austria upon request. If you are planning to travel with a caravan, it's wisest to find out in advance on which roads and passes these vehicles are prohibited. Trailers need a *carnet de passage*.

Camping and Caravaning Club Austria (CCA), 5, Wien, Mariahilfer Straße 180, tel: (0222) 89121.
Österreichischer Camping Club (ÖCC), 1, Wien, Schubertring 1-3, tel: (0222) 71199.

Youth Hostels

Austria has many more youth hostels then those mentioned here. Information can be obtained from:

Österreichischer Jugendherbergsverband, 1010 Wien, Schottenring 28, tel: (0222) 533-5353; fax: (0222) 535-0861.

Vienna

Jugendgästehaus, Fr. Engels-Platz 24, tel: (0222) 330-0598.
Jugendherberge, Myrthengasse 7, tel: (0222) 523-9429.
Gästehaus Ruthensteiner, R. Hamerling-Gasse 24, tel: (0222) 893-2796.
Turmherberge Don Bosco, tel: (0222) 713-1494.
Jugendgästehaus Hütteldorf, Schlossberggasse 8, tel: (0222) 877-0263.

Burgenland

Neusiedl am See, Herbergsgasse 1, tel: (02167) 2252.
Rust, Am Seekanal 1, tel: (02685) 245.
Purbach, Türkenhain, tel: (02683) 5538.

Lower Austria

Annaberg, Annarotte 77, tel: (02728) 8496.
Klosterneuburg-Gugging, tel: (02243) 83501.
Melk, Abt Karl-Strasse 42, tel: (02752) 2681.
Krems, Kasernstr. 6/1, tel: (02732) 83452
St Pölten, Kranzbichlerstr. 18, tel: (02742) 73010.

Upper Austria

Ampflwang, Stefan-Demuth-Haus, Hüblstrasse 11, tel: (0732) 772-633.
Bad Ischl, Am Rechensteg 5, tel: (06132) 26577.
Freistadt, Schlosshof 3, tel: (07942) 4365.
Gosau 168, Bischof-Dr.-Eder-Haus, tel: (06136) 352.
Hallstatt, Lahn 50, tel: (06134) 279.
Hinterstoder, Mitterstoder 137, tel: (07564) 5227.
Linz, Kapuzinerstrasse 14, tel: (0732) 282-720.
Mondsee, Krankenhausstrasse 9, tel: (06232) 2418.
Steyr, Hafnerstrasse 14, tel: (07252) 45580.
Admont, Schloss Röthelstein, tel: (03613) 2432.

Styria

Bad Aussee, Lerchenreith 148, tel: (06152) 52238.
Graz, Idlhofgasse 74, tel: (0316) 914-876

Riegersburg 3, Im Cillitor, tel: (03153) 217.

Carinthia

Klagenfurt, Kumpfgasse 20, tel: (0463) 513-172.
Heiligenblut, Hof 36, tel: (04824) 2259.
Villach, Dinzlweg 34, tel: (04242) 56368.

Salzburg City

Aignerstrasse 34, tel: (0662) 23284.
Eduard Heinrich-Strasse 2, tel: (0662) 25976.
Glockengasse 8, tel: (0662) 876241.

Salzburg State

Badgastein, Ederplatz 2, tel: (06434) 2080.
Hallein, Schloss Wispach, tel: (06245) 80397.
St Gilgen, Mondseer Str. 7-9, tel: (06227) 365.
St Johann im Pongau, Alpendorf JH Weitenmoos, tel: (06412) 513.
Zell am See, Seespitzstrasse 13, tel: (06542) 7185.

Tyrol

Innsbruck, Radetzkystrasse 47, tel: (0512) 395 882.
Glockenhaus, Weiherburggasse 3, tel: (0512) 286 515.
Studentenheim, Reichenaustrasse 147, tel: (05222) 46180.
Kufstein, Schloss Hohenstaffing, Thierbergweg 28, tel: (05372) 52514.
Reutte, Prof. Dengl-Strasse 20, tel: (05672) 3039.
Sillian, Arnbach Nr. 84, tel: (04842) 6321.

Vorarlberg

Bregenz, Belruptstrasse16a, tel: (05574) 42867.
Feldkirch-Levis, Reichsstrasse 111, tel: (05522) 73181.

Eating Out

What to Eat

Culinary Phrases

The following is a list of various culinary terms, dishes and foods:

Backhendl	breaded and baked chicken
Beinfleisch	cooked beef
Beuschel	a lung and heart ragout
Erdäpfel	potatoes
Faschiertes	minced meat
Fritatten	sliced pancakes
Germ	yeast
Geselchtes	smoked
Grammeln	dripping
Gugelhupf	ring-shaped poundcake
Häuptlsalat	lettuce
Karfiol	cauliflower
Kohlsprossen	brussel sprouts
Kren	horseradish
Krenfleisch	boiled young pork with bacon in a horseradish sauce
Kukuruz	corn
Marillen	apricots
Obers	cream
Palatschinken	pancakes
Paradeiser	tomatoes
Powidl	plum sauce
Ribisel	blackcurrants
Ringlotten	Mirabelle plums
Schlagobers	whipped cream
Schöpsernes	mutton
Schwammerl	mushrooms
Selchfleisch	smoked meat
Tafelspitz	a special cut of cooked beef
Topfen	a soft curd cheese
Zwetschken	plums

Where to Eat

Restaurants

Austrian cooking is generally rich and wholesome. Almost every large town has at least several nationally-known restaurants. Listed here by provincial capital are some of the leading dining establishments:

Mautern near Krems: Landhaus Bacher, 3512 Mautern bei Krems, tel: (02732) 829370.
Graz: Plabutscher Schlössl, Göstlinger Str. 129, tel: (0316) 684858.
Salzburg: Goldener Hirsch, Getreidegasse 37, tel: (0662) 8084.
Innsbruck: Kapeller, Phil.-Welser-Str. 96, tel: (0512) 343106.
Bregenz: Zoll, Arlbergstr. 118, tel: (05574) 31705.
Vienna: Restaurant Korso, 1, Mahlerstr. 2, tel: (0222) 515-16546.
Restaurant Steirereck, 3, Rasumofskygasse 2, tel: (0222) 713-3168.

It is only feasible to recommend a small selection of other restaurants here. The following ones serve regional specialities as well as international specialities:
In Vienna: Korso, Vier Jahreszeiten, Altwienerhof, Gottfried, Hauswirth, La Scala and the Drei Husaren.
In Lower Austria: Schafelinger, located in the town of Haag.
In Upper Austria: The Allegro in Linz.
In Carinthia: Kellerwand in Kötschach-Mauthen and the Bleiberger Hof in Bad Bleiberg.
In the Salzburg Area: Villa Hiss in Badgastein, the Mesnerhaus in Mauterndorf, Lebzelter-Obauer in Werfen, the Weisse Kreuz in Mondsee and the Brunnwirt in Fuschl.
In Tyrol: The Unterberger Stuben in Kitzbühel.

Regional Cuisine

The culinary specialities of Austria are distinguished by region. Here are some of the leading restaurants which offer a selection of dishes characteristic of their respective regions:
Burgenland: Taubenkobel, 7081 Schützen/Geb, tel: (02684) 2297.
Lower Austria: Jamek, 3610 Joching, tel: (02715) 2235.
Villa Schratt, 4820 Bad Ischl, tel: (06132) 7647.
Styria: Zum Klein-Hapl, 8580 Köflach, tel: (03144) 3494.
Salzburg: Braugasthof Sigl, 5162 Obertrum, tel: (06219) 5162.
Restaurant Döllerer, 5440 Golling, tel: (06244) 2200.
Tyrol: Lendbräu, 6130 Schwaz, tel: (05242) 72002.

International Cuisine

Asia, 1, Himmelpfortgasse 27, tel: (0222) 512-7277.
Bambus, Auerspergstr. 2, tel: (0222) 433-337.
Dalmatia, 1, Riemerg. 12, tel: (0222) 513992.
Grotta Azzurra, 1, Babenbergerstr. 5, tel: (0222) 586-1044.
Italienische Weinstube, 7, Mariahilfer Str. 80, tel: (0222) 930-322.
Koh-I-Noor, 1, Marc Aurel Str. 8, tel: (0222) 533-0080.
Kiang, 1, Falkestr. 5, tel: 512-0783.
K2 Sushi, 1, Fleischmarkt 6, tel: (0222) 535-6828.
Lechaim, 2, Hollandstr. 7, tel: (0222) 214-6745.
Oxensteak, 4, Prinz-Eugen-Str. 2, tel: (0222) 504-7121
Ristorante Firenze, 1, Singerstr. 3, tel: (0222) 513-4374.
Siam, 1, Rotenturmstr. 11, tel: (0222) 533-5235.
Sorbas, 1, Opernring 3-5, tel: (0222) 587-245.

Health Food

Vienna: Wrenkh, 1, Bauernmarkt 10, tel: (0222) 535-3362.
Siddharta, 1, Fleischmarkt 16, tel: (0222) 513-1197.
Linz: Getreidemühle, Klammstr. 3, tel: (0732) 275-646.
Carinthia: Alpenrose, 9872 Obermillstatt, tel: (04766) 2500.
Römerbad, Bad Kleinkirchheim, tel: (04240) 8235.
Tyrol: Philippine, Innsbruck, Müllerstr. 9, tel: (0512) 58915.
Schwarzer Adler, Innsbruck, tel: (0512) 587-109.

Viennese Hot-Spots

Alt-Wien, 1, Bäckerstr. 9, tel: (0222) 512-5222.
Daniel Moser, 1, Rotenturmstr. 14, tel: (0222) 513-2823.
Kaktus, 1, Riemergasse 1-3, tel: (0222) 533-1938.
Krah-Krah, 1, Rabensteig 8, tel: (0222) 533-8193.
Oswald & Kalb, 1, Bäckerstr. 14, tel: (0222) 512-1371.

Palaces & Castles

A number of first-class restaurants have been established in old palaces and castles, many of which also offer overnight accommodation.

These are just some of the possibilities available:

VIENNA

Palais Schwarzenberg, tel: (0222) 784-515.

LOWER AUSTRIA

Schloss Rosenau, 3924 Rosenau, tel: (02822) 582210.
Schloss Dürnstein, 3601 Dürnstein, tel: (02711) 212.

STYRIA

Schloss Ober-Mayerhofen, Sebersdorf, tel: (03333) 25030.

CARINTHIA

Schloss Leonstain, 9210 Pörtschach, tel: (04272) 2816.

SALZBURG

Schloss Mönchstein, 5020 Salzburg, tel: (0662) 848-555-0.
Schloss Prielau, 5700 Zell am See, tel: (06542) 72609.
Schloss Hellbrunn, 5020 Salzburg, tel: (0662) 820-3720.

Romantic Cellars

VIENNA

Piaristenkeller, 8, Piaristengasse 45, tel: (0222) 406-01930.
Urbanikeller, 1, Am Hof 12, tel: (0222) 533-9102.
Wiener Rathauskeller, 1, Rathausplatz 1, tel: (0222) 405-12190.

EISENSTADT

Schlosstaverne, Esterházyplatz 5, tel: (02682) 63102.

RUST

Rathauskeller, Hauptplatz, tel: (02685) 261.

SALZBURG

Zum Mohren, Judengasse 9, tel: (0662) 842-387.

GRAZ

Hofkeller, Hofgasse 8, tel: (0316) 832-4390.

DORNBIRN

Günthers Vinotek, Riedgasse 10, tel: (05572) 22679.

Viennese Specialities

COFFEE HOUSES

Bräunerhof, 1, Stallburggasse 2, tel. (0222) 512-3893.
Café Central, 1, Herrengasse 14, tel: (0222) 533-3763.
Café Dommayer, 13, Auhofstr. 2, tel. (0222) 825-465.
Café Frauenhuber, 1, Himmelpfortgasse 6, tel: (0222) 512-4323.
Café Hawelka, 1, Dorotheergasse 6, tel: (0222) 512-8230.
Café Landmann, 1, Dr.-Karl-Lueger-Ring 4, tel: (0222) 532-0621.
Café Museum, 1, Friedrichstr. 6, tel: (0222) 565-202.
Café Prückl, 1, Stubenring 24, tel. (0222) 512-6115.
Café Sacher, 1, Philharmonikerstr. 4, tel: (0222) 5145-7846.
Café Sperl, 6, Gumpendorfer Str. 11, tel: (0222) 564-158.

CONCERT CAFÉS

Café Bräunerhof, 1, Stallburggasse 2, tel: (0222) 512-3893.
Café Dommayer, 13, Dommayergasse 1, tel: (0222) 877-5465.
Konzertcafé Schwarzenberg, 1, Kärntner Ring 17, tel: (0222) 512-7393.
Walzerkonzertcafé, DDS Johann Strauss, 1, on the canal next to the Marienbrücke, tel: (0222) 639-367.

CAKE & PASTRY CAFÉS

Demel, 1, Kohlmarkt 14, tel: (0222) 6335-516.
Gerstner, 1, Kohlmarkt 14, tel: (0222) 524-963.
Heiner, 1, Kärntner Str. 21-23, tel: (0222) 5126-863.

Drinking Notes

Austria has a long tradition of wine. The Romans are known to have tended vineyards in the old region of Vindobona. One thousand years later, this tradition was taken over and continued by the local monasteries. Particular types of wine grapes have proved themselves to be hardy in the Austrian climate. More than a third of the total area used for the cultivation of grapes is devoted to Grüner Veltliner, of which it is said the taste is tangy and slightly peppery. Blaufränkische, a hearty, fruity red wine, is also very popular.

Vineyards are cultivated in the following four provinces: Vienna, Lower Austria, Burgenland, and Styria.

Wine in Austria is separated into four different categories: *Landwein* (table wine), *Qualitätswein* (wine of certified origin and quality), *Kabinettwein* (high quality white wine) and *Prädikatswein* (special quality wine).

In most vineyard areas you can pay a visit to one of the wine cellars for a little sampling. Or, better still, sit out in the open, under the shade of old trees and have the wine-grower himself serve you a glass.

Further information is available from the **Austrian Weinmarketing Servicegesellschaft**, 6 Gumpendorfer Str. 8, tel: (0222) 587-4767.

White Wine

Riesling – a lively, piquant wine with a flowery bouquet; grown in Wachau.
Grüner Veltliner – full-bodied, fruity and piquant; produced in Lower Austria and in Burgenland.
Traminer – aromatic.
Zierfandler – a rich bouquet.
Müller-Thurgau – light and sweet with a flowery bouquet.
Welschriesling – finely full-bodied; from Burgenland and Styria.
Weisser Burgunder – with a nut-like bouquet.
Neuburger – full and hearty; produced in Lower Austria and Burgenland.

Red Wine

Zweigelt blau – fine and fruity.
Blauer Portugieser – mild; produced in Lower Austria.
Blauer Burgunder – fiery, with a nutty bouquet; found in Lower Austria and in Burgenland.
Schilcher – fruity and sharp; produced in Styria.

Heurige

You'll find *Heurige* (cosy wine bars which serve new wine) in Vienna and in the wine-growing region.

VIENNA

Fuhrgassl-Huber, tel: (0222) 440-1405.
Mayer am Pfarrplatz, tel: (0222) 371-287.

GUMPOLDSKIRCHEN

Melkerhof Melk, (private parties only) tel: (02252) 62108.

Weinstadl, tel: (02252) 62218.

PERCHTOLDSDORF

Killermann, tel: (0222) 868-181.

KREMS

Kremser Sandgrube, tel: (02732) 3191.

DÜRNSTEIN

Alter Klosterkeller, tel: (02732) 5362.

DONNERSKIRCHEN

Liesserhof, tel: (02683) 8636.

PURBACH

Pauli's Stuben, tel: (02683) 5513.
Türkenkeller, tel: (02683) 5112.

GRAZ

Stiegelmar, (private parties only) tel: (02173) 2203.

Wine Holidays

Eastern Austria (Lower Austria, Vienna, the Burgenland and Styria) is a wine growing region. Twelve different "Wine Routes" open them up and acquaint you not only with the different tastes of their wines but also with the ancient background of the trade. Driving along the "Wine Route" is a cherished weekend pastime for the locals.

LOWER AUSTRIA

The Therme region around Baden bei Wien.
The wine route along the Kamptal.
The Carnuntum region east of Vienna.
The Weinviertel.
The Wachau.

BURGENLAND

The Neusiedlersee region.
The Neusiedler-hill region.
Central Burgenland.
South Burgenland.

STYRIA

South Styria.
West Styria.
Southeast Styria.

Each region has wine academies, fairs, tours and tasting events. Detailed information is available through: **Vinoveritas-Austria**, Prof.-Kaserer-Weg 333, 3491 Straß im Straßertal, tel: (02735) 553-514, fax: (02735) 700-614.

Pubs

Bastei-Beisel, 1, Stubenbastei 10, tel: (0222) 5124-319.
Figlmüller, 1, Wollzeile 5, tel: (0222) 5126-177
Ofenloch, 1, Kurrentgasse 8, tel: (0222) 5338-844.
Salzamt, 1, Ruprechtspl. 1, tel: (0222) 533-5332.
Wein-Comptoir, 1, Bäckerstr. 6, tel: (0222) 512-1760.
Wrenkh, 1, Bauernmarkt 10, tel: (0222) 533-1526.
Zum Suppentopf, 1, Wipplingerstr. 21, tel: (0222) 533-2435.

Attractions

Culture

Castles & Palaces

Because of its position at the crossroads of the trade routes used in the Middle Ages and later, and as the centre of an empire which encompassed Europe, many castles and palaces were erected at strategically important and naturally beautiful places in Austria. These grand edifices have, for the most part, all been renovated and these days serve as a most graphic display of the country's history.

The castles and palaces mentioned here are only the largest and most beautiful of the many situated throughout Austria:

VIENNA

Belvedere Palace, the Palace of Prince Eugene (1714–16 and 1721–23).
Hofburg, the Imperial Residence, centre of the Habsburg Empire.
Schönbrunn Palace, the summer residence (1695–1713).

BURGENLAND

Eisenstadt, Schloss Esterházy (1663–1972).
Forchtenstein Castle (17th century).
Güssing, Hochburg (16/17th century).
Halbturn, baroque palace (1711).
Landsee Keep (1772).
Lockenhaus Castle (13th century).

LOWER AUSTRIA

Aggstein, castle ruins (13th century).
Heidenreichstein, moated castle (16th century).
Marchegg, country house (1733).
Mödling, Castle Liechtenstein (12th century).
Orth a. d. Donau, keep (13th century).
Rosenburg, Renaissance palace (1583–1604).
Schallaburg, Renaissance palace (1572–1600).
Schlosshof, summer residence of Prinz Eugene (1725–29).
Seebenstein, Höhenburg (1600).
Wiener Neustadt, castle (13th century).

STYRIA

Graz, Eggenberg Palace (1635).
Herberstein, castle (13th-17th century).
Riegersburg, castle (17th century).

CARINTHIA

Friesach - Petersberg, ruins of the archiepiscopal castle (12th century).
Launsdorf, Hochosterwitz Castle (1570-86).
Spittal an der Drau, Schloss Porcia (1533-1602).

UPPER AUSTRIA

Gmunden, lake palace (17th century).
Linz, castle (1481).
Wels, former ducal castle (late-Middle Ages).

SALZBURG

Hellbrunn Pleasure Palace (1615).
Hohensalzburg Fortress (1077).
Residence (1595).
Schloss Mirabell (1606).

SALZBURG STATE

Goldegg, castle (1536).
Schloss Moosham, Doppelburg (13th century).
Werfen, Hohenwerfen Castle (1077).

TYROL

Hall i. T., Hasegg Castle (1480).
Heimfels, ruins (13th century).
Innsbruck, Hofburg (1776).
Kufstein, fortress (1504).
Landeck, castle (Middle Ages).
Lienz, Bruck Castle (1280).
Schloss Ambras, (1564-1789).
Schwaz, Freundsberg Castle (1472-75).
Stans, Tratzberg Castle (16th century).

Foundations & Monasteries

Because Austria is a strictly Catholic country, it is densely packed with numerous seminaries and monasteries. Most of the monasteries were founded at the beginning of this millennium and many still possess Romanesque elements of style. These are some of the most beautiful and historically-signficant edifices to be found anywhere in Austria (the dates in parentheses refer to the year of foundation).

VIENNA

Capuchin Monastery (1618).
Scots Church (1155).

BURGENLAND

Eisenstadt, Franciscan monastery (1625).
Güssing, Franciscan monastery (1648).
Loretto (1651).

UPPER AUSTRIA

Engelszell, Cistercian monastery (1293).
Lambach, Benedictine monastery (1056).
Mondsee, former Benedictine monastery (church 748).
Reichersberg, Augustinian canonical foundation (1048).
Schlägl, Premonstratensian canonical abbey (1218).

STYRIA

Admont, Benedictine abbey (1074).
Göss, former Benedictine convent (ca. 1000).
Neuburg an der Mürz, former Cistercian abbey (1327).
Pöllau, former Augustinian canonical foundation (1504).
Rein, oldest Cistercian monastery in Austria (1129).
Seckau, Benedictine monastery (1140).
Vorau, Augustinian canonical foundation (1163).

CARINTHIA

Friesach, Dominican monastery (1217).
Millstatt, former Benedictine Abbey (1060).
Ossiach, former Benedictine monastery (1028).
St Paul i. Lavanttal, Benedictine monastery (1028).

SALZBURG CITY

Benedictine Abbey of St Peter (696).
Franciscan Monastery (1220).
Nonnberg, Benedictine abbey (715).

SALZBURG STATE

Matsee, Collegiate foundation (770).
Michelbeuern, Benedictine abbey (817).

TYROL

Innsbruck, Franciscan monastery (1553).
Stams, Cistercian foundation (1273).
Vomp - St Georgenberg/Fiecht, Benedictine monastery (1138).
Wilten, Premonstratensian canonical foundation (1138).

VORARLBERG

Bregenz–Mehrerau, Cistercian monastery (1097).
Hohenweiler/Gwiggen - Maria Stern, Cistercian convent (1856).

On the Baroque Trail

Visitors can follow the Baroque trail in a circle throughout Austria. The stretch from Salzburg over Upper Austria, Lower Austria, Vienna, Burgenland, Styria, Carinthia Tyrol and Vorarlberg has countless baroque masterpieces. Baroque music is performed in many Austrian cities.

Information regarding concert dates and detailed literature pertaining to the "Barockstrasse" is available at the **Austrian Tourist Office Centre** in Vienna 5, Margaretenstrasse 1, tel: (0222) 587-2000, and at Austrian Tourist Office agencies in other countries as well.

Baroque Concerts

VIENNA

Baroque concerts in Vienna take place throughout the year in two large concert halls:
Musikverein (Music Society), 1, Bösendorferstr. 12.
Konzerthaus, 3, Lothringerstr. 20.

LOWER AUSTRIA

Internationale Kirchenmusiktage (International Festival of Church Music), 3100 St Pölten, Lilienfeld and Herzogenburg, tel: (02742) 324-345.
Schlosskonzert Grafenegg (Graffenegg Palace Concerts; May-October), tel: (02735) 220-587.

Konzertring Göttweig, 3511 Furth, tel: (02735) 6161.
Sommerkonzerte auf der Schallaburg (Summer Concerts on the Schallaburg), 3382 Schallaburg, tel: (02754) 63170.
Pfingstkonzerte in Stift Melk (Whitsun Concerts in Melk Abbey), 3390 Melk, tel: (02752) 523-120.

UPPER AUSTRIA

Oberösterreichische Stiftskonzerte (Upper Austrian Monastery Concerts), 4060 Leonding, Holzbergerweg 18, tel: (07327) 81044.
Österreichische Donaufestwochen (Austrian Festival of the Danube, August–September), Schloss Greinburg, 4360 Grein an der Donau, tel: (07268) 680.

SALZBURG

Salzburger Festspiele (Salzburg Festival in July/August), 5010 Salzburg, tel: (0662) 80450.
Salzburger Schlosskonzerte (Salzburg Palace Concerts), 5024 Salzburg, Markartplatz 9, tel: (0662) 848-5860.
Salzburger Festungskonzerte (Salzburg Fortress Concerts; May–October), 5020 Salzburg, Anton Adlgasser-Weg 4, tel: (0662) 842-43010
Mozart Serenaden (Mozart Serenades), 5071 Siezenheim 342, tel: (0662) 851-168.

TYROL

Ambraser Schlosskonzerte (Ambras Palace Concerts; July-August), 6020 Innsbruck, Blasius Hueber-Str. 12, tel: (0512) 571032.
Festwoche der Alten Musik (during the second half of August), 6020 Innsbruck, Blasius Hueber-Str. 12.

Museums

The country's museums are veritable treasure troves. The Austria which survived following the collapse of the monarchy had always been the centre of the enormous empire. Whatever object or work of art was considered to be of artistic value was usually taken to Vienna.

There were many art patrons in the imperial family as well as in the houses of various aristocratic families who had the means with which to acquire art objects of extraordinary value. Today, Vienna alone has more than 50 museums and practically

every small city in Austria has a local museum in which are housed the relics of its own lengthy history.

The following Viennese museums all belong in this latter category; in addition to these is a list of many others, which may correspond to certain individual interests.

Vienna

Gemäldegalerie und Kupferstichkabinett der Akademie der Bildenden Künste (Painting Gallery and Engravings Cabinet of Academy of Fine Arts), 1, Schillerplatz 3, tel: (0222) 588-160,
Graphische Sammlung Albertina (Albertina Graphics Collection), 1, Augustinerstr. 1, tel: (0222) 534-830.
Bundessammlung alter Stilmöbel (National Collection of Old Period Furniture), 7, Mariahilfer Str. 88, tel: (0222) 923-240. (The museum is closed until 1999.)
Erzbischöfliches Dom-und Diözesanmuseum (Cathedral and Diocesan Museum), 1, Stephansplatz 6, tel: (0222) 51552/598.
Sigmund-Freud-Museum, 9, Berggasse 19, tel: (0222) 319-15960
Historisches Museum der Stadt Wien (Vienna Historical Museum), 4, Karlsplatz, tel: (0222) 505-8747.
Hoftafel und Silberkammer (Imperial Tableware and Silver Treasury), 1, Hofburg, tel: (0222) 533-7570.
Geschichte der Medizin (History of Medicine), 9, Währinger Str. 25, tel: (0222) 403-2154.
Kaisergruft bei den Kapuzinern (Kaiser's Crypt), 1, Tegetthoffstr. 2, tel: (0222) 526-853.
Kunsthistorisches Museum (Museum of Art History), 1, Burgring 5, tel: (0222) 521-770.
Weltliche und geistliche Schatzkammer (Imperial Treasury), 1, Hofburg, Schweizerhof, tel: (0222) 533-7931.
Wagenburg, 13, Schloss Schönbrunn, tel: (0222) 877-32440.
Museum des 20. Jahrhunderts (Museum of the 20th Century), 3, Schweizergarten, tel: (0222) 317-69000.
Museum moderner Kunst Palais Liechtenstein (Museum of Modern Art in Palace Liechtenstein), 9, Fürstengasse 1, tel: (0222) 317-69000.
Museum für Völkerkunde (Museum of Ethnology), Neue Hofburg, tel: (0222) 534-300.
Naturhistorisches Museum (Museum

of Natural History), 14, Burgring 7, tel: (0222) 521-770.

Österreich Galerie (Austrian Gallery), 3, Prinz-Eugen-Str. 27, Schloss Belvedere, tel: (0222) 795-570.

Österreichische Nationalbibliothek (Austrian National Library), 1, Josephsplatz 1, tel: (0222) 534-100.

Österreichisches Museum für angewandte Kunst (Austrian Museum of Applied Art), 1, Stubenring 5, tel: (0222)711-360.

Schatzkammer des Deutschen Ordens (Treasure Chamber of the Teutonic Order), 1, Singerstr. 7, tel: (0222) 512-165.

Schauräume der Hofburg (Display Rooms of the Hofburg), 1, Hofburg, tel: (0222) 587-5554/515.

Schloss Schönbrunn (Schönbrunn Palace), 13, Schloss Schönbrunn, tel: (0222) 811-130.

The following museums are also located in Vienna:

The Baking Museum, 24 **district museums**, numerous commemorative rooms and memorials. The **Museum of Funerals**, a **Museum of Circuses and Clowns**, the **Viennese Phonograph Museum**, the **Tile Museum**, the Bohemian Forest Museum, a **Museum of Electro-Pathology**, the **Museum of Copy Machines**, the **Museum of Radios**, a **Fire Brigade Museum**, the **Museum of old Horse-drawn Carriages**, a **Museum of Criminal Investigations**, a **Museum for the Blind,** the **Museum of the Institute for Forensic Medicine**, the **Theatre Museum**, a **Museum of Esperanto**, the **Museum of Horticulture**, the **Gendarmerie Museum**, the **Museum of Society and Economics**, a **Museum of Photography**, the **Folk Art Museum**, a **Tobacco Museum**, the **Tape Recorder Museum**, the **Prater Museum**, a **Museum of Clocks**, a **Railway Museum, Mail and Telegraph Museum**, and a **Trolley Museum.**

For further information contact the **Vienna Tourist Board**, A-1025 Obere Augartenstr. 40, tel: (0222) 211-140.

Burgenland

Burgenländisches Landesmuseum (Burgenland State Museum), Museumsgasse, tel: (02682) 62652.

Haydnmuseum, Joseph-Haydn-Gasse 21, tel: (02682) 62652.

Jüdisches Museum (Jewish Museum), Wertheimerhaus, Unterbergstr. 6, tel: (02682) 65145.

● **7131 Halbturn**
Schloss Halbturn, tel: (02172) 8577.

● **7062 St Margarethen**
Römersteinbruch (Roman Quarry), tel: (02680) 2188.

Lower Austria

● **3400 Klosterneuburg**
Chorherrenstift Klosterneuburg (Neuburg Monastery), Stiftsmuseum, Stiftsplatz, tel: (02243) 4110.

● **3321 Kolmitzberg Heeresgeschichtle Museum** (Museum of Military History), tel: (07479) 2239.

● **2151 Asparn an der Zaya Museum für Urgeschichte** (Museum of Prehistory), Schloss Asparn, tel: (02577) 80390.

● **Marchegg Grosswildjäger und Afrika Reisender/Abententeuerer, Schloss Marchegg** (Museum of Game Hunters and African Travellers and Adventurers), tel: (02285) 710-011.

● **3511 Furth**
Graphisches Kabinett Stift Göttweig (Museum of Graphic Art), tel: (02732) 855-810.

● **3454 Reidling**
Niederösterreichisches Barockmuseum (Lower Austrian Baroque Museum), Schloss Heiligenkreuz-Gutenbrunn, tel: (02782) 4097.

● **3130 Herzogenburg**
Kunstsammlung und Schatzkammer (Art Collection and Treasure Chamber), Stift Herzogenburg, tel: (02782) 31120.

● **3382 Loosdorf**
Schloss Schallaburg, tel: (02754) 6317.

● **3390 Melk**
Museum des Stiftes Melk (Melk Abbey Museum), Stift Melk, tel: (02752) 2312.

● **3924 Rosenau Österreichisches Freimaurermuseum** (Museum of Austrian Freemasons), Schloss Rosenau, tel: (02822) 582-210.

Upper Austria

● **4020 Linz**
Landesmuseum (State Museum), Museumstr. 14, tel: (0732) 774-482.

Neue Galerie (Museum of Modern Art), Blütenstr. 15, tel: (0732) 707-03601.

● **8430 Hallstatt**
Prähistorisches Museum (Museum of Prehistory), Seestr. 56, tel: (06134) 208480.

● **4210 Gallneukirchen Afrika Museum in Schloss Riedegg**, Mariannhiller

Missionshaus, tel: (07235) 622240.

● **5310 Mondsee**
Pfahlbaumuseum (Museum of Lake Dwellings), Marschall-Wrede-Pl.

● **4582 Spital am Pyhrn**
Felsbildermuseum (Museum of Rock Paintings), tel: (07563) 318.

Styria

● **8010 Graz**
Johanneum (Provincial Museum), Rauberg 10, tel: (0316) 80170.

Diözesanmuseum (Diocesan Museum), tel: (0316) 713-99440.

● **8911 Admont**
Naturhistorisches- und Kunsthistorisches Museum des Benediktinerstiftes (Natural History and Art History Museum of the Benedictine Abbey), Benediktinerstift, tel: (03613) 231-235.

● **8992 Altaussee**
Salzbergwerk (Salt Mines), tel: (0362) 371-3320.

Carinthia

● **9020 Klagenfurt**
Landesmuseum für Kärnten (Museum of the Federal state of Carinthia), Museumgasse. 2, tel: (0463) 536-305-52.

Kärntner Landesgalerie (Provincial Art Gallery), Burggasse. 8, tel: (0463) 5360.

Diözesanmuseum (Diocesan Museum), Haus am Dom, Lidmanskygasse 10/III, tel: (0463) 502498.

● **9843 Döllach**
Goldbergbaumuseum (Museum of Gold Mining), Schloss Grosskirchheim, tel: (04825) 226.

● **9063 Maria Saal**
Kärntner Freilichtmuseum (Carinthian Open-air Museum), tel: (04223) 31660.

Salzburg

● **5020 Salzburg**
Hohensalzburg, tel: (0662) 844-145.

Dommuseum (Cathedral Museum), Pf. 62, tel: (0662) 844-1890.

Mozarts Geburtshaus (Mozart's Birthplace), Getreideg. 9, tel: (0662) 844-3130.

Salzburger Barockmuseum (Salzurg Baroque Museum), Orangerie des Mirabellgarten, tel: (0662) 877-432.

Residenzgalerie, Residenzplatz. 1, tel: (0662) 840-4510.

Museum Carolino Augusteum, Museumsplatz 6, tel: (0662) 843-1450.

● **5400 Hallein**

Bergwerkmuseum (Museum of Salt Mines), Dürrnberg, tel: (06245) 852-8515.
Keltenmuseum (Celtic Museum), Pflegerplatz 5, tel: (06245) 807-830.

Tyrol
● **6020 Innsbruck**
Hofburg, Rennweg 1, tel: (0512) 27186.
Hofkirche with the Silver Chapel, Rennweg, tel: (0512) 583-092.
Kaiserschützenmuseum (Museum of Imperial Marksmen), Klostergasse 7, tel: (0512) 583-386.
Bergisel Museum, Bergisel 3, tel: (0512) 582-312.
Kunsthistorisches Museum Schloss Ambras (Art History Museum of Schloss Ambras), tel: (0512) 348-446.
Tiroler Landesmuseum Ferdinandeum (State Museum), Museumstr. 12, tel: (0512) 59489.
Zeughaus Maximilian I (Imperial Arsenal), Zeughausgasse, tel: (0512) 587-439.

Vorarlberg
● **6900 Bregenz**
Vorarlberger Landesmuseum (State Museum), Kornmarkt, tel: (05574) 46050.

Festival Performances

Classical music was born in Austria and a large number of annual, traditional music festivals pay tribute to this fact. The majority of these festival performances and week-long celebrations naturally take place during the summer months. The **Austrian Tourist Information Centre** will send you a printed summary of events scheduled for the year including a list of one-time only performances. (Tel: (0222) 587-2000).

A respective schedule of events for the following festivals are also available at the addresses listed below, tickets can be reserved here as well:

Vienna
Wiener Festwochen (Vienna Festival), 6, Lehargasse 11, tel: (0222) 589-220.
Bundestheater (National Theatre), 1, Goethegasse 1, tel: (0222) 514-440.
Wiener Musik-Sommer (Vienna Music Summer), Kulturamt der Stadt Vienna, 1, Rathaus, tel: (0222) 4000-8400.

Haydn- und Schuberttage, Tage der Sakralen Musik (Sacred Music Days), 1, Bösendorferstr. 12, tel: Musikverein (0222) 505-86810.
Viennale, 1, Uraniastr. 1, tel: (0222) 526-59470.
Festival Wiener Klassik (Vienna Classical Festival), 3, Preindlgasse 1, tel: (0222) 825-208.
Sommerspiele im Schönbrunner Schlosstheater (Summer Fesival in Schönbrunn Palace Theatre), 1, Fleischmarkt 24, tel: (0222) 811-130.

Burgenland
Seefestspiele Mörbisch (Lakeside festival performances), 7072 Mörbisch, tel: Eisenstadt (02682) 662-100. July and August tel: Mörbisch (02685) 81810.
Haydn Festspiele (Haydn Festival), 7000 Eisenstadt, Schloss Esterházy, tel: (02682) 61866.

Lower Austria
Badener Operettensommer (Baden Summer Operettas), 2500 Baden, Kurdirektion, tel: (02252) 445-3142.

Upper Austria
OÖ Stiftskonzerte (Upper Austrian Monastery Concerts), 4060 Leonding, tel: (0732) 781-044.
Operettenwochen Bad Ischl (Operetta Festival), 4820 Bad Ischl, Herrengasse 32, tel: (06132) 23839.
International Brucknerfest in Linz, 4010 Linz, Untere Donaulände 7, tel: (0732) 775-236.

Styria
Styriarte Graz, 8010 Graz, Palais Attems, tel: (0316) 812-9410.
Schladminger Musiksommer (Schladming Music Summer), 8970 Schladming, Stadtamt, tel: (03687) 22508.

Carinthia
Carinthischer Sommer (Carinthian Summer), 9570 Ossiach, Stift Ossiach, tel: (04243) 8664.
Internationale Musikwochen in Millstatt (International music week), 8972 Millstatt, Rathaus, tel: (04766) 2021.

Salzburg
Salzburger Festspiele (Salzburg Festival), 5010 Salzburg, Festspielhaus, tel: (0662) 80450.
Salzburger Schlosskonzerte (Salzburg

Palace Concerts), 5024 Salzburg, Makartplatz 9, tel: (0662) 848-5860.
Mozart-Woche in Salzburg (Mozart Week), 5024 Salzburg, Mozarteum, tel: (0662) 876-585.
Salzburger Festungskonzerte (Salzburg Fortress Concerts), 5020 Salzburg, Thumeggerstr. 26c, tel: (0662) 842-43010.
Mozart Serenaden (Mozart Serenades), 5071 Siezenheim 342, tel: (0662) 436-870.
Salzburger Kulturtage (Salzburg Culture Days), 5010 Salzburg, Waagplatz 1a, tel: (0662) 845-346.
Jazzfestival Saalfelden, 5751 Maishofen, tel: (06582) 74963.

Tyrol
Ambraser Schlosskonzerte (Ambras Palace Concerts), 6020 Innsbruck, Blasius Hueberstr. 12, tel: (0521) 571-032.
Kammermusikfestival Pertisau (Pertisau Festival of Chamber Music), 6213 Pertisau, **Fremdenverkehrsverband**, tel: (05243) 5260.

Vorarlberg
Bregenzer Festspiele (Bregenz Festival), 6901 Bregenz, Festspiel- und Kongresshaus, tel: (05574) 413-0.
Schubertiade Hohenems (Hohenems Schubert Festival), 6845 Hohenems, Schweizer Str. 1, tel: (05576) 72091-0.
Montafoner Konzertsommer (Montafon Summer Concerts), 6780 Schruns, Siberthalerstr. 1, tel: (05556) 2253.

TICKET PURCHASE
Tickets can bought from the following box offices in Vienna:
Kartenbüro Alserstrasse, tel: (0222) 405-1372.
Kartenbüro Augustinerstrasse, tel: (0222) 533-0961.
Kartenbüro Flamm, tel: (0222) 512-42250.
Verkehrsbüro, tel: (0222) 588-000.
Fremdenrekehrsbüro, tel: (0222) 211-140.
National Theatre Ticket Reservations: 1, Goethegasse 1, tel: (0222) 514-440. Open 9am–5pm Monday–Saturday.
Advance ticket sales: Bundestheaterverband, 1, Hanuschgasse 3, A-1010 Wien, tel: 514-442960 VISA, Eurocard/Mastercard, Diners, AMEX. Book minimum seven days in advance.

Pubs & Bars

VIENNA

Bristol Bar, 1, Kärntner Ring 1; first-class address.

Eden Bar, 1, Liliengasse 2; men are required to wear ties, live-music.

Klimt Bar, Hilton Hotel, 3 Am Stadtpark; Art Nouveau decor.

GRAZ

Ernst Fuchs Bar.

Hotel Erzherzog Johann, Sachstrasse 3-5.

VELDEN

Schlossbar, Schlosshotel; friendly, warm ambience.

Discos

VIENNA

Queen Anne, 1, Johannesgasse; not for young people.

Volksgarten, 1, Volksgarten; for young people.

GRAZ

Ska, Grabenstr. 8; Ex-New-Wave.

VELDEN

GIG, Klagenfurter Str. 46.

KLAGENFURT

Scotch Club, Pfarrplatz 20.

KITZBÜHEL

Take Five, Heroldstr. 1.

Night Clubs

VIENNA

Nina's Club Bar, 1, Bauernmarkt 21; a well-managed hostess bar.

Orient Bar, Orient Hotel, 1, Tiefer Graben 30-32; the most well-cared for flophouse in Vienna.

Orchidee, 5, Schönbrunnerstr. 137; live show, private rooms.

Renz, 2, Zirkusgasse 50; Vienna's Montmartre, shows, private rooms.

LINZ

Club Emanuela, Rudolfstr. 90; Roman baths.

GRAZ

Nummer 1, Triesterstr. 25.

SALZBURG

Cats Club, Esshauerstr. 5; more like a plush drawing room.

Jazz

VIENNA

Jazz-Club Opus One, Mahlerstr. 11.

Jazzland, 1, Franz Josephs-Kai 29.

Casinos

Baden: 2500 Baden, in the Kurpark.

Badgastein: 5640 Badgastein, Grand Hotel d'Europe.

Bregenz: 6900 Bregenz, Symphonikerplatz.

Cercle Vienna: 1010 Vienna, Kärntner Str. 41.

Graz: 8010 Graz, Landhausgasse 10.

Kleinwalsertal: 6991 Riezlern.

Kitzbühel: 6370 Kitzbühel, Hotel Goldener Greif.

Linz: 4020 Linz, Rainerstr. 12-14.

Salzburg: 5020 Salzburg, Mönchsberg 3.

Seefeld: 6100 Seefeld, Hotel Karwendelhof.

Velden: 9220 Velden, Casino.

Sports & Leisure

Activity Centres & Camps

Sport Camp Tyrol, 6500 Landeck, tel: (05442) 646-360.

Alpines Rafting-Camp Iseltal, 9951 Ainet, tel: (04853) 5231.

Club Alpin Extra, 5441 Abtenau, Markt 79, tel: (06243) 3088.

Kajak und Rafting-Fun-Center, 5090 Lofer, tel: (06588) 7524.

Balloon Trips

Erster Oberösterreichischer Ballonfahrerverein, 4693 Desselbrunn 21, tel: (07673) 37300.

Österreichischer Alpenballonsportclub Salzburg, 5033 Salzburg, tel: (06212) 7786.

Tiger-Heissluftballonclub Weinviertel, 1100 Vienna, Felix-Grafe-Gasse 4/147/7, tel: (0222) 688-1387.

Bicycle Tours

The Austrian Federal Railway has bicycles to rent at various railway stations, which can then be returned to any train station. The rental price is reduced by 50 percent if you've arrived by train.

Danube Bicycle Route: Passau-Vienna, 1300 km (90 miles).

Neusiedlersee Bicycle Route: Mörbisch-Rust-Neusiedl-Illmitz, 70 km (45 miles).

Pinzgau Bicycle/Walking Route: Zell am See-Kaprun-Mittersill-Neunkirchen am Grossvenediger, 50 km (30 miles).

Inn Valley Bicycle Route: Innsbruck-Hall-Wattens-Schwaz-Brixlegg-Kufstein, 75 km (50 miles).

Ziller Valley Bicycle Route: Fügen-Zell am Ziller-Mayrhofen and back, 30 km (20 miles).

Canoeing

Canoeing or rafting along Austria's many rivers has developed into one of the most popular sporting activities today. Equipped with an inflatable raft (small and light enough to be transported in a knapsack), with or without a guide, you drift or paddle through white water rivers. There are maps and literature available to inform you of the degree of difficulty of any particular river. The most popular rivers are:

LOWER AUSTRIA

The Zwettl, Kamp, Mühlkamp, Pielach and Thaya.

UPPER AUSTRIA

The Alm, Aschach, Innbach, Grosse Mühl, Steyr and the Traun.

STYRIA

The Enns, Laming, Mur, Mürz and the Salza.

CARINTHIA

The Drau, Gurk and the Möll.

SALZBURG

The Lämmer, Saalach, Salzach and the Torrenerbach.

TYROL

The Inn, Isel, Upper Isar, Kössener Ache and the Lech.

Golf

VIENNA & LOWER AUSTRIA

GC Vienna/Freudenau (18-hole), tel: (0222) 728-9564.
GC Schloss Ebreichsdorf (18-hole), Ebreichsdorf, tel: (02254) 73888.
GC Föhrenwald (18-hole), Wiener Neustadt, tel: (02622) 29171.

BURGENLAND

GC Neusiedlersee-Donnerskirchen (18-hole), Donnerskirchen, tel: (02683) 8171-0.

UPPER AUSTRIA

GC Am Mondsee (18-hole), St Lorenz Drachensee, tel: (06232) 3835.
Salzkammergut GC (18-hole), Bad Ischl, tel: (06132) 26340.
GC Linz (18-hole), St Florian, tel: (07223) 82873.

STYRIA

GC Schloss Pichlarn (18-hole), Irdning, tel: (03682) 24393.
GC Bad Gleichenberg (9-hole), Bad Gleichenberg, tel: (03159) 3717.

CARINTHIA

GC Austria Wörthersee (18-hole), Moosburg-Pörtschach, tel: (04272) 834860.
GC Wörthersee (18-hole), Velden, tel: (04274)7045.

SALZBURG

GC Bad Gastein (9-hole), tel: (06434) 33260.
Golf & Country Club Salzburg-Klessheim (9-hole), tel: (0662) 850-851.
Jagd und Golfclub Schloss Fuschl (9-hole), tel: (06226) 8206.

TYROL

GC Seefeld-Widmoos (18-hole), tel: (05212) 2777.
GC Kitzbühel-Schwarzsee (18-hole), tel: (05356)71645.

Hang & Para Gliding

LOWER AUSTRIA

Danneberg Fred, 3264 Gersten, Brettl 28, tel: (07485) 973-170.

UPPER AUSTRIA

Drachen und Paraflugschule Garstnertal, 4582, Spital am Phyrn, 132, tel: (07562) 7066.

STYRIA

Hängegleiterclub Styria, 8010 Graz, Steinfeldgasse 20, tel: (0664) 337-2880.

SALZBURG

Pinzgauer Drachen und Paragleitschule, 5733 Bramberg 211, tel: (06566) 8522.

TYROL

Himberger Sepp, 6345 Kössen 252, tel: (05375) 6559.
Girstmaier Bruno, 9900 Lienz, Patriasdorferstrasse. 8, tel: (04852) 37355.

VORARLBERG

Greber Kaspar, 6863, Egg, Bühel 853, tel: (05512) 3322.

Horse Riding

For general information contact **Reitarena Austria**, 4121 Altenfelden, Tel: (07282) 5367.

BURGENLAND

Neusiedler Csarda, 7100 Neusiedl, Obere Wiesen 1, tel: (02167) 8659.

LOWER AUSTRIA

Höldrichsmühle, 2371 Hinterbrühl, tel: (02236) 262740.
Schloss Ernegg, 3261 Steinakirchen am Forst, tel: (07488) 71214.

UPPER AUSTRIA

Reitergut Weissenhof, 4563 Micheldorf, Atzelsdorf 3, tel: (07582) 62609.

STYRIA

Islandpferdehof Hoyos, 8102 Semirach, Windhof 70, tel: (03127) 88350.

CARINTHIA

Trattlerhof, 9546 Bad Kleinkirchheim, tel: (04240) 8173.

SALZBURG

Brandlhof, 5760 Saalfelden, Tel: (06582) 780-0555.

TYROL

Haflingerhof, 6311 Wildschönau-Mühltal, tel: (05339) 8810.
Stanglwirt, 6353 Going am Wilden Kaiser, tel: (05358) 2000.

VORARLBERG

Auhof, 6780 Schruns, Auweg 14, tel: (05556) 72269.

Mono-Skis, Snowboards & Swingbos

UPPER AUSTRIA

● **4842 Gosau**, Ski School (Skischule), tel: (06136) 88540.
● **4582 Spital am Pyhrn**, Ski School Wurzeralm, tel: (07563) 4732.

STYRIA

● **8665 Langenwang**, Ski School Mürztal, tel: (03854) 2337.
● **8630 Mariazell**, Tourist Association (Verkehrsverein), tel: (03882) 2366.
● **8785 Hohentauern**, Ski School Moscher, tel: (03618) 204.

CARINTHIA

● **9546 Bad Kleinkirchheim**, Tourist Association, tel: (04240) 8212.
● **6920 Hermagor**, Tourist Office (Verkehrsamt), tel: (04282) 2043.

SALZBURG

● **5441 Abtenau**, Club Alpin, Markt 16, tel: (06243) 2939.
● **5640 Badgastein**, Ski School Badgastein, tel: (06434) 2260.

- **5550 Radstadt**, Ski School Radstadt, tel: (06452) 7382.

TYROL

- **6094 Axams**, Ski School Olympic, tel: (05234) 67415.
- **6632 Ehrwald**, Ski School 200, tel: (05673) 2620.
- **6080 Igls**, Ski School, tel: (0512) 292-439.
- **6365 Kirchberg**, Ski School, tel: (05357) 2209.
- **6631 Lermoos**, Ski School, tel: (05673) 2840.
- **6380 St Johann i. T.**, Ski School, tel: (05352) 64777.

VORARLBERG

- **6764 Lech**, Ski School, tel: (05583) 2007.
- **6952 Hittisau**, Ski School, tel: (05513) 8254.
- **6787 Gargellen**, Ski School, tel: (05557) 6401.

Mountain Climbing Schools

UPPER AUSTRIA

Alpenschule Laserer, 4824 Gosau, tel: (06136) 8835.

STYRIA

Bergsteigerschule Dachstein-Tauern, 8972 Ramsau am Dachstein 273, tel: (03687) 81424.

CARINTHIA

Alpinschule Mallnitz, 9822 Mallnitz, tel: (04784) 290.

SALZBURG

Club Alpin Extra, 5441 Abtenau, tel: (06243) 2939.
Alpin und Bergsteigerschule Oberpinzgau, 5741 Neukirchen, tel: (06564) 8221.

TYROL

Bergsporthochschule Kaisergebirge, 6353 Going, tel: (05358) 2750.
Alpin und Wanderschule Kitzbühel, tel: (05356) 62496.
Bergsteigerschule Piz Buin-Silvretta, 6563 Galtür 74a, tel: (05443) 8260.

VORARLBERG

Alpinschule Montafon, 6780 Schruns, tel: (05556) 76676.
Bergschule Kleinwalsertal, 6993 Mittelberg, tel: (05517) 5860.

Panning for Gold

There are opportunities to join the gold rush, but don't expect a fortune.
Tourist Association (Fremdenverkehrsverein) Heiligenblut, 9844 Heiligenblut, tel: (04824) 200-121.
Tourist Association Rauris, 5661 Rauris, tel: (06544) 62370.

Pools & Baths

VIENNA

Amalien Pool, Oberlaa Thermal Pool.

BURGENLAND

Deutschkreuz Water World.

LOWER AUSTRIA

Baden and Bad Vöslau Thermal Water Beaches, City Club Vienna, Vösendorf.

UPPER AUSTRIA

Bad Ischl Salt Water Pool, Bischofsberg Indoor Rock Pool.

STYRIA

Radkersburg and Waltersdorf Thermal Pools.

CARINTHIA

Bad Bleiberg Crystal Pool, Bad Kleinkirchheim Thermal Roman Pool, Villach Thermal Adventure Pool.

SALZBURG

Badgastein Rock Pool, Bad Hofgastein Thermal Pool, Kaprun Thermal Optimum.

TYROL

Axams Leisure Centre, Stubai Aquarena, Seefeld Olympic Sport Centre.

VORARLBERG

Brand and Mittelberg Water Worlds, Gargellen.

Rafting

CARINTHIA

Oberfellach (Möll, Gail, Isel), tel: (04782) 2510.

EAST TYROL

Lienz (Isel), tel: (04853) 5231.

SALZBURG

Abtenau (Salzach, Lammer), tel: (06243) 2939.
Taxenbach, tel: (06534) 6215.

Lend, tel: (0641) 66152.
Saalbach-Hinterglemm (Saalach), tel: (06541) 7008.

STYRIA

Pruggern (Gesäuse) Tel: (03685)-22245.
Schladming (Enns), tel: (03687) 22574.

TYROL

Haiming (Inn, Ötztaler Ache) Tel: (05266) 88661.
Ötz (Ötztaler Ache) Tel: (05252) 6035.
Gerlos (Lech, Gerlos, Salzach), tel: (05284) 5361.

UPPER AUSTRIA

Bad Goisern (Traun, Lammer, Koppentraun), tel: (06135) 8254.

VORARLBERG

Lech (Lech), tel: (05583) 2161-0.

Ski Areas

People don't only come to Austria just for conventional skiing these days. In addition to "just skiing", they come to go **tobogganing**, **bobsleding**, **cross-country skiing** and **curling**, and even to take classes to learn how to manage a snowboard at one of the 190 snow resort areas. No fewer than 112 areas offer **Swingbo courses**, at 160 places there are instructors to teach you how to use a **mono-ski**, in 138 areas you can rent a **bobsled** and in Feld am See in Carinthia you can learn how to **ice-surf**. Listed here are just a few of the countless addresses; local tourist information centres can provide you with further information.
7142 Illmitz, Tourist Information Office (Fremdenverkehrsbüro), tel: (02175) 2383.
7100 Neusiedl/See, Tourist Information Office, tel: (02167) 2229.
7071 Rust, Tourist Information Office, tel: (02685) 202.
7072 Mörbisch/See, Tourist Information Office, tel: (02685) 8201.
7141 Podersdorf, Tourist Information Office, tel: (02177) 2227.

Snow & Ice Sports

There are around 1,000 areas in Austria which offer excellent opportunities for skiing. The following is a list of tourist information centre telephone numbers of the best-known:

STYRIA

8623 Aflenz, tel: (03861) 2265.
8992 Altaussee, tel: (03622) 71643.
8990 Bad Aussee, tel: (03622) 54040.
8163 Fladnitz, tel: (03179) 7160.
8962 Gröbming, tel: (03685) 22131.
8993 Grundlsee, tel: (03622) 8666.
8920 Hieflau, tel: (03634) 294.
8785 Hohentauern, tel: (03618) 335.
8665 Langenwang, tel: (03854) 615521.
8972 Ramsau am Dachstein, tel: (03687) 81833.
8970 Schladming, tel: (03687) 2268.
8982 Tauplitz, tel: (03688) 2446.

CARINTHIA

9601 Arnoldstein, tel: (04255) 2314.
9546 Bad Kleinkirchheim, tel: (04240) 8212.
9843 Grosskirchheim, tel: (04825) 521-21
9844 Heiligenblut, tel: (04824) 200-121.
6920 Hernagel, Karnische Skiregion, tel: (04282) 2043.
9640 Kötschach-Mauthen, tel: (04715) 8516.
9821 Obervellach, tel: (04782) 2510.
9565 Turracher Höhe, tel: (04275) 8216.

UPPER AUSTRIA

4843 Ampflwang, tel: (07675) 2479.
4864 Attersee, tel: (07666) 7719.
4822 Bad Goisern, tel: (06135) 8329.
4820 Bad Ischl, tel: (06132) 277570.
4810 Gmunden, tel: (07612) 64305.
4824 Gosau, tel: (06136) 82950.
4830 Hallstatt, tel: (06134) 8208.
4573 Hinterstoder, tel: (07564) 5263.
4831 Obertraun/Dachstein, tel: (06131) 351.
5360 St Wolfgang, tel: (06138) 2239.
4582 Spital am Pyhrn, tel: (07563) 249.
3574 Vorderstoder, tel: (07564) 8255.

SALZBURG

5630 Bad Hofgastein, tel: (06432) 6481-0.
5640 Bad Gastein, tel: (06434) 25310.
5671 Bruck an der Glocknerstr, tel: (06545) 72950.
5632 Dorfgastein, tel: (06433) 7277
5532 Filzmoos, tel: (06453) 8235.
5672 Fusch a. d. Glocknerstr, tel: (06546) 236.
3440 Golling, tel: (06244) 356.
5771 Leogang, tel: (06583) 8234.
5090 Lofer, tel: (06588) 832.
5722 Niedersill, tel: (06548) 8232.
5562 Obertauern, tel: (06456) 8252.
5162 Obertrum, tel: (06219) 8307.
5550 Radstadt, tel: (06452) 305.
5661 Rauris, tel: (06544) 6237.
5760 Saalfelden, tel: (06582) 725130.

TYROL

6060 Absam, tel: (05223) 3190.
6274 Aschau im Zillertal, tel: (05282) 2923.
6094 Axamer Lizum, tel: (05234) 8178.
6230 Brixlegg, tel: (05337) 62581.
6262 Bruck am Ziller, tel: (05288) 72500.
6644 Ellmau, tel: (05358) 2301.
6563 Galtür, tel: (05443) 8204.
6353 Going, tel: (05358) 2438.
6444 Gries im Ötztal, tel: (05253) 5103.
6263 Hart im Zillertal, tel: (05288) 62309.
6654 Holzgau, tel: (05633) 5244.
6080 Igls, tel: (0512) 59850.
6460 Imst, tel: (05412) 6910.
6020 Innsbruck, tel: (0512) 59850.
6561 Ischgl, tel: (05444) 5266.
6365 Kirchberg i. T, tel: (05357) 2309.
6370 Kitzbühel, tel: (05356) 62272.
6345 Kössen, tel: (05375) 6287.
6330 Kufstein, tel: (05372) 62207.
6183 Kühtai, tel: (05239) 222.
6764 Lech, tel: (05583) 2161-0.
5090 Lofer, tel: (06588) 8321.
9971 Matrei i. O, tel: (04875) 6527.
6414 Mieming, tel: (05264) 5274.
6162 Mutters, tel: (0512) 573-744.
6465 Nassereith, tel: (05265) 5253.
6433 Oetz, tel: (05252) 6669.
6380 St Johann i. T, tel: (05352) 63335.
6100 Seefeld, tel: (05212) 2313.
6450 Sölden, tel: (05254) 2212.
6762 Stuben, tel: (05582) 761.
6293 Tux, tel: (05287) 85060.
6280 Zell am Ziller, tel: (05282) 2281.

VORARLBERG

6787 Gargellen, tel: (05557) 6303.
6793 Gaschurn, tel: (05558) 8201.
6952 Hittisau, tel: (05513) 6354.
6764 Lech, tel: (05583) 2161-0.
6991 Riezlern, tel: (05517) 5114-0.
6780 Schruns, tel: (05556) 722530.
6762 Stuben, tel: (05582) 761.
6763 Zürs, tel: (05583) 2245.

Powder-Snow Skiing

You can find out by telephone just how deep the snow is in Tyrolean ski areas.

In Austria, call either of the automobile organisations ÖAMTC, tel: (0222) 711-997, or ARBÖ, tel: (0222) 891-277.

The number to call for the **Tyrolean Post and Telegraph Service Snow Report** is (0512) 1585.

In Germany you can get this information from the **ADAC**, tel: (089) 7676-2687; in Switzerland it is available through the **Austrian Tourist Information Office** in Zurich, tel: (01) 272-3331.

If you want to do any powder-snow skiing, it is important to be well-informed as to the current avalanche situation. Information regarding **avalanche conditions** in Tyrol are available by calling (0512) 1567 (recorded message), or (0512) 581-839 (person-to-person information). For the weather forecast in Tyrol, call (0512) 1566.

Summer Skiing

TYROL

Kaunertal, 2,750–3,100 metres (9,020–10,170 ft), tel: (05475) 2530.
Pitztaler Glacier, 2,840–3,440 metres (9,320–11,290 ft), tel: (05413) 86288.
Ötztaler Glacier, 2,800–3,200 metres (9,190–10,500 ft), tel: (05254) 2219.
Stubaier Glacier, 2,600–3,200 metres (8,530–10,500 ft), tel: (05226) 8113.

SALZBURG

Kitzsteinhorn, 2,450–3,030 metres (8,040–9,940 ft), tel: (06547) 8700.

STYRIA

Dachsteingletscher, 2,300–2,700 metres (7,550–8,860 ft), tel: (03687) 81241.

CARINTHIA

Mölltaler Glacier, 2,700–3,100 metres (8,860–10,170 ft), tel: (04785) 615.

Ultralights

Ultralight instruction and training is available from the **Österreichische Aero Club**, Sektion Amateur und Ultralight, Vienna 4, Prinz-Eugen-Strasse 12, tel: (0222) 505-102.

Further Reading

General

Journeys, by Jan Morris. Oxford University Press, 1984. Collection includes an essay on Vienna.

Austrian Cooking, by Gretel Beer. André Deutsch.

History

The Fall of the House of Habsburgs, by Edward Crankshaw. Penguin, 1983.

The Hapsburg Monarch, by Arthur J. May. University of Pennsylvania, 1966.

Clash of Generations, by Lavender Cassels. John Murray, 1973.

Austria, Empire and Republic, by Barbara Jelavich. Cambridge University Press.

Nightmare in Paradise: Vienna and its Jews, by George E. Berkley. California University Press.

Mayerling: the Facts behind the Legend, by Fritz Judtman. Harrap, 1971.

Dissolution of the Austro-Hungarian Empire, by J. W. Mason. Longman.

The End of Austria-Hungary, by L. Valani. Knopf, 1973.

A Nervous Splendour, by Frederic Morton. Little, 1979.

The Habsburg Monarchy, by A.J.P. Taylor Penguin, 1990.

Biography

The Life and Work of Sigmund Freud, by Ernest Jones. Penguin.

Gustav Mahler – Memories and Letters, by Alma Mahler. Collins.

Maria Theresa, by Edward Crankshaw. Constable.

W.A. Mozart: Letters, edited by Hans Mersmann. Dover Publications.

Prince Eugene of Savoy, by Nicholas Henderson. Weidenfeld.

Art & Literature

Austrian Life and Literature: Eight Essays, edited by Peter Branscombe. Scottish Academic Press.

From Vormarz to Fin de siècle: Essays in 19th-century Austrian Literature, edited by Mark G. Ward. Lochee Publications.

The Austrian Mind: An Intellectual and Social History 1848-1938, by William M. Johnstone. University of California Press.

The Age of the Baroque, 1610–1660, by Carl J. Friedrich. Greenwood Press, London.

Music Guide to Austria & Germany, by Elaine Brody. Dodd, 1975.

Baroque and Rococo, edited by Anthony Blunt. Granada.

Fiction

The Third Man, by Graham Greene. Viking 1950.

The Little Comedy, and other stories, by Arthur Schnitzler. Ungar, 1977.

Other Insight Guides

Europe is comprehensively covered by the 340 books in Apa Publications' three series of guidebooks which embrace the world.

Insight Guides provide a full cultural background and first rate photography.

Insight Guide Vienna provides a real insight to this busy cosmopolitan city and its way of life.

Insight Pocket Guide

The **Insight Pocket Guide** series contains personal recommendations from a local host and comes with an invaluable full-size fold-out map.

Insight Compact Guides

The **Insight Compact Guide** series, which packs easily accessible information into a small format, together with carefully referenced pictures and maps includes titles on Vienna and Salzburg

Art/Photo Credits

Photography by
Tony Anzenberger 66.67.
275, 281L
Anzenberger/Caputo 159, 234
Anzenberger/Horvath 70/71, 157,
161, 173, 250, 253
Anzenberger/Kraus 27, 145
Anzenberger/Lehmann 185R
Anzenberger/Mathis, -/Pretsch 138
Anzenberger/Reismann 23
Anzenberger/Sattlberger 22, 24, 26,
72/73, 91, 124/125, 158
Anzenberger/Trumler 184,
216, 220, 243, 274, 290 169,
177L, 177R
Anzenberger/Wiesenhofer 11, 79, 81,
96/97, 142, 162, 190,
202/203, 207, 208, 218, 219, 221,
226, 237, 266/267,
268/269, 277, 279, 291,
292/293, 295, 297, 298, 300, 301,
302, 305, 309
Anzenberger/Zach-Kiesling 25, 120/
121, 135, 144, 146, 182, 183, 230,
278, 280, 306
Art and History Collection 42, 44, 48,
62
Augsberg City Archives 30
Basta 12/13, 100/101, 107L, 236,
242, 276
Bodo Bondzio 52, 132, 143, 252, 255,
256, 259, 288
Bundeskanzleramt 64, 78, 129
Contrast 98/99, 103, 104, 105, 109,
222/223, 229, 238, 241, 258, 271,
281R, 287, 299, 303, 304, 307, 311
Annabel Elston/Apa 16/17
Wolfgang Fritz 1, 85, 160, 164/165,
166, 174, 175, 176, 178, 180, 185L,
284
Christian Hager 6/7, 82, 107R
Robert Harding Picture Library 2

Janos Kalmar 20/21, 92, 93, 94, 111,
116, 117, 118, 119, 133, 136, 137,
140, 141, 147, 149, 154, 156, 168,
172, 181, 186, 187, 188, 192/193,
197, 204, 206, 209, 211, 214, 215,
Wilhelm Klein 28/29, 31, 33, 41, 43,
46, 50, 63, 65, 76/77, 126, 76L,
76R, 77, 126, 127, 128, 254, 272,
296
Deiter Maier 14/15, 18/19, 32L, 37,
83, 84, 113, 199 205, 210, 217,
224, 235, 239, 240, 263, 264, 273,
283, 285, 289
OFW 112, 74
Gustav Sonnewend 179. 282, 312 88,
89, 90, 103, 130, 155, 163,
Evelyn Tambour 170, 194, 227, 231,
232
Topham Picturepoint 32R, 40, 47, 54,
55, 56, 57, 58, 59, 61
Transglobe 106, 112, 152, 153, 191,
196, 198, 233, 260, 261, 262, 286
US Press 110, 189, 246, 247, 248,
252, 171
Vienna City Museum 34/35,
45, 53
VFW/ Wiesenhofer 68/69
WARCH 38, 39, 51
The Wallace Collection 49

Maps Berndtson & Berndtson

Visual Consultant V. Barl

337

Index

A

Aggstein Castle 180
Abbey of Lambach 80
Abbey of Mehrerau 297
Abbey of Melk 81, 179
Abfaltern 242
Abfaltersbach 242
Aflenz 214
Aggsbachdorf 180
Aigen-Schlägl 190
Albeck Fortress 237
Alberndorf im Pulkautal 176
Alberschwende 299
Albrecht 38
Allend 168
Allgäu 281
Altausser See 199
Altdorfer, Albrecht 75
Altenfelden-Mühital Nature Park 190
Altlengbach 167
Altenmarkt 188
Ambras Castle 278
Ampflwang 191
Angelbach 177
Anras 241
Anschluss 24, 64, 78
anti-Semitism 67
Arlberg 290
Arlberg Pass 307
Arlberg Railway 308
Arnsdorf 180
Asch 241
Aschau 183
Asparn an der Zaya 175
Assling 241
Attersee 195
Austrian Open Air Museum,
    Stübing 217
Axams 286

B

Babenbergs 33, 168, 175, 179, 185
Bachmann, Ingeborg 78
Bad Aussee 199
Bad Deutsch Altenburg 173
Bad Gams 219
Bad Gleichenberg 221
Bad Goisern 187
Bad Hofgastein 257
Bad Ischl 197
Bad Leonfelden 190
Bad Radkersburg 220
Bad St Leonhard 234

Bad Vöslau 170
Baden 170
Baroque architecture 76, 80–84
Bassett, Richard 25, 66, 67
Bassgeigensee 228
Batholmäberg 310
Battle of Lechfeld 33
Beer Museum, Laa Castle 175
beer 88, 178
Beethoven 77
Berg im Drautal 239
Berndorf 170
Bernstein 163
Berzau 299
Biberweier 282
Biedermeier age 52, 129, 142
Bischofshofen 254
Black Hand (Serbian nationalist
    organisation) 60
bobsleigh 106
Böckstein 258
Bohemian Woods 190
Brahms, Johannes 226
Brand 307
Braz 308
Bregenz 294–298
Bregenz Festival 297
Breitenbrunn 158
Brenner Pass 23
Breu, Jörg 75
Brixen Valley 277
Bruck and der Leitha 173
Bruck and der Salzach 261
Brückl 227
Bruckner, Anton 77, 185
Brueghel, Pieter 135, 163
Brunnbach 188
Buchburg 306
Bücher, Wilhelm 206
Burgenland Wine Academy 161
Burgtheater see Vienna
Byzantine culture 75

C

Café Raimund 79
cakes 93
canyoning 110
Carlone Family 83, 155, 185
Carlone, Bartolomeo 190
Carlone, Carlo Antonio 76
Caspar, Mitzi 56
Celts 31, 112, 126, 185, 253
Charlemagne 32
Charles IV (Emperor) 23
Charles V 43
Charles VIII of France 40
Christianity 31, 127
coffee (history of) 49
coffee houses 49, 95
confectionery 88
Congress of Vienna 51
Counter-Reformation 43, 44
Cranach, Lukas 75
Crusaders 33, 75
curling 105

D

Dachstein 103
Dachstein Ice Caves 198
Dachstein Massif 198
Dalaas 308
Damüls 299
Danöfen 308
Danube 24, 31
Danube school of painting 75
de Paula Penze, Franz 286
death (Austrians' attitude
    to) 26, 148
Deix, Manfred 79
Dellach im Drautal 239
Deutsch Griffen 236
Deutsch-Wagram 173
Diet (election to) 32
Diocletian 31
Disraeli, Benjamin 67
diving 110
Dobersberg 177
dog sledging 106
Döllach-Grosskirchheim 232
Dollfuss, Engelbert
    (Chancellor) 63, 131
Dölsach 241
Donnersbach 205
Donnerskirchen 160
Dornbirn 300
Drosendorf 176
Dualism 55
Duel Hill 238
dumplings 89
Dürnstein Monastery 82

E

East Tyrol 241–243
Eastern March 32
Ebene Reichenau 237
Ebensee 195
Edict of Worms (1521) 43
Eggern 177
Ehrenhausen 217
Einsiedeln Abbey 306
Eisenerz Alps 207
Eisriesenwelt Caves 254
Elisabeth, Empress 55, 58
Erzberg Alps 207
Erzberg 208, 209
Esterhàzy family 155
Eugene, Prince 45–46, 83, 84, 129,
    132, 137, 172
Europa Bridge 284

F

Faistenberger, Benedikt 275
Falkenstein Castle 231
Fallbach 177
Family Law, the (1839) 52, 58
Fascism 63–65, 131
Feistritz 238
Felber Tauern 265
Feldkirch 302
Ferdinand I 51–52
First Repubic of Austria 23

Fischer von Erlach, Johann Bernhard 58, 80, 83, 84, 129, 137, 171, 214, 252, 261
Fischer von Erlach, Joseph Emanuel 80, 83, 84
Flattach 231
Flattnitz 236
Fontanella 366
food 86–95
Forchtenstein Castle 162
Frankenburg 191
Franz Ferdinand, Archduke 58–60, 139
Franz II 26, 50
Franz Jozef 26, 52, 53, 55, 129, 131, 168, 197, 290
Frauenkirchen 84
Fraunberg 213
Frederick II (the Quarrelsome) 33
Frederick III 39, 40
Frederick the Great 48
free climbing 108
Freistadt 189
French Revolution 50
Freud 78
Friebitz 175
Fulpmes 286
funerals 26, 148
Fürstenfeld 221
Fuscher Lake 234
Fux, Joseph 76

G

Gaicht Pass 281
Gamlitz 220
Gamsberg Nature Path 233
Gargallen 310
Garsam Kamp 179
Gastein Valley 112
Gayenhofen Castle 305
gemutlichkeit 52
Gerloss Pass Toll Road 265
Germans, the 23
Germany 53, 63
Gesäuse Ravine 206
Glödnitz 235
Gmund 178
Gmunden 196
Göfis 304
Goldberge 233
Goldegg Castle 257
Goldenes Dach, Innsbruck 75
Gollinger Waterfalls 253
Gössl 199
Götzens 286
Götzis 302
Graz 215-218
    Archduke Johann Fountain 215
    Arsenal 215
    arts festival 216
    Castle 216
    Cathedral 216
    Conservatory for Music and Performing Arts 216
    Eggenberg Château 84, 217
    Eisernen Tor 216
    Franciscan Church 215

Herrengasse 216
Karl-Franzens University 216
Landhaus 215
Old Town 215
Old University 216
restaurants 216
Schlossberg 216
Türkensäule 216
Great Depression 63
Greifenburg 238
Gröbming 205
Groppenstein Castle 231
Gross Gerungs 178
Grossarl Valley 257
Grossenzersdorf 170
Grossglockner 107–108
Grossglockner Alpine Road 232
Grossraming 188
Grossvenediger 243
Grosswalsertal 305
Grundlsee 195, 199
Gstatterboden 207
Gumpolskirchen 169
Gunther, Matthäus 286
Gurk Valley Railway Museum 235

H

Hagenburg 175
Hagengebirge 254
Hainburg 172
Halbturn 157
Haldensee 281
Hallein 257
Hallstatt 197
Hallstätter See 195, 198
hang-gliding 111
Hanslick, Eduard 77
Hard 177
Hardegg 176
Hasegg Castle 278
Hàsek, Jaroslav 78
Haus im Ennstal 205
Hausruch mountains 191
Haydn, Joseph 155, 173
Haydn Museum 173
Heidenreichstein 177
Heiligenblut 233
Heiligenkreuz 168
Heinfels 242
Heintz, Josef 75
Heller, André 79
Hermagor 230
Herrensee 177
heurige 95
Hieflau 206
High Tauern 243
hiking 112
Hinterbrühl 168
Hintertax 283, 284
Hirschegg 307
Hirschenwies 177
historicism 78
Hitler 23, 24, 53, 63, 65
Hittisau 299
Hochgurgl 288
Hochosterwitz Castle 75, 228
Hochrindl 237

Hochschwab 214
Hochtannberg Pass 300
Hochtor 234
Hohe Tauern National Park 234
Hohenems 301
Hohensalzburg 75, 251
Hohenwerfen 75
Hohenwerfen Castle 254
Hoher Göll 253
Holy Roman Emperor (title and role) 32
Holznechtmuseum 188
Hopfgarten 277
Hoyos, Count 56
Hueber, Andrä 284
Hundertwasser, Friedensreich 133
Hungarian border 154
Hvars 32

I

Ice Age 258
ice-hockey 105
ice-skating 105
Illmitz 156
Innergschlöss-Alm 243
Innsbruck 270–274
    Cathedral 270
    Goldenes Dachl 270
    Herzog Friedrichstrasse 270
    Hofburg 272
    Hofkirch 272
    Maria Theresienstrasse 273
    Tyrol Museum of Popular Art 273
    Wilten 273
    Wilten Basilica 274
International Haydn Festival 156
Irdning 205, 209–210
Iron Age 197

J

Jasomirgott (Henry II) 33, 127, 132
Jerzens 288
Jews 39, 50, 64, 67, 129, 131, 135
Jochberg 275
Joching 181
Johnsbach 207
Jois 158
Joseph II 26, 50
Judenberg 213

K

Kafka, Franz 78
Kaiserbach Valley 275
Kaltenbrunn 288
Kaning 228
Karl Eidler Private Museum of Pannonia 158
Karwendel Range 279
Kaschauer, Jakob 75
Kasternreith 188
Kauner Valley 288
Kautzen 177
Kefermarkt 190
Kellerberg 238
Keutschach 228

Kirchberg 277
Kirchheim Castle 232
Kitzbühel 102, 274
Kitzbühel Alps 259
Klagenfurt 225
Klammer, Franz 102
Klapotetz 218
Kleinreifling 188
Kleinwalsertal 305
Kloster Valley 296
Klosterneuberg 167
Klostertal 307
Knab, Michael 75
Kokoshka, Oskar 78
Kolm 227
Kölnbrein Barrage 229
Kolschitzky 49
Kramau am Kamp 179
Krampendorf 226
Kreisky, Bruno 66
Krems 181
Kreuzeck Range 239
Krieglach 214
Krimml 265
Krippenstein 198
Kundl 277
Kundlerklamm 277
Kurfstein Fortress 277

L

Laa an der Thayer 175
Lagenfeld 288
Lainach 232
Lake Constance Line 297
Lake Fuschl 194
Lake Hafner 228
Lake Hintersteiner 275
Lake Keutschach 228
Lake Klopeiner 227
Lake Millstatt 228
Lake Neusiedler (Neusiedlersee) 105,
    108, 156–163
Lake Ossiach 228
Lake Piburger 287
Lake Pressager 230
Lake Turner 227
Lake Wörther 225
Landeck 290
Langbathseen lakes 197
Lange Lacke 157
Langenegg 299
Larisch-Wallersee, Marie 56
Laussa 187
Lavanmünd 235
Lavant 241
Lavant Valley 234
Laxenberg 169
Lech 280
Leisach 241
Leiser Mountain Nature Park 175
Leoben 210–213
Leopold I 44, 45, 76
Leopold of Babenberg 33
Leopoldsteiner See 207
Lermoos 282
Liebnitz 217
Liechtenstein Castle 174

Liechtensteinklamm 257
Lienz 241
Lienzer Dolomites 241
Liezen 205
Linz 184–186
Lippizzaner Museum 134
Lippizzaner stallions 217
loden 205
Lodron, Paris (Archbishop) 249
Loipersdorf Therme 220
Losenstein 187
Loser 199
Louis XIV of France 44
Lüner See 307
Luther, Martin 39, 41, 43, 128

M

Maissau 179
Mallnitz 231
Malta 229
mannerism 75
Mari Alm 260
Maria Wörth 227
Mariahilfkirche 84
Mariazell 214
Marie Theresa, Empress 46–48, 50,
    86, 129, 135, 158, 169, 172, 237,
    270, 272, 297, 310
Matrei 242, 284
Maulbertsch, Franz Anton 77
Maultern 181
Maulterndorf 255
Mausoleum of Ferdinand II 84
Mausoleum of Ruprecht von
    Eggenberg 84
Maximilian I 39–41, 242, 270, 303
Mayerling 56–58, 168
Mayrhofen 283
Mellau 299
Metternich 50–52
Michaelbeuren 80
Mieders 286
Miller, Abraham 275
mining 208, 210
Miracle Plays 25
Mittelberg 307
Mittersil 263
Mittewald 241
Mödling 168
Möll Valley 230
Möll Valley Glacier 231
Monastery of Klosterneuburg 84
Monastery of St Florian 81
Monsee 195
Mooserboden Reservoir 263
Moosham Castle 255
Morawetz, Fritz 108
Mörbisch 161–162
mountaineering 106–108
Mozart 77, 249, 251
Mühlviertel 188–191
Münichtal 208
music 25
Mussolini, Benito 63
Mustapha, Kara 44

N

Napoleon Bonaparte 33, 50, 129,
    173, 237
Napoleon III 53
Navis Valley 284
Nazism 63–65
Neo-Nazism 67
Neusiedl 158
Neusiedlersee see Lake Neusiedler
Niederweiden Castle 171
Nierdersulz 174
Nikolsdorf 241
Noreaia (Noricum) 31
Nussdorf 196

O

Oberdrauburg 239
Obergurgl 287, 288
Obertraun 198
Obervellach 231
Oberwart 163
Oggau 160
Opera Ball, Vienna 136
Ossiach 84, 228
Ottakar II of Bohemia 33, 37
Ottenstein Reservoir 178
Otto the Great, Emperor 33
Ötz 287
Ötztal 287

P–Q

Pacher, Michael 75, 195, 241, 250
Packsattel Mountain Road 234
Panzendorf 242
paragliding 111
Paris Revolution 52
Partenen 310
Pastertze Glacier 233
Paternion 238
Paznaun Valley 290
Peasants' Wars (1525–26) 43
Petronell-Carnuntum 173
Pfaffstätten 169
Pfandhütte 236
Philip of Coburg 56
Piegarten Castle 177
pigs 26
Pilgram, Anton 75, 161
Piz Buin 310
Plansee 282
Pöckstein Castle 235
Podersdorf 157
Pöllau 76
Porcia Castle 238
Porsche Museum 229
Pörtschach 226
Poysdorf 174
Präbichl Pass 210
Praundtauer, Jakob 80, 81, 179, 187
Preitnegg 234
Pressbaum 167
Prince Eugene see Eugene, Prince
Princip, Gavrilo 66
Prugg Castle 173

Prussia (rise of) 48
Puchsbaum, Hans 75
Puster Valley 241
Qualtinger, Helmut 79

R

Raab-Ödenburg–Eberfurt Railway 162
Radkersburg 220
Radstätter Tauern Pass 255
Ragall 305
Ragga Gorge 231
Ramsau 205
Rangersdorf 232
Rankwiel 302
Rattenberg 277
Reder, Walter 67
Reformation 43–44, 75
Reichenfeld 234
Reichersberg 191
Reichraming 187
Reichraminger Mountains 187
Rekawinkel 167
Renaissance, the 41, 75
Reutte 281
Richard the Lionheart 82, 128,
    179, 181
Ried 283
Ried im Innkreis 191
Riegersburg 221
Riezlern 307
Ringstrasse (Vienna) 131
Robber Barons 33, 128
Rococo 76
Rohrau 173
Rohrback 190
Romans 31, 126, 185, 261
Rosanna Valley 290
Rosegger, Peter 77, 214
Rosswiese Reservoir 230
Rudolf, Crown Prince 55–58
Rudolf of Habsburg 37
Rudolf IV 38, 127, 132

S

Saalbach-Hinterglemm 259
Saalfelden 260
Sachertorte 93
Sachsenburg 238
Sailer, Toni 102, 274
St Anton 290, 310
St Christoph 308
St Florian 31
St Florian (place) 75, 76, 81
St Georgen 213
St Georgen am Längsee 227
St Gilgen, Lake Wolfgang 195
St Johann 275
St Johann im Pongau 257
St Leonhard 288
St Martin 260
St Martin's Day 94, 160
St Mary of Loreto 235
St Paul im Lavanttal 235
St Peter 213
St Primus an Turnersee 227
St Ulrich 235

St Veit an der Glan 227
St Wolfgang 195
Salzach Valley 253
Salzburg 80, 88, 249–265
    Bishop's Palace 249
    Burgberg 249
    Cathedral 249
    Collegiate Church of St Peter 250
    Domplatz 249
    Franciscan Church 250
    Getreidegasse 251
    Glockenspiel 250
    Hellbrunn Palace 249
    Hohensalzburg 249, 251
    Judengasse 252
    Mirabell Gardens 252
    Mönchsberg 249
    Mozart's birthplace 251
    Nonnberg 251
    Old Market 252
    Pilgrimage Church of Maria
        Plain 252
    St Mark's church 80
    St Peter's Churchyard 251
    Schloss Klessheim 80
    Schloss Mirabell 80, 249
    Town Hall 252
Salzkammergut 194–199
Sandl 189
Sandstein–Wienerwald Nature
    park 167
Schadonna Pass 305
Schafberg 195
Schattenburg Castle 303
Schladming 204
Schloss Eggenberg, Graz 84
Schloss Halbturn 84
Schloss Sachsengang 171
Schlosshof 84, 172
schnapps 88, 95
Schneeberg 167
Schnitzler, Arthur 78
Schoenberg, Arnold 78
Schönbühel 180
Schoppernau 300
Schröcken 300
Schruns 310
Schruns-Tschagguns 310
Schubert, Franz 77, 168, 219
Schuschnigg 63
Schwanberg 219
Schwanthaler, Thomas 80
Schwarzenberg 299
Schwarzsee 213
Schwaz 278
Seckau 213
Second Republic 66
Sedlnitzky, Joseph 51
Seeschloss 196
Seetaler Alps 234
Seewalchen 196
Seisenegger, Jako 75
Seyss-Inquart 63
Sforza, Bianca 40, 270
Sichelsee 241
Siege of Vienna 44–45
Silian 242
Silvretta Alpine Road 290

Silvretta Reservoir 308, 310
Sirnitz 237
skeleton riders 106
Skiing 102–104
skijoring 104
snowboard riding 104
Solari, Santino 76, 252
Sölden 288
Sonnleitner, Sissy 230
Sonntag 306
Sophienalpe 167
Sound of Music, The 67
South Styrian Wine Country 217
Spittal 230
Spittal an der Drau 238
Spitz 180
Spitzeralm 236
Spranger, Barholomäus 75
Steinbach 196
Stephanie of Coburg (Crown
    Princess) 55, 57
Steyr 186
Stockneboi am Weissensee 238
Stoob 163
Stoss, Veit 251
Strass 283
Strassburg 235
Strauss, Johann 25, 26
Streif Run, the 102–104
Strobl 195
Strudel von Strudendorff, Peter 77
Stubai Valley 286
Stuben 290, 308
Stubing 217
Sturm und Drang (literary
    movement) 77
Styrer Kripperl 187
Styria 204–221
Styrian Iron Road 186–188
Suleiman the Magnificent 43
swingbo riding 104

T

Tamsweg 257
Tannheim Mountains 281
Tauplitz 205
Tausendeimerberg 180
Techendorf 229
Telfes 286
Tennengebirge 254
Teufenbach 213
Thal 241
Thaya Valley Nature Park 177
Third Man, The 147
Third Reich 64
Thirty Years' War 44, 80
Timmelsjoch 287, 288
Toplitzsee 198
Trabuschgen Castle 231
Trakl, Georg 78
Traunsee 195, 196
Trisanna 290
Trofaiach 210
Trofeng 208
Troger, Paul 81
Tullenerback 167
Türkenturm 158

Turkish Empire 39, 43, 75, 76, 126, 128–129, 160, 221
Turracher See 213
Tuxer Grund 283
Tyrol 270–290

U

Und 181
Unterach 196
Unterried 241
Upper Gail Valley 230
Urslau Valley 260
Ursulinenkirch 84

V

van der Nüll 135, 136
Velden 226
Vent 287
Vetsera, Mary (Baroness) 56–58
Viebergelauf (Four Mountain Course) 26
Vienna 82, 83, 92, 93, 95, 124–148
  Austrian National Gallery 139
  Baroque architecture 82–83
  Belvedere 129, 137
  Burgtheater 76, 139, 140
  Church of St Charles 137
  City Hall 139
  Ethnological Museum 135
  Graben 132
  Hofbibliothek 84
  Karlskirche 83
  Karlsplatz 137
  Kirch am Hof 83
  Kohlmarkt 134
  Landtmann coffee house 140
  Michaelerplatz 134
  Museum of Baroque Art 139
  Museum of Medieval Art 139
  Music Association Building 137
  National Gallery of Art 135
  National Library 135
  New Château 135
  Parliament Building 139
  Plague Column 83, 133
  Sachwarzenberg 83
  St Stephen's Cathedral 38, 75, 127, 131, 132
  Schloss Belvedere 83
  Schönbrunn Palace 129, 142–143
  Schottenhof 140
  Schwarzenbergplatz 137
  Scots' Gate 140
  Spanish Riding School 134
  Vienna Ball 136, 167
  Vienna Boys' Choir 135
  Vienna State Opera 135
  Vienna Woods 131
  Votive Church 140
  Winter Riding School 84
Villach 237
Visalpsee 281
von Alt, Salome 252
von der Vogelweide, Walther 127
von Hildebrandt, Johann Lukas 81, 83, 137, 171, 173, 252
von Horvath, Ödön 78
von Raitenau, Wolf Dietrich 249
von Schernberg, Graf Christoph 257
von Werdenberg, Count Rudolf 304
Vorarlberg 294–310
Vordenberg 210

W

Wagner, Otto 131
Wagner, Richard 77
Wagner–Bacher, Lisl 94, 181
Waidhofen an der Thaya 177
Waldenstein Castle 234
Waldheim, Kurt 24, 64, 67
Waldviertel 176–179
Waldviertel Narrow Gauge Steam Railway 178
Walgau 303
walking 112
Waltersdorf Therme 221
Weaving Museum 177
Weiden 157
Weigel, Hans 79
Weimar Republic 63
Weinberg Castle 190

Weissbriach 230
Weissenbach 196
Weissensee 105, 229
Weissenstein Castle 242
Weit Valley Waterfall 239
Weitra 178
Wenns 288
Wetterstein Range 280
Weyer 188
white water sports 108, 110
Wiener schnitzel 86
Wiesen 241
Wildbach Castle 219
Wildenstein Waterfall 227
Wilfersdorf 174
Wilhelm II 56
windsurfing 108
Wine Country 95, 174, 217–220
wine 95, 96, 160, 218–220
wine scandal 67
Winkelau 175
Winklern 232
Wolfsberg 234
Wolkenstein Castle 205
Wolkersdorf 174
Wörgl 277
World War I 24, 60, 78, 131, 134
World War II 64–65, 79, 135, 198, 199, 239, 263, 299
Wörschach 205

Z

Zeiller, Franz Anton 282
Zell 284
Zell am Moos 195
Zeller See 195, 258, 259
Zemmgrund 283
Ziller Valley 282
Zillergrund 283
Zillertal Mountain Road 283
Zirknitz Valley 232
Zweig, Stefan 78
Zwettl 178
Zwieselalpe 199
Zwieselstein 287
Zwischenwässern 235